Donald M. McKale is Associate Professor of History at Georgia College and the author of *The Nazi Party Courts: Hitler's Management of Conflict in His Movement, 1921-1925*, as well as numerous articles in the professional journals.

THE SWASTIKA OUTSIDE GERMANY

The Swastika
Outside Germany

Donald M. McKale

THE KENT STATE UNIVERSITY PRESS

Library of Congress Cataloging in Publication Data

McKale, Donald M. 1943-
  The Swastika outside Germany.

  Bibliography: p.
  Includes index.
  1. Nationalsozialistische Deutsche Arbeiter-Partei. Auslands-
Organisation. I. Title.
DD253.41.M3   329.9'43   77-22304
ISBN 0-87338-209-9

For Emily Anne and
David Marshall

CONTENTS

PREFACE

This book deals with the origins and activities of Nazi party organizations formed in many countries in the 1930s by German Nazis. Small as they were, the party groups received much attention from the foreign press and political leaders who were convinced that the groups in the United States, Latin America, and elsewhere were a serious menace to freedom and democracy.[1] Their story, which can now be told from captured German records, makes a contribution to the study of the diplomacy of totalitarian regimes and the effort of Adolf Hitler's Nazi movement to organize the thirty million racial Germans living outside Germany for his aggressive foreign policy. The rationale for the groups centered around the Nazis' conviction that blood and race made foreign Germans natural allies of Hitler, particularly if the Germans were educated in the *völkisch* ideology of National Socialism and encouraged to back Hitler. Once he took over the German government in 1933, the groups also developed from the belief of certain Nazi officials like Rudolf Hess that the party must dominate German diplomacy.[2]

The following pages reveal more extensive action on the part of the Nazis in foreign lands than has commonly been assumed. The success of their groups abroad was, however, largely minimal. The branches found it impossible to turn German neighborhoods and communities in foreign countries into miniature Third Reichs. In their zeal to nazify foreign Germans and spread Hitler's gospel of authoritarianism, anti-Semitism, anti-Communism, and anti-liberalism, they encountered obstacles unknown to Nazis in Germany—differing cultures, life styles, political systems, and moral values. In most instances the Nazis found themselves alienated from their milieu, but they refused to adjust their objectives or modify their practices accordingly. The consequences were the banishment of the Nazi party from many countries by 1939 and the arrest of party members in neutral nations during World War II. But the failure of the foreign party organizations should not be a reason for ignoring them. Although they never came close to dominating German diplomacy or foreign Germans, their story illustrates what can happen when extremist and irresponsible elements claim control of a government. Their experience is yet another sad reminder of the Nazi folly of basing Germany's foreign relations solely on the ideas of race and power.[3]

Analyzing these foreign Nazi branches involves the pitfall of overemphasizing their significance in German foreign policy. Hans Nieland and Ernst Wilhelm Bohle, the leaders of the central party agency in Germany entrusted with the directing of the groups, were never confidants of Hitler. Nor did they enjoy authority among elite Nazis like Himmler, Bormann, Goebbels, Göring, and Ribbentrop. The party affiliates abroad never determined foreign policy. This was done by Hitler, his foreign ministers and advisers, and professional diplomats of the German Foreign Ministry.[4] The function of the groups was to carry out what they believed was the desire of Hitler and his party for foreign Germans. But while Hitler rarely took the branches seriously as a mechanism of foreign policy, the groups' leaders outside Germany viewed their work as crucial to the Reich. Often, they acted without the approval of Bohle or Nieland, which meant that the groups were hardly the monolithic apparatus their foreign critics claimed them to be.

They also revealed a basic flaw in Hitler's regime: it rewarded blind dedication and suppressed initiative and compromise. Time and again the groups' meddling in the affairs of foreign countries and their blundering activities undermined Germany's reputation, yet the Nazis equated this with devotion to Hitler and Germany. What is amazing about the groups is the support (and even reward) given by leaders in Germany to the incompetency that dominated much of their work. The more they were opposed abroad, the more praise they received in Germany. Each foreign reaction against the branches fed the belief of Hitler, Hess, Bohle, and other Nazi officials that Germans were persecuted by the world and that there existed a global conspiracy of Jews, Communists, and "liberals" to destroy the German race.

I wish to clarify the citations in the book that include newspapers and original documents I have used. Purposely, I cited full titles of newspaper articles where I felt such citations would be useful evidence in themselves. The same inconsistency is present in the citing of primary source materials (for example, letters, orders, and other correspondence of the Nazi party, German cultural agencies, and German Foreign Ministry). Some valuable documents stated the subject of their contents, and in such cases I have given the original statements of subject as they appeared in letters or official directives. When noting microfilm collections, which form the bulk of the evidence for the study, I have listed the microcopy, roll, and (where possible) frame or folder numbers.

D.M.M.

ACKNOWLEDGMENTS

It is a pleasure to note the many institutional and personal contributions that made this study possible. A large part of the book is based on unpublished records of the Nazi party and German Foreign Ministry, and I wish to express my gratitude to the Georgia College Faculty Research Committee for several grants that enabled me to purchase most of these documents on microfilm. I would also like to express my deep appreciation to Dr. Arnold Ebel and the *Deutscher Akademischer Austauschdienst* for a grant that made possible the completion of my research in Germany and England.

During my visit to Germany, I was helped significantly by Dr. Klaus Weinandy and the staff at the *Politisches Archiv des Auswärtigen Amts* in Bonn; by Daniel P. Simon and Richard Bauer at the Berlin Document Center; and by the library of the *Historisches Seminar* at the University of Bonn. I also wish to thank Dr. Anton Hoch of the *Institut für Zeitgeschichte* in Munich and the staff of the *Bundesarchiv* in Koblenz (most of whose records on the AO are on microfilm and cited in this study as Microcopy T-81, T-82, and T-580) for their advice and correspondence. In addition, I would like to thank the Wiener Library and Institute for Contemporary History in London, and particularly M. Johnson and Janet Langmaid, for their courtesy and helpfulness.

For their valuable advice and archival assistance, I wish to thank Robert Wolfe of the National Archives, Washington, D.C.; Dr. Arnold H. Price of the Library of Congress, Washington, D.C.; Nancy Dyer of the Interlibrary Loan Department at the Georgia College Library; Penny Berger of Lincoln, Nebraska; and the staffs of the libraries at the University of Nebraska-Lincoln, Emory

University, and University of Georgia. John Mendelsohn of the National Archives was gracious enough to supply me with records on Bohle's trial. My appreciation especially extends to those who were kind enough to read the manuscript and offer suggestions for revision: Professors Earl R. Beck of Florida State University; Hans-Adolf Jacobsen of the University of Bonn; Kenneth R. Calkins of Kent State University; and my colleagues at Georgia College, William I. Hair and David G. Mead. Whatever I may owe to the above mentioned, all errors of fact and judgment in this study are my responsibility.

Finally, it is a special delight to thank my wife and children. This work could not have been completed without the personal encouragement and enjoyment only they could give. My wife, Janna, also proofread the manuscript and designed several charts.

Donald M. McKale
Milledgeville, Georgia
January 1977

ABBREVIATIONS

AA   *Auswärtiges Amt*; German Foreign Ministry with headquarters in the *Wilhelmstrasse* in Berlin

AO   *Auslands-Organisation*; Foreign Organization of the NSDAP, 1934-1945 (called the *Auslands-Abteilung* [Foreign Department], 1931-1933; and the *Abteilung für Deutsche im Ausland* [Department for Germans Abroad], 1933-1934)

APA   *Aussenpolitisches Amt*; Foreign Policy Office of the NSDAP

BA   *Bundesarchiv*, Koblenz

BDC   Berlin Document Center, Berlin

BKA   *Bundeskanzleramt* Austria; Federal Chancellery Office of the Austrian Government

Chef AO   *Büro des Chefs der Auslands-Organisation im Auswärtigen Amt*; Office of chief of the AO in the AA (1937-1941)

DAF   *Deutsche Arbeitsfront*; German Labor Front

DAI   *Deutsches Auslands-Institut*; German Foreign Institute, Stuttgart

DBFP   *Documents on British Foreign Policy, 1919-1939* (London: H. M. Stationery Office 1954), Third Series

DGFP   *Documents on German Foreign Policy, 1918-1945* (Washington, D.C.: U.S. Government Printing Office 1949–), Series C and D

Diplogerma   German Diplomatic Mission

DZA   *Deutsches Zentral Archiv*, Potsdam

FRUS   *Foreign Relations of the United States* (Washington, D.C.: U.S. Government Printing Office, 1951–)

FZ	*Frankfurter Zeitung*
Gestapo	*Geheime Staatspolizei*; Secret State Police
GL	*Gauleitung*; district leadership of the NSDAP
HA	NSDAP *Hauptarchiv*, Hoover Institution, Stanford University (Microfilm Collection)
HJ	*Hitler-Jugend*; Hitler Youth
IfZ	*Institut für Zeitgeschichte*, Munich
KK	*Kulturkammer*; German Chamber of Culture
LC	Library of Congress, Washington, D.C.
LG	*Landesgruppe*; country group of the NSDAP in a foreign land
LGL	*Landesgruppenleiter*; country group leader of the NSDAP in a foreign land
MF	Master File
NA	National Archives, Washington, D.C.
NG	Nazi Government Ministries Series (Nuremberg Documents)
NI	Nazi Industrialists Series (Nuremberg Documents)
NP	Nazi Propaganda Series (Nuremberg Documents)
NSDAP	*Nationalsozialistische Deutsche Arbeiterpartei*; National Socialist German Workers' Party, or Nazi party
NS	*Nationalsozialistische*; National Socialist
NSLB	*Nationalsozialistische Lehrerbund*; Nazi Teacher's League
NSPK	*Nationalsozialistische Partei-Korrespondenz: Pressedienst der NSDAP*
NYT	*The New York Times*
O.Gr.	*Ortsgruppe*; local group of the NSDAP
Ogrl.	*Ortsgruppenleiter*; leader of a local group of the NSDAP
OKW	*Oberkommando der Wehrmacht*; Supreme Command of the German Armed Forces
OPG	*Oberstes Parteigericht*; Supreme Court of the NSDAP
PA	*Politisches Archiv des Auswärtigen Amts*, Bonn
PK	*Parteikorrespondenz*; party correspondence
PO	*Oberste Leitung der Politische Organisation der NSDAP*; Supreme Leadership of the Political Organization of the NSDAP
PS	Paris-Storey Series (Nuremberg Documents)
RFSS	*Reichsführer* SS; Reich Leader of the SS

RG   Record Group (collections of documents in the NA)

RL   *Reichsleitung*; national leadership of the NSDAP, Munich

ROL   *Reichsorganisationsleitung*; national organization leadership of the NSDAP

RPA   *Reichspropagandaamt Ausland*; National Propaganda Office for Foreign Countries

RuSHA   *Rasse- und Siedlungshauptamt*-SS; Race and Settlement Main Office of the SS

SA   *Sturmabteilung*; storm troopers of the NSDAP

SD   *Sicherheitsdienst*; Security Service

Slg. Schu.   *Sammlung Schumacher*

SS   *Schutzstaffeln*; elite guards of the NSDAP

Stüpu.   *Stützpunkt*; support point of the NSDAP

TMWC   International Military Tribunal, *Trial of the Major War Criminals* (Nuremberg, 1947-1949)

Uschla   *Untersuchungs- und Schlichtungsausschuss*; Investigation and Conciliation committee of the NSDAP

VB   *Völkischer Beobachter*; national newspaper and major propaganda organ of the NSDAP

VDA   *Volksbund für das Deutschtum im Ausland*; League for Germandom Abroad, Stuttgart

VOBL   *Verordnungsblatt der Reichsleitung der Nationalsozialistischen Deutschen Arbeiter-Partei*

VoMi   *Volksdeutsche Mittelstelle*; central agency of the SS for dealing with persons of German descent outside Germany

WL   Wiener Library and Institute for Contemporary History, London

1

INTRODUCTION: EARLY ORIGINS OF THE NAZI PARTY IN FOREIGN COUNTRIES

"Smash Hitler's International!" This battle cry of a group of concerned Americans in 1941 was aimed at alerting the United States that Hitler's war machine in Europe was about to be unleashed on America. The frightening prophecy was soon to become a reality.[1] Those voicing the warning believed with many people that Hitler possessed a political and military organization (i.e., a Nazi International) that would destroy whatever its lord and master commanded. Since January 1933, when Hitler was named German Chancellor and his National Socialist German Workers' Party (*Nationalsozialistische Deutsche Arbeiterpartei*, or NSDAP) began its takeover of the Weimar government, the world had been conditioned by his Propaganda Minister, Joseph Goebbels, to believe this view of the Third Reich. The belief was further strengthened by Hitler's rapid consolidation of his regime in Germany, his bringing a sudden and shocking diplomatic revolution to Europe in the 1930s, and his quick victories during the early months of World War II.

Still another source for this view of Nazi Germany was the arsenal of agencies Hitler employed in his plans for world conquest. This study focuses on one of those institutions, the Nazi party's Foreign Organization (*Auslands-Organisation*, or AO), and its creation in the 1930s of a network of small and boisterous Nazi groups outside Germany.

An analysis of any agency of Nazi foreign activity must begin with a summary of the attitudes held by Hitler and his party on foreign affairs. His ideas had been securely formed before his appointment in 1933. During the 1920s, as the NSDAP struggled to become a prominent force in German politics, the movement included several factions—ranging from the so-called "Wilhelmine imperialists" through the "agrarian radicals" to the "revolutionary socialists" —which entertained different positions on foreign policy. All, however, shared a common goal in that they attempted to gain influence in shaping Hitler's ideas.

The imperialists were mainly officers from the Wilhelmine Reich who urged Germany's expansion overseas to win back the colonies in Africa and islands in the Pacific Ocean that Germany had lost by the Versailles Treaty in 1919. The socialist faction, eliminated from the party by the summer of 1930, held several views on foreign affairs that differed from Hitler's. Although the socialists rejected colonialism and supported an attempt by Germany to find *Lebensraum* ("living space") in central Europe, they were anti-Western and anti-British, and their bias lay towards the east and Russia. Cooperation with Russia, it was hoped, would enable Germany to assert her claims against the West and to revise the hated Versailles Treaty.

The group nearest Hitler was the agrarian radicals, who emerged after 1930. They were committed to Nazi racial theories and to the party's worship of German "blood and soil"; they argued that, to keep the German race pure, the future of Germany did not lie in capturing overseas colonies, but in the conquest of land in eastern Europe and Russia. Stressing racism and power politics, the agrarians pushed for Germany to ally with England to enable the Reich to conquer the living space in eastern Europe that was necessary for the settlement of German peasants and for the racial preservation of the German people.[2]

Before 1933, Hitler's ideas too centered on the doctrines of race and living space. In *Mein Kampf* (1925) and in his later and less publicized writings (which were little more than chapters from his memoir published separately), *Die Südtiroler Frage und das deutsche Bündnisproblem* (1926), *Der Weg zum Wiederaufstieg* (1927), and *Hitlers zweites Buch* (1928), he discussed the cornerstones of his foreign policy: anti-Semitism, anti-Bolshevism, and conquest of *Lebensraum* in the east.[3] By renouncing colonies overseas and Germany's claims to the South Tirol, he hoped to purchase the support of Britain and Italy for his overrunning of Europe and Russia, and for his later conflict with the United States over world supremacy. According to his racial plan, the German people were to be bred into a superior, Germanic elite, and the struggle for

world power could only end in a German triumph and in the fulfill-
ment of the racial purpose of world history.[4]

Nazi foreign activity after 1933 was pursued in two separate directions: the orthodox channels of intergovernmental diplomacy
represented by the German Foreign Ministry (*Auswärtiges Amt*, or
AA), and the propaganda and subversive work of the Nazi party
among Germans outside the Reich and among native fascist or
Nazi-like movements in many countries. The basic goal was always
to increase Germany's influence around the world. The many agencies operated or controlled by the NSDAP that were involved
abroad included the AO, the party's Foreign Policy Office (*Aussenpolitisches Amt*, or APA), the *Dienststelle Ribbentrop*, the
German Foreign Institute (*Deutsches Auslands-Institut*, or DAI)
as well as the League for Germandom Abroad (*Volksbund für das
Deutschtum im Ausland*, or VDA) in Stuttgart, and the Volksdeutsche Mittelstelle (VoMi), the central agency of Hitler's elite
guard (*Schutzstaffel*, or SS) for dealing with persons of German descent outside Germany.[5]

As this study will illustrate, the dualism between the diplomatic
service and NSDAP resulted in a lack of unity in German foreign
policy, and in opposition among the party's leaders abroad and
German diplomats. It also lessened the power of the *Auswärtiges
Amt*, whose aristocratic tradition and professionalism were despised by Hitler and prompted him to call the Ministry an "intellec-
tual garbage dump." The independence of the AA was attacked
after 1933 by party leaders like Goebbels, Rudolf Hess, Alfred
Rosenberg, Martin Bormann, and Heinrich Himmler, and the Ministry was forced to compete with the AO and the other agencies
mentioned above. Even Joachim von Ribbentrop, on becoming
Foreign Minister in 1938, employed the AA as a private or personal
apparatus along with his *Dienststelle*.[6]

Particularly after 1933, when Rosenberg had eliminated himself
as the party's candidate to head the AA, Hess and Goebbels viewed
the AO as a weapon for "coordinating" the Ministry and filling
it with loyal National Socialists. As the AO expanded to include
several hundred small affiliates abroad, which clashed with the
AA's foreign missions, Hess and the German Foreign Minister,
Constantin von Neurath, convinced Hitler to bring some unity to
the party-state dichotomy by placing Ernst Wilhelm Bohle, head of
the AO after May 1933, in the Ministry. But while Bohle worked
hard to have party men appointed to the AA and while he was able

to make a few of his AO leaders abroad consuls or attaches, he failed to "nazify" the Ministry. He maintained to foreign governments that were suspicious of the AO that the NSDAP had little interest in the Foreign Ministry or its missions. Yet his assurances were hardly the truth. He explained to another party leader in 1941 that the cloaking of AO officials abroad with diplomatic titles (which had begun in 1936) was to enable such functionaries "to accomplish" their "activity for the NSDAP under the protection of [diplomatic] extraterritoriality." In fact, he added, uniting party and diplomatic offices abroad was only "a camouflaging in the interest of performing party work."[7]

On the other hand, the view that the AA was reduced by the Nazis to impotence, as asserted by two of Hitler's diplomats, Franz von Papen (the former Chancellor and the Ambassador to Austria and Turkey) and Ulrich von Hassell (the Ambassador to Italy), is untrue. Intrusions by the party caused frequent conflicts and confusion, but the basic apparatus of diplomacy (including the AA's career personnel) remained intact; the embassies and consulates continued to perform their normal functions, and dispatches, recommendations, and instructions flowed to and from the AA's headquarters in Berlin. The confusion, the duplication of effort, and the ideological interference certainly contributed to the problems of the diplomats, yet their role was not destroyed and the day-to-day routine of the AA was not impaired. The Ministry remained a significant agency of German foreign policy.[8]

Control of foreign Germans was the principal source of competition and friction among the National Socialists and the AA. By 1930 approximately thirty million Germans (i.e., German citizens or *Reichsdeutschen*) and those of German descent who were citizens of foreign countries (*Volksdeutschen*) lived outside Germany. Technically, according to Nazi usage, such terms carried racial implications. *Reichsdeutschen* were German nationals "residing in the Reich," while *Volksdeutschen* were "Germans by race of foreign citizenship" and were a "racial elite" allegedly "enjoying privileges of German citizens." The National Socialists, when discussing foreign Germans, also employed the term *Auslandsdeutschen*, which meant "German nationals residing abroad."[9]

Large German minorities existed in eastern Europe, particularly in Poland and Czechoslovakia (parts of which had formerly belonged to Germany), and in many countries outside Europe Germans lived together in closely-knit communities (or colonies) that had developed since the middle of the nineteenth century. Large colonies, for example, had sprouted in southern Brazil, Argentina, South Africa, Egypt, and parts of the Far East (namely China, Japan, Australia, and Netherlands East Indies), where emigrant German farmers and businessmen had not been assimilated into the foreign cultures. Divided after World War I into supporters of the German monarchy and followers of the Weimar Republic, these self-contained colonies were nonpolitical in nature and were designed to preserve the cultural heritage of the Fatherland and to further the economic interests of foreign Germans.

The colonies were not only proud of their private German schools (*Deutsche Schule*), but also of their sports groups, book clubs, women's societies, youth organizations, and chambers of Commerce.[10] Each colony was incorporated according to the laws of its resident country, and most were operated by elected chairmen and executive committees. Such democratic principles were to be attacked after 1933 by the NSDAP and its foreign groups, which hoped to establish in the colonies an administration based on the party's authoritarian maxim of organization, the *Führerprinzip* ("leader principle").

The unofficial head of each colony was its local German consul or diplomatic representative, who often addressed his colony to celebrate a national holiday and invited it to be his guest in the mission building. An example was the arrival in London in November 1925 of Gustav Stresemann, the German Foreign Minister, to sign the Locarno Pact between Germany, England, and France. Conclusion of the agreement, which guaranteed Germany's western borders and allowed her to negotiate as an equal with the other European powers for the first time since World War I, was a momentous occasion, and the German Embassy in London invited the local German community to a reception.[11]

The Weimar government attempted wherever possible to establish close ties with the colonies and to aid them in retaining their cultural identity. After Germany's entry into the League of Nations in 1926, Stresemann became the champion of European minorities in the world body. Through his controversial "minorities diplomacy" (*Minderheitenpolitik*), he was able to call world attention to the problems of German communities in eastern Europe (particularly Poland) and to secure certain concessions for them. The German government also utilized the foreign communities for Germany's political and economic advantage. Although it did not use the small groups of German settlers in such areas as the Near East, it cared for communities that were being recreated in China after World War I. Following the German inflation of 1922 and 1923, a large number of Germans emigrated to China, finding considerable work with American industry and escaping worthless paper mark salaries. Accordingly, Berlin contributed to the re-establishment of the colonies in the Far East by subsidizing German schools, churches, and newspapers. Moreover, although treaties between Germany and China in 1921 and 1924 made German citizens in China subject to Chinese law, the Weimar regime tried to give as much legal protection as possible to its nationals there.[12]

The movement of Germans to China was not unusual; many also left the Weimar Republic and settled in the United States and Latin America. Between 1919 and 1933, for instance, roughly 430,000 Germans arrived in the United States. Alienated by inflation, civil strife, political murders, chronic unemployment, and political factionalism at home, disillusioned proletarians and recently proletarianized elements of the middle class dreamed of finding a better life elsewhere. Not every German who emigrated to America or other foreign lands, however, was looking for a place to live permanently. Some were "self-proclaimed emigres" who hated the Republic, others were right-wing nationalists or members of Hitler's movement, and still others hoped to raise money for German causes.[13]

In addition to the German government, foreign Germans during the Weimar period were administered by two large cultural agencies in Stuttgart, the German Foreign Institute and the League for Germandom Abroad. The Institute, with its massive research facilities and library on foreign *Deutschtum* (translated variously as "Germandom," "Germanism," or "Germanness"), focused its attention on cultural Germanism abroad and concerned itself with preserving the German language and way of life among foreign German communities. But some of the more important studies on Germanism during the 1920s were written for the Institute by writers whose emphasis on *Deutschtum* was toward *völkisch* solidarity among foreign Germans rather than on culture and ethnicity. Such persons, perhaps unwittingly, contributed to the later Nazi transformation of the meaning of *Deutschtum* into a racial and political concept.[14] They also developed an ethnic vocabulary to describe the various classifications of Germans outside the Reich; these terms (*Reichsdeutsche, Volksdeutsche, Auslandsdeutsche*) were to be used extensively after 1933 by the AO and its party branches abroad, and when the National Socialists seized power, these too took on distinct racial overtones.

Thus, the fanatical concern of the NSDAP for foreign Germans was in part a continuation of German tradition. On the other hand, the National Socialists sought to disassociate themselves completely from the policies of the Weimar government, and they repeatedly asserted that their predecessor had paid little official attention to Germans outside the Reich. Shortly after Hitler became Chancellor, his Deputy Führer, Hess, remarked to an audience, "You know as well as I that the greatest mistake of the former regime was its refusal to keep up ties of blood which connect the Germans in their homeland with Germans abroad." Bohle argued that under the Wilhelmine and Weimar regimes there had "existed such a massive gulf separating the foreign Germans and the native people, that one could rightly speak of a foreign German tragedy."[15]

Hitler, Hess, and Bohle believed that it was Germany's mission to unify the thirty million Germans outside the Reich into a worldwide German *Volksgemeinschaft* ("racial community"); or, as Bohle stressed, to mold "foreign Germandom" into "a racial community in the sense of the Third Reich."[16] In his few foreign policy addresses dealing with Germans abroad, Hitler revealed the broad interpretation and *völkisch* character which the Nazis applied to them by lumping them together under the term "foreign Germandom" (*Auslandsdeutschtum*). Although this word was also utilized in the 1920s by *Deutschtum* theorists, in Hitler's view it meant the superiority of blood ties to political or state ties among Germans abroad. Nazi theorists were indeed blunt on this point. Waldemar Damer's *Unsere Brüder jenseits der Grenzen* (probably 1938), explained that *Auslandsdeutschen* were "all [persons] of German blood who are conscious of being German, and who possess German citizenship."[17] Like Hitler, Bohle's interpretation was equally broad and confusing for the outside world. Speaking to a group of leaders from his party organizations around the world who were assembled at the Nazi party rally in Nuremberg in 1934, he bewildered even his listeners when he announced that all "Auslandsdeutschen are National Socialists!" On another occasion, he remarked that *Auslandsdeutschen* were persons "who think German and feel German."[18]

The Nazis, just as they became obsessed with saving the Reich's Germanic population, were determined to preserve the persons of

German descent living abroad from the anti-German "conspiracy" of world Jewry, Communism, and liberalism. Moreover, the Nazi groups outside Germany were created as bases from which the historic struggle against the alleged plot could be carried on world-wide. The Jew, Nazi officials firmly believed, was out to enslave the world's Aryan population; thus, it was crucial in fighting such a menace to confront it not only in Germany but throughout the world.

In addition to supporting Nazi racism, the groups abroad functioned as instruments of German expansion. After 1934 the AO created party organizations (comprised mainly of German citizens) in Austria, Poland, and Czechoslovakia, and their propaganda, political agitation, and economic work among local Germans were aimed at building strong Pan German movements in each country.[19] The objective was the same as Hitler's more noted diplomatic and military tactics; the party branches, despite their small size and limited significance, were to help push forward the day when eastern Europe would lie in National Socialist hands and when the German minorities there would become a part of a "Greater German Reich."

What was disturbing to world leaders was that such activities were scarcely limited to Poland and the small democracies on Germany's eastern border. Nazi groups in the Latin American countries, the United States, the former German Southwest Africa, and the British dominion, the Union of South Africa, alarmed many foreign officials. Already in November 1934 the American Ambassador to Germany, William Dodd, informed his government, "It is not improbable that a guiding principle which is present in this constant agitation [of the AO] is political—to protect Germany in case of future war and to further her prestige and possible territorial expansion." Four years later Cordell Hull, the American Secretary of State, warned that "the [German] danger to the Western Hemisphere is real and imminent."[20]

Although the NSDAP initially formed its foreign affiliates in the spring of 1931, their ideological origins lay much earlier in the party's history. Foreign Germandom had already caught the eye of the extreme right-wing party in Munich in February 1920. The official program of the party, drafted partially by Hitler, made little distinction between German citizens and *Volksdeutschen*. While the party's racial ideology was not yet fully developed, the program nevertheless suggested the volatile ethnic nationalism that was later to stamp Hitler's Reich and its aggressiveness toward foreign Germans. The program demanded "the consolidation of all Germans . . . into a Greater Germany," and it maintained that "every citizen of the [German] State" must live "for the usefulness of all" the people.[21]

Hitler won full control over the NSDAP in July 1921, and prior to his abortive *Putsch* in Munich two years later, when he attempted to strike down the Weimar democracy with his semi-militarized and brown-shirted "storm troopers" (*Sturmabteilung*, or SA), he mentioned little in public about foreign policy and foreign Germans. His attention was riveted solely on seizing power at home and making himself the lord of Germany. But following his *Putsch* and resulting imprisonment, his philosophy matured into the racial and nationalist principles that were to become the basis of his party's later efforts to organize Germandom on a worldwide scale.[22]

Just as his thoughts on foreign affairs were developed significantly in the pages of *Mein Kampf*, so were his attitudes toward world Germandom and toward its role in his future Reich.[23] "As a State," he remarked, his Empire would have to include "all Germans," because it was only by unifying the world's Germans that his historic mission could be accomplished. His great task was "assembling and preserving the most valuable racial elements of this nation [Germany]" and "raising them gradually and securely to a ruling position" in the world.[24] This radical stress on a racially-oriented foreign policy, the aims of which included disseminating Germandom abroad and establishing its supremacy among the other races of the world, was further acknowledged by Hitler in 1928. The foreign policy of the NSDAP, he argued, would know "no Germanizing or Teutonizing . . . but only the spread of its own people." Moreover, the party's "national conception" was "not determined by former patriotic ideas of government, but rather by völkisch racial views."[25]

Some Nazi ideologues were even more explicit about the party's concept that it was blood and race that would tie Germans around the world to a common destiny under Hitler. In Nitz Volker's *Unser Grenz- und Auslanddeutschtum* (published in 1931 by the party press in Munich), it was maintained that Hitler's birth outside the Reich was a "warning" that the future Nazi racial community would include more than simply Germany. Volker argued that for "all who are of German blood, we demand the right of sovereignty of peoples, and we renounce therefore no Germans, whether in

the South Tirol or in North Schleswig, in the West or in the East."
Bohle, in a speech commemorating Hitler's birthday in 1944, explained that for Germans there was "no greater sin than the
voluntary relinquishing of German blood." To justify the wooing
of foreign Germans by the AO, he maintained: "Thus we firmly
believe and we know that a German is everywhere a German,
whether he lives in the Reich, in Africa, in Denmark or in China
or elsewhere in this world. Not countries or continents, not climate
or environment, but blood and race decide the thoughts and the
obligations of Germans."[26]

Nazi policy toward foreign Germandom was not aimed at turning foreign peoples into Germans, but instead, as Hitler explained
publicly, making loyal National Socialists out of persons "who belong to our people, who are of our blood, and who speak our
language."[27] His ideas had been stimulated by Germany's crushing
defeat in World War I and his persistent feeling that Germans had
been discriminated against by the rest of the world following the
war. He and his followers were convinced that Germans abroad
had been so little cared for by the Kaiser's government that they
had failed to support the Reich fully during the conflict. In a sense,
when foreign Germans were accused by the National Socialists
and other right-wing extremists in Germany of being disloyal to
the Fatherland in the war, they were being cast by the rightists
into that unfortunate class of Germans who had allegedly "stabbed
the Reich in the back" in 1918. Obviously the Nazis did not relish
a repetition of such behavior; consequently, when they seized
power in Germany in 1933, they worked through the *Auslands-
Organisation* and its affiliates abroad to "coordinate" foreign Germandom, hoping thereby to assure Hitler of its support.[28]

Hess and Bohle were also quick to tie the concept of "class
struggle" to the NSDAP's efforts to organize foreign Germans.
As the party stressed, one of its chief concerns at home was to
replace the Weimar Republic, which was torn by deep conflicts,
with a *Volksgemeinschaft* united by German blood and a fanatical
loyalty of the people to their superman Führer, Hitler. The Nazis
further believed that foreign Germans were threatened by Com-
munist-inspired political differences and social antagonisms. How
else could one explain why German communities abroad were
structured along democratic lines, why they seemed to hold little
respect for the Weimar regime or Fatherland, and why many were
split between monarchists and republicans? According to Bohle,

testifying at his trial in Nuremberg in 1948, "whenever three or four Germans get together they think they must form some sort of a society or club, and the chief object of these societies seemed to be to fight one another, thereby forgetting altogether the question of national patriotism as such."[29]

If the theoretical foundations were present in National Socialism to encourage its interest in foreign Germans, the NSDAP was slow in realizing the value of such a resource for the party. From its inception it paid scant attention to Germans abroad. Except for the creation in 1927 and 1928 of party organizations and storm trooper units in Austria, Poland, and the Sudetenland in Czechoslovakia,[30] it made little effort to mobilize Nazi members and Reich citizens abroad until 1931. The party was deeply involved in its quest to overthrow the German government and capture the latter for itself. Throughout its short history its energies had been focused on putting Hitler into power.

Progress toward this coveted goal was difficult and slow, however; in the *Reichstag* ("national legislature") elections of May 1928, the NSDAP received a disappointing 2.6 percent of the national vote and placed only twelve deputies in the assembly. Hitler, ranting against the Treaty of Versailles and emphasizing the doctrines of race and *Lebensraum*, formulated little on foreign affairs that he had not already discussed in *Mein Kampf*.[31] The party reflected his overriding concern to conquer Germany; its money, for example, went almost exclusively for propaganda and for building its organizational apparatus inside the Reich.[32]

Its initial interest in foreign Germans came from individual party members abroad and from Gregor Strasser, the organization chief of the NSDAP and second in line to Hitler. Following the dismal showing of the party in the *Reichstag* election in 1928, Strasser became head of an office in the NSDAP's national leadership (*Reichsleitung*) in Munich, which handled foreign press and organizational matters. He was also named the special expert on foreign affairs in the Nazi *Reichstag* fraction. Beyond Strasser, the party's pseudoforeign service in the 1920s included Rosenberg, Kurt Ludecke, and Ernst (Putzi) Hanfstaengl, each having a degree of influence on Hitler's foreign policy ideas.[33]

Although the NSDAP's interest in foreign German communities was to reach its peak in 1933 and 1934, its efforts to penetrate them began sporadically and much earlier at the instigation of individual party members. Dedicated members who left Germany in the 1920s because of political frustrations with the Weimar regime or to escape the authorities often attempted to organize the particular colony in their local area by recruiting Reich citizens for party membership. Wherever they could discover "political friends" (*Gesinnungsgenossen*), they formed small groups that concerned themselves with publicizing Hitler to foreign Germans and with contacting offices of the NSDAP in Germany.[34] A willingness of foreign party members to act independently of the NSDAP was therefore revealed early, as some members interpreted the party's aims as they saw fit (i.e., without orders from Germany). Such behavior was to manifest itself throughout the party's history abroad.

The earliest activity among foreign Nazi members developed in the Americas, South Africa, and China. In Latin America, nearly 1.5 million persons of German descent and roughly 180,000 Reich citizens lived chiefly in southern Brazil, Argentina (especially in Buenos Aires), Chile, Paraguay, and Uruguay. Particularly alarming to the Latin Americans was the refusal of the German settlers to be assimilated fully into the Latin way of life. Not only did the Germans reveal a strong national loyalty to their original homeland, but they held steadfastly to the German language in everyday speech, and they formed compact and isolated settlements that possessed their own cultural organizations. In many instances this strong cultural and political attachment to the Fatherland conflicted with (and even displaced) similar feelings felt for the local Latin American nation.[35]

Such conflicts were slowly sharpened with the arrival of fanatical members of the NSDAP. Groups of Nazi members in Brazil and Paraguay first developed ties with the Munich *Reichsleitung* in 1928. In July Hans Asanger, a doctor in Benedito Timbo in southern Brazil, created what the NSDAP later called its first *Ortsgruppe* ("local group") abroad. In Paraguay a small collection of party members formed an "organization center," which was headed until 1930 by Otto Künze and an emigrant Danzig SA man, Bruno Fricke. Each party branch in Paraguay and Brazil was soon designated by the *Reichsleitung* as a foreign *Gruppenleitung* ("group leadership").[36]

The most active organization at the end of the 1920s arose in Blumenau, a city in southern Brazil near the Atlantic coast. The leader of the group was a doctor who succeeded in recruiting from local German nationals twenty-one members for the NSDAP by

December 1930. The group established close contact with Munich, which sent the Blumenau organization propaganda materials for its theater group and monthly *Sprechabende* ("discussion evenings," in which the group and its prospective members heard speeches on National Socialism by party leaders).[37]

Nazi activities in the United States also began in the 1920s. The large number of Germans who had migrated to the United States since the nineteenth century (including almost a half million during the Weimar years) offered promising recruitment possibilities for the National Socialists. Like the Germans in Latin America, German emigrants to the United States had settled in large, tightly-knit clusters in the developing industrial cities of Pittsburgh, Detroit, Cleveland, Cincinnati, New York City, and Los Angeles. Party theorists in the AO, DAI, and VDA estimated that roughly seven million German-Americans in 1930 still spoke German as their principal language and that approximately a quarter of America was of German descent. Bohle and the AO believed that the sons and daughters of millions of German settlers who had arrived in America in the eighteenth and nineteenth centuries could be unified into a vital political force for Germany. But never having visited America nor studied it closely, Bohle and other Nazis anxious to form party groups there never understood that such efforts were jeopardized seriously by the rapid and thorough assimilation of the Germans into American culture.

Although a number of loyal Nazis fled to America after the Hitler *Putsch*, neither the NSDAP nor Hitler paid much attention to the United States until 1928. In *Mein Kampf* Hitler had written as if America hardly existed. It was only in the summer of 1928, with the appearance in Germany of increasing numbers of American-made automobiles (cars always caught Hitler's eye), that he noted the United States was a product of European migration and a great meeting place of the Aryan race. Also believing that he saw a powerful Jewish population in America, he suddenly began viewing the Americas as the chief threat to the German domination of the world, and he concluded that following Germany's conquest of France and Russia (which he had outlined in *Mein Kampf*), a war with America would be inevitable. The AO, in its hopes of furthering Nazi influence in the United States by creating party groups and supporting German-American organizations there, applied to its policy Hitler's racial interpretation of American history. Accordingly, the United States was a Jew-ridden plutocracy whose salvation could only come from its large German element, which, the Nazis were convinced, was still untainted by Jewish influence.[38]

From the American side, the anti-German hysteria that had been touched off in the United States by World War I had disappeared by the mid-1920s. The debate over the Versailles Treaty had hardly closed when Americans began to doubt Germany's responsibility for causing the war. Many German-Americans made the most of this opportunity. Although they had been subjected to harsh treatment during the war, they formed such organizations as the Steuben Society, which grew rapidly, emphasized the contribution of German emigrants to American institutions, and distributed literature. The Society, for example, republished Albert Bernhardt Faust's *The German Element in the United States: With Special Reference to Its Political, Moral, Social, and Educational Influence* (1927), a massive study that stressed the German contribution to such American causes as abolition, civil service reform, sound money policy, peace congresses, and personal liberty. Similar works included F. Eiselmeier's *Das Deutschtum in Angloamerika* (1926) and C. E. Dale's *Amerikanisches Auskunftsbuch* (1923).[39]

Hitler, except for dispatching Ludecke, one of his political fund raisers and foreign policy advisers, to Detroit in 1924 to obtain money from Henry Ford (who had attracted Nazi attention by his anti-Semitic writings),[40] made no effort in the 1920s to expand National Socialism to the United States. While it is true that as early as the fall of 1922, a tiny NSDAP group was founded in the northeast section of the Bronx, it was created independently of Munich and it hardly flourished. Nevertheless, some of Hitler's followers tried to rally Germans in America to their hero. One was Edmund Fürholzer, who emigrated from Germany to America in December 1926 and founded a newspaper in New York, the *Deutsche Zeitung*, which he hoped would attract local Germans to National Socialism.[41]

But even before Fürholzer had arrived, a cover organization for Nazi members and other extreme rightists from Germany had been formed in October 1924 in Detroit. Three Nazi and German emigrants, Fritz and Peter Gissibl and Walter Kappe, founded the National Socialist Association of Teutonia (*Nationalsozialistische Vereinigung Teutonia*). It was no accident that the Teutonia was established in Detroit, because the city was undergoing what many American cities were experiencing in the 1920s—rapid industrialization, mass production, and temporary unemployment.

Immigrant German laborers, especially those working for the Ford Motor Company, were dismissed from their jobs, and after 1929 and the beginning of the Depression, the situation worsened. A handful of workers, some looking for security, others because of a belief that their problems had been caused by a Jewish-capitalist plot, joined the Teutonia. Fritz Gissibl, head of the ultra-conservative organization, had arrived in America in December 1923, but he did not join the NSDAP until three years later.

The Teutonia, even before its leader became a National Socialist, celebrated Hitler's birthday by collecting money for the NSDAP in Munich. Sometimes, as in May 1926, the Association was rewarded for its financial sacrifices with a note of appreciation from Hitler. The Teutonia's ideology and propaganda were thoroughly National Socialist. Through handbills, pamphlets, and its newspaper, *Vorposten*, its leaders attacked the Jews, Communists, Weimar Republic, and German revolution of 1918. But in Germany, it proclaimed, the teachings of one man, Adolf Hitler, were emerging, and soon this "real German man" would come to power and crush such enemies.[42]

Some hard-core National Socialists in America, many of whom were social misfits and political extremists like the Gissibls, chose not to join the Teutonia; instead, they worked to form their own *Ortsgruppe*, which they hoped might someday be officially recognized by Munich. An example was Christoph Klausfeldner, an "old fighter" from the early Nazi movement in Germany. A member of the militant *Rossbach Freikorps* (one of the many paramilitary and *völkisch* organizations formed in Germany after World War I) at seventeen years old, Klausfeldner entered the SA in Bavaria, became a personal courier for the Nuremberg Nazi chief, Julius Streicher, and participated in the Hitler *Putsch*. He fled to the United States soon after the Munich uprising. Klausfeldner, who could never free himself of his extreme political activism, organized a party group in Cincinnati in 1932 that was finally acknowledged by the *Reichsleitung* as an *Ortsgruppe* of the NSDAP.[43]

Many more America-bound National Socialists in the 1920s decided to join Gissibl's Teutonia. One was Heinz Spanknöbel, later boss of the widely publicized German-American group of the mid-1930s, the Association of the Friends of the New Germany (*Bund der Freunde des Neuen Deutschlands*). Spanknöbel, an employee of the Ford Motor Company, had arrived in the United States in 1929, but as the Depression deepened, he lost his job and began

working full-time for the Teutonia. Concurrently, he joined the
NSDAP and became close friends with Gissibl. By 1932 Teutonia
had branches in Chicago, Los Angeles, New York City, Hudson
County, and Cincinnati, and claimed a membership of roughly
five hundred.

The Hudson County group was located in Union City, New Jersey
and was led by a dedicated Nazi transplanted from Frankfurt,
Wilhelm Schneider. When he arrived in the United States in 1927,
Schneider dreamed of developing a party organization that would
have the official sanction of Hitler and Munich. The local German
language newspapers, however, refused to cooperate with him; as he
investigated further, he discovered that Hitler was hardly known to
Germans in New Jersey and that there was very little interest in
National Socialism. Unlike the Germans in South America, those
in the United States were quickly and completely transformed into
persons who felt themselves a part of the native way of life. Many,
in fact, could not have cared less about the Fatherland or a political
figure who was still barely known to Germans inside the Reich.
Schneider, disappointed but undaunted, finally contacted Gissibl,
and later formed the Teutonia affiliate in Hudson County.[44]

The reaction of the party in Germany to the efforts by foreign
members to spread Hitler's ideas was to encourage them wherever
possible and to begin plans for organizing them. Himmler, the
party's propaganda leader and chief of the SS, sent the Teutonia
Nazi placards and pamphlets, and in September 1930 he issued the
first set of directives for "foreign propaganda" (*Auslandspropa-
ganda*).[45] Munich also assembled a small mailing list of foreign members, and the Propaganda Department demanded and received
political reports from the party branches abroad. A Nazi group in
Windhoek, the capital of former German Southwest Africa, reported on its work among local German clubs and societies by noting
optimistically, "The acceptance of the [Nazi] view is not unfavorable, with a larger increase in and stronger effect on [German]
associations definitely to be expected."[46] Moreover, new *Gruppenleitung* were created in China, Southwest Africa, and New York
City; each organization was headed by someone approved by Munich
and was responsible for party members and German citizens in its
country.[47]

Yet, despite the party's growing awareness of its foreign members, the main problem facing it abroad until 1930 was its anonymity and total lack of publicity outside Germany. Just as Hitler's

views on foreign affairs were barely known inside Germany until his alliance with Alfred Hugenberg (the film and newspaper czar) and the German nationalists against the Young Plan in 1929, so most Germans around the globe had rarely heard of the Nazi Führer. As party officials in Munich noted, any penetration of foreign Germandom with Nazi ideology would take time and money, elements with which the NSDAP was hardly endowed once the Depression began. What Nazi leaders recognized even more was that their party badly needed a dramatic success in national politics. Above all, this would take it closer to its supreme goal of gaining power in Germany. Strasser, Ludecke, and a few others believed that it could also help awaken world Germandom to Hitler and his historic mission.

2

HANS NIELAND AND THE
AUSLANDS-ABTEILUNG, 1930-1933

As Hitler climbed his way to power in Germany between 1930 and 1933, his party took its first steps to attract and organize foreign Germandom. Although by no means a serious concern of the party, small groups (ranging in number from a few persons to fifty) of German citizens and Nazi members abroad were formed in many countries under Munich's direction. While tiny and hardly significant to the NSDAP's fortunes at home, the groups were nevertheless dedicated to Hitler, proud of their contact with the parent movement, often quarrelsome and unruly, and led by authoritarian-minded party bosses.

The impetus for creating them came from Hitler's surprising triumph in the *Reichstag* election in September 1930. Exploiting the misery caused by the Depression in Germany, the NSDAP suddenly became the second largest party in the national assembly. The victory, which made headlines in the foreign press,[1] was also vital in arousing for the National Socialists at least the attention of a few Germans abroad. The party's foreign members greeted the breakthrough with excitement. Some wrote the *Reichsleitung* offering their "heartiest good wishes for the powerful success that was achieved."[2]

CREATION OF THE *Auslands-Abteilung*

Only weeks after the election, a handful of Hamburg National Socialists met to discuss the development of a new Foreign Department (*Auslands-Abteilung*) in the NSDAP that could organize and guide the party's foreign members. The group was led by Willy

Grothe, an SA man and local party bigwig who had been a private import-export dealer in Africa. His nationalism and sense of persecution had been kindled when he was imprisoned in Africa during World War I by the British. He was convinced that a future *Auslands-Abteilung* should have its headquarters in Hamburg, the historic Hanseatic city from which ships left daily for all corners of the world. It was a symbol, he noted, with which foreign Germans could identify.[3]

To persuade Munich that an *Auslands-Abteilung* was needed, Grothe and his circle approached a Nazi *Reichstag* deputy from Hamburg, Hans Nieland. Nieland received the idea with enthusiasm, particularly after he began entertaining visions that he might become head of the Department and add to his stature in the party. At the beginning of 1931 he contacted the party's organization leader, Strasser, proposing that such a Department be created and that he, Nieland, be commissioned its chief. To prove his sincerity he traveled to Munich in the spring and obtained the *Reichsleitung*'s list of roughly fifty addresses of foreign party members (most living in the United States and Canada).[4]

Strasser, after discussing the affair with Hitler, fully agreed, and on 28 April 1931 he issued an order creating the *Auslands-Abteilung* with its headquarters in Hamburg, subordinating it to his office and handing the job of leader to Nieland. Although Strasser had always been hopeful of doing something for National Socialists outside Germany, he was mainly pleased for selfish reasons about the Department. Since the party's victory the previous fall his office had been swamped with correspondence from foreign Germans sympathetic to Hitler and from foreign members, and he openly admitted, "I needed someone to answer the letters from abroad."[5]

Nieland's availability, however, hardly meant that he was qualified to organize the foreign members or to lure other Germans abroad into the party. Described derisively by a party opponent as an "ambitious little bourgeois," he had never set foot outside Germany nor did he speak a foreign language.[6] Except for holding a doctoral degree in political science and for having pursued a brief study of law, he had little to offer in dealing with and understanding the problems of Germans abroad. He had been born the son of a merchant on 3 October 1900 in Hagen, a small town in Westphalia. After serving for a few months in World War I, he spent several years in school and settled in Hamburg to become an export trader and legal adviser. Fancying himself an extreme German patriot and an opponent of the Weimar regime (which, he believed, had been forced on Germany after the war), he had joined the party in 1926.[7]

Strasser's directive gave the *Auslands-Abteilung* control over foreign members who were not under district party organizations in Austria, the Saar region in western Germany, and the free city of Danzig. At the beginning of June, Nieland issued his first command to the foreign members, proudly announcing that Hitler had shown "his interest in you and your happiness" by forming the *Auslands-Abteilung* and that the NSDAP now challenged the National Socialists abroad to become active for the movement. Involving oneself for the party, he maintained, was the most noble goal members abroad could achieve, and it would enable them to "join the battlefront of the German people."[8]

The order also laid down guidelines for financial dues to be paid by the members to Hamburg and for establishing *Ortsgruppen* of twenty members or more and "support points" (*Stützpunkte*), which were groups comprised of fewer members. In places with only a tiny number of Nazis there were no *Ortsgruppen* or *Stützpunkte*, but party cells (*Zellen*) that were subordinate either to a nearby *Ortsgruppe* or directly to the *Auslands-Abteilung*. As soon as enough members were available or had been recruited to form an *Ortsgruppe* or *Stützpunkt*, a list of members was forwarded to the *Auslands-Abteilung* for approval.

Once the group had been created, it chose the "most capable leader" (i.e., an *Ortsgruppenleiter*, *Stützpunktleiter*, or *Zellen-leiter*) from its midst, and his selection was confirmed by Nieland. The foreign leaders were commissioned to assemble "a staff of assistants" who would handle the local party treasury, secretarial duties, and propaganda.[9] Soon, these small affiliates abroad would find themselves subordinated to national party organizations called *Landesgruppen* ("country groups"), led by *Landesgruppenleiters* ("country group leaders") who were responsible to Hamburg.

Nieland also assembled his own staff. His only salaried employees were his father and sister, who were hired as office manager and bookkeeper; making the office a "family affair," however, was to bring him a barrage of criticism later. The remainder of his staff included his special advisers (*Referate*), who headed regional divisions in the *Auslands-Abteilung* and corresponded with party members in their regions. While Grothe was the adviser for Africa, there were similar officials for Europe, North America, Latin America, Australia, India, and East Asia.[10] By late September the staff had been expanded to include divisions for foreign propaganda, membership, financial affairs, and the press.[11] Most of the staff were recruited from the party organization in Hamburg, while others were not even Nazi members but offered their services free to the Department. An example was Bohle, a young, foreign-born commercial employee; he joined the NSDAP and began work in December 1931 with the Department as a specialist on the Union of South Africa.[12]

It became apparent very quickly that one of the most important offices was the Propaganda Division. It busily collected a lengthy list of German newspapers abroad and sent them free articles on Hitler and his movement. This was to become a popular method for disseminating propaganda among foreign Germans, particularly after a number of party groups abroad began publishing their own papers. The Division and Nieland also sent crudely typewritten information sheets to members abroad entitled the *National-sozialistische Auslandsbrief* (*National Socialist Foreign Letter*). A frequent contributor to the letters was Otto Langmann, an Evangelical pastor from Guatemala and a later AO official who became Germany's Minister (*Gesandter*) to Uruguay.[13]

By the fall of 1931 the recruiting of new Nazi members abroad and the forming of foreign affiliates had registered small gains. Nieland reported to Munich that his Department had 751 foreign members enrolled in the party, including *Volksdeutschen* as well as German citizens.[14] Enlisting Germans with foreign citizenship, however, was criticized by Strasser and the *Reichsleitung's* legal adviser, Hans Frank. Although Strasser issued an order directing the *Auslands-Abteilung* to recruit only Reich nationals and to command them not to intervene in the affairs of their host country,[15] the question was to arise repeatedly in the future. Many groups abroad were unable to resist the temptation of expanding their membership by signing up interested ethnic Germans who were foreign citizens. But as Hitler informed the editor of the *Leipziger Neueste Nachrichten*, Richard Breiting, in an interview in May 1931, Nazi policy abroad would never be based on the views of foreign governments, world opinion, or long-range effects of the policy. It would instead be Machiavellian in nature and "dictated by the needs of the moment" of the party and German government.[16] Translated into practice, this meant that Nazi groups outside Germany applied the selfish party law that said the "needs of the Nazi community came before those of the individual" (*Gemeinnutz geht vor Eigennutz*),[17] and they continued to direct their efforts at foreign citizens.

SMALL PARTY BRANCHES IN THE AMERICAS AND EUROPE

The first party affiliates outside Germany recognized by the *Auslands-Abteilung* were in Argentina, Brazil, and Paraguay. In addition to the large *Volksdeutsch* population (roughly 1.5 million persons), the Latin American penchant for dictatorships, for political parties led by a charismatic hero, and for militarism, combined with a depressed socio-economic development to breed a certain sympathy for the Nazi groups.[18] In Argentina the situation seemed particularly favorable for the NSDAP. The party's heavy nationalist propaganda complemented the extensive *Deutschtum* campaign that had been carried on since World War I (which had stressed that Germany was an anti-imperialist nation and not responsible for the war) by leaders of the German communities. Furthermore, German influence since Wilhelmine days on the Argentine army appeared to ensure the government's friendliness toward the Nazi groups.

The large German colony in Buenos Aires had been formed since the 1870s, and it possessed a heterogeneous political, economic, and social structure. Upper class Germans in the colony, many of them German citizens, were wealthy businessmen and employees of leading German firms. This elite group held its distance from the majority of the colony's members, which included lesser employees, small merchants, artisans, shopkeepers, and laborers. Politically the colony was conservative, with many strong monarchists who outnumbered liberals and socialists. During World I a cultural organization for *Deutschtum* work, the *Deutsche Volksbund* ("People's League"), and a German Chamber of Commerce had been organized, the latter as a defense for German economic interests against "blacklisting" by the Argentine government. The November revolution of 1918 in Germany had far-reaching effects on the colony, as the formation of the Weimar Republic sharpened the old political divisions in the community. The social and economic leadership despised the Weimar regime and criticized the government vehemently in its major newspaper, the *Deutsche La Plata-Zeitung*. The paper of the democrats and republicans in the colony was the pro-Weimar *Argentinisches Tageblatt*, whose subscribers numbered roughly half those of its competitor.

The breach continued throughout the 1920s and was widened further by the appearance of the first Nazi *Ortsgruppe* in Buenos Aires in the spring of 1931. It included 59 members. The group grew slowly, held meetings and demonstration marches, and attracted the opposition of the Argentine press and German diplomats by its members' wearing Nazi uniforms publicly. Local authorities also disliked the infiltration of some Nazis into Argentine fascist and conservative movements. The *Ortsgruppe's* public debut was a memorial service in May 1931, held jointly with German veterans' groups like the *Stahlhelm* ("Steel Helmet"), for Albert Leo Schlageter, a former German officer executed by the French for sabotage during the French occupation of the Ruhr region in 1923 and worshiped as a hero by the NSDAP. Two months later the group held its first mass meeting, where nationalist speakers attacked and berated the Weimar Republic. In the days that followed, the *Ortsgruppe* became increasingly active. A demonstration of the local in November attracted over eight hundred persons, and a similar event in January 1932, held with other nationalist German organizations, attracted five thousand colony members.

In May 1932 Nieland ordered a thorough reorganization of the party in Argentina, and he established a national party unit or *Landesgruppe*. It published a special information sheet which every party member was expected to read and purchase. A "leadership school" was created to educate and train officials for the *Landesgruppe*. By September 1932 the party had expanded outside the Buenos Aires local to include seven *Stützpunkte* and 278 members.[19]

Affiliates were also formed in Brazil. A group in Rio de Janeiro was assembled in October, and similar branches developed among the settlements of German farmers and merchants in the large southern states. In May a fifteen-member *Stützpunkt* was created in São Paulo, and it held weekly meetings in the homes of its leading members. It was directed by a young businessman, Hans-Henning von Cossel, whose political activism and German nationalism could be traced to his earlier service in the German army and his membership in the Free Corps. The group's work included spreading Nazi philosophy in the German colony, indoctrinating party members in the ideology of National Socialism, and pressuring local German newspapers to halt criticism of Hitler. By the end of 1931 the group had doubled its membership and its meetings were drawing over a hundred visitors.[20] A similar success was taking shape in Paraguay, where party affiliates had existed for two years. In August 1931 the *Auslands-Abteilung* created a *Landesgruppe* in Asuncion, under the guidance of a retired army officer, Franz Reitzenstein.[21] An organization also sprouted in Santiago, Chile behind the leader of the local German Railway Office, Karl Hübner, and *Landesgruppenleiter* Willi Kohn.[22]

In the United States, where the political situation was the reverse of that in South America, Nieland believed that the best method for developing *Ortsgruppen* and not attracting the attention of the authorities was to use Gissibl's Teutonia group as a "cover organization, with the [Nazi] local the heart." Gissibl, above all, entertained hopes of leading the entire Nazi movement in the United States. But some party members there, like Klausfeldner in Cincinnati, noted for Nieland that Teutonia had never been designated a unit of the party. They had never joined Teutonia, but had created disorganized party cells in the major cities with large German populations. These members numbered less than two hundred, but they claimed that they were the nucleus of a party structure in America and that the Teutonia's membership was composed largely of nonparty people.

As Ludecke observed, Nieland was greatly interested in the United States, seeing in it a goldmine for acquiring new party members and dues. He also saw a chance to increase his authority in America by forcing Gissibl's group and the disorganized cells of party members to compete for his approval of their leadership of a future party in the United States. Ignoring Teutonia, he placed the New York *Gruppenleitung* in the summer of 1931 under the *Auslands-Abteilung* and designated it the official *Ortsgruppe* of the NSDAP in New York.[23] He also searched for a trusted *Vertrauensmann* ("confidential agent") for America, who could be counted on to expand the membership and report faithfully to him.

His choices for such a leader were limited. One candidate was Alfred Krinn, commissioned by Strasser in 1930 to operate the *Gruppenleitung* New York.[24] Another possibility was the editor of a German newspaper in Cincinnati and a ranking member of Teutonia, Walter Kappe.[25] But for a time the strongest bet for the job seemed to be Ludecke, a personal friend of Hitler and one of the Führer's campaign fund raisers who had spent considerable time after 1922 touring the United States and speaking to German organizations about Hitler. At the beginning of 1931 he had joined the Teutonia and taken control of its propaganda for the states along the eastern coast.[26]

Unfortunately for Ludecke, he proved to be too well qualified for the post; he also appeared to Nieland to be overly ambitious. Krinn was eliminated from consideration in July 1931 when he became involved in a bitter quarrel with other members in New York and was ousted as their leader. In a rowdy meeting that was characteristic of the *Ortsgruppe*, a Long Island janitor named Paul Manger was chosen to succeed Krinn. The New York group was particularly prone to bickering and factionalism, which led some members to leave it and organize a new Nazi cell in Yorkville, a predominantly German-speaking section in Manhattan. This left Kappe, who finally became *Vertrauensmann* for North America until the beginning of 1932, when he was replaced by Manger. Nieland's naming of Manger, however, hardly encouraged Gissibl; it ruined Teutonia's hope of taking over the NSDAP in America, and any move by Gissibl to counter Hamburg's decision would end completely his dream of leading the entire movement.[27]

Such instability as shown by the party in America was hardly uncommon in the NSDAP's foreign groups. Their members were equally dogmatic and subjective in their political beliefs and uncompromising in their tactics as were the party bosses directing the show from the Reich. The "totalitarian mind-set" of Nazi leaders made personal conflict and struggles for power commonplace in the NSDAP at home, and the situation differed little in its small foreign groups.[28] But while the Nazis were experiencing a less than spectacular beginning in America, their affiliates created by the *Auslands-Abteilung* during 1931 in Europe revealed a bit more promise. This was especially true of the organizations that sprang up in Switzerland and Italy. Although some groups had begun meeting unofficially in Switzerland during the previous year, the first party branch was formed by National Socialists in Zurich in September 1931 and acknowledged by Hamburg several months later.

The *Ortsgruppe* had a small staff that had been "trained in Munich," which busily spread propaganda about Hitler throughout the colony. The local also recruited party members among the German citizens, and here too, the staff showed what it had learned in Munich. By compiling a list of persons who had fled from Germany to Zurich to escape paying income taxes or other financial obligations, the local was able to blackmail wealthy Germans and force them to join the party or to give donations to it. There were also small *Stützpunkte* in St. Gallen, Tessin, Davos, Berne, Geneva, and Basel, and the *Auslands-Abteilung* flooded every major Swiss city with copies of the NSDAP's national propaganda organ in the Reich, the *Völkischer Beobachter*.[29] One of Hitler's most fervent disciples in Switzerland was Wilhelm Gustloff, a German national from Mecklenburg who had settled in Davos in 1917. An extreme German nationalist and conservative, he had joined the virulently anti-Semitic German Racist League for Defense and Attack (*Deutschvölkischer Schutz- und Trutzbund*) in 1921, but after Hitler's *Putsch* he became a convert to the NSDAP and sought to spread Hitler's ideas in Switzerland. He spent his vacations in Germany, drilled with the SA, and eventually built a tiny *Stützpunkt* in Davos in 1930.[30]

The growth of the party in Italy also began in 1931. Since 1929 small clusters of party members had met in Rome, Milan, Meran, Bozen, Genoa, and Florence. Many members complained that Germans in Catholic Italy had a problem in maintaining their national and cultural heritage.[31] Their greatest protest, however, was over the South Tirol. By the Treaty of St. Germain of 1919, the southern portion of the Tirol had been transferred from Austria to Italy, with the frontier drawn at the Brenner Pass. Roughly 230,000 German-Austrians were included in Italy, which created the "problem" of the South Tirol (or *Alto Adige* as Italians called it) and formed the major stumbling block to an Italo-German alliance. There is ample evidence that following the "march on Rome" in October 1922 the Fascist government treated the German-Austrians badly. Beginning in 1923 Mussolini's regime sought to "italianize" the Germans in the Tirol: Italian was declared the official language; family names were italianized; school instruction in German was forbidden; and German newspapers, journals, and cultural groups were suppressed. Persons who protested or sabotaged the Fascist effort were imprisoned.[32]

Hitler, fascinated with Mussolini, was determined both to ally with Italy and to absorb Austria into Germany. Consequently he carefully avoided an Italo-German confrontation over the Tirol. In 1922 he had learned from Ludecke, who visited Mussolini for the Nazi leader, that the Duce was sensitive about the Tirolean question. Subsequently, writing in *Mein Kampf* and in a brochure he drafted in 1926, *Die Südtiroler Frage und das deutsche Bündnisproblem* (most of which has been lost but was a chapter from his memoir), he made no secret that his plan to unify Germans in Europe did not include those in the Tirol.

His position apparently had a positive effect on Mussolini. Although he was hardly an admirer of Hitler, the Duce sent money and secret shipments of arms to the NSDAP, and by 1928 and 1929 a pleasant relationship had developed between Fascist and Nazi leaders.[33] But Hitler's view was not shared by many members of his own party in Germany, Austria, and the Tirol. Hans Frank flatly disagreed with Hitler in a letter to his boss in August 1926, and in the summer of 1931 he spoke to the Nazis in Innsbruck, demanding that Germany annex the Tirol (for which the NSDAP later apologized). Similar feelings were rampant among Nazi groups in Milan, Bozen, and Meran.[34]

At the end of 1930 Hitler and Strasser dispatched a *Vertrauens-mann* to Italy to look into the creation of *Ortsgruppen* there. Since Hitler was already convinced that Italy must be one of the Reich's allies when the National Socialists came to power, the *Reichsleitung* gave the *Auslands-Abteilung* strict orders to ensure that the groups in Italy would run smoothly and cause no trouble for the Fascist government.[35] Despite Hitler's demand for caution, the Department quickly organized a *Landesgruppe* during the latter half of 1931, the heart of which was a *Stützpunkt* created in Rome in October, which by the year's end had enrolled twenty-five members. The *Stützpunkt* even attracted attention in Germany. The liberal press in Munich noted its appearance and claimed that its leaders were forming a political alliance with the chieftains of the Fascist party. Although the *Völkischer Beobachter* grudgingly acknowledged that an affiliate existed in Rome, the paper maintained that "all of the [other] assertions are lies."[36]

Nieland also appointed *Vertrauensmänner* to build Nazi organizations in England, Poland, Denmark, Latvia, Spain, Portugal, and Yugoslavia.[37] In England the party's agent was Otto Bene, a personal acquaintance of Hess who had spent considerable time in London after 1927 as a representative for Trylisin hair tonic. Acting on orders from the *Auslands-Abteilung*, he organized a party group in the German community of London, and he established the party's headquarters in the offices of a local German newspaper, the *Neue Londoner Zeitung*. His efforts were soon rewarded; in April 1932 the *Auslands-Abteilung* made him head of the London *Ortsgruppe*.[38]

From their inception the Nazi affiliates abroad resembled the party groups inside Germany because the foreign groups developed not around the ideology of Nazism, but around strong-willed party bosses and men like Bene, Gustloff, Reitzenstein, Kohn, and Friedhelm Burbach (the party's leader in Portugal and Spain) who proclaimed their total loyalty to Hitler. The groups abroad were rigidly organized according to the *Führerprinzip*, and the authority of their leaders depended principally on each man's charisma and his ability to convince his local German colony that he was Hitler's personally anointed chieftain by virtue of his support from Hamburg.[39] This was particularly true for party leaders outside Europe. One of the first branches to arise in Africa, for example, was an *Ortsgruppe* in the Cameroons that was erected in December 1931 around Bernhard Ruberg, a former German war hero, Free Corps leader (who once belonged to the group of right-wing assassins in Germany, the *Organisation Escherich*), and fanatical National Socialist.[40]

Despite the work of such ambitious personalities, not every affiliate abroad was established successfully or permitted by foreign authorities to operate. The Swedish government flatly refused to allow the NSDAP to form a branch in its country. When the *Auslands-Abteilung*'s contact man for Sweden, Willy Meyer-Donner, entered Stockholm in December 1931 and began speaking to local Germans in his SA uniform, the government quickly imprisoned him and later ordered his expulsion from the country. Nieland's stubborn response was to ask Hitler's right arm and head of the Nazi *Reichstag* fraction, Herman Göring, if he would use his friendship with the King of Sweden to get Meyer-Donner readmitted to Sweden.[41] Already the NSDAP was revealing its insensitivity to the opinion of foreign governments, and the party's silly games were attracting official hostility abroad.

1932: HARD WORK AND FRUSTRATION

The Swedish blunder notwithstanding, Nieland and the *Reichsleitung* greeted the beginning of 1932 with great optimism and confidence that this would be the crucial year when the party seized control of the German government. They noted that the Depression was deepening in Germany and causing massive unemployment and misery and that the democratic government in Berlin was helpless to halt the crisis. Walter Buch, head of the NSDAP's intraparty courts for keeping order in the movement and for punishing disobedient members, the Investigation and Conciliation committees (*Untersuchungs- und Schlichtungsausschüsse*, or *Uschla*), proclaimed to a member in east Africa that "any child can see that we

will take control of the government in the not-too-distant future."
Nieland celebrated the arrival of the new year by traveling outside
Germany for the first time to visit *Ortsgruppen* in Amsterdam,
Rotterdam, The Hague, and London; at each he told his listeners
that Hitler would soon be the lord and master of Germany.[42]

Such presumptions proved to be a fool's paradise. Not only was
1932 to be a frustrating year that saw the NSDAP become embroiled in a series of costly and demoralizing elections (particularly
the *Reichstag* election in November, in which the party lost seats
in the legislature), but Hitler failed to take control of the government as his leaders had prophesied. Furthermore (and less important from the party's viewpoint), the ensuing months were to
be troublesome for Nieland, the *Auslands-Abteilung*, and its strug-
gling affiliates abroad. A number of the groups were plagued with
factionalism and organizational troubles, and had Hitler not come
to power in early 1933 they would probably have collapsed.

Troubles for the *Auslands-Abteilung* began in February when
Hitler personally ordered Strasser to take over from the Department complete control of the Nazi groups in Italy and Switzerland
and to appoint *Landesgruppenleiters* for each country. The reasons
for Hitler's directive centered around the significance he attached
to both countries and around Nieland's personal disagreements with
several party officials in Italy. Another factor in his decision may have
been the party's troubles (which were unrelated to the *Auslands-
Abteilung*) in Austria. In September 1931 the Nazis supported a
coup against the Austrian government of Engelbert Dollfuss. The
uprising was led by Walther Pfrimer, leader of the national-radical
section of the Styrian *Heimwehr* and advocate of the use of force
to oppose the regime. This "march on Vienna" failed, and Pfrimer
and his associates were tied to the National Socialists by a court at
Graz.[43]

The new *Landesgruppenleiters* chosen by Munich, Heinrich Brand
in Italy and Gustloff in Switzerland, devoted themselves to collecting contributions for the upcoming German presidential election,
where Hitler was opposing the incumbent, the military hero Paul
von Hindenburg. Combining propaganda with blackmail, both leaders raised noticeable sums of money from Germans in Italy and
Switzerland. Gustloff's organization participated in provincial Swiss
elections by spending several thousand marks and using propaganda
from Germany to elect politicians who were pro-German.[44] Payments from Brand's organization, however, were discovered by a

Munich journalist, Werner Abel, who accused Hitler of receiving money from Italian citizens and other foreign nationals. In a libel suit brought by the Nazis against Abel following Hitler's loss to Hindenburg in a runoff election, Hitler denied the accusations.[45]

Evidently Hitler believed his denial that the NSDAP was meddling in the affairs of foreign nations was not convincing enough. The *Reichsleitung* ordered party members abroad to carry special passbooks issued by the *Auslands-Abteilung* that directed members to "follow the laws of the country in which you are a guest."[46] The leadership also created in June 1932 an organization to which foreign citizens who were sympathetic to Hitler could belong. This was the League of Friends of the Hitler Movement (*Bund der Freunde der Hitler-Bewegung*), and it represented a front group through which the Nazis could influence persons abroad who were not German nationals.[47]

The new passbook and the League scarcely lessened the noisy and often trivial activity generated by the *Auslands-Abteilung* and its affiliates. More small groups were formed, and the veteran branches that had been created the previous year continued their dual task of spreading Nazi propaganda and gathering new members among foreign Germans. The first group in the Far East was founded in Shanghai by Franz Hasenöhrl, a German salesman, an outspoken nationalist, a friend of Hess, and a party member beginning in October 1931. Born in Vienna, he had fought in World War I on the eastern front and been taken prisoner by the Russians.[48]

Considering the large number of German communities in China, recruitment prospects for the party appeared excellent there. Since the end of the nineteenth century, closely-knit colonies had sprouted in Tientsin, Tsingtau, Hong Kong, Hankow, and Shanghai. Each colony had developed around branches of the German-Asiatic Bank and the trade of large German business firms like I.G. Farben and Krupp. In addition, the settlements were proud of their own consulate, small shops, school, men's choir, town hall (*Rathaus*), women's auxiliary, and church. Although some Germans had lost their property to the Chinese government during World War I, Sino-German trade revived after the conflict, and included in the exchange was a considerable supply of weapons, armaments, and military advisers shipped from Germany. In return the Chinese sent to the Reich high grade tungsten, wood-oil, sesame seeds, tallow, cotton, and animal skins.[49]

Several small *Stützpunkte* also appeared during the early months of 1932 in the Union of South Africa and in Southwest Africa. In the latter, which had been a German colony before World War I and had been taken from the Germans in 1919 and mandated to England's dominion, the Union of South Africa, a tiny group of National Socialists in Windhoek agitated among the country's ten thousand Germans for a return of the former colony to the Reich. In the nearby Union, a busy *Stützpunkt* was formed in May, and its leader was Hermann Bohle, a German national and professor of electrical engineering at South African College in Capetown. He was the elderly father of Ernst Bohle, the *Auslands-Abteilung*'s adviser for the Union and the later chief of the AO. Bohle had been born of peasant origins in western Germany and had emigrated to England to seek a college degree. After teaching at colleges in Birmingham, Walsall, and Bradford, he had moved his family to Capetown in 1906.

Despite his joining the ranks of foreign Germandom, he retained a deep national feeling for his Fatherland, and he sought to instill this quality in his children by rigidly demanding that they speak only German at home. When his family was mistreated by the Capetown authorities and he was released from his professorship during the World War, he rapidly became a fanatical German nationalist and anti-Semite. In fact, he attempted to return to Germany in January 1920. Once he learned of Hitler's radical right-wing philosophy through his son Ernst, who had applied for membership in the NSDAP in November 1931, the elder Bohle quickly became a Hitler convert. Bitter from the feeling that he had been persecuted because he was a German living in a foreign land and believing that the NSDAP held the key to Germany's rebirth as a powerful nation, he began dabbling in South African politics. When he was refused by a group of German Jews the chance to address the Capetown German colony about the Hitler Youth Movement (*Hitler-Jugend*, or HJ) at the colony's community hall, he promptly held his speech (which was virulently anti-Semitic) at a nearby hotel. By the end of the summer he had formed a number of *Stützpunkte* in the Union, and the *Auslands-Abteilung* had promoted him to *Landesgruppenleiter*.[50]

Still another *Landesgruppe* that revolved around a dominant personality was that in the Netherlands, where party locals were formed in Amsterdam, The Hague, and other Dutch cities. The Hague *Ortsgruppe* quickly became a model of the busy activity that pleased the *Auslands-Abteilung* and Munich. Its thirty devoted members met each Friday evening in a rented hall for a *Sprechabend*, where Nazi ideology and the problems of foreign Germans were discussed. For its main project, however, it arranged the supreme thrill for its members and their guests—in March 1932 the group crossed the German border to see and hear Hitler speak at a party rally in Düsseldorf.[51] The *Landesgruppenleiter* was an Amsterdam sales-man, Martin Patzig, appointed in May and who operated his or-ganization in a rigidly dictatorial fashion. He printed elaborate propaganda brochures on Hitler for the Dutch public (stressing Hitler's Catholic background and his potential for saving western Christendom from Bolshevism), and he sought to encourage Ger-mans to become active in the native Dutch National Socialist move-ment led by Anton Mussert. Nor did his work stop there; in June he arranged for Nieland to speak to the *Ortsgruppe* Amsterdam, and when anyone opposed his authority he ruthlessly employed his Party Court (*Uschla*) to expel them from the party.[52]

Patzig's propaganda efforts were aided considerably because Germany was just across the border, and plenty of propaganda could be smuggled into the Netherlands from Hamburg or Munich through various channels. But the *Auslands-Abteilung*'s supplying its groups outside Europe with such material posed a far more difficult problem. How could Nazi books, pamphlets, and newspapers, for example, be dispatched safely to the affiliates in faraway Argentina, Brazil, Southwest Africa, or China? Already in 1931 the staff of the *Auslands-Abteilung* began wrestling with the question, and it soon decided that the answer lay with the German merchant marine. The NSDAP, as it sought to do with all groups in German society, did its utmost to attract the German seamen into its ranks. Its efforts in this regard started in the fall of 1931, when a special Seafarer Section (*Abteilung Seefahrt*) was formed in the *Auslands-Abteilung*. The party saw in the hardy travelers of the world's seas a vital instrument for carrying propaganda to Germans in foreign lands and for serving as the connecting link between Ger-many and the Nazi affiliates abroad.

But the *Reichsleitung*, reacting to a financial scandal in the lead-ership of the Section and to what appeared to be Nieland's failure to administer the seamen effectively, reorganized the Section and freed it from the *Auslands-Abteilung* in March 1932. Under Kurt Thiele, a Nazi *Reichstag* deputy from Bremen, it busily enlisted shiphands and seamen—of whom roughly thirty-four percent were unemployed because of the Depression—in the large harbors of

Hamburg, Bremen, Bremerhaven, Kiel, Rostock, and Stettin. The Section placed *Vertrauensmänner* on the Baltic and North Sea waterfronts, and among other duties they held public "recruiting evenings" and placed packets of propaganda aboard freighters bound for overseas ports. From the ships the packets were smuggled ashore and sent to party groups and German colonies inland. By May the Section counted 688 members working loyally on 175 ships to sign up new seamen for the NSDAP.[53]

The Section smuggled increasing supplies of propaganda onto the ships, and it erected a sophisticated courier service whereby the material could be transferred among ships docked in overseas harbors. As the Depression intensified and Nazi political fortunes rose at home (with the party winning big in the *Reichstag* election in July), the membership rolls of the Section expanded correspondingly. By the close of 1932 it had enrolled 2,505 shiphands who were distributed among 371 ships.[54] Not surprisingly, when the Third Reich began in January 1933, the NSDAP possessed a well-constructed nucleus of seamen to carry its propaganda around the world. But it was only in March 1934 that the AO (or the successor to the *Auslands-Abteilung*) regained administrative control over the Seafarer Section.

Nieland's inability to rule the Section was a tipoff of graver difficulties that emerged at the end of 1932 to plague him. One of his problems was his membership in the *Reichstag*, which was work that ate heavily into his schedule and left him little time to devote to his rapidly growing Department in Hamburg. By the fall of 1932 it had established 150 *Ortsgruppen* and *Stützpunkte*, most of them very small. Added to the affiliates that had emerged earlier in the year in the Netherlands, China, and South Africa, *Vertrauensmänner* had organized branches in Sweden, Finland, Estonia, Norway, Lithuania, Iceland, Belgium, the Canary Islands, Morocco, Turkey, Palestine, Greece, Bulgaria, Hungary, Colombia, Guatemala, Peru, Uruguay, Netherlands East Indies, Australia, India, Manchuria, and Siam.[55] Unfortunately for the *Auslands-Abteilung*, the rapid proliferation brought it far more headaches and problems than success.

One of the worst troubles was the party in the United States, which was without firm leadership and was the object of several would-be chieftains who were maneuvering to take control of it. Manger's appointment by Hamburg to head the *Ortsgruppe* New York and the party in America brought a brief pause in the power struggle and eventually restored a semblance of order to the

New York local. Regular meetings were held every Saturday night by the latter, attended by eighty to ninety members. But as the effects of the Depression became increasingly severe in 1932, attendance dropped and the group became disorganized and again riddled with factionalism and dissension. Despite its meager financial resources, it did possess a newspaper, *Amerikas Deutsches Post*, which published articles sent from Hamburg and from party papers in Germany.[56]

The final blow to Gissibl's dream of leading the party in America was the defection from Teutonia of Spanknöbel, his old friend. Spanknöbel had lived in Detroit since 1929, and a year later he had joined the local Teutonia branch and the NSDAP. When Gissibl moved to Chicago and took Teutonia's national headquarters with him, Spanknöbel became head of the Detroit unit. He also organized at the beginning of 1932 and led a Nazi *Ortsgruppe* in Detroit, while simultaneously currying the favor of Nieland and the *Auslands-Abteilung*. His ambition had become identical with Gissibl's—to replace Manger and become the official leader of the NSDAP in the United States. The conflict was also organizational in nature. Many party members belonged to Teutonia, and small party locals (outside New York and Detroit) acknowledged by Hamburg had appeared alongside Teutonia groups in Chicago (under Gissibl's leadership), Los Angeles (Dr. Breiting), Hudson County (Schneider), and Paterson, New Jersey (Bredfeld).

Spanknöbel spent the early part of 1932 laying the groundwork for his move to seize power. With a flurry of activity he traveled around the United States speaking to party branches and Teutonia groups and collecting funds to be sent to the *Auslands-Abteilung*. Nieland wired him several enthusiastic telegrams urging that he collect more money for dispatch to Germany. Nieland's view of the members in America was typical of most Nazis in the Reich; they were convinced that Americans—the Depression notwithstanding— were wealthy and that the NSDAP could do very well financially by tapping the pocketbooks of the German population in the United States. Most of the members in America, however, were fairly poor, and some were without jobs.

Spanknöbel, bursting with importance behind his Hitler-style moustache, hustled contributions from Teutonia groups and played favorites with their members, who gave him special information or gifts that he could forward to Hamburg. Although some Teutonia members disliked Spanknöbel's aggressiveness, Gissibl at the end of February was forced to announce the dissolution of the Teutonia and to suggest that it become the core of the party groups across the country.[57] Elated with the news, Spanknöbel made a whirlwind trip to Germany, probably to confer with Nieland, and he returned to the United States to enroll in the NSDAP the Teutonia members who had not yet joined the party.

He arrived in New York in early April, just in time to help the *Ortsgruppe* there celebrate the opening of its new party headquarters. The local had converted an old store into a meeting hall and decorated its windows and walls with swastika emblems. The celebration, which included over a hundred party members, was opened by Manger, the *Ortsgruppenleiter* and the nominal head of the party in America, who turned the program over to Spanknöbel. Speaking with authority, the latter discussed Nazi ideology and described the worsening economic and political situation in Germany. Apparently, Manger never suspected that his guest was pushing to succeed him and that Spanknöbel had made himself popular in Hamburg. The festivities brought the local for the first time to the attention of *The New York Times*, which noted the rally and misspelled Spanknöbel's name.[58]

The old Teutonia people were welcomed into the party groups. This was particularly true in Hudson County, where the former local Teutonia boss, Schneider, formed a Nazi *Ortsgruppe*. The trademark of the group became its weekly *Sprechabende*, indoctrination meetings, and public rallies, each ending with Nazi songs and "Sieg heils" to Hitler. To protect its affairs from disruption by outsiders or opponents, the local established a storm trooper unit modeled along the lines of the SA in Germany. Comprised of the *Ortsgruppe's* roughest elements, the members of the unit wore uniforms that included black trousers, white shirts, and swastika armbands. It was used to distribute party literature and newspapers sent from Germany like the *Völkischer Beobachter*, *Der Angriff* (Goebbels's sheet in Berlin), and *Der Stürmer* (Streicher's anti-Semitic paper in Nuremberg). The storm troopers became notorious in nearby Union City and west New York City. Not only did they parade in public wearing uniforms and carrying swastika flags, but when they became involved in confrontations with the police and "communists" (as Schneider called the *Ortsgruppe's* enemies), the authorities banned the party from holding public meetings.

Even some Nazi members were displeased with such belligerence. Ludecke himself, dreaming of one day commanding the party in the United States, was critical of the tactics of the Schneiders, Spanknöbels, Gissibls, and Mangers. In the summer of 1932 he went to Munich and urged Strasser to expel the older members in America and re-establish the movement along less activist lines. Regarding the elder members (of which Ludecke counted between sixty and seventy), he bluntly informed the Reich organization leader, "They're no credit to the Party. . . . They strut through the streets of German neighborhoods puffed up and loud-mouthed, parading their Storm Troop uniforms. As propaganda, they're pretty bad. America doesn't like strong-arm agitators, especially aliens."[59]

But Strasser refused to listen. He and others in the *Reichsleitung* were told by Spanknöbel that there were hundreds of German-Americans waiting anxiously to be led to Hitler's bandwagon.[60] As the party in Germany was to do throughout its history, it fully accepted many of the exaggerated claims of its foreign groups about their successes, membership numbers, and recruitment possibilities. Moreover, it was extremely difficult to entertain ideas of restraint when Munich believed dogmatically that its mission was to win the support of foreign Germans for Hitler, and alienating a few Americans hardly mattered as long as the NSDAP's colors were being paraded. As for Spanknöbel, the rosy picture he painted for Hamburg and Munich was to help vault him past Gissibl and Manger and into the leadership of the party in the spring of 1933.

Petty clashes and power struggles also surfaced in 1932 in groups in Turkey, Brazil, and Southwest Africa. In Windhoek in July, the *Ortsgruppenleiter*, Ernst Wandke, was accused by dissident party members of having sexual relations with a black native. It was only after Nieland threatened to use the *Uschla* to expel the troublemakers that they dropped their attack. From Rio de Janeiro the *Auslands-Abteilung* was informed in November that its local branch was creating a hotbed of discontent in the German community because of the party's blatant distribution of propaganda and its attempt to dominate the German School. Among other demands placed on the school, the local pressured the teachers to refrain from using the anti-World War I novel, *All Quiet on the Western Front*, in their classes. In a sharp letter to the party leader in Rio, Willi Meiss, Nieland's chief aide in the *Auslands-Abteilung*, Bohle, ordered the group to stop causing trouble. Establishing discipline in the foreign groups was never easy, particularly when the branches had disagreements with the *Auslands-Abteilung*. During the fall the leader of the *Ortsgruppe* Constantinople, Franz Reiner, quarreled with Nieland and a local German newspaper, the *Türkische Post*, over the type of propaganda sent to the group by Hamburg and printed in the *Post*.[61]

About the only bright spot among the affiliates in 1932 was the *Ortsgruppe* Colombia, led by a German business representative in Barranquilla, Erwin Ettel. His success as a party leader was in large measure the result of his ventures as a businessman and traveler. After serving on a submarine in the Mediterranean in World War I, he worked during the 1920s for the Junkers Aircraft Company in northern Europe, Turkey, Persia, and Iraq. In February 1930 he became a top official in the German-Colombian Air Transportation Society, making frequent business trips to New York and aiding the Colombian government in its war with Peru. During the brief conflict he supplied the Colombians with German weapons and arranged for the training of Colombian pilots in Germany and the United States. Consequently, he was well known to German circles in many countries, and his entering the Nazi movement and forming an *Ortsgruppe* was greeted with enthusiasm by the German colony in Colombia.[62] One of the few pre-1933 Nazi functionaries who could speak several foreign languages, Ettel was destined to become a ranking official in the AO and the German Foreign Ministry.

AUTHORITARIAN ANARCHY: NIELAND AND LOWER LEVEL PARTY POLITICS

Nieland's troubles with the foreign groups scarcely stopped with the strife and factionalism he encountered in them. On top of clashes (involving the *Türkische Post* affair) with the party's Press Office and the Propaganda Department in Munich, he squabbled with other party offices over who possessed the authority to operate Nazi organizations in foreign countries. As his experiences illustrated, politics at the lower levels of the NSDAP were not the battles for power (about which much has been written) such as those fought among Goebbels, Strasser, Ernst Röhm (the SA chief), Göring, Himmler, and Franz Schwarz (the party's treasurer). Instead, politics in the lesser organizations was a chain of tiny wars interrupted by armistices and alliances that had little effect on either Hitler or the *Reichsleitung*. Despite the Nazi claim that the party was a totalitarian movement that functioned according to the

Führerprinzip, it was in fact a picture of authoritarian anarchy caused by the dogmatism and ambition of party leaders and by the administrative chaos that characterized it.[63]

Nieland's competence in party affairs outside Germany overlapped with that of several party offices. In Danzig and Austria the *Reichsleitung* had formed party districts that were answerable to Munich, and since February 1932 it had taken over control of National Socialists in Italy and Switzerland. Munich had also created in November 1931 a so-called Eastern Department (*Abteilung Ostland*) under Karl Motz, to administer Germans in Scandinavia and eastern Europe. The Department, because of its encroachment into territory also under the jurisdiction of the *Auslands-Abteilung*, became the object of a complaint by Nieland to Strasser.[64]

Nieland's lack of popularity in the party also extended by the end of 1932 to several individual party officials. In the summer he tangled with Joseph Wagner, district leader in South Westphalia, and the argument became so heated that Nieland offered to duel his rival "with weapons." Wagner accused him of failing to appear for speaking engagements with party groups in Westphalia, and the head of the *Auslands-Abteilung* believed that his "honor" as a National Socialist had been called into question. Discord even surfaced inside the Department, as his employment of his sister and father in the Hamburg office aroused a mountain of criticism against him. One in the Department who resented the "family affair" arrangement was Nieland's close aide, Bohle, who believed that none of the Nielands understood their business, particularly since they had rarely been outside Germany. Bohle eventually resigned in disgust in May and only returned in the fall when Nieland asked him back to become a "district inspector" for the Department and promised to pay him.[65]

Such strife was closely observed by Strasser, whose major concern was to build an efficiently administered party apparatus that would help Hitler win the massive electoral victories needed to make him Chancellor. To this end Hitler and Strasser announced in June 1932 an impressive reform of the offices and departments in the *Reichsleitung*. The overhaul of the leadership came just in time, as the party soon found itself involved in costly *Reichstag* elections in July and November and a series of *Landtag* ("state legislature") elections. Strasser also hoped to improve the administration of the foreign branches, but he believed this could be achieved only by Nieland's submitting his choices for party leaders abroad to

Strasser's office for final approval. The trouble in several of the groups, in Strasser's view, could be traced to Nieland's appointment of "unsuitable people" as foreign leaders (e.g., Georg Wagner, a non-Nazi in Budapest, and Hans Sachsenberg, a suspected criminal in Constantinople).[66]

Although the *Reichsleitung* received pressure during the autumn of 1932 to replace Nieland, it refused and even gave him a promotion. For one thing, in dismissing him, his superior, Strasser, would be admitting his bad judgment in hiring him. The fact remained, furthermore, that despite its mounting troubles, the *Auslands-Abteilung* had formed over 150 small groups outside Germany (an impressive expansion, despite their size, over the fifty addresses of foreign members Nieland had acquired in the spring of 1931), and was adding more daily. But this was only a tiny part of Strasser's worries; his thoughts were focused mainly on the NSDAP's worsening position inside Germany and on his own future.

Still, he extended his organizational reforms of the summer by renaming the *Auslands-Abteilung* the Department for Germans Abroad (*Abteilung für Deutsche im Ausland*). At Nieland's urging, moreover, he upgraded the newly designated Department in mid-November to the status of a district organization and called it the Foreign District (*Gau Ausland*); a *Gau* ("district") was the highest administrative level in the NSDAP below the *Reichsleitung*. Nieland was also promoted from Department Chief (*Abteilungsleiter*) to *Gauleiter*, and he thus joined in rank such party notables as Goebbels and Streicher.[67]

But his advancement was short-lived. Strasser suddenly resigned on 8 December following the NSDAP's demoralizing setback in the *Reichstag* election the previous month and Hitler's refusal to compromise and form a new government with the German Chancellor, General von Schleicher. Since Nieland and the *Gau Ausland* had been intimately tied to Strasser, the latter's resignation weakened seriously the position of the new *Gau* and its boss. Hardly had Strasser's letter of withdrawal to Hitler become public than several party leaders (among them Rosenberg, the party's philosopher and rapidly emerging foreign affairs "expert") began efforts to remove Nieland and place his *Gau* in their hands.

Meanwhile, Nieland's troubles were compounded by difficulties which several of his affiliates suddenly experienced with foreign authorities. The Brazilian government dissolved the Porto Alegre local, and in January 1933 the government threatened to close the

German School in Rio de Janeiro because of National Socialist infiltration of the school and the opposition to the Nazis from the German colony.[68] When Karl Kudorfer, the *Vertrauensmann* in Greece, held a rowdy and provocative "Hitler meeting" in Athens, the police banned him from further party work. Another action that caught the eye of foreign authorities was the racial discrimination practiced by the branches; following strict orders from Hamburg the groups categorically refused to admit Germans who were "of Jewish descent."[69]

Even the groups in Italy caught the mistrustful eye of the authorities, greatly displeasing Munich. When the Weimar government banned the SA from Germany in the spring of 1932 and the party dissolved the SA for a time, a number of unemployed and aimless storm troopers filtered into Italy and caused troubles for the local party groups (e.g., by stealing from members), native Fascist organizations, and the Italian police. The problem became so acute, in fact, that the *Landesgruppe* Italy agreed to permit the Italian Ministry of Interior to arrest unemployed SA men and other "doubtful elements" who did not possess the NSDAP's foreign passbook. By mid-February 1933 the affair forced Munich to dissolve several *Ortsgruppen*.[70] The *Landesgruppenleiter* Brand, acting on orders from Germany, threatened to expel unruly members and to "proceed with all recklessness" in the punishment of "undisciplined behavior."[71]

Above all, the *Reichsleitung* hoped to assure Mussolini and the Italians that Nazis in Italy—despite their questionable conduct—posed no threat to the Duce's regime. Before the Nazi seizure of power in Germany, foreign officials hardly suspected the party groups abroad of subversion or clandestine activity that would undermine the sovereignty of foreign nations. Although some governments observed the groups' presence, rarely were the branches officially banned, and only occasionally were Nazi members expelled from foreign countries for illegal political activities.[72]

This was not unusual. Most of the groups abroad were extremely small, their noisy and visible work hardly made them a serious danger, and they represented a party which had never governed Germany. On the other hand, there was little official intelligence work or "spying" done by the groups prior to 1933 that might have aroused suspicions abroad against them. Except for a few contacts with minor officials in German embassies and consulates,[73] the NSDAP possessed no espionage network abroad until after Hitler became Chancellor. In part, its lack of foreign intelligence activity was because of its failure to infiltrate the *Auswärtiges Amt*; until 1933 only sixty-four of the roughly 2,500 employees of the Ministry and its foreign missions were National Socialist members.[74]

While it became well known that very few of the Reich's diplomats joined the NSDAP, a fact particularly disconcerting to Hitler and fueling his innate suspicion of them, this was not totally unfavorable for the party. The small number of National Socialists in German missions abroad helped further to conceal the true nature of Nazism to foreign governments and to preserve the party's relative obscurity outside Germany. Especially as the movement formed its foreign groups during 1931 and 1932, this anonymity proved profitable, helping the branches to remain free from harassment by foreign officials.[75]

On New Year's Day of 1933 the NSDAP counted 3,102 members living outside Germany, who represented the core of each party organization abroad. Most of them lived among the large German populations in South America, southeastern Europe, Southwest Africa, the United States, and China.

TABLE I
Countries with the Largest
Number of Nazi Members (January 1933)

Country	Number of Members
Brazil	348
Chile	189
Italy	168
Austria	159
Argentina	156
Southwest Africa	149
United States	115
China	83
Spain	80
Paraguay	62
England	59
Netherlands	52
Guatemala	51
Czechoslovakia	50
Mexico	41
Portugal	40

Sources: AO, "Parteimitglieder, Stand 30.6.1937.," T-120/78/60145-60148; and Jacobsen, *Nationalsozialistische Aussenpolitik*, pp. 661-64.

Despite the advantages encouraging their growth, the Nazi groups abroad found themselves in the same demoralized state as that of the NSDAP at home. Many were split with factionalism and found it difficult to attract followers with their blatant propaganda and rowdy methods. They were also hurt because they represented a movement that had never governed Germany, and after the NSDAP's reversal in the national election of November 1932 the party appeared to be further away than ever from ruling the country. Still, the groups remained convinced that Germans abroad could be won for Hitler's sacred racial and political cause by the same tactics that the party was employing at home. As future history revealed, the Nazis abroad had landed on a treadmill of chiefly meaningless and trivial activities that was soon to have far more influence on foreign opinion toward Germany than it warranted. Although buoyed by propaganda sent regularly from Hamburg worshiping Hitler and National Socialism, the foreign branches had not yet received the information they anxiously awaited: that Hitler had been named Chancellor and the head of a National Socialist government. But such news was not long in coming.

3

ERNST BOHLE AND THE EXPANSION AND ADMINISTRATION OF THE PARTY GROUPS ABROAD, 1933-1934

Upon hearing that Hitler had been commissioned Chancellor on 30 January 1933, the small party groups outside Germany reacted with a flurry of enthusiasm and activity. In the months that followed, the Nazi political and social revolution inside Germany was accompanied by a determined (but disorganized and not always effective) effort by the affiliates abroad to win for Hitler total control over German colonies, clubs, and organizations. The three thousand National Socialists outside the Reich, with their Führer now in power at home, believed that all Germans and persons of German descent abroad must be made to accept the Nazi ideology and support the new Hitler government.

Foreign members watched with excitement as Hitler exploited the burning of the *Reichstag* building to give him a pretext to unleash a "reign of terror" in Germany against Communists, Jews, and "liberals." The hated *Geheime Staatspolizei* ("Secret State Police," or Gestapo) emerged, and the SA and Himmler's SS took over the remainder of the important police positions. The new government set forth to capture the minds of Germans. On 13 March a Ministry for People's Enlightenment and Propaganda was created, headed by Goebbels. After the *Reichstag* election on 5 March and the coercion of the legislature into voting Hitler dictatorial power for four years, many Nazi opponents landed in concentration camps, and the Nazis began the *Gleichschaltung* ("coordination") of the German state governments. Hitler even moved to destroy the opposition in his own party; on the "night of the long knives" in June 1934 he coldly ordered the execution of the

SA leader, Röhm, and other SA and party officials. With the SA leadership decimated, the SS suddenly emerged as the party's most powerful military arm.

As Hitler sought to "nazify" Germany, the government began removing from its bureaucracy Jews, Communists, Socialists, and Weimar loyalists. Similar purges occurred in the professions; teachers, for example, were forced to enter the Nazi Teacher's League (*Nationalsozialistische Lehrerbund*, or NSLB). To replace labor unions and rule the German working class the government created the much publicized German Labor Front (*Deutsche Arbeitsfront*, or DAF). Hitler's aims were to destroy the Weimar Republic and bring Germany firmly under his authoritarian thumb. This, he believed, would enable him to revise the Versailles Treaty, rearm Germany, and transform the nation once again into a world power.

His first moves in this regard came in the autumn of 1933 when he pulled Germany out of the League of Nations and withdrew it from the European Disarmament Conference at Geneva. The world reaction to the new regime and its policies was hostile. Particularly in the Western democracies, the suppression of freedom and political dissent, the attacks on the Jews, the dismissal of prominent university professors, the abolition of trade unions, the public burning of books, and the campaign against the Christian churches combined to provoke anti-German sentiment among public opinion. Much of the respect for Germany among the Western powers that had developed during the Weimar years now reversed itself.

This foreign response was heightened by aggressive and thoughtless activities of the NSDAP groups abroad and their attempted *Gleichschaltung* of local German communities. Most party members outside Germany eagerly welcomed the nationalism, anti-Semitism, and revisionist foreign policy of the Reich government, and they made their admiration for the "new Germany" clear— often too clear—to their fellow Germans and non-Nazis abroad.[1] This campaign to dominate the foreign colonies was encouraged by Berlin and Munich, and particularly by the *Gau Ausland* in Hamburg. The inspiration from Germany, however, was disorganized and haphazard, and the resulting work of the foreign party groups established a pattern of senseless behavior that was to hurt the branches throughout the Third Reich.

HESS AND THE EMERGENCE OF BOHLE

The poor communication between Germany and the groups resulted in part from a shake-up in the leadership of the *Gau Ausland*. In early March Nieland was named police president of Hamburg, and considering his difficulties during the previous months, it was not surprising that he was removed as head of the *Gau* two weeks later. The explanation for the dismissal was that his new post would prevent him from devoting adequate time to the *Gau*. His release, however, was more the result of intraparty politics and rivalries among several party leaders. Strasser's successor as organization leader, Robert Ley, fired Nieland because Ley despised Strasser and hoped to rescind many administrative procedures that his predecessor had established.

Another who wanted to strengthen his hand by subordinating the *Gau* to himself was Rosenberg, head of the NSDAP's Foreign Policy Office (APA) formed in Berlin in April,[2] who dreamed of one day becoming Hitler's foreign minister. Although Nieland protested the loss of his job, Ley replaced him with a close friend in the *Reichsleitung*, Rudolf Schmeer. Schmeer worked with Ley and Rosenberg; they ordered the dissolution of the party branches outside Germany and planned to rebuild the groups under the guidance of the APA. Ley added to the confusion by renaming the *Gau* the Department for Germans Abroad and removing its prestigious *Gau* status.[3]

The beleaguered Department and its independent control over Nazis abroad were saved only by the efforts of Hess, Hitler's Deputy Führer, and Nieland's former assistant, Bohle. Hess was himself a foreign German, born in Egypt. Having met Hitler in 1920 he immediately worshiped the beer hall agitator as Germany's future political savior. Already in 1921 he had proclaimed to Germans living in Spain that Germany's "most vital task is the recovery of the German reputation in the world." To achieve this goal, he was convinced that foreign Germans could play a crucial role if they were mobilized for Hitler and made to support him.[4]

His protege in the NSDAP was Bohle, who met Hess for the first time in March 1933. Bohle, whose thick brown hair, long face, slender body, swarthy complexion, and protruding ears made him resemble Hess more than "the legendary blue-eyed, fair-haired beautiful Nordics among the important party personages," was born

in Bradford, England on 28 July 1903; three years later he moved
to the Union of South Africa.[5] Strongly influenced by his domineer-
ing father, he was raised in a family where only German was spoken
at home and where the greatness of Germany was continually
stressed to the children. His sense of nationalism was also stimulated by his English schoolmates at Capetown High School; during
World War I they ridiculed him with the nickname "Kaiser Will."
Because of his English education, he became a youthful admirer of
the British Empire, which later prompted him to note that "I was
absolutely fascinated and dominated by the conception of a German
Reich which, in spite of a completely different structure, would, in
every respect, enjoy absolute equality with England in the concert of
world powers." Upon graduating from high school in 1919 he was
urged by his father to attend a German university.[6]

He arrived in Germany during the following year and studied
economics and political science at the Universities of Cologne and
Berlin, graduating in December 1923 with a degree in commerce.
After working with several export and merchandising firms in
Hamburg, he purchased in 1930 his own automobile accessories
shop, and he worked occasionally as an interpreter for the local
Egyptian consulate. In November 1925 he married Gertrude Bachmann from Cologne, a marriage that he claimed later was "a love
match opposed by both families."[7] For both practical and philosophical reasons, he joined the NSDAP at the end of 1931 and
began working in the *Auslands-Abteilung*. He firmly believed that
he could be of great service to the party because of his knowledge
of England, Africa, and other foreign countries—something, he noted,
that was almost totally lacking among the provincial Nazi leadership. As a foreign German who had retained his British citizenship,
he was greatly interested in the party's Department for Germans
Abroad and in the problems of his countrymen outside Germany.[8]

He was also attracted to the party by its radical philosophy that
mixed a fanatical German nationalism with an intense hatred of
Communism and the Jews and a worship of Hitler as a "superhuman" Führer who would rebuild Germany into a world power.
In 1931 and 1932, as the Depression deepened and the Weimar
government proved itself incapable of meeting the crisis, Bohle became convinced that democracy could not succeed in Germany.
He was firmly persuaded that it could never protect the nation from
the danger of a Communist revolution; his glorification of Hitler,

in fact, centered around his deep fear of Communism (shared by many Germans) and his belief that only Hitler could rearm Germany and rescue the country from the "red peril." He was also attracted to the Führer because of Hitler's anti-Semitism. Although he was not as openly crude in his denunciation of the Jews as were other Nazi officials, Bohle nevertheless disliked Jews and believed in the myth of a "Jewish conspiracy" against Germany, which said that the small Jewish minority in Germany dominated the important professions and controlled the larger cities like Berlin and Frankfurt.[9]

Nor was Bohle solely against Communists and Jews. He had a profoundly hostile attitude toward religion, and after 1933 he was to become a fanatical supporter of the NSDAP's campaign to destroy the Christian churches in Germany. He maintained that the Christian religion was unsuitable for Germans because it had been founded by and received its orders from an "Asiatic" (i.e., Christ), and not an "Aryan." He demanded the creation of a state religion where baptisms, marriages, and funerals would be secularized. His antagonism toward religion originated in his boyhood home; his mother was a Catholic, his father a Protestant, and the children were baptized in different faiths. The family had little religious education and never attended church or read the Bible.[10]

When Nieland was removed and Ley and Rosenberg threatened to destroy the independence of the Department for Germans Abroad, Bohle asked to meet with Hess. They met in March, and Bohle made an appeal that the Department be preserved and that foreign Germans not be forgotten by the NSDAP. He maintained to Hess that dissolving it would cause troubles for the Hitler government, because foreign Germans would create their own political organizations that would operate independently of Germany. It would be better, he suggested, to erect a disciplined organization controlled by the party than to permit groups in other countries to function on their own.[11]

He also argued that the Department had a great potential value in foreign affairs. Its affiliates, for example, were "in the position to give the offices of the Reich party leadership vitally important material" on political and economic matters abroad, and they could take a "special interest" in "the question of the appointment of our representatives in foreign countries [i.e., ambassadors, consuls, and ministers of the Auswärtiges Amt]."[12] Thus Bohle had visions of using the Department to "nazify" the foreign service, and because the AA had always been hostile ground for the party, his idea was pleasing to Hess and other leaders like Goebbels and Schwarz.

Hess was obviously impressed with the young and aspiring Bohle, who informed Hess that he would welcome the chance to lead the Department. In sharp contrast, Bohle's chief rival, Rosenberg, was making a very unpleasant showing in London, where he visited in May as a personal goodwill envoy from Hitler to the English government. The would-be diplomat was criticized by the British press, indicating the failure of his mission, and he cut short his trip to return home a much weaker candidate for a leading post in the AA. In June the bombastic and drunken Ley created a number of ugly incidents at the International Labor Organization Conference in Geneva, which resulted in Germany's leaving the meeting prematurely.[13] As future history revealed, the record of such party men wishing to be diplomats was to be none too good, a lesson that Bohle was to learn.

On 8 May 1933 Hess startled Rosenberg and Ley by naming Bohle the new head of the Department for Germans Abroad, but keeping the latter subordinate to Ley. When Rosenberg protested and tried to undermine Bohle by forming a Nazi *Ortsgruppe* for diplomats and the AA, he was thwarted by Hess and Schwarz.[14] But the greatest example of Bohle's newly found authority was his meeting with Hitler in Munich in July, when a conference was held among Hess, Bohle, and party leaders from Portugal (Burbach), London (Bene), the Cameroons (Ruberg), China (Hasenöhrl), and Egypt (Hess's brother, Alfred), to discuss "new directives" for the Nazi groups abroad.

Meeting with Hitler had the effect of legitimizing Bohle with the Nazi hierarchy and solidifying him in his new position, although he was never to become one of Hitler's inner circle or close friends. Soon thereafter, on 3 October, Bohle was raised to the rank of *Gauleiter* and made directly responsible to Hess. Reacting to his promotion, he quickly claimed that his Department for Germans Abroad was now "the sole authoritative party office for all foreign countries," and he informed his groups abroad that Hess had resolved "many uncertainties in the movement regarding the competencies" of the Department. He also made his debut as an emerging party figure by addressing a special conference (*Sondertagung*) of the Department at the annual party rally in Nuremberg in August. He discussed the "future tasks" of his organization, and making it appear like a gigantic global structure, he boasted that it possessed over 230 party groups around the world (which was to expand to four hundred by the following summer).[15] Already he was making extreme public claims, rarely tempered with qualifying remarks, that could only arouse foreign suspicion toward himself and his country.

THE AO AND ITS ADMINISTRATIVE STRUCTURE

Bohle's hard work, the elimination of Rosenberg as a rival, and his cordial relationship to Hess soon brought major organizational changes to the Department for Germans Abroad. In mid-February 1934 Hess reconfirmed Bohle's status as a *Gauleiter*, and he changed the name of the Department to that of *Auslands-Organisation* (AO). Subject to Hess's directives, the AO was granted total control over correspondence between party agencies in Germany and the foreign groups, and Nazis traveling abroad were ordered to report to the AO before their departure.[16] A month later Hess reaffirmed the AO's authority over the German seamen who were enrolled in the Seafarer Section, and by mid-1934 the Section had a membership of ten thousand.[17]

While the changes meant little in expanding the AO's decision-making powers, they were noted in the foreign press. But the AO's growing prestige was especially underscored when Hess gave an address to a national conference (*Reichstagung*) of three thousand foreign Germans at the Nuremberg party rally in September 1934. Several nights later Hitler visited with twenty foreign party leaders at a reception. The attention from the Führer was announced in the Nazi press, and it further legitimized the position of Bohle, the AO, and its affiliates abroad among the National Socialist hierarchy.[18]

Throughout 1934 and the early months of 1935, the AO's organizational apparatus was expanded. A new information sheet or *Mitteilungsblatt*, containing orders from Hamburg for its groups abroad, was published monthly and dispatched with secrecy to the branches.[19] The *Landesgruppenleiters* also found their duties defined. Following the *Führerprinzip*, they were made subordinate to Bohle, yet, simultaneously, they were granted authority over the party groups in their country. No communication between their groups and Germany was allowed without their permission. If a *Landesgruppenleiter* disobeyed Bohle or proved "politically unreliable," he was replaced. But to avoid such problems, Bohle personally selected and trained the party leaders, and when possible, they were asked to travel to Hamburg for conferences with the AO staff. Many *Landesgruppenleiters* were businessmen who lived abroad and mixed politics with business when they returned to Germany. Others returned for the Nuremberg rallies.[20]

The restructuring of the AO also involved an increase in the staff and offices in Hamburg. In May 1934 Bohle appointed Alfred Hess, the brother of Hitler's Deputy and the founder of the party's groups in Egypt, his Deputy *Gauleiter* and Commissioner for Economic Questions; Ruberg (who had returned to Germany from the Cameroons) his Staff Leader; and a young Ph.D. in English philology, Emil Ehrich, his Adjutant. Several new departments were formed, including a Personnel Office (*Personalamt*), Inspection Office (*Inspektionsamt*), Foreign Trade Office (*Aussenhandelsamt*), Legal Office (*Rechtsamt*), Party Court (*Parteigericht*), Cultural Office (*Kulturamt*), Welfare Office (*NS-Volkswohlfahrt*), Repatriation Office (*Rückwandereramt*), Working Association of German Women Abroad (*Arbeitsgemeinschaft der deutschen Frau im Ausland*), Youth Office (*Jugendamt*) affiliated with the HJ, and section of the German Labor Front.[21]

Financing for the expansion came from several sources. Since the AO could no longer rely on monthly dues of its members to support it, the party Treasury in Munich took care of most of its expenses. Funds were also contributed for special purposes from the Propaganda Ministry and from donations of wealthy Germans abroad. The foreign groups were financed through the monthly dues of their members, special subsidies from the AO, and covert *schwarze Kassen* (small collections employed for local work and never reported to the AO or Treasury in Munich).[22]

The new departments that were most active in administering the groups abroad and in carrying the customs of the Third Reich to foreign Germans were the Welfare Office, Legal Office, Foreign Trade Office, and Party Court. The Welfare Office concerned itself with mobilizing foreign Germans for the NSDAP's annual *Winterhilfswerke* ("Winter Relief Program"). The Program was begun each fall, and the AO's Welfare Office collected money and other items from Germans abroad and German businesses that could be distributed to needy families in Germany. Those who failed to contribute were recorded by the *Landesgruppen* and blacklisted. In a few instances, as in Argentina, considerable native opposition arose to the branches abroad sending the money gathered to Germany. But the Winter Relief collection was often a profitable operation for the Germans; in October 1934 Bohle proudly informed Goebbels that the *Landesgruppe* China had collected 165,000 marks (roughly 40,000 dollars) for the Fatherland.[23]

Since the Nazis believed that foreign Germans were not administered adequately by the AA and its foreign missions, it was not surprising that the AO developed a Legal Office to look after the legal problems of Germans abroad. The Office was headed by Wolfgang Kraneck, a judicial assessor and government bureaucrat, and it was designed to give legal advice to foreign party organizations, cooperate with the German government in supplying Germans abroad with private legal counsel, and draft legislative proposals for the government dealing with foreign Germans.[24] But such admirable goals notwithstanding, the Office concerned itself chiefly with juridical questions arising from the dual citizenship of foreign Germans (i.e., persons holding both German citizenship and nationality in the country where they resided). In a number of instances Kraneck and Bohle encouraged Nazi officials abroad to acquire dual citizenship to make their infiltration of foreign political organizations easier.[25]

The Nazis were also convinced that foreign Germans could be used more extensively in Germany's economic plans.[26] While the government began to rearm Germany and make the country economically self-sufficient, the AO's Foreign Trade Office, led by Alfred Hess and a retired army major, Eberhard von Jagwitz, tried to contribute to the policy of autarky by mobilizing the economic support of foreign Germans. The Foreign Trade Office appointed an economic adviser who was generally a local German businessman (*Wirtschaftsstellenleiter*) in each of the Nazi groups abroad. The advisers, according to Nazi publications, sent monthly economic reports to the AO, worked to conclude foreign trade agreements for German firms, ensured the economic interests of foreign Germans, and publicized "the National Socialist economic view." But most *Wirtschaftsstellenleiter* hardly worked toward such vital and noble goals. While many filed economic reports with the Foreign Trade Office (which always stressed the number of Aryans, Jews, and Freemasons that were employed in German firms and whether or not the firms contributed financially to the NSDAP), the bulk of their time was spent coercing foreign German businesses to release Jewish or anti-Nazi employees and placing trusted

National Socialists at the head of German Chambers of Commerce abroad.[27]

With respect to the latter, the advisers spent a great deal of energy coordinating the Chambers, which were associations of German businessmen interested in encouraging German trade. Many Chambers had developed during World War I, mainly to protect German commerce and businesses abroad from hostile governments. But following a conference of AO leaders with representatives of the Chambers (a meeting that featured an address by Hess) in Berlin in June 1934, an agreement was reached that placed the Chambers fully in the clutches of the NSDAP.[28] For Chambers that failed to knuckle under to the AO, the reward was unmerciful harassment and pressure from foreign party groups. When Gustav Adolf Wulff, chairman of the Chamber in Chile who had influential connections to Chilean business, criticized the terrorism and stifling of freedom of speech in Germany, the AO attacked Wulff and ousted him from office. Wulff unfortunately learned that the Nazis could suppress the freedom of speech of foreign Germans as well as Germans at home.[29] The episode, furthermore, illustrated that the AO worked at cross-purposes with the economic policy of the AA and German government. While the AA hoped to expand Germany's trade (especially in the Americas and Far East), the AO and its groups eliminated (mainly for political reasons) German businessmen abroad who possessed extensive commercial contacts and who could have benefitted the German economy significantly.

A similar policy was pursued toward German firms in foreign countries. The Foreign Trade Office did its utmost to control the selection of representatives abroad of German companies. Before I. G. Farben employees could be sent abroad, they had to receive "no objection" certificates from the AO, which judged the agents according to their "political reliability" (i.e., their racial purity and dedication to Nazism) rather than their commercial contacts or business prowess.[30] When Hans Gast, an agent in Bogota, Colombia for the *Gutehoffnungshütte*, refused to cooperate with his Nazi local, the AO ordered the industry's central office in Oberhausen to replace Gast and recall him to Germany. To settle the affair and save Gast's job, the firm had to appeal to the AA.[31]

The Foreign Trade Office forced German businessmen abroad to join the NSDAP by threatening them with reprisals against relatives in Germany. The Office also blacklisted foreign German firms that were anti-Nazi or that employed Jews. In the Balkans, Brazil, Denmark, Spain, and the Netherlands, the rabid anti-Semitism of the AO and its party groups became especially pronounced as German companies were pushed to release their Jewish workers or face the threat of boycotts organized by local party organizations. If the barons of big business in Germany disapproved of such policies, they did little to stop it. Hermann Waibel, a director of Farben, praised the AO's work publicly by noting that it "will result in the betterment of the entire nation."[32] Thus the racism of Hitler's Germany affected the outside world as well as the Reich; Alfred Hess and his subordinates in the Foreign Trade Office were determined to play a key role in destroying what they alleged was the Jews' stranglehold over the world's economy.

The Office in the *Landesgruppe* Spain was a model organization. It dominated the German Chamber of Commerce in Barcelona and pressed for the release of Jews and Freemasons from German companies like Siemens, AEG, Telefunken, Farben, and banks and shipping firms. Already by the end of 1935 the Jewish director of AEG in Madrid, David Falk, was forced to resign. The Office even dabbled in commercial espionage against foreign companies and governments. When Spain and Uruguay were about to sign a trade agreement in February 1935, it ordered its agents in Spain to learn the secret list of articles for trade in the pact, which the German government could use in bargaining for a more favorable commercial agreement with Uruguay and in easing out Spanish trade.[33]

A serious difficulty posed by this increasing party work was the disciplining of the foreign groups and their members. The AO, to ensure that the *Führerprinzip* would dominate the affiliates, established a special Party Court in Hamburg headed by Kraneck. The Court was created following the reorganization of the old *Uschla* system in December 1933, and the Tribunal was subordinated to the party's Supreme Court (*Oberstes Parteigericht*) in Munich. The AO Court had specially appointed arbitrators (*Schlichter*) in the branches abroad, and their chief duties were to settle quarrels among party members, investigate cases of insubordination to party authority, and examine the worthiness of a foreign German to become a party member.[34] Uppermost was the goal of concealing from foreign authorities (and Germans) any disunity or discontent in the Nazi organizations; at all costs the party's image as a totalitarian movement of fanatical Hitler followers had to be upheld.

The Court and its arbitrators were especially careful to protect the racial "purity" and political unity of the foreign groups. They expelled or banned from entering the groups Germans who were Freemasons or Jews, Germans who appeared to be "politically unreliable," and Germans who held foreign citizenship. On the race issue the Court was explicit. In a circular to the arbitrators in January 1934, Kraneck instructed, "Predominant for the judgment of every case [i.e., membership] is the question whether or not the German reputation or the prestige of the white race has been jeopardized. . . . A German who still insists on marriage with coloreds or halfbreeds proves thereby that he consciously ignores the dominant view of the German people on the racial problem. He cannot become a party comrade."[35]

Bohle used the Court to remove unsatisfactory party leaders. At the beginning of 1934 he replaced the *Ortsgruppenleiter* in Budapest, Wagner, and a year later the Court expelled him from the party (whereupon he fell under the surveillance of the Gestapo).[36] But along with the Court, the AO had several other methods for handling troublemakers. On numerous occasions it sent special commissioners to groups that were experiencing difficulties; in the spring of 1935 it dispatched the Evangelical pastor, Langmann, to Mexico and Guatemala. In extraordinary instances, it cooperated with the AA in returning to Germany disobedient party members. Also, in checking the political attitudes of party leaders abroad, it worked with the Gestapo. The latter collected information for the AO and harassed relatives in Germany of unruly foreign officials to force them into line.[37]

INSTITUTIONAL WARFARE AND PERSONAL AMBITIONS

If the Third Reich was characterized by massive power struggles among the Nazi elite, a similar but less significant series of battles was waged among lower level officials and institutions. The AO, despite its rise to a degree of prominence in the Nazi world in 1933 and 1934, fell into the latter category, and its less than amicable relations with other agencies illustrated much about the everyday operation of Nazi bureaucracy. When it suddenly emerged as a contender for the control of the large foreign German population, the AO became the adversary of several cultural and political organizations whose work also involved Germandom abroad. Bohle, often with the aid of Goebbels, sought to eliminate such rivals by destroying their independence and by placing trusted National Socialists in key positions in each agency.

First to be coordinated was the League of Foreign Germans (*Bund der Auslanddeutschen*), a cultural society formed in World War I as a community of interest of German citizens who had been pushed out of foreign countries by the war.[38] The AO also infiltrated the German Foreign Institute (DAI), which possessed a large library for research on every aspect of German life abroad. With the appointment of a National Socialist, Richard Csaki, as its leader, the agency was quickly nazified. But Bohle and Karl Strölin, the president of the DAI and Lord Mayor of Stuttgart, quarreled frequently, and the AO never viewed the Institute as a political opponent. Wishing to be self-sufficient and collecting its own information on foreign Germans through its party affiliates, the AO rarely used the DAI's research material. Much of it was published in an extensive statistical study, the *Handwörterbuch des Grenz- und Ausland-Deutschtums*. But Bohle's interest in foreign Germans was political, and he had little use for the academic work of the DAI.[39]

One of the bitterest enemies of the AO was the League for Germandom Abroad (VDA), whose purpose since its inception in 1881 had been aiding foreign Germans in the areas of education and youth work. Headed by Hans Steinacher, it had cultural clubs and youth groups of foreign Germans. The conflict broke out in the summer of 1933 when the AO and Hitler Youth campaigned to undermine the VDA's prestige by portraying the League's leadership as being "aged" and out of touch with foreign Germans.[40] The VDA particularly resented the efforts by the AO's Youth Office and the Hitler Youth to build foreign HJ groups that were subject to the party branches abroad. HJ groups blossomed in 1933 and 1934 in association with the party in Greece, Belgium, Bulgaria, Holland, Sweden, Switzerland, Turkey, China, Southwest Africa, Argentina, and Brazil. Their activities included hiking, listening to short wave broadcasts from Germany, celebrating Hitler's birthday, learning HJ and national songs, dominating German schools, and training students in the German language.[41]

Hess, in an effort to resolve the differences between the VDA and AO and unify Germany's policy toward persons of German descent abroad, created in October 1933 a special *Volksdeutsch* Council, which was subject to him and led by Karl Haushofer, the geographer, and Steinacher. The Council's liaison to Hess's office was Heinrich Kersken, an SA officer.[42] Although the Council was later reduced to an insignificant advisory body for Hess and the AA, it controlled temporarily the AO in matters concerning *Volksdeutschen* and handled questions that dealt mainly with German minorities in eastern Europe.

The main examples were the roughly three million Sudeten Germans in Czechoslovakia and the large minority (about one million) in Poland, some of whom had been cut off from Germany by the peace treaties of 1919. In the former, ties of the Sudeten National Socialist party to Germany had forced the Czech government to pressure the movement into dissolving itself in September 1933. But the Council, Steinacher, and AA tried to implement a moderate or "traditionalist" policy among the Sudeten Germans, which stressed the welfare and protection of the minority by encouraging its integrity with the Czech government. According to Steinacher, both German-Czech relations and interests of the Sudeten Germans would best be served if Germany avoided interference in Sudeten German affairs by the NSDAP or any other unauthorized agency. Here he contacted and supported Konrad Henlein, leader of the moderate Sudeten German *Heimatfront*, which was dedicated to creating a united Sudeten German community to combat what it regarded as Czech oppression of Germans. This collaboration reached its peak in the spring of 1935, when Steinacher contributed large sums of VDA money to the Henlein movement's campaign in the Czech national elections. The stunning victory of the movement (renamed the *Sudetendeutsche Partei*, or Sudeten German party) in the May election led many observers to conclude that Henlein had now become a tool of the Germans.

But Henlein's moderate policy of assuring the Czechs of the loyalty of his party and of denying ties to Germany proved self-defeating. The Czechs remained unconvinced, and he found himself the object of a massive attack by radicals in his party who demanded the union of the Sudetenland with Germany and the destruction of Czechoslovakia. The radicals were encouraged by Bohle and the AO, who worked through the Nazi consul in Reichenberg, Walter von Lierau, and mission official in Prague, Sigismund von Bibra. Not only did Lierau (who had joined the NSDAP in 1921 and the SS in 1932) and Bibra (who entered the party in May 1933) seek to subvert the relations between the AA and the *Volksdeutsch* Council, but they radicalized Sudeten German youth and student clubs, supported anti-Henlein newspapers, and fomented discontent among Sudeten German nationalists. By the end of 1935 the Sudeten German party was badly split between the traditionalists and the radicals, a conflict that mirrored the fight in Germany between Bohle and Steinacher and which had serious future consequences for Henlein.[43]

In Poland Bohle and the AO pursued a similar policy, despite Germany and Poland's signing an agreement in January 1934 for the protection of the German minority. German nationals in Poland were headed by a Nazi mission official in Nromberg, Hans Bernard, whose effort to spread propaganda among the German minority favoring its reunification with Germany was concentrated in two *Volksdeutsch* groups, the *Deutsche Vereinigung* ("German Association") and *Jungdeutsche Partei* ("Young German party"). Although the Polish government officially recognized the older unity organization, the *Vereinigung*, as the sole representative of the minority, Bernard and the AO supported the *Jungdeutschen*, a group of radicals that held racial and political ideas similar to the NSDAP and that demanded reunification with Germany. Bohle, operating through Bernard, tried to establish the AO's supremacy over the *Volksdeutsch* Council in Polish affairs by infiltrating the *Deutsche Vereinigung* with *Jungdeutschen*. To nazify the *Vereinigung* and the major German cultural organization in Poland, the *Deutsche Volksbund* ("People's League"), Bohle also relied on his *Ortsgruppenleiter* in Warsaw, Carl Burgam.

But by the spring of 1935 Burgam and Bernard had only brought greater disunity to the minority. The AA and Steinacher, alarmed at the NSDAP's apparent willingness to compromise the integrity and unity of the German community, opposed the AO vigorously. In April the German Foreign Minister, Neurath, warned Hess that the Polish government would not agree to its German minority being organized by the AO's groups. Evidently, Hess was impressed with the threat to Polish-German relations, and he directed Bohle to halt his policy of "coordinating" the minority; increasingly the AA now intervened.[44]

Conflict also surfaced over the AO's activity among German minorities in several other eastern European countries. By the end of 1933 it possessed party groups in Bulgaria (led by Karl Brausewetter, a doctor in Sofia, and Walter Rosengart in Plovdiv), Hungary (headed by Wagner in Budapest, who contented himself with harassing the local German mission and German-Hungarian

Chamber of Commerce), and Rumania. In the latter, the authorities had banned Nazi activities but the AO continued to operate an undercover *Ortsgruppe* in Bucharest. The party leader in Rumania, the Russian-born Artur Konradi, cooperated with the pro-Nazi *Volksdeutsch* leader, Fritz Fabritius, in spreading propaganda among the large German minority and in creating by 1935 a new nazified organization of German-Rumanians, the *Volksgemeinschaft der Deutschen in Rumänien* ("Racial Community of Germans in Rumania").[45]

But while Steinacher, the VDA, and the *Volksdeutsch* Council worked with the AA to unify the German minorities in eastern Europe, Bohle undermined Steinacher's position at home by extending his influence with Hess and the latter's Staff Leader, Martin Bormann. In the spring of 1934 the NSDAP replaced the VDA's traditional designation of *Auslanddeutsch* with the Nazis' more racial oriented term, *Auslandsdeutsch*, and in countries like Norway, VDA groups and the AO's branches competed for the support of German nationals. When the exasperated Steinacher and Haushofer complained to Hess, the Deputy Führer responded by removing Kersken from his staff and naming Bohle his chief of *Volksdeutsch* affairs.[46]

Bohle immediately took his promotion to mean that he possessed full control over all foreign Germans, and he increased his attack on the VDA. His *Landesvertrauensmann* for Canada, Karl Gerhard, after talking with Bohle while Gerhard was visiting Germany, bragged of having "primacy in all questions of foreign Germandom" in Canada. Without success, however, Gerhard tried to capture the leadership of Canada's principal *Volksdeutsch* organization, the *Deutsche Bund* ("German League").[47] Eventually, in October 1937, Steinacher was informed by Hess that he had been given a "leave of absence" from his position as head of the VDA; this prompted one of Bohle's close associates to remark gleefully to the AO leader that another "bristly pillar" had fallen from competition with the NSDAP.[48]

For the moment, during early 1935 at least, Bohle had expanded his power beyond administering German citizens abroad, and he had won a major (albeit temporary) victory in the *Volksdeutsch* question. He later explained his ambition and drive to amass personal authority by noting that the AO was not taken very seriously by many party officials, including Hitler. Bohle was known in party circles as the "gentleman Gauleiter," and he was frequently twitted for having been born in England. Indeed, he was never to be completely "at home" with the party hierarchy, except for Hess, nor did he become an intimate friend of any of the highest Nazi officials.[49]

He was blessed, however, with a love of power and an undying devotion to Hitler, necessities for survival in the brutal world of Nazi politics. At the beginning of 1935 he was secretly dreaming of one day becoming German Foreign Minister and using the AO to reconstruct the AA along National Socialist lines. Many of his *Landesgruppenleiters* and other functionaries abroad were beginning to view themselves as "party diplomats" whose jobs were more vital to Germany than its mission leaders. A series of petty battles was already brewing at the consular and legation level between the AO and AA over which agency was to be the official German representative to the thirty million foreign Germans.

In part, the hostility between the AO and *Wilhelmstrasse* was traced back to the suspicion with which the party and AA had observed one another before 1933. In Hitler's eyes the career diplomats' extensive education, international background, personal friendships with foreigners, and knowledge and appreciation of other countries made them highly suspect. The mission officials were also taught a principle that Hitler detested as weakness: they believed in compromise, not only as a fundamental aspect of foreign policy, but as a general rule of life.[50]

Despite such antagonism, Hitler did not purge the AA of its leading officials. Realizing that the diplomats could play vital roles in helping Germany project a peaceful image in foreign affairs and relieve the anxiety of its foreign critics, he saw little reason to bring wholesale changes to the agency. Also, many in the AA became convinced after 1933 that their own foreign policy goals were not entirely different from those Hitler publicly announced. They particularly sympathized with his stress on peace and moderation, his anti-Marxism, and his demand for a revision of the Versailles Treaty. Examples of leading diplomats who were retained were Neurath, Bernhard Wilhelm von Bülow, Werner Otto Freiherr von Grünau, Richard Meyer, Gerhard Köpke, Hans Heinrich Dieckhoff, Friedrich Stieve, and Karl Ritter.[51]

The party officials abroad viewed the diplomats with the same petty contempt as Hitler, and the party men urged already in 1933 a major housecleaning of the AA, whereby only trustworthy Nazis would assume leadership of the Ministry and support without hesitation Hitler's foreign policy. The trivial everyday conflicts that surfaced between the party chieftains and diplomats centered in part around the desire of the former to replace the diplomats as the official leaders of the German communities.

But tension among them was also personal in nature. Both groups lived in entirely different worlds that were not easily harmonized. The privileged position of the mission officials—their social opportunities and high standards of living—often aroused feelings of envy among the Nazi leaders. The latter attached great value to their social status, which was partly because of their personal ambitions and partly because of their desire to be considered influential by Bohle and others in Germany. Consequently, they made it a point to be invited to the social functions of the diplomatic missions, and in affairs where the party was formally acknowledged (e.g., at gatherings celebrating Hitler's birthday), its leaders expected to be treated with the pomp and dignity accorded the mission officials.

The party functionaries also reproached the diplomats for their alleged indifference to the interests of foreign Germans, and following Bohle's order of 28 February 1934, *Landesgruppenleiters* sent reports to the AO that contained personal data about the diplomats and that had the potential of having a decisive influence on the party's attitude toward the officials and their families. According to the directive, *Landesgruppenleiters* were to collect information about their mission officials' activity in the NSDAP, membership in Freemasons lodges (which the Nazis deemed Jewish organizations), racial background, and politics during the Weimar period. Bohle instructed that the material be sent to him and that it contain a "summary judgment [of each diplomat] from the viewpoint of the movement [i.e., party leaders abroad]" and a comment on whether or not the diplomats "would be found worthy to be accepted into the ranks of our movement." It was hardly surprising that the diplomat under Hitler discovered, in the words of Andor Hencke, the AA's political expert for eastern Europe and Russia, that "more diplomacy and greater psychology were generally required . . . in his relations with the Party leaders than with the Governments of foreign countries."[52]

The resentment on both sides appeared in the spring of 1933. While some party leaders reported they were receiving friendly cooperation from their mission leaders, others complained bitterly to Bohle. Willi Meiss, the local leader in Rio de Janeiro, criticized the new German Minister to Brazil, Arthur Schmidt-Elskop, and demanded that the German Legation in Rio be nazified immediately. The party chieftain in Southwest Africa, Wandke, protested vigorously when the German Consul in Windhoek refused to fly the swastika flag atop the Consulate. He attributed the Consul's action to his "republican attitude" and "Jewish wife." Similar denunciations came from the Union of South Africa and China.[53]

When Hess subordinated the AO to his office, a few diplomats became more friendly to the party leaders. In the fall Bohle proposed to his boss that a new Reich Ministry for Foreign Germandom be created that would be supervised by the AO and would handle the official government work with Germans abroad normally performed by the AA. When Hess refused to push the idea with Hitler, Bohle began holding private meetings with the head of the AA's Personnel Department, Grünau.[54] From the conferences there developed in December 1933 a special agreement between the AO and AA regarding the membership of Foreign Service officials in the NSDAP. Accordingly, diplomats who wished to join the party were obliged to apply through the AO.[55]

But the meetings and agreement failed to improve the unhappy relationship between the diplomatic missions and party leaders abroad.[56] The party and AA especially clashed over efforts by the AO and Nazi Teacher's League (NSLB) to infiltrate foreign German schools. During 1934 and 1935 there were 1,519 German schools abroad that were financially supported by the German government (with many more that were not); the total enrollment of the schools exceeded 82,000 students.[57] While many teachers in the schools were well-educated German citizens or ethnic Germans, the schools' students included large numbers of non-German children, or "foreigners." The latter, the Nazis felt, made the penetration of the schools crucial: through the children, the AO and NSLB aimed at influencing favorably the parents and older generation, thus improving the image of the "new Germany" abroad.

The approach of the NSLB to the schools was simple and straightforward. It sent them membership cards for the League and forms for ordering propaganda. Each school contacted was asked to select a group leader (who was, preferably, a German citizen and loyal Nazi) to organize its teachers along Nazi lines and recruit members for the NSLB. The group leaders were to form "working associations" from among their fellow teachers, and the leaders were to hold meetings that would be indoctrination sessions on Nazism, and especially on the "racial foundations of the German people." Some party leaders made their objectives explicit to the teachers. The *Ortsgruppenleiter* in Havana, Cuba instructed local German teachers that "pedagogy has to acknowledge that the chief function of education is political." Determined to impress the point on his listeners, he continued, "With all educational activity, the National Socialist ideology must be represented. The significance of education in the school is that the teacher must be associated with the [racial] community."[58]

While this blunt approach produced marked opposition from German communities in Rio de Janeiro, São Paulo, Guatemala, and Athens, it eventually worked well in schools in Tokyo, Yokohama, Bolivia, Uruguay, and several other Latin American nations.[59] The NSDAP even built new schools abroad.[60] Such activities, however, angered the AA, which began to fear that it would lose its cherished position as the official agency for placing teachers in German schools abroad. Already in November 1933 the Ministry had criticized the efforts of the NSLB to politicize the schools, but the clash especially heated up during the following summer.[61]

The AO, supported by Rosenberg and the APA, campaigned to have the head of the AA's School Department, Stieve, replaced. He was anathema to the NSDAP on two counts: he was not a Nazi member nor did he agree to support blindly the party's policies. Furthermore, the AO's Cultural Office, led by Bohle's protege, Ehrich, had several fanatical National Socialists to recommend as Stieve's replacement.[62] Surprisingly (and much to the anger of the AO), he was able to retain his job, and the AA continued to have the final word on the appointment of teachers to the schools.

But Stieve's situation was threatening to become commonplace for diplomats who refused to hide their anti-Nazi sympathies. They began feeling considerable pressure to join the NSDAP to secure their jobs. In February 1934 Bohle approached Neurath about transferring Curt Prüfer, a friend of the AO leader and a Ministerial Director in the AA, to the Personnel Department of the Ministry. As Bohle complained to Goebbels later, "we as you also are well aware, have in the Foreign Service a severe deficiency in National Socialist representatives of the Reich [i.e., diplomats]." Nazi appointments to the AA, he lamented further, were a "great rarity," a fact whose change was an "unconditional necessity" for the AO.[63] Hans Kroll, an official in the AA and later Embassy Counselor in Turkey, noted that before 1933 "it was difficult and dangerous to enter the party," but once Hitler became Chancellor, "it was difficult to remain out of the party, [so] that I knew where my place was." The diplomats were strongly urged to become Nazi members for several reasons. Sometimes, receiving promotions was aided by membership, and it was argued that membership would strengthen the authority of the mission leaders over German nationals and party functionaries under their jurisdiction.[64]

Despite the developing pressure, there was no stampede by the diplomats to join the party in 1933 and 1934. The party leader in Spain, Walter Zuchristian, reported to Bohle that only four persons (out of twenty-two) in the German Embassy in Madrid belonged to the movement. Leading mission officials who acquired membership included Erich von Luckwald (Albania), Edmund Freiherr von Thermann (Argentina), Otto Reinebeck (Estonia), Ulrich von Hassell (Italy), Heinrich Ruedt von Collenberg (Mexico), Viktor Prince zu Wied (Sweden), and Emil Wiehl (Southwest Africa). Yet, the foreign party leaders remained suspicious of the diplomats, and they recommended that only a few be admitted. In October 1933 the *Ortsgruppe* London informed the AO of fifteen officials in the German Embassy who were unworthy of membership, including Hilger van Scherpenberg, the son-in-law of Hjalmar Schacht, Hitler's chief economic adviser.[65]

ORGANIZED CONFUSION: THE
PARTY IN THE AMERICAS AND THE FAR EAST

While Bohle and Hess struggled to expand the influence of the AO, its groups outside Germany received little guidance from the Reich. As they had in the *Kampfzeit* ("years of struggle," as the period before 1933 was called in the NSDAP), the branches took a back seat to the party's more important activities inside Germany. When the groups began their campaign to seize control of local German communities and to replace the latter's democratic administration with the *Führerprinzip*, the groups were aided little by Bohle or the AO. By the spring of 1934, despite the poor communication, the AO had succeeded in impressing on the affiliates that Germans abroad must be coordinated and made totally loyal to Germany. Zuchristian instructed his groups in Spain that they "must be in the position to rule the life of [their] entire German colony. The necessary strength for this will never express itself in numbers, but solely in the unity, in the internal discipline, and in the resulting striking force that develops [against German enemies]."[66]

During the spring of 1933, several groups, eager to act and to prove their loyalty to the new regime by disseminating National Socialism, tried to contact the AO for orders on how to proceed, but they received no reply. Since close ties with the NSDAP in Germany had always been a source of pride for the groups, many (like the *Ortsgruppe* Mexico City and locals in Southwest Africa) became disconcerted when they received "no answer from Hamburg."[67] Without support from Germany, some party leaders abroad, such as the *Landesgruppenleiter* of Brazil, Cossel, found themselves helpless in disciplining their members. Several in the São Paulo local refused to obey Cossel's orders when they learned he had not heard from Germany for several weeks, and it appeared he no longer had the sanction of the NSDAP.[68]

Operating party groups and organizing local Germans were only two aspects of Nazi policy in Brazil and Latin America. The German government also sought to establish closer political and diplomatic ties there, to support native fascist movements (e.g., Integralism in Brazil), and to develop Germany's trade relations. By 1935 the economic policy in particular had become so successful in South America that it began to alarm the United States.[69] In Brazil Cossel's efforts were focused on the large communities in the south, where German-Brazilians numbered 520,000 in Rio Grande do Sul, 275,000 in Santa Catarina, and 126,000 in Paraná. The Nazis used the communities, which were strong in import and retail trade, local manufacturing, and farming, as a major component in their rapid expansion of trade with Brazil. In March 1933 Cossel was instrumental in drafting a plan for the AA that would have settled 40,000 families from Germany in Rio Grande do Sul and Paraná and created a unified German state in the southern provinces. Although the project came to nothing, the NSDAP and Cossel pushed the plan, maintaining it would protect the racial purity of the Brazilian colonies from the threat of the large influx of Japanese settlers.

Apparently, Hitler himself was intrigued with developing a strong racial outpost in Brazil and with displacing North American and Hispano-Portuguese influences throughout Latin America. On Brazil, he explained in private circles, "We shall create a new Germany there . . . . We shall find everything we need there."

He added that establishing a Nazi foothold in Brazil could be achieved best through the local German colony: "We shall not land troops like William the Conqueror and gain Brazil by strength of arms. Our weapons are not visible ones. Our conquistadores . . . have a more difficult task than the original ones, and for this reason they have more difficult weapons."[70]

The goal of the *Landesgruppe* Brazil was to coordinate the German settlements in São Paulo, Rio de Janeiro, and the southern states. Cossel began by founding a weekly newspaper for the *Ortsgruppe* São Paulo, the *Deutsche Morgen* (which later became the paper of the *Landesgruppe*), and by sponsoring a beer party on 1 April for the local colony to celebrate the birthday of Bismarck.[71] Although many in the colony were conservative and nationalistic and therefore enjoyed such gatherings, most Germans deeply resented the *Ortsgruppe* when it began making extreme demands on the colony's school. While the school's director and teachers were German citizens, Cossel denounced the staff as being Marxists and insisted that the teachers become Nazi members. Also, he campaigned for the school to fly the swastika flag and for it to teach anti-Semitism in its classes. Such agitation quickly aroused the wrath of many parents, and after a hue and cry from both sides, the Nazis softened their demands as the parents withdrew their children from classes and complained strenuously to the AA in Berlin.[72]

Similar unpleasant clashes occurred in other cities and villages where Nazi groups, totally unrestrained and receiving few orders from Germany on what tactics should be employed, antagonized their German communities. In Rio de Janeiro tension arose in March between the *Ortsgruppe* on the one hand, and Schmidt-Elskop, the German Minister to Brazil, and leaders of the colony on the other. The head of the local, Meiss, attempted to have himself elected the leader of the colony, but failed. To restore order, that summer Bohle finally transferred to Rio the *Landesgruppenleiter* of Chile, Kohn.

Such shenanigans did not go unnoticed by the Brazilian government. Since 1930 it had sought to initiate mild measures to nationalize the large minorities (including the Germans) in the country, and in July 1934 a major step was taken when the President, Getulio Vargas, proclaimed a new constitution limiting the influx of foreigners into the country. Coupled with later laws, the constitution opened the way toward the official nationalizing of the country's large number of private (and particularly German) schools and the controlling of the number of foreigners in the labor market.[73] Still, while local party groups seemed determined to make political pests of themselves without attracting much sympathy, their efforts were periodically crowned with success. When Cossel spoke on relations between National Socialism and foreign Germans in Curitiba, he drew twelve hundred persons; weekly meetings of the *Ortsgruppe* Porto Alegre (re-established after its ban in 1932) had over eighty members attending regularly.[74]

The wide range of belligerent activities in Brazil was matched by party groups in other Latin American countries. In November 1933 the party in Bolivia was reorganized; because of complaints from the German Legation in La Paz about Helmuth Knips, the unemployed and unpopular *Landesgruppenleiter*, he was replaced by Bohle with a highly decorated veteran from World War I, Captain Achim von Kries. Prior to Bohle's reforming of the method for choosing *Landesgruppenleiters*, the NSDAP's leadership abroad was recruited haphazardly, and anyone who was willing to serve was chosen. Consequently, numerous social misfits (e.g., Knips) and persons who were morally disreputable became party leaders, reflecting badly on the foreign groups and contributing to their failure. In Chile the party sponsored brief radio broadcasts, supplied a weekly propaganda page to the German newspaper in Santiago, published its own paper (the *Westküsten Beobachter*), and held weekly *Sprechabende*.[75] Nazi groups in Uruguay tried to seize control of German schools, which brought forth the usual resistance of many *Volksdeutschen* who despised the Nazis' interference and who feared repression from the Uruguayan government.[76]

But it was in Argentina that Nazi penetration became especially apparent. During 1934 Germany established close trade relations with Argentina and dispatched a new minister to Buenos Aires, Thermann. Thermann's appointment was welcomed by Bohle, who was visited by Thermann before he left for his assignment, and by the *Landesgruppe* Argentina. Bohle, in discussing the minister with Hess, noted that "our entire work abroad would be much simpler if all Reich representatives were as positive toward the new state as Herr v. Thermann." The minister was also greeted warmly by the conservative *Deutsche La Plata-Zeitung*, but when the German government and he were attacked by the *Argentinisches Tageblatt*, he pushed the Argentine government to prosecute the paper. Hoping to destroy the nagging *Tageblatt*, the *Landesgruppe* pressured local Germans not to buy it, had the paper banned in Germany, and forced German banks and businesses not to place advertisements in it.

Since several local Spanish newspapers criticized Berlin, the AO, Foreign Press Office (*Auslandspresseamt*) of the NSDAP, Ministry of Propaganda, and Press Department of the AA began a concentrated campaign to counter the anti-German sentiment. Articles painting a grossly pro-Nazi picture about Germany were sent to the principal party newspapers in Latin America, *Der Trommler* (published by the *Landesgruppe* Argentina), *Deutsche Morgen*, and *Westküsten Beobachter*.

But party activity in Argentina was not limited to spreading propaganda. Some of its groups allied with native right-wing extremist organizations, and the result was often violence. In September 1934 bomb attempts were made on the *Tageblatt*, synagogues, and leftist organizations in Buenos Aires. Several months later a theater that had shown a controversial movie attacking Nazi anti-Semitism was bombed. Much to the anger of the German community, the *Landesgruppe* descended on the German schools and the *Deutsche Volksbund*, which was exposed in large headlines by the *Tageblatt*. It was only when Bohle sent his troubleshooter for South America, Kohn, to Buenos Aires, that the furor in the community subsided, and order was restored.[77]

Kohn and his choice as *Landesgruppenleiter*, Gottfried Brandt, began the coordination of the *Volksbund* by forcing its chairman and a large number of its members to resign. In July 1934, Wilhelm Röhmer, a physician at the German Ministry and a National Socialist sympathizer, was chosen the new chairman, and he gave permission for *Volksbund* members (most being *Volksdeutschen*) to enter local NSDAP groups. Although Brandt and Röhmer represented the core of the party's leadership, they contrasted sharply in their political views. Brandt's specialty was Jew-baiting; he regularly carried in his pocket the latest edition of Streicher's *Der Stürmer*, and his speeches at party meetings were anti-Semitic tirades. Röhmer had been one of the founders of the *Volksbund*, and while he was not a fanatical anti-Semite like Brandt, he was Brandt's equal as an opportunist. Before 1918 he had been a monarchist, but during the Weimar years he had supported democracy for Germany. Following Hitler's seizure of power, however, he had suddenly taken up the cause of National Socialism, prompting one of his fellow Nazis to observe: "Indeed whatever direction the political wind blows in Germany, he [Röhmer] blows with it."

Through the *Volksbund* the NSDAP camouflaged its coordination of the roughly two hundred German schools in the country. The party also organized a large demonstration with the *Volksbund*, which celebrated Germany's withdrawal from the League of Nations and Disarmament Conference and sent a congratulatory telegram to Hitler. A section of the German Labor Front was formed in the *Landesgruppe*, and it enrolled workers, technicians, and commercial employees of German firms and acted as a kind of labor union for the workers. Finally, the party infiltrated youth groups and sports clubs in German colonies and sponsored a sports contest in October 1933 that attracted 1,400 German and *Volksdeutsch* youth.[78]

Outside Argentina, similar activities that appeared to meddle in the internal affairs of Latin American countries led to official government measures against the National Socialists. When the party in Guatemala caused an uproar in the local German colony by demanding that the German school accept several Nazi members on its executive board, the government closed the school. Part of the uproar centered around the rabid Nazism of the party's leader and a teacher, Walter Lehne, who was also head of a local Hitler Youth association.[79] The foreign press also noted for the first time the NSDAP groups in South America. *The New York Times* riveted its attention on Nazi propaganda being smuggled into Brazil and Argentina. In future articles the *Times* would significantly prepare the way for the myth later to arise in the United States that the Nazi organizations in South America represented a serious threat to the safety of the Western hemisphere and America.[80]

Part of the myth rested on deliberate tales of sinister Nazi intrigue spread by anti-German elements, part originated with sensational reporting by liberal and left-wing newspapers, and part came from honestly held but erroneous impressions which many Americans had regarding Nazi activities in Latin America. But it was the party groups in the United States, with their thoughtless antics beginning in 1933, that also contributed to the myth. Throughout the 1930s Hitler and his subleaders generally ignored and underestimated "the significance of the United States;" as Bohle woefully admitted after World War II, "I did not know enough about America."[81]

From its beginning the Hitler regime progressively destroyed the favorable attitude that had developed in the United States toward Germany in the 1920s. A number of factors arose quickly in 1933 to undermine German-American relations: differences over disarmament, problems involving trade and tariffs, conflicts over international payments, and sharp clashes between the political ideologies of the American and German governments. Nazi persecution of the Jews, hostility toward democracy, attacks on cultural and literary freedom, and the campaign to destroy the churches repulsed many Americans. In early March 1933 a delegation from several major Jewish organizations complained to Secretary of State Hull, and on 27 March they held a large rally in Madison Square Garden protesting Nazi anti-Semitism. The Department of State was bombarded with protests, and while Schacht was visiting the United States in May. an anti-Nazi demonstration with 100,000 participants was held in New York City.[82]

Amidst a public relations campaign by the AA, the new German Ambassador to America, Hans Luther, and the Consulate General in New York to improve Germany's image in the United States, the local party affiliates moved in the opposite direction. They alienated Colonel Edward Emerson, an old friend of Fürholzer who possessed connections to the influential United German Societies in Yorkville and the German-American Board of Trade, and the groups' leaders began encountering difficulties from the American authorities. Manger, the nominal *Vertrauensmann* for America, lost his job and began thinking about returning to Germany.

Manger was also attacked by his bickering *Ortsgruppe* New York. Neither he nor the AO could control the local, and by March a chaotic situation had developed. Even Spanknöbel was forced to halt his work in Detroit, and in mid-March he sent an envoy to Hamburg to ask if he should return to Germany or try to carry on his activity by attaching himself to a German consulate in America.[83] Hess, when informed of the mounting problems, instructed Bohle that a continuation of the party groups in the United States was "asking for trouble," and he ordered him to dissolve them.[84] As it was to do in the future in other countries, the NSDAP quickly began a pseudoretreat in response to the American reaction to Nazism.

On the other hand, Spanknöbel traveled to Germany sometime in late March or the beginning of April and made the exaggerated claim to Hess and Bohle that thousands of German-Americans were eagerly waiting for Berlin to form a genuine Nazi movement in the United States. Nothing could have been further from the truth, but Spanknöbel's view prevailed, and he returned to America with an order allegedly signed by Hitler to dismantle the NSDAP groups and to permit Nazi members to enter the *Volksdeutsch*-oriented Friends of the Hitler Movement (formed a year earlier and controlled by Hamburg). Some members joined the Movement while others, like the leader of the faction-ridden Hudson County local, Schneider, became disillusioned and returned to Germany.[85]

Since the Movement was soon dissolved by Hamburg, most Nazi members joined a new organization, the Association of the Friends of the New Germany (*Bund der Freunde des Neuen Deutschland*), created in May by Spanknöbel. Although led by Spanknöbel and apparently acknowledged as a Nazi group by the *Reichsleitung*,[86] the Friends included in its membership a catchall array of Reich nationals, Germans with American citizenship, party members, and non-Nazis. While the Friends was under orders from Germany to be less militant and less public than the former Nazi *Ortsgruppen*, Spanknöbel exceeded his authority and became far too aggressive. To crush opposition to his rule among local Nazis, he employed the threat of force and violence; at the end of May he created a special Fighting Division (*Ordnungsdienst*), which wore Nazi-style uniforms and was modeled after the SA.

Throughout the summer he toured the eastern United States, boasting that his new group was the sole Nazi organization in North America. Hoping to preserve a semi-American identity, he distributed leaflets and bumper stickers showing the swastika alongside the insignia of the Ku Klux Klan. Accompanying him was a small unit of the *Ordnungsdienst*, and during one of his anti-Semitic speeches in Newark, the presence of the storm troopers provoked a bloody brawl. In July the Friends of the New Germany held a convention in Chicago and it began publishing its own newspapers, the *Deutsche Zeitung* and *Das neue Deutschland*.[87]

Spanknöbel also carried his bellicose methods outside the party. He sought to seize control of the United German Societies (consisting of seventy clubs and 10,000 members) in New York and the German-American Society in Chicago, but his racist demands that German-Jewish groups be expelled from the societies and that they display swastika flags at their meetings were received with a flood of opposition. In September 1933 the Jewish members left the

United German Societies in protest against him. He attempted, in addition, to force the *New Yorker Staats-Zeitung und Herold,* America's most prestigious German newspaper, to publish material favorable to the Third Reich.

His downfall came in the autumn. At the end of September the *Reichsleitung* bowed to the furor he was creating by removing him as head of the Friends and ordering him "to refrain from any activity until further notice."[88] He was also undercut from Germany by Bohle, who directed two of Spanknöbel's accomplices from America, who were visiting Germany, to inform him to halt his activity. One visitor was John Wuerz, a former member of the defunct *Ortsgruppe* New York; the other was Captain Frederick Mensing, who had been Bohle's *Landesvertrauensmann* for America since the summer. An official in the New York branch of the North German Lloyd shipping firm, Mensing had no party groups to control, and his only functions were to register party members in the United States and forward their dues and other contributions to the AO.[89] It is also probable that he was to spy on Spanknöbel and the Friends and report to Hamburg; his appointment, which was made without Spanknöbel's knowledge, was a further signal of the latter's fall from grace with Bohle and Hess.

In mid-October Mensing and the German consul in New York, Otto Kiep, asked Bohle to halt immediately all party work in America. They secured his agreement, mainly because they were supported by the senior counselor for American affairs in the AA and by the announcement of the opening of an investigation by the American House of Representatives (led by Samuel Dickstein) into pro-Nazi activities in the United States. Bohle agreed to a list of demands from Mensing and Kiep: only German citizens in America could become NSDAP members; Bohle would strictly prohibit the members from engaging in any party work; Spanknöbel would be ordered to relinquish his leadership of the Friends in favor of an American citizen; and Mensing would ensure that the Friends refrained from all political work while party members remained in the organization.[90]

But many of the demands were more easily adopted than carried through. Before Mensing could return to implement the new policy, Spanknöbel became embroiled in a public argument with the mayor of New York over celebrating "German Day" in the city, and the Nazi leader was charged by a federal grand jury with failing to register as an agent of the German government. His antics were even discussed among President Roosevelt's inner circle of advisers and noted in the foreign press. On the night of 29 October he quietly fled on a German freighter to Germany. Once home, the NSDAP gave him a hero's welcome, and he became one of Himmler's SS officers.[91] Although the affair had done severe damage to Germany's reputation in the United States and had given considerable support to allegations by rabid anti-Nazis like Dickstein that Hitler had sent hundreds of Nazi spies to the United States, German leaders were fiercely proud of anyone who demonstrated blind loyalty to Hitler.

Spanknöbel escaped just in time. The night he set sail American customs officials began searching German ships for Nazi literature and propaganda. While the searches continued periodically into early 1934 and produced little evidence against the German government, a massive cache of anti-Semitic pamphlets was uncovered in New York in February on a German freighter, the *Este*.[92]

By 1934 the Nazi movement in America was probably doomed to failure; it had attracted public attention and was observed with suspicion by the American government. First the Nazi *Ortsgruppen*, and later the Friends of the New Germany, revealed to many Americans a political and racial philosophy that seemed totally alien, and the groups played a significant role in conditioning many Americans to view National Socialism as a threat to the United States. But as the history of the groups was already revealing, this could hardly be true. Their work, much of it bordering on the ridiculous, was futile, and it alienated both Americans and German-Americans. In Germany Bohle, Hess, and other leaders were out of touch with reality in America (or else they did not care what happened there), because they stubbornly refused to dissolve their organizations in that country and held to the belief that German-Americans were waiting by the hundreds to join Hitler.

While bigger troubles were brewing in the United States, the NSDAP found it impossible to form its groups in Russia and to penetrate the iron wall of security around the country that was Hitler's archenemy. Hamburg was even forced in October 1933 to quit dispatching mail across Siberia to its groups in the Far East because the mail was falling into the clutches of the Communists. Since the Hitler government hardly relished a confrontation with the Soviet Union while the Nazis were immersed in consolidating their power at home and beginning rearmament, the AO commanded its *Landesvertrauensmann* for East Asia, Hasenöhrl, to direct his branches in northern China near the Russian border not to engage in any "provocative" activities.[93]

But in southern China the party made little effort to hide its intense hatred of Communism. While Sino-German relations were close during 1933 and 1934 and included strong military and commercial ties (e.g., German military advisers and weapons were sent to Chiang Kai-shek's government in exchange for raw materials needed for Germany's rearmament), the party penetrated German colonies and exploited the strong fear of Communism shared by local Germans, Chinese, and the government. The largest and most active *Ortsgruppe* was Hasenöhrl's branch in Shanghai, which spent most of its time winning support from the local German colony and Consul General, R. C. W. Behrend. On 16 March several hundred members of the colony attended a ceremony at which the nationalist "black-white-red" flag of pre-World War I Germany and the swastika flag were raised atop the Consulate General. In keeping with the order a few days earlier from the German president, Hindenburg, the "black-red-gold" flag of the Weimar regime was removed. Behrend and Hasenöhrl spoke at the festivities, both denouncing Communism, and the *Ortsgruppe* sang the Horst Wessel song (the official tune of the NSDAP honoring an SA youth killed in Berlin in 1931).[94]

Hasenöhrl was also kept busy arranging for the formation of Nazi groups in other parts of the Far East. In 1934 he visited Japan and scouted the possibility of creating an organization there. Because of the close ties of the AA and the German army to China, the Berlin government had few contacts with China's archrival, Japan. But beginning in 1933 and 1934 the NSDAP openly favored Japan and the establishment of stronger relations with Tokyo. While the party had been interested in Japan since the 1920s, the sudden fancy in her had developed because of the Japanese withdrawal from the League of Nations and the party's speculation that Japan would soon go to war with Russia over imperialist possessions in the Far East. Hitler spoke about Japan on several occasions with Ribbentrop and Rosenberg, and Hiroshi Oshima, a highly pro-German diplomat, was appointed the military attache in Berlin. As a small part of this growing awareness of Japan, the first Nazi groups there arose in mid-1934 in Tokyo and Yokohama; appointed *Landesgruppenleiter* was a middle-aged businessman and recent convert to the NSDAP, Rudolf Hillmann.[95]

About the only concession Hitler made to Japan in 1933 was to dispatch a "party diplomat" and adventurer supported by the APA and Göring, Ferdinand Heye, to the Japanese puppet state of Manchuria. It was Heye's scheme to shift German policy away from China to Japan; he hoped to do this by his government's recognizing officially Manchuria and developing stronger German-Manchurian trade (which centered around Manchurian soybeans). Over the objections of the AA, which feared alienating China, Heye blindly arranged a German-Manchurian trade agreement and promised German recognition of the country. But because of Germany's ties with China, the Reich government refused recognition, the Manchurian regime responded politely by refusing the trade agreement, and Heye was so discredited that Hitler withdrew him from his mission in February 1935. The AO was also active in Manchuria. Its groups in Mukden, Darien, and Harbin, organized in June 1934 by Hanns von Kirschbaum, pursued further commercial contacts and pushed for Manchuria's recognition by Germany.[96] The results, however, were as unimpressive as Heye's.

The encouragement of trade became a principal task of numerous branches in the Far East. Foreign agents of the Krupp Steel Works and I. G. Farben were appointed *Stützpunktleiters* in Calcutta and Bombay, and German commercial employees headed party groups in the Dutch East Indies. Yet, the party was never to exclude political tasks for economic functions. Its affiliates in Australia and New Zealand became involved in bitter struggles when they sought to remove anti-Nazi officials from local German clubs. The *Stützpunkt* Auckland forced the president of the German Association to resign because of his "wavering attitude toward Germany."[97]

MINOR SUCCESSES IN EGYPT AND EUROPE

If the main objective of the groups abroad was to nazify German communities and persuade them to support Hitler's regime, nowhere did the policy work better than in Egypt and in several European countries. But here again, such assertions must be qualified. It was only in Spain in 1936 and 1937 (and to a lesser extent in Austria) that the foreign organizations became significant agencies for aiding German political and economic expansion. Although an official Nazi policy toward the Middle East was not formulated until later, the AO commissioned party members there in the spring of 1933 to build *Stützpunkte* in Palestine and Iran and to reorganize the small branches in Turkey.

Both the APA and Hamburg urged that Germany expand her activity in the Arab countries, and one of the most ardent advocates of this policy was Alfred Hess. He and several other Nazis had formed in 1932 active locals in Cairo and Alexandria.[98] Following closely in his older brother's footsteps, Hess had joined the NSDAP in August 1920; having served in World War I where he was wounded and decorated for heroism, he returned to Egypt in 1926 and joined his family's wholesale firm. After the Nazi seizure of power, he and several party friends began "coordinating" the major German colonies in Egypt.

Aided by the German Minister to Egypt, Eberhard von Stohrer,[99] the party in Alexandria gained complete domination over its colony and reorganized the community according to the *Führerprinzip*. After a similar triumph over the colony in Cairo, the new *Landesgruppenleiter*, Hans Schröder, happily reported to Bohle that "all German associations in Egypt" had given the party "unlimited authority," thus revealing that "all of Germandom has been united."[100] Schröder's groups were also busy spreading propaganda among the Arabs in Egypt and Palestine; it was anti-Jewish and anti-British and aimed at undermining England's hold over the Suez Canal. The Germans in Egypt were also proud of the Arab National Socialist party which the NSDAP had helped to construct in Palestine. Anti-Jewish material printed in the Arabic language was supplied to the native party through the Egyptian NSDAP.[101]

Along with its progress in Egypt, the AO concentrated its efforts on Germany's neighboring lands in Europe. In several instances the results were noticeable, and they helped bring the progressive consolidation by 1935 of the intraparty power of the agency. Mainly because of the large masses of Germans in Europe and because they were within easy reach of the Reich, the NSDAP's efforts there were more carefully coordinated from Germany than was its work elsewhere.

Europe also ranked higher on the party's list of priorities (than, for example, did South America or the Far East) because of its proximity to Germany and because of the latter's being forced to deal extensively with the European countries to maintain security. But part of the party's expansion in Europe was the result of the Nazi government's massive propaganda campaign waged abroad to counter foreign opinion against Hitler's regime, and especially against its brutality, anti-Semitism, and persecution of the churches. Throughout 1933 and 1934 meetings on "the influencing of public opinion abroad" to soften foreign antagonism were held involving Hitler, Goebbels, the AA, and party agencies like the AO and APA. Hitler, in a remarkable moment of reflection on the situation, explained at a conference in May 1933, "We find ourselves politically in an isolation in the world from which we can only emerge if we are able to improve the mood abroad."[102]

The answer, he surmised, was to flood Europe and the world with propaganda. All his fantasies notwithstanding, he was enough of a realist to recognize that his revolutionary goals (both at home and abroad) would be opposed vehemently in many foreign lands. To achieve his aims he cleverly combined throughout his regime propaganda, power politics, and a Machiavellian principle that said "justice is only that which serves the needs of the Nazi movement and German nation."[103] The party's response to his call was to unleash in April 1933 what it termed "a defensive struggle" against the "campaign of slander" being waged against Germany by foreign Jews and Marxists. Hamburg ordered its affiliates in Europe to counter criticism of Germany by planting articles in the European press and by talking with discretion to "available foreign Germans" and "citizens of the native country" who were known friends of party members. Aiding the AO was the Fichte *Bund*, a highly nationalistic organization in Hamburg formed in 1914 in memory of the nineteenth-century philosopher and used as a secret cover after 1933 for Nazi propaganda.[104]

Although few National Socialists in Europe had been in Germany since Hitler became Chancellor to witness for themselves what was happening, they combatted hostility in their countries to the *Reichstag* Fire affair, the purge of Röhm and the SA in June 1934, and other controversial incidents. Party groups tackled their propaganda tasks with fanaticism, and the opposition to their efforts from foreign Germans was summarized by a report of the German mission in Berne to the AA: "In the understandable zeal to advertise for their idea, National Socialist organizations and locals in Switzerland make entirely too much noise. All too boisterously do they seek on foreign ground to attain a rapid development of the former German associations in their understanding of the terms."[105]

While the groups focused on propaganda matters, they also tried to nazify German colonies and influence diplomats in German missions. They made sporadic progress. The *Ortsgruppe* Copenhagen functioned as an intelligence service for the AO. As German Communists fled for protection to Denmark following the *Reichstag* Fire, the group sent Hamburg reports and press clippings with names of refugee Germans and stories of their accusing the Nazis of starting the blaze. The information was filed in the NSDAP's records, and if the Communists (or their families) were unfortunate enough to be caught returning to Germany, it was used to arrest them.[106] In London, Bene, the *Landesgruppenleiter* of Great Britain, developed friendly relations with Leopold von Hoesch, the German Ambassador. Considering Hoesch's anti-party feelings, Bene's accomplishment was no small feat. Described by Bohle as the party's "most respectable local leader abroad," he traveled to Ireland in May 1934, and with the aid of the German Legation in Dublin (and over the objections of the Irish President, Eamon De Valera), secretly formed a *Stützpunkt* in the Irish capital.[107]

The party built more organizations in the Netherlands, which fell under the skeptical eye of the Dutch government and were eventually banned. Not only did the groups infiltrate the police department in The Hague and become involved in street brawls with Communists, they followed their dictator, Patzig, who commanded them to coordinate at all costs their respective German communities. By the autumn of 1934 the groups had conquered and reorganized colonies according to the *Führerprinzip* in Amsterdam, Eindhoven, Utrecht, Rotterdam, The Hague, Helmond, Tilburg, and Alkmaar. As a result, the government outlawed foreign political organizations, but the NSDAP countered by creating undercover branches called the *Reichsdeutsche Gemeinschaft* ("Assocation of Reich Citizens").[108]

Although the party's work brought a deterioration in official German-Dutch relations, Patzig continued to act like Hitler's personal "governor" for the Netherlands, and he became too brazen and bombastic for even his German superiors. When he wildly demanded in party propaganda that Germany annex the Netherlands and when the Dutch threatened to expel him, Bohle dismissed him as *Landesgruppenleiter*. He was replaced by a retired army officer in Rotterdam, Major A. R. Witte, who became the party's "Foreign Commissioner for the Netherlands." Witte supported native pro-Nazi movements like Mussert's Dutch National Socialist party and the National Socialist Netherlands Workers' party, which campaigned for a "greater Netherlands, including Flemish Belgium, affiliated with the Third Reich."[109]

While party groups in Belgium, Bulgaria, Greece, and Albania sought to coordinate their German colonies,[110] active branches in Italy placed their men at the head of communities in Rome, Naples, Genoa, Florence, and Milan. Brand, the *Landesgruppenleiter*, sent trains carrying several hundred party members and Germans from Rome, Florence, and Milan to Munich to vote for the Nazis in the *Reichstag* election on 5 March 1933.[111] While Brand ordered his groups not to alienate Mussolini's government by wearing uniforms, flying swastika flags, or holding provocative meetings, the AO instructed the locals, "The National Socialist movement is sympathetic to Fascism. The German people are pleased that both nations are bound by the same foreign policy aims." When Brand proved incapable of ensuring that the branches in the South Tirol would follow the pro-Fascist line, he was relieved of his post, and the most troublesome affiliate, Meran, was dissolved and reorganized under new leadership.[112] Because of feelings of *irredenta* and because of repression by the Fascists, German-Austrians in the Tirol were hardly as enthusiastic about Mussolini as were Hitler and the NSDAP.

When it came to Austria Mussolini correctly suspected that the Hitler government would be a danger to Italian interests. In Austria, the party had operated since August 1926 an organization of German nationals that had agitated for the unification of Austria with Germany. Led by Alfred Frauenfeld, the *Gauleiter* of Vienna, and Theo Habicht, a *Reichstag* member, the party created SA formations, Hitler Youth groups, and student clubs. Frauenfeld also helped to develop an Austrian National Socialist movement, which aimed at overthrowing the Austrian government headed by the Christian Socialist Chancellor, Dollfuss. Habicht undermined the Dollfuss government by distributing propaganda, holding demonstrations, and radicalizing the Austrian Nazis. By the summer of 1933 such activity had expanded to include bombings and other acts of terrorism. The government reacted sharply by banning the NSDAP, SA, SS, and other rightist groups. Habicht quickly fled to Germany, and Frauenfeld was later arrested and imprisoned on suspicion of high treason; he was released in January 1934, and he too escaped to Germany.

The ban of the party forced it to move underground and to claim to the Austrian authorities (and Mussolini) that Germans in Austria had nothing to do with the Austrian National Socialists who were allegedly causing the trouble. But Habicht continued to lead the subversive campaign from Munich, piping propaganda by radio into Austria and dropping leaflets by plane which attacked Dollfuss and called on the Austrians to rise against their weak government. Hitler pushed hard toward a Nazi takeover in Austria, primarily through internal disruption and terror supported by outside pressure from Germany.[113]

To complicate matters, Nazi groups in the South Tirol were caught smuggling propaganda, explosives, and weapons across the border to the illegal Austrian Nazis. In February 1934 the Italian police arrested the *Ortsgruppenleiter* of Trieste, Berger, and found his house full of ammunition and propaganda earmarked for Austria. Although the AO removed Berger from his post and Hess ordered a halt to the smuggling, arrests of party members continued, and Nazi work in Italy came under the close scrutiny of the Italian press. As late as September Nazi activists like Richard Koderle, deprived of his Austrian citizenship in 1933 for illegal activities, were expelled from the South Tirol.[114] Koderle was rewarded for his "sacrifice" with a leading position in the AO in Hamburg.

But after the brutal murder of Dollfuss and the attempted overthrow of the democratic regime by the Austrian Nazis on 25 July 1934, Bohle began secretly to rebuild the NSDAP's group of German nationals in Austria. In October and November 1934 he negotiated with Hess and the German Minister in Vienna, Papen, to prepare the groundwork for the AO's takeover of the major German organization for Reich citizens, the *Bund der Reichsdeutschen in Österreich* ("League of German Citizens in Austria"). The League, formed in 1919 and headquartered in Vienna, had numerous clubs and associations and claimed the allegiance of roughly 27,000 Germans. Bohle's negotiations (which involved a visit to Vienna to confer with Papen) were crowned with success in April 1935, when Hess gave him full authority over German nationals in Austria.

The expansion of his authority to Austria was particularly disconcerting to Papen, who had been sent by Hitler to Vienna to centralize Germany's Austrian policy and to return it to the pre-July tactic of "peaceful infiltration." Before accepting Hitler's appointment, Papen had laid down several conditions, including the severing of all relations between the German and Austrian Nazi movements and the establishing of the union of Germany and Austria through strictly evolutionary means. Such a policy was necessary, he maintained, to relax international tension following the Dollfuss murder and until Austria could be removed from the world spotlight.[115] But, if Papen had visions of centralizing Germany's effort in Austria, Bohle had other ideas. While the AO used the League of German Citizens in Austria as a cover for its organizations, it decided early to recruit Austrians for its groups. Although Hess had ordered Frauenfeld and Habicht in August 1934 to "have nothing at all to do with the National Socialists in Austria," Bohle informed the AA at the end of the year that his groups in Austria could include Austrians.[116]

The AO wasted little time in coordinating the League of German Citizens. In August 1935 the League's chairman was forced out by an internal rebellion of pro-Nazi radicals led by *Vertrauensmänner* of the AO. The latter included the new director of the League, Robert Günther, and an ambitious SS doctor and HJ leader in Lindau, Otto Butting. They purged the League's membership rolls of Austrian names, communicated closely with Hamburg, sent dues collected from Nazi members to the Reich, and quarreled with Papen. Butting, who had been active in the *Landesgruppe* Switzerland, reorganized the League into *Ortsgruppen* led by loyal Nazis and directed centrally from Vienna by Günther. Butting was also an agent of the German Security Service (*Sicherheitsdienst*, or SD).[117]

As the Germans continued to work in Austria (despite Hitler's public claims to the contrary), the NSDAP developed branches in France and Spain, and it expanded its activity in Portugal. In Paris, above the disapproval of the German Ambassador Roland Köster, a group of one hundred members celebrated (on Bohle's order) the murder of Dollfuss. In Spain most of the large German population was comprised of persons who had emigrated in the nineteenth century or Germans who had moved from the Cameroons following their expulsion from Africa in World War I. But Burbach, the party's "Foreign Commissioner for Portugal and Spain," built his organizations from young Germans who detested the Weimar Republic and who had fled Germany since 1920.[118]

In June 1933 Burbach and Bohle named Zuchristian, an employee of the Siemens corporation in Madrid, as *Landesgruppenleiter*, and he rapidly created twenty-seven *Ortsgruppen*, twelve *Stützpunkte*, and eight *Zellen* in the country and in Spanish

Morocco. Under his orders the groups met regularly each month at *Kontrollversammlung* (meetings closed to nonparty members), *Werbeversammlung* (propaganda meetings attended by outsiders or guests of members), and *Kameradschaftsabende* (social gatherings for cultivating the "spirit of comradeship" of the groups). The Madrid local was divided into *Zellen*, each operated by a cell fore-man (*Zellenobmann*) responsible for knowing the members in his area of the city, their ability to perform party work, and their "special relations" to the press. The cell leader also made certain that his people were ready to participate in party jobs. When the *Ortsgruppe* Madrid demanded such services, the members were instructed that "private and social interests must be largely de-ferred" and that those who refused to work would be expelled from the NSDAP.

The groups in Spain devoted a great deal of time to propaganda and press work. They sent reports to the AO about Spanish news-papers, radio, and film; the political stance of the papers was noted, and the *Landesgruppe* informed Hamburg which papers were sus-ceptible to Nazi influence. The party also harassed German busi-nesses that advertised in papers that were anti-German. The left-wing and republican press, in response to the party's work, attacked the *Ortsgruppe* Madrid's propaganda and infiltration of the German school.[119]

The *Landesgruppe* rapidly developed into a model organization. It became involved in a variety of matters that included arranging for the arrest by Spanish police of Germans who were anti-Nazi and spying on Nazi political enemies. In September 1935 it success-fully infiltrated Otto Strasser's *Schwarze Front* ("Black Front") and destroyed the group's system for smuggling anti-Hitler propa-ganda to Germany.[120] The party also kept German diplomats in Spain under surveillance, thereby following the directive from Bohle in February 1934 ordering *Landesgruppenleiters* to make character studies of the diplomats.[121]

The party in Spanish Morocco was comprised of German busi-nessmen, engineers, and former officers of the *Schwarze Reichswehr* ("Black Army"), the illegal units of the German army during the Weimar Republic. Led by the *Ortsgruppenleiter* of Tetuan, Adolf Langenheim, the party developed intimate contacts with local Italian Fascists. The anti-Jewish propaganda of Langenheim and another party official, Karl Schlichting, attracted considerable atten-tion from the authorities. When the police in French Morocco learned that propaganda denouncing the Jews and Versailles Treaty had been sent from the *Ortsgruppe* Tetuan, the French appealed to the Spanish to prevent the local from continuing its work. In response, houses of Germans in Tetuan were searched and local party functionaries like Schlichting, whose guilt he would admit only to Zuchristian, were interrogated. Nor was the party's handiwork ignored outside Morocco. The foreign press ran sensational headlines about "Nazi Propaganda in Morocco" and about the arrest of German agents, which only damaged further Germany's reputation and fueled the impression that Nazi spies were everywhere.[122]

The events of 1933 and 1934 were vital to the future of the Nazi party abroad, its ultimate failure to conquer foreign Germandom, and its feud with the AA. Amidst the confusion caused by the seizure of power in Germany and by the lack of restraint on the party's foreign branches, the latter embarked on a pattern of behavior that could only be harmful to Germany. Most of their work among foreign Germans—from spreading blatant racial and political propaganda to threatening the freedom of German firms and businessmen abroad—was futile, because its base was far too narrow and selfish to contain anything attractive to the outside world.

While alienating both Germans and foreigners, such activities fed (with the brutal nature of Hitler's regime) the suspicion of many in the Western world that Germany was aggressive and potentially dangerous. In this respect, the groups already exercised an influence over foreign opinion that was vastly out of proportion to their small organizations, which had poor communication with Germany, lacked discipline, and were dominated by petty quarrels. Bohle, with his bombastic claims about the size of the AO and how it ruled all Germans abroad, compounded the comedy of errors. The fact that he and higher ranking leaders (like Hess and Hitler) refused to restrain foreign party members indicated that the Germans cared little about earning the world's respect and cooperation. By seeking to carry the customs and attitudes of the Third Reich to Germans outside Germany, the NSDAP was contributing to the other factors in Hitler's policies that were to undermine feelings of security in the world and to prepare the atmosphere for war.

4

THE AO: MIXING PARTY AFFAIRS
WITH DIPLOMACY, 1935-1937

By the beginning of 1935 Hitler had consolidated his dictatorship and started his bid to make Germany a world power. Although he stressed his desire to live at peace with Europe (as shown by his treaty with Poland), Germany's withdrawal from the League of Nations and European Disarmament Conference had suggested otherwise. His confidence was strengthened by the domestic troubles in 1934 of the Austrian and French governments and by the death of his only political superior in Germany, Hindenburg. In immodest fashion he seized the powers of the Presidency and took the title of "Führer and Chancellor."

He wasted little time in shocking the world by bringing a revolution to the power relationships of Europe. Making a shambles of the Versailles Treaty and Locarno Pact, Germany increased its armed forces, signed a naval agreement with the English, moved its army into the demilitarized Rhineland, unleashed a rearmament program, and established the Anti-Comintern Pact with Japan and Italy. By the end of 1936 Germany had replaced France and Britain as the major power in Europe.

A hint of what had happened was revealed in the summer of 1936 when Hitler and Mussolini supported General Franco's forces in the Spanish Civil War. The democracies chose to appease the dictators by refusing to help the Spanish Republicans. By November 1937 Hitler had become so bold because of his foreign successes that he secretly informed his generals that Germany needed more *Lebensraum* to support her people; Austria and Czechoslovakia, he noted, must be conquered soon if the international situation permitted.[1]

One indication (among the many) of Germany's growing belligerency in foreign relations was the persistent work of the Nazi party abroad, the meddling by its foreign groups into the domestic affairs of their host countries, and the sharpening of the attack by the AO on the *Auswärtiges Amt*. As 1935 dawned the AO boasted of possessing five hundred groups abroad and of employing over 170 officials and secretaries in its offices in Hamburg. On 20 March it moved its headquarters to Berlin, where Bohle and other functionaries were ceremoniously welcomed to the busy political life of the capital by representatives from the city, the AA, and the Propaganda Ministry, and by the President of the Iberian-American Institute (*Ibero-Amerika Institut*), the retired General, Wilhelm Faupel.[2] Bohle's rising significance brought him a private discussion on foreign Germandom with Hitler, which resulted in the upgrading of the AO to the status of a *Gau* organization in the party. Hitler, to identify AO leaders, even approved a special insignia, the so-called "AO diamond" (*Raute*) for them to wear on party uniforms.[3]

ANTI-COMMUNISM IN LATIN AMERICA AND THE *Bund* IN THE UNITED STATES

The AO was especially proud of the progress of its organizations in Latin America. From the larger states pleasant news often trickled into Berlin; on 1 May the party led rallies allegedly involving twenty-five thousand persons in São Paulo and eleven thousand in Buenos Aires. Particularly friendly relations were established between Germany and Brazil. Trade between them increased sharply, and the authoritarian government of Vargas moved closer to Berlin politically by opening a strong campaign against Communism in Brazil. Following a Communist uprising in November 1935 Vargas dissolved the local Communist party and forced it underground. The government extradited to Germany a group of Brazilian revolutionaries of German descent, including the wife of the chairman of the Communist party, Olga Benario.

At the beginning of 1936 the Gestapo started unofficial negotiations with Felinto Müller, chief of police in Rio de Janeiro, and Captain A. H. Miranda Correa, head of the Brazilian police, for an agreement that would provide for an exchange of German and Brazilian police for training purposes and for an exchange of information about the Communists and their activities. A year later a group of Brazilian secret police were Himmler's guests in Germany to learn about the methods of the Gestapo. Such contacts were aided by the *Landesgruppe* Brazil, which negotiated during 1937 with the Brazilian Minister of Justice, F. Luis da Silva, to arrive at a formal agreement whereby Brazilian police units could be trained in Germany to detect and battle Communism.[4]

Much of this was a part of Germany's campaign to persuade Brazil (together with Argentina and Uruguay) to sign a so-called Anti-Comintern agreement, similar to that concluded by Germany with Japan and Italy. Another aspect of German policy toward Brazil was the *Landesgruppe*'s support of pro-Nazi elements in the Brazilian army and of the Brazilian fascist movement, Integralism. The Integralists, a fairly large group comprised of many Brazilian-Germans, were led by Plinio Salgado, a Brazilian nationalist. They demanded the strengthening of the Brazilian government, family life, property, Catholicism, and intellectuals, and they advocated ousting foreign capital from the country. The Nazis wished to use the large *Volksdeutsch* element in the movement to push it into influencing the Vargas government toward closer relations with Germany.

But one of the German headaches in Brazil was the growing appeal of Integralism to young Brazilian-Germans. Although Salgado maintained that his mother had descended from a German family and that his movement did not intend to rival either the Nazis or Italian Fascists in Brazil, Cossel and Schmidt-Elskop complained to the AA that Integralism could damage Germany's efforts to organize Brazilian-Germans.[5] Cossel and the *Landesgruppe* also had other problems. When a group of Nazis in Rio de Janeiro criticized him, he expelled twenty-nine from the party. Because of the *Ortsgruppe* Curitiba's propaganda campaign among its German colony and its insistence that the colony's social clubs open their doors to National Socialists, both the colony and local authorities threatened to abolish the affiliate. Of the twenty-five thousand Germans in Curitiba, fifteen hundred were German citizens and only 150 were party members. Thus, much of the antagonism arose from the claim of the small local to leadership over the *Volksdeutschen*.[6]

Such difficulties notwithstanding, Berlin hoped to make Brazil an example of the cooperation of all elements of Germany's expansion: friendship with the Brazilian government, supported by German positions in Brazilian trade, banks, and transportation, by influence on the army and police, and by developing a strong fascist movement.

Until the Vargas regime turned against the National Socialists at the beginning of 1938, Brazil was one of the few countries where foreign Germans became a threat to the state. In the absence of a German military invasion, the Brazilian-Germans became important through the only other method they could—influencing the government, army and police, and local fascist movements.[7]

In Chile and Argentina, too, the Germans cultivated ties to native institutions and fascist organizations; the right-wing Chilean National Socialist party (or Nacistas) included Chilean-Germans who were friendly to the *Landesgruppe*. Between 1935 and 1937 the Nazis increased their contacts with the Argentine army and air force, opening the way for military delegations to visit Germany. German policy toward Argentina also emphasized the extension of close commercial relations (aimed at undercutting British and American trade), the founding of German firms, and the investment by divisions of AEG, Siemens, and Farben in the electrical, chemical, transportation, and construction industries.

Politically the Germans hoped to exploit the anti-Communism of the authoritarian government of Agustin Justo, which banned the left-wing press and crushed Communists and democrats. Another cornerstone of German policy was its support (particularly through propaganda) of anti-North American attitudes, which produced some success at the Inter-American Conference for the Maintenance of Peace in Buenos Aires in December 1936. Although President Roosevelt received a warm welcome from over a half million persons on his arrival for the meeting, the Argentine government refused to approve a proposal by the United States for an alliance of the Americas against the threatening situation in Europe. But an aspect of German activity that was particularly alarming to the United States was the continued penetration of Argentine-Germans by the AO's groups; during 1935 and 1936 the *Landesgruppe* Argentina enjoyed a free hand from harassment by local authorities to complete the coordination of the *Deutsche Volksbund*. Its executive committee now included several Nazi members, among them Brandt (who retired as party leader and was replaced by a merchant, Fritz Küster), Gottfried Sanstede, head of the Central German Railway Office, and Heinrich Volberg, the *Landesgruppe*'s economic adviser.

Küster had been active as a foreign representative for German firms since before World War I. He produced both local suspicion and hostility in the United States by contributing to the growing friendliness between the German and Argentine armies. Argentine army units and officers went to Germany for "study trips" and military training, and in 1937 the chief of the Argentine air force visited Germany as Göring's guest. The *Landesgruppe* also helped to establish contacts with a number of influential Argentine civilian leaders, including the government's ministers for agriculture and finance, the directors of several banks, and the head of the Argentine Academy of War.[8]

Despite the apparent success of the *Landesgruppen* and of German policy in Latin America, serious troubles were brewing there by 1937 for the National Socialists. It must be recalled that the Nazi groups remained extremely small in Latin America, that their noisy and visible activities helped them exercise a greater impact on public opinion than they should have, and that the majority of *Volksdeutschen* were not Nazi sympathizers. Opposition existed particularly from German Catholics, democrats, socialists, and Communists. In the spring of 1936, a Catholic bishop in Chile, Guido Beck, publicly attacked National Socialism and informed his parishioners: "In Germany a furious Kulturkampf has swept over the nation. The sanctuary of the conscience has been raped. One political party, National Socialism, has brutally destroyed all other parties and now leads a very frightening dictatorship." In Argentina a priest from Caldera, Peter Fuchs, discouraged German Catholics from joining the *Volksbund*.

Although the *Landesgruppe* Chile countered Catholic opposition by using its paper, the *Westküsten Beobachter*, to accuse priests and religious orders of homosexuality, anti-Nazi activity mounted. On May Day in 1936 one hundred thousand leftists attended a demonstration in Buenos Aires. Several months later special relief committees were organized to aid the Republicans in the Spanish Civil War, and a new anti-Nazi newspaper, *Neues Spanien*, appeared that boasted sixty thousand readers. Furthermore, the *Argentinisches Tageblatt* continued its scathing criticism of the *Landesgruppe* Argentina and *Volksbund*.

The Germans also began to feel opposition in Latin America from the United States. During the early months of 1936 the American government made plans to respond to the extensive German penetration, and using the Pan American Conference in December, it sought to counter German policy by applying pressure on the Latin American states to convert the Monroe Doctrine into a formal defensive alliance of the Americas.[9] This sharpening of resistance by the United States was to contribute significantly to the outlawing of the Nazi party and other foreign political organizations in Argentina and Brazil in 1938 and 1939.

Nazi-supported groups in the United States also added to America's anti-German feeling. Although the AO had been forced to dissolve its branches there in April 1933 and to order party members to refrain from activity in the Friends of the New Germany, Bohle retained a personal agent in New York, Frederick Mensing. Despite a worsening of German-American relations (in part because of the earlier party groups) and a statement by the United States government condemning Mensing's operating in America, Bohle directed him to continue. Mensing himself suggested to the AO that it should not function in America, but his idea fell on deaf ears.[10]

The most serious bone of contention centered around the Friends of the New Germany, led after 1933 by Gissibl and a German-American Ph.D. from Yale University, Herbert Schnuch. During the early months of 1934 antagonism toward the Friends increased because of press reports from Germany that stressed the militarization of German life, persecution of the Jews, struggle against the Christian churches, and murders of Röhm and Dollfuss. The result of a Congressional investigation of fascist and Communist activities, spearheaded by Dickstein and Representative John McCormack of Massachusetts, was widely publicized and revealed that native right-wing groups had adopted Nazi ideas, such as the belief in a worldwide Jewish-Communist conspiracy.

During the investigation Schnuch had boasted to McCormack that he (Schnuch) was the head of the Nazi movement in the United States, when in fact he was not, as this post was held by Mensing. Then came the mock trial on 7 March against Hitler, held before twenty thousand persons in Madison Square Garden and sponsored by the American Federation of Labor and the American Jewish Congress. Hitler, when interviewed on the same day by Dodd, the American Ambassador in Berlin, did not mention the trial, but he denounced accusations that Nazi propaganda was being spread in the United States, and he blamed the Jews for them. But Luther, Dodd's counterpart in Washington, protested to Secretary of State Hull, about what the Ambassador termed the wild "anti-Germanism" of the American public and government. A month later, alarmed at what was happening, President Roosevelt conferred about Nazi activities with his top advisers.[11]

The Friends themselves contributed to the unrest with their propaganda that emphasized anti-Semitism, racist politics, equating Jews with Communists, and raising the specter of Negro domination of America. Much of its propaganda was sent from Germany, and it was published by newspapers or scandal sheets of the Friends. The membership of the Friends fluctuated between five and six thousand persons, with many being skilled industrial workers or artisans who had been hit hard by the Depression. Although most members had been anti-Semites and National Socialists since they left Germany in the 1920s, their hatred of the Jews was stimulated by their individual economic troubles.[12]

Bohle and Hess responded in February 1934 to the clamor caused by the Friends by publicly ordering all party members in the United States to resign from the group and to quit spreading "propaganda among non-Germans."[13] But simultaneously, Bohle continued the NSDAP's involvement in America by secretly collecting from Mensing and other sources (e.g., Nazi seamen and officials traveling in the United States for the DAI) information about the "political reliability" of the German consuls in New York (Hans Borchers), Cleveland (Hinrichs), Detroit (Hailer), Chicago (Jäger), St. Louis (Freytag), and Pittsburgh (Loibl). Realizing the AO's shaky position, Bohle planned to use the officials (whose diplomatic immunity offered them protection from the authorites) as further contacts with the Friends and Nazis in the United States. Except for Borchers and Jäger, who were not Nazi members, the consuls impressed the AO and DAI as being "convinced National Socialists;" Bohle received favorable reports on the Vice Consul in New York and Mensing's assistant, Friedhelm Draeger.[14]

At the end of October, news of the difficulties in America with the Friends reached Hitler. In a conversation with Theodore Hoffmann, the head of the Steuben Society, he was told that the leaders of the Friends were young Germans who were not American citizens and that Americans "assumed that they received their instructions from a superior authority in Germany." Hitler was evidently surprised at the news, but did little to remedy the situation. He told Hoffmann that he "had given strict instructions that National Socialists were in all circumstances to refrain from political activities in the country which was their host," and he ordered Hess to question Bohle about the AO's ties to the Friends. Bohle denied any connections to the latter, which his superiors accepted without question, and he suggested that Hess investigate ties to the Friends of the Gestapo, Propaganda Ministry, and APA.[15]

His claim to Hitler and Hess that the AO had nothing to do with the Friends was false. Although the AO had no public dealings with the group, it nevertheless retained contacts with individual members. While visiting or vacationing in Germany, members were indoctrinated with Nazi propaganda at leadership schools operated by the AO near Hamburg, and when a delegation from the Steuben Society visited Germany, the AO, DAI, and Propaganda Ministry gave it the red carpet treatment to lure it into a more favorable attitude toward the NSDAP. Another bridge to the Friends was Ulrich von Gienanth, an SS leader assigned to the German Embassy.[16] The AO also corresponded with German nationals who had left the NSDAP (at Bohle's earlier command) so as to enable them to remain active in the Friends. However, during 1935, Bohle had their party membership suspended (instead of cancelled) to reward them for their work and to allow the AO to claim that only Americans were leading the Friends and that German citizens had withdrawn from it. Roughly three hundred Nazis had their membership suspended.[17]

Throughout early 1935 the Friends flaunted its sympathy for National Socialism. It angered many Americans when it supported the German-born carpenter, Bruno Hauptmann, during his trial for the kidnap-murder, three years earlier, of the infant son of Charles Lindbergh. It also organized new groups in upstate New York, which the Jewish War Veterans sought to block with legal action. In April it sponsored a dance to celebrate Hitler's birthday, and at a mass meeting in New York, the group adopted resolutions defending German rearmament and denouncing international Communism. By the late spring, such futile agitation had combined with a wave of new attacks in Germany on the Jews and churches (which culminated with the Nuremberg rally in September) to cause renewed tension between America and the Reich and to increase the pressure applied by the American authorities on the Friends.[18]

The days of the Friends were numbered. Bohle and Hess withdrew their support from the organization when it began expanding in membership and splintering into hostile factions. The internal conflicts finally persuaded Bohle to wash his hands of the group; the AO refused to answer letters from it, and Bohle forwarded such mail to the DAI and made it responsible for the Friends. On 11 October 1935 the AO, Hess's office, and AA ordered all *Auslandsdeutschen* to resign from the Friends, and Mensing documented for the American authorities the NSDAP's intention not to spread propaganda in the United States.[19]

Since the Friends was comprised of roughly sixty percent German nationals, the directive from Berlin threatened to decimate the organization. While several of its leaders protested to Bohle and Hess (including Gissibl, who went to Germany to complain personally), Hess released a letter to the Associated Press that officially confirmed the earlier order and divorced the NSDAP from the group.[20]

But America had not seen the last of Nazi-manipulated groups. By the beginning of 1936 many in the Friends, seeing the apparent futility of continuing the group and learning that it was in serious financial difficulty, started transforming it into a successor organization, the German American *Bund* (*Amerika Deutscher Volksbund*), led by a man who loudly proclaimed himself the "American Führer" and who was to become the great symbol of un-Americanism, Fritz Kuhn. As the heir to Gissibl, Manger, Spanknöbel, and Schnuch, Kuhn was to help make Americans believe that National Socialism was a direct threat to the United States. Amazingly enough, he achieved this without much support from the NSDAP and German government, the very things that Americans feared most.

A chemical engineer and former Free Corps soldier from Munich, Kuhn had arrived in the United States in 1927 and entered the Friends of the New Germany in 1933. Shortly thereafter he became an American citizen. He took official command of the *Bund* on 29 March 1936, when he was elected *Bundesleiter* ("Federal Leader") at the first annual convention of the group in Buffalo. Despite his claims to leading a mass movement of thousands of German-Americans, the *Bund*'s membership never exceeded twenty-five thousand persons, and the majority of it was comprised of German citizens who had formerly belonged to the Friends. Revealing Bohle and Hess's apparent lack of control over German citizens in America, only ten percent of the *Auslandsdeutschen* in the Friends had withdrawn from it following the October directive, and the remainder entered the *Bund*. Flamboyant, forever proclaiming himself the "American Führer," and maintaining that he was backed by Berlin, Kuhn built the *Bund* into a self-supporting, money-making operation.

It was organized into fifty-five local groups (each with units of uniformed strong-arm men whom Kuhn called his SS), whose members paraded in brown shirts, flew the swastika flag, made anti-democratic and anti-Semitic speeches, praised Germany, and distributed to German communities questionnaires received from the NSDAP. It also operated a vigorous youth group, large summer camps for youth, a publishing company in Yorkville, newspapers, and several interlocking corporations that hid the membership of its German citizens. Kuhn, in his bombastic speeches, denounced the New Deal as a "Jew Deal," and he maintained that Roosevelt and his Jewish advisers were tools of Moscow. His hatred also extended to American Blacks, who he alleged were allied with the Jews, were highly susceptible to Communism, and had been infiltrated by Jews and Communists.[21]

Despite his repeated assertion in public that the *Bund* was approved and supported by Berlin, the claim was untrue. The AO, which now agreed with the AA that the group was too great of a liability to back, sent only insignificant amounts of cash and a few party speakers (e.g., the DAI official, Karl Götz) to the *Bund* and other German-American groups, and it had little direct contact with the organization. Its chief connection with the *Bund* was through the Consulate General in New York and its leaders, Borchers and Draeger.[22] But if the AO and other Nazi agencies had reversed their attitude toward the German-American movement, the American public believed that Germany's stance on Nazi-type groups in the United States had not changed.

The view that Kuhn and his group were dangerous Nazi agents was heightened when the "American Führer" met the German Führer in Berlin on 2 August 1936. Although Hitler did not announce his support of Kuhn or promise him the backing of Germany, news pictures of the German leader and Kuhn shaking hands had other effects. The meeting aroused increasing excitement in the United States, it enabled Kuhn to deceive his followers by making them believe that he took orders directly from Hitler, and it strengthened the popular American feeling that Hitler fully endorsed the *Bund*.

The *Bund* was only one aspect of the deteriorating German-American relations during 1936 and the beginning of 1937. If the American public was hostile to Germany because of Nazi barbarism at home and Berlin's sponsoring (as Americans believed) of groups like the *Bund*, the United States government was increasingly alienated from Germany for economic and diplomatic reasons. In the summer of 1936 the Germans tried and failed to extract significant trade concessions from the United States. Furthermore, because of Germany's remilitarization of the Rhineland and her extensive involvement in Spain, sentiment grew in America toward isolationism, and Roosevelt began exploring an American role in a search for peace in Europe.[23] Such antagonism toward Germany as had been provoked in the United States was eventually to become of great significance.

FAILURES: GERMAN SCHOOLS
ABROAD, SOUTH AFRICA, AND SWITZERLAND

While the NSDAP sought to disengage itself from German-American activities, the stubborn refusal of its foreign groups to halt their harassment of German colonies and mission officials led to the further alienation of foreign Germans from National Socialism. Yet, while the groups' shenanigans were damaging to Germany, the AO's work was praised by Hitler and Hess.[24] A serious bone of contention among the branches and German communities remained the party's effort to dominate German schools and youth clubs abroad. In addition to petty quarrels between Nazi and non-Nazi teachers in Afghanistan (Kabul) and Buenos Aires, conflicts arose in Havana, Cuba and Guadalajara, Mexico between party locals and schools that sharply divided the German communities.[25]

The perpetual uproar in many schools resulted from the continued infiltration of them by the AO and NSLB. On top of pressing the AA to send teachers to the schools who possessed "unconditional National Socialist qualities," the party agencies gave the schools numerous books, curriculum plans, and other teaching aids. For use by teachers, the NSDAP sent "examination copies" of books about politics, geography, and subjects dealing with the alleged racial inferiority of the Jews and east European Slavs. To schools whose students were mainly children of foreign citizens, it generously dispatched books in foreign languages (e.g., *Anglo-American Criticism on the Treaty of Versailles* and *Brave Fighters on the Western Front*). In August 1935 the AO, HJ, and Propaganda Ministry sponsored a visit to Germany of twelve hundred German students residing in other European nations. The young people saw "historical sites of the [Nazi] movement" in Munich, and they were urged by party leaders to "be and remain a German!"[26] In some instances, however, such projects backfired. When the *Landesgruppe* Chile sent a group of girls from the German-Chilean Youth League (*Jugendbund*) to the Nuremberg rally in September and the girls were forced to parade in HJ uniforms, a wave of indignation swept over the German colony and provoked demands that the Nazis end their work with the League.[27]

Despite Bohle's claim at the rally that "foreign Germandom" was totally "united behind Adolf Hitler," the assertion was untrue; numerous *Volksdeutsch* clubs (e.g., in Manila, Winnipeg, and Montreal) refused to cooperate with the Nazis.[28] But while the AO ignored the disruption caused by its affiliates, it could not turn a deaf ear to the failure of the party organizations in South Africa, which agitated for a return of Southwest Africa and Tanganyika (formerly German East Africa) to Germany. Although such demands were echoed by several ranking officials in Germany (e.g., Ribbentrop, Göring, Schacht, Franz Ritter von Epp, and Heinrich Schnee), who urged Hitler to press England to give the lands back to the Reich, Hitler's attitude toward overseas colonies was one of caution, authorizing only low-key propaganda that stressed Germany's rights but did not attack England or other colonial powers.[29]

Unfortunately for the Nazi groups in South Africa, they rejected his moderation. The *Landesgruppe* Southwest Africa and its locals in Windhoek, Swakopmund, Lüderitz, Usakos, Otjiwarongo, and Walvis Bay, and cells among German farmers, criticized the British and campaigned for a German takeover of the territory. On 8 August 1933 the *Landesgruppenleiter*, Major Weigel, reported to the German Consul General in Pretoria: "South-West is yearning for Germany. It wants to be German South-West Africa again. South-West has to have Germany, otherwise it will be dead soon. And the saddest part of it is that a portion of the second generation of Germans, the German youth, is in danger of becoming Afrikaners." The *Landesgruppe* took control of the major German organization, the *Deutsche Bund*, established a prominent doctor, Schwietering, as its chairman, and pushed the *Bund*'s leadership (many of whom held German and British citizenship) to swear "a solemn oath of allegiance" to Hitler.

The party demanded the same from German youth who held dual citizenship and who were organized into HJ units. When the *Bund* and parents of the youth protested about the oath, Weigel replied that it was necessary because it was an order from Germany. The *Landesgruppe* also collected information against local Germans who were anti-Nazi; the material was forwarded to the AO, which pressed the German government to withdraw Reich citizenship from the rebels. Threats, too, were used. A local farmer was informed by a *Bund* leader, "If you and your wife do not sign [a *Bund* membership card] immediately, both of you will be driven from the country with a whip, should it become German again."

Germans were also encouraged to join several anti-Semitic and nationalist organizations like the South African Grey Shirts and South African National Socialist Movement. The *Landesgruppe* supported the Grey Shirts financially, and both cooperated in distributing vulgar anti-Semitic propaganda urging the government of Southwest Africa to deprive Jews of their citizenship, positions in government and the professions, and property. Such propaganda also maintained that the *Protocols of the Elders of Zion* were authentic and that the Jewish religion used the blood of Christian children for ritual purposes. Other right-wing organizations infiltrated by the Nazis were the South African People's Movement, National Democratic party (or "Blackshirts"), Fascists, and Gentile Protection League.

But the most dangerous work of the party was its effort to seize control of Southwest Africa's economy. While much of the country's commerce lay in German hands, the *Landesgruppe* tried through propaganda and rumor-mongering (which advertised that Germany would soon regain Southwest Africa) to persuade British and African farmers to sell their land to Germans and resettle in the Union of South Africa. The *Landesgruppe* and AO drafted plans in March 1934 for "a more extensive [German] settlement" that would "create a German majority" in Southwest Africa; as Weigel informed the AO, the proposal could soon become a reality if Germans purchased farms by using the small downpayment for land required by the State Land Bank. According to the party leader, "The possibility exists . . . of acquiring through cleverly concealed manipulation comparatively cheap farms for German settlement purposes."[30]

Similar activity was carried on in the Union of South Africa under Hermann Bohle. Already in 1933 the police in Southwest Africa had searched the offices of the *Ortsgruppe* Windhoek and found letters from Bohle discussing Nazi strategy in the former German land. By mid-1934 the party had caused tremendous resentment among local Germans. In a moment of frustration, one person noted: "Here in South-West the Nazis have produced a deep division among the Germans, and this is not in the spirit of [their] Leader, Adolf Hitler."[31] Hostility to the AO from the Germans

focused around the *Deutsche Afrika-Post*, a pro-monarchist paper
that identified local Nazi leaders and demanded that Bohle be removed as head of the AO and that the organization be dissolved.
Following a wild Nazi youth meeting in Windhoek (which included
a torchlight parade, speech by Weigel, short wave broadcasts from
Germany, and "heils" to Hitler) in early July, the offices of the local
were searched again by the police. Within hours the HJ was
banned, and its leaders (including Weigel) were expelled from the
country. On the heels of another police raid in October the entire
NSDAP was outlawed.[32]

The ban was an embarrassment to Germany and to Hitler's low
profile on the colonial issue. Obviously it revealed a sad lack of
coordination among Hitler, his government, and the party, and
the latter's belligerency in South Africa threatened to alienate
England, a country that Hitler still hoped to woo in 1934 and 1935.
Even before the party's expulsion, Neurath had complained to Hess
about the undisciplined work in Southwest Africa of the NSDAP's
Colonial Policy Office (*Kolonialpolitisches Amt*, headed by Epp)
and the AO. He had described the situation as "unbearable"
and warned Hess that the ban was imminent.[33]

Hess, refusing to understand what had happened and displaying
a hardheadedness that was typical of the party leadership, placed
the blame for the blunder on the Colonial Policy Office, APA, and
HJ, and he commanded each agency to subordinate its future work
to the AO (which was now to camouflage its activity through the
Deutsche Bund), AA, and Special Commissioner appointed by
Hitler for Disarmament Questions, Ribbentrop. The AO also sent
two "troubleshooters" to Africa, a decorated naval commander,
Heinz Menche, and the hereditary Archduke Friedrich von Mecklen-
burg, who were to act as mediators between the party and local
German communities.[34]

The sudden rise to prominence of the smooth, snobbish, and aspiring Ribbentrop was no accident. The man who was to become
after 1937 the bitterest opponent of the foreign party groups, the
AO, and Bohle, was Hitler's chief foreign affairs adviser and head of
his own private Foreign Office in the NSDAP, the *Dienststelle Ribbentrop*. Following his role in concluding the Anglo-German Naval
Agreement in June 1935, Hitler granted him complete control over
Germany's colonial policy and presented him with the flowery title
of Ambassador Extraordinary and Plenipotentiary of the German
Reich. In a prelude to his later attempt to crush the AO, Ribben-

trop immediately attacked Bohle by visiting the AO's headquarters on 3 July 1935 and informing Bohle that the "entire colonial policy in the future will officially be directed by me." Commanding the AO to organize its work in South Africa strictly within the *Deutsche Bund*, he insisted that the tensions among Germans there and between the Germans and the authorities be eliminated. Orders from Germany to the *Bund* were to be given only with his agreement and sent through the AA and its missions in South Africa.

Two weeks later Bohle was dealt another blow when he demanded at a meeting with Hess, Ribbentrop, and Haushofer that the AO be granted jurisdiction over all *Volksdeutschen*. Hess refused the request, whereupon Bohle threatened to resign his offices. But Hess was apparently able to soothe his protégé by reminding him that the AO was still the supreme agency for Germandom in Latin America. Another result of Ribbentrop's directives was a shake-up in the party leadership in the Union of South Africa. Hermann Bohle was replaced as *Landesgruppenleiter* by a Ribbentrop man, Helmut Kirchner, and Bohle was asked to return to Germany to join his son in Berlin.[35] Like most Nazi leaders abroad who were deported or recalled, he was welcomed home as a hero and given a position as head of the AO's *Amt für Technik* ("Office for Technicians").

The sudden subordination to Ribbentrop also undermined the AO's authority over the VDA and *Volksdeutsch* Council. In October Hess dissolved the Council and redistributed the duties of the VDA between the AO and the *Dienststelle Ribbentrop*. In agreement with Ribbentrop and Himmler, the powerful leader of the SS and German police, Hess ordered the AO to limit its work to German citizens abroad (i.e., *Auslandsdeutschen*), and he granted increasing authority in *Volksdeutsch* matters to the SS and its central agency for dealing with persons of German descent abroad, the VoMi.[36] Bohle himself was admitted to the SS in September 1936, and in the months that followed numerous AO officials became SS members. Bohle, obviously interested in solidifying his own position, actively pursued Himmler's friendship, and the SS began penetrating the AO, as it did many of the NSDAP's organizations. Himmler's primary motive in coming to terms with Bohle was to use the party groups abroad as espionage mechanisms for the SS and for Reinhard Heydrich's SD.[37]

In view of what lay ahead during 1936 Bohle sorely needed Himmler's support. Although the party insisted publicly that its groups outside Germany were following Hitler's wish by obeying strictly the laws of their host countries, there was strong evidence that suggested otherwise. During the spring the leader of the NSDAP in Costa Rica, Herbert Knoehr, was caught red-handed cooperating with the Communists in an election campaign, and shortly thereafter in Venezuela, the entire party organization was prohibited by the state police. A flourishing campaign of the liberal press in the Netherlands East Indies and Australia attacked Germany's racial laws and the anti-Semitism of the party's locals. Nor was this all. The king of Rumania complained about the party's encouragement of right-wing groups in his country, and the AO aroused further suspicion against itself in Czechoslovakia by contributing to radicalism and disunity in the Sudeten German community.[38]

The most profound indication of the resentment building outside Germany against the meddlesome NSDAP was the murder on 4 February 1936 of Wilhelm Gustloff, the Swiss *Landesgruppenleiter*. But the assassination was only the culmination of hostility that had been mounting among the Swiss since 1933 against Gustloff and his organization. The party had infiltrated several Swiss "front" groups, coordinated German societies, and reported local Germans who were anti-Nazi to the Reich police, thus assuring their arrest if they visited Germany. By May 1934 the *Landesgruppe* was organized into forty-five subgroups and units of the HJ, and it published a propaganda paper, *Der Reichsdeutsche in der Schweiz*, which stressed that all officials in the party had sworn an oath of loyalty to Hitler.[39]

Its work drew considerable publicity during 1935, when Berthold Jacob, an emigrant German journalist (and friend of the Communist publisher and writer, Willi Münzenberg), was kidnapped and sent to Germany by a Gestapo agent, Hans Wesemann. In December, Hans Kittelmann, a member of the *Landesgruppe* and the chief stenographer for the Swiss Federal Assembly, was dismissed for secret activities as a Nazi. It was further discovered that the *Landesgruppe* was using as spies German students in Swiss universities. Such revelations stimulated a wave of anti-German feeling among the democratic-oriented Swiss and local German socialists.

Just before his assassination, Gustloff was threatened with expulsion from Switzerland, and the NSDAP was in danger of being outlawed.[40] But the man who idolized Hitler and who "often looked at the 'Führer's' picture for hours on end . . . 'to gain strength,' " was suddenly shot to death by a young Jewish-Yugoslavian student, David Frankfurter.[41] The murder created a sensation in Germany;

not only did it increase the Nazis' fanatical belief that Germans were persecuted abroad, but Hitler, Hess, Bohle, and the NSDAP made a martyr out of the slain party leader.

For the funeral and the cremation, Bohle and an impressive entourage from the AO went to Switzerland to accompany the body back to Gustloff's home in Schwerin. The funeral service, which was paid for by the NSDAP and German government and broadcast on German and Swiss radio, was highlighted by an address from Hitler. Amidst one of his most vicious attacks on the Jews, he asserted that "now every local [NSDAP] group in foreign countries has its National Socialist patron, its holy martyr, who died for this Movement and for our idea. In every office now his [Gustloff's] picture will hang, his name each will carry in his heart, and for all time he will never be forgotten."[42] The NSDAP did its best to fulfill Hitler's pledge and make Gustloff a sort of Horst Wessel of the AO. It worked with the Propaganda Ministry and AA to unleash a major propaganda campaign that portrayed Frankfurter as the evil tool of the Communist International and the worldwide Jewish conspiracy against Germany.[43]

Not everyone in the party and government was upset by the murder. The German Minister to Switzerland, Ernst von Weizsäcker, had deeply resented Gustloff and his organization. Weizsäcker wrote a lengthy report to the AA criticizing the Landesgruppe, and he later maintained that the Nazis had harassed the German Legation in Berne and himself unmercifully, saying that they had accused him of being a Francophile and of being unpatriotic, and that Gustloff had sent "official party reports" to Berlin dealing with politics, economic questions, non-Aryan Swiss businesses, attitudes of Germans in Switzerland, and officials at the Legation.[44]

The uproar in Germany over the loss of Gustloff alarmed the Swiss government enough that it banned the NSDAP in mid-February. The Landesgruppe, while claiming to have dissolved itself, continued undercover and under the direction of the new German Charge d'Affaires in Berne, Bibra (who was transferred, over Neurath's protest, from Prague), and Erwin Kuske, a special "Commissioner of the AO for the Affairs of Reich Citizens in Switzerland." Taking a cue from the Swiss, the Dutch government quickly demanded the separation of the AO from its cover organization in the Netherlands, the Association of Reich Citizens. Also, despite efforts of the AA to prevent it, Sweden expelled the Landesgruppenleiter in Stockholm, Heinrich Bartels, and three aides. They were accused of seeking to nazify the local German colony, distributing propaganda among Swedish citizens, and wearing Nazi uniforms in public.[45]

Neither the setbacks in Switzerland nor the troubles with the Swedish, Dutch, and Swiss governments daunted the determination of the foreign Nazi groups to operate at full throttle. On the contrary, the actions against the groups spurred them to even greater activity. In retaliation against the Swedes, the Germans expelled (at the proposal of Alfred Hess) two Swedish businessmen from the Reich. Only in Spain, where elections in mid-February strengthened the left-wing Republican government and aroused fears in the Nazi leadership that the *Landesgruppe* Spain might be outlawed, was the party abroad directed to curtail its work.[46] The AO trespassed against the independence of the AA, and following the scare in Spain, the party extended its influence deeper into that country and Austria. The renewed interest in Austria reflected Hitler's budding friendship with Mussolini (who was willing to drop his opposition to German domination of Austria) and his wish to prepare for the *Anschluss* ("union").

PARTY ATTACHES AND THE FOREIGN MINISTRY

One result of Gustloff's assassination was its encouragement of the AO to encroach on the freedom of the AA. An indication of this was Hitler's suggestion to Neurath on 19 March 1936 that *Landesgruppenleiters* be attached for their safety to Germany's diplomatic missions. Wherever they were endangered by foreign opposition, such leaders were to be taken into the staff of their mission to enable them to enjoy extraterritoriality and other diplomatic immunities. According to Hitler's idea, the leaders would be appointed to the missions as "Party attaches;" they would, however, still report to Bohle and be paid by the NSDAP.[47]

Hitler made it clear, therefore, that he fully supported the party abroad and that he was willing to ensure its success at the expense of the AA. Whether or not he had other motives for the suggestion to Neurath is not clear. It seems unlikely that he was considering the AO a mechanism for one day reorganizing the AA along party lines, but he may have entertained the thought of using it as an instrument of competition to keep the Ministry in line. At any rate, the significance of his backing was not lost on Bohle. On 27 February 1936 the AO chief had talked to Hitler about incorporating the AO into the AA and giving Bohle a high post in the Ministry. Arguing that Gustloff's murder had made the unification of party and state in foreign affairs an "absolute necessity," Bohle maintained to Hitler that the AO must be granted an official (i.e., governmental) status to strengthen its authority over foreign Germans and its relations with other governments.

He also reminded the Chancellor that the AO administered over five hundred groups abroad and that its work was encouraged by Hess, Goebbels, and Göring. He emphasized too that in 1928 Mussolini had united the foreign groups of the Fascist party with the Italian Foreign Office. His arguments were apparently well received. Although Hitler did not combine the AO with the AA, he issued his opinion favoring the insertion of party leaders in German missions, and he asked for a detailed memorandum from Bohle concerning his ideas. In the months that followed, discussions were held among Bohle, Hess, Neurath, and Heinrich Lammers, head of Hitler's Reich Chancellery.

Neurath, to establish a degree of control over Bohle and bring *Deutschtum* work more within the scope of the AA, agreed to the party attache solution only on certain conditions. Such demands included the attaches' renouncing all "propaganda or organizational activity [among Germans abroad]," their subordination to German mission chiefs, and a major role for the mission leaders in the choice of the attaches. While Bohle and Hess recognized that the acceptance of the conditions would mean a capitulation to the AA, they continued the conferences and even suggested that several *Landesgruppenleiters* be granted diplomatic status, including Heinrich Diehl (Luxemburg), Konradi (Rumania), and Gerhard Hentschke (Guatemala).[48]

A more subtle form of pressure was placed on the Ministry by the AO's sharpening of its insistence that diplomats become party members or resign their offices. During 1936 Bohle suggested to Borchers (Consul General in New York), Herbert von Dirksen (Ambassador to Japan), and Kroll (a leading AA official) that they join. Other mission leaders who entered the party included Stohrer (Egypt), Herbert von Richthofen (Belgium), Eugen Rümelin (Bulgaria), Hans Frohwein (Estonia), Johannes von Welczeck (France), Hans Georg von Mackensen (Hungary, later State Secretary in the AA), Victor von Heeren (Yugoslavia), Count Zech-Burkersroda (Holland), Heinrich Sahm (Norway), and Friedrich Werner von der Schulenberg (Russia). Officials in other government positions were even threatened. Ernst Adolf Hepp, a reporter in New York for the German news agency *Deutsches Nachrichtenbüro*, was informed by Mensing that he would lose his job if he did not apply immediately for membership.[49]

Further intrusion into the AA involved the intelligence reports received by Bohle from the *Landesgruppenleiters* that dealt with the political, economic, and military life of their nations and with the attitudes of German diplomats abroad. The reports, some apparently being sent from Bohle to Hess, Himmler, and even Hitler, were used in confirming some lower echelon appointments in the AA, pressuring it to release less significant diplomats suspected of being anti-Nazi, and having several party leaders admitted to it (e.g., Bene, named Consul General in Milan; and Schröder, named to the Personnel Department).[50]

Although the reports were never as significant in decisions on appointments and promotions as the AO led the diplomats to believe, they were thoroughly resented by the AA. Their existence was called to Neurath's attention by complaints from the diplomats, and on investigating their nature and final destination, he learned that some were sent to Hitler. Neurath allegedly approached Hitler about the subject and "protested against this illegal news service." But Hitler was not impressed.[51] The Foreign Minister, who appears to have been kept in the dark about the reports, consequently attached far more importance to them than they warranted.

SPAIN AND AUSTRIA

The conflict with the AA was expanded by the Spanish Civil War, which exploded in July 1936 and continued until 1939. The war involved a bitter attack by rebels in the Spanish army, led in southern Spain by General Francisco Franco, and the Spanish fascists, the Falange, against the Republican government that had ruled in Madrid since 1931. Franco and the army, shortly after they launched their assault on the government from Spanish Morocco, appealed to Hitler for military aid. The request was presented to Hitler by two officials from the *Ortsgruppe* Tetuan, Langenheim, head of the branch, and Johannes Bernhardt, chief representative in Spanish Morocco of the AO's Foreign Trade Office who owned an export company and possessed close ties to Spanish army officers.[52]

Prior to the outbreak of the war the Nazi government had shown little interest in Spanish affairs. But the NSDAP, working through the *Landesgruppe* Spain, had retained intimate contact with the Falange and anti-government elements in the army, and there was evidence uncovered during the war that suggested the *Landesgruppe* anticipated it a month before it began. In mid-June, among other preparations for the war, it informed Berlin of the pending conflict and assembled a large contingent of former SA men, German army officers, and pilots in Spain to act as technicians, engineers, and propagandists for the rebels. Also, two party officials in Madrid, Erich Schnaus and Heinrich Rodatz, had been smuggling weapons and ammunition to Franco. Rodatz, Spanish representative for the Junkers Aircraft Factory, was a friend of the General, and he served as one of the *Landesgruppe*'s propaganda agents.[53]

On 22 July 1936 Franco sent Bernhardt and Langenheim with letters to Germany appealing to Hitler to send airplanes and weapons to the rebels. The emissaries flew to Berlin where Bohle and Hess quickly arranged for them an audience with Hitler and Göring, who were attending the Wagner music festival in Bayreuth. Accompanying Bernhardt and Langenheim to Bayreuth were the leaders of the AO's Legal Office, Kraneck and Robert Fischer, who argued that Germany had every legal justification for intervening in Spain. Meanwhile, the AA had been informed that the couriers were on their way to see Hitler. Since the AA favored a neutral attitude and believed it too risky for Germany to become involved in an international conflict, Neurath rushed to Bayreuth to argue against the aid to Franco. But he failed in his mission; on 26 July key conferences among Hitler, Göring, Werner von Blomberg (German Minister of War), and Admiral Canaris (a friend of Franco and chief of German military intelligence, *Abwehr*), produced the decision to assist Franco. A few days later the AA was informed of the decision and told that Germany would eventually recognize the Junta government in Burgos that Franco had joined; such recognition was to follow in October.[54]

In the meeting with Hitler, it was decided that all operations for moving weapons, planes, and troops to Franco would be conducted through a semi-official trading company, *Compañia Hispano-Marroqui de Transportes* (Hisma), which would be developed from Bernhardt's export firm in Seville. It was also agreed that a company called Rowak (*Rohstoffe-und-Waren-Einkaufsgesellschaft*) would be created in Berlin with Göring's assistance to handle the German end of the economic cooperation with the rebels. German aid was not agreed on without strings attached; the Nazis intended to extract copper and other valuable minerals and raw materials from Franco in return for Germany's aid. On 2 August Hisma began the transport of rebel troops from Morocco to Seville, enabling Franco to achieve his first victories in southern Spain. Supplies also began reaching Spain by ship from Germany. The planning for full-scale operations began a day later, when German naval officials, Fischer (who had been attached temporarily to the German Embassy in Spain), Bernhardt, and Langenheim met Franco and his staff in Tetuan.[55]

While Rowak and Hisma were organized for logistical purposes, the party groups in Spain, German merchant marine, and navy evacuated hundreds of German nationals and *Volksdeutschen* from Spain who had been caught in the crossfire of the war. The AO also constructed a special "relief committee" (*Hilfsausschuss*) for the refugees, which was headed by a young import dealer in Barcelona and long-time Nazi, Hans Hellermann. The committee also became a propaganda weapon for the AO, which never missed a chance to parade its work before Germans in the Reich. During the first months of the war fifteen thousand Germans were evacuated from Spanish harbors.[56]

The sudden flurry of German activity in Spain earned a notorious reputation among foreign governments. In late August correspondence among the party groups was seized by the Republican government and printed in London newspapers; immediately the AA ordered that party documents be stored for better protection in German missions in Spain and in other European countries.[57] Despite such problems, the AO worked feverishly with Göring (who was named chief of the Reich's Four-Year-Plan in October), Hess, and the Ministries for Finance and Economics to coordinate trade with Franco and private Spanish markets. At Göring's direction, Hess placed the entire personnel of the AO at the disposal of Rowak to handle the deliveries of materials to and from Spain.

The influence of the party on the intervention in the war expanded in November 1936. Hitler, at the urging of Hess, Bohle, and Kohn, the former party leader in Chile and an official of the Propaganda Ministry assigned to Spain, named the head of the Iberian-American Institute, Faupel, German Ambassador to Franco's Nationalist government in Salamanca. Although a professional diplomat, Karl Schwendemann, served as Faupel's chief counselor, Bohle was able to affect substantially Germany's official policy-making in Spain through Faupel, Kohn, and the *Landes-gruppenleiter*, Arthur Dietrich. When Faupel experienced opposition from the AA or Schwendemann, he quickly appealed to Bohle. In March 1937 Bohle reminded Schwendemann that Faupel and Kohn were his (Bohle's) personal agents in Spain and that the "NSDAP must occupy the same predominant position in a Nationalist Spain as it has been allowed in Fascist Italy."[58]

As Italy, Russia, England, and France became involved in the Spanish conflict, Faupel soon joined with the AA and German High Command in urging that Germany press Franco for agreements that would bring a larger and steadier volume of Spanish trade to Germany. Faupel and several officials in Hisma pushed Bernhardt to exploit his "very close relations" with Franco and his brother, Nicolas, in acquiring such agreements. Although Bernhardt stubbornly refused to approach Franco, it was argued that Germany must insist on copper pledges from the Spanish leader while he was still in a precarious position and under pressure in the war. The time was ripe, Faupel and others maintained, to look out for Germany's interests in Spain; otherwise, it was believed, Italy and England would "turn up at the last moment and pose as the real moving spirit."[59]

While the NSDAP was busy in Spain and while the world was focusing its attention on the Civil War, the party began to intensify its penetration of Austria. In October 1936, shortly before the Anti-Comintern Pact was concluded between Germany and Japan (and later Italy), which reflected the determination of those nations to ensure allies for themselves, Bohle looked increasingly like a professional diplomat. Acting as a sort of party emissary, he made a whirlwind tour to Vienna and Rome to discuss politics with the Austrian government and with Mussolini. The Anti-Comintern pact had been made possible by the worsening of relations between Italy and the Western democracies over Mussolini's invasion of Ethiopia, by Italo-German support of Franco, and by Italy's willingness to drop much of its hostility toward Germany's interference in Austria.

The latter had been secured primarily through a major Austro-German agreement signed on 11 July 1936, which provided for German recognition of Austria's independence, for Austria to follow a path closer to Germany in foreign affairs, and for the preparation of further economic and cultural exchanges. Yet, while Hitler promised not to interfere in Austrian affairs and while he informed the illegal Austrian Nazis that they would have to keep silent until Germany was ready to annex Austria, the AO quietly expanded its party groups of German nationals in the country under the cover of the League of German Citizens in Austria. Through the League Bohle staunchly supported the radical or militant faction among the Austrian Nazis, centered after 1935 around its new leader, Josef Leopold. This faction, which opposed the more gradualist and peaceful approach to *Anschluss* stressed by the Vienna lawyer, Arthur Seyss-Inquart, still belonged to the pre-1934 era of activism, violence, propaganda, and infiltration.[60]

The significance Bohle attached to Austria became clear in September, when he invited the "unofficial" (i.e., not publicly named by the AO) *Landesgruppenleiter* of Austria and German Consul at Salzburg, Bernard, to speak to four thousand foreign party members at the fourth annual conference of the AO in Erlangen.[61] He also worked to persuade Schuschnigg's government to legalize his undercover groups in Austria and to permit the AO to supervise them. Although such plans were questioned by the AA,[62] he scored a major breakthrough with the Austrians when he visited Vienna on 23-24 October. On top of addressing a Thanksgiving Day festival of the local German colony and urging its members to be loyal Nazis and refrain from mixing in Austrian politics, he conversed with Austrian leaders and with Papen. Through his discussions with Guido Schmidt, the pro-Nazi Austrian Foreign Minister, permission was granted for the AO to continue building a Nazi organization in Austria for the roughly seventeen hundred German citizens there who were National Socialists. After securing the concession, he was convinced by the AA to postpone raising questions with Vienna about further privileges for German Nazis in Austria such as displaying the German flag and wearing uniforms and insignia.[63]

But acquiring such rights was no problem. When Schmidt visited Berlin at the end of November, he met with Bohle, and later he and Neurath signed a secret protocol (which Bohle helped to draft) that gave the owners of Austrian inns and hotels the permission to fly the German flag when German citizens were their guests.[64] The protocol and July agreement opened the door in a legal manner to the most massive intervention by the German Nazis since the terrorism of 1933 and 1934. Even Austrian nationalists began calling Schmidt the "Judas of Austria." The AO, which formed a special

Austrian Section in its Berlin offices to coordinate its work across the border, founded numerous *Reichsdeutsch* newspapers in Austria that published *Anschluss* propaganda. It also retained close contact with the armed and illegal Austrian Nazis by working within the large League of German Citizens in Austria (which had become the *de facto Landesgruppe* Austria).[65]

The League was reorganized in January 1937, and its leadership was placed in the hands of the unofficial *Landesgruppenleiter*, Bernard, and local party leader in Vienna, Schliephack (who possessed an office in the German Embassy). Camouflaged in the League were four *Ortsgruppen* in Vienna, numerous other party branches around the country, and Nazi affiliated organizations like the Student's League, HJ troop, Gymnastics Section, League of Disabled German War Veterans, and social club of the DAF.[66] While the small number of German citizens in the League (roughly 27,000 of the 44,000 Germans in Austria) signified little direct danger to Austria, the League's ties to the Austrian National Socialists were a different matter.

Many of the League's leaders had been long-time members of the Austrian movement and had been arrested, imprisoned, or fined in 1933 and 1934. Such elements also formed a radical and irresponsible wing in the League that secretly planned a new *Putsch* against the Austrian government. The group was tied closely to the militant faction in the Austrian NSDAP around Leopold; it met frequently in the German mission in Vienna but was fairly small and included a ranking League official, Peetz, an SA leader, Precheisen, and two legation counselors at the mission, Engelbert and von Heinz. With connections to undercover Austrian SA and SS units, the would-be *Putschists* planned to use in their insurrection the notorious Austrian Legion (political exiles from Austria) headquartered in Bavaria. The conspiracy, which failed to get off the ground, included smuggling weapons from Germany to the SA and SS in Austria.[67]

The League's activities prompted Bohle in January 1937 to ask the AA and Austrian government to approve the formal commissioning of Bernard as *Landesgruppenleiter*. But the request evoked immediate opposition from both. The AA rejected the request (and Vienna agreed) on the basis that the foreign NSDAP groups were subordinate to the laws of their guest nation, while German missions enjoyed extraterritoriality and diplomatic immunity. Combining consular and party offices abroad, it was argued by the *Wilhelmstrasse*, could only destroy foreign respect for German diplomats and lead to serious difficulties with foreign governments.[68]

But Hitler, Bohle, and the NSDAP viewed the problem in reverse. To them the party was the state in Germany,[69] and according to German law, its leaders abroad were representatives of the German Reich and equal in status to their diplomatic counterparts. While this extremely narrow interpretation acknowledged only German law (and the German political situation) and refused to respect what had been known by the world for centuries as international law, it reflected the sharp party-state dualism in Germany. As for the NSDAP, it was apparently convinced of the AO's argument and of its growing importance; in December 1936 the party Treasury tripled its financial support of the organization.[70] But most significant, the party's insistence that its officials abroad were as authoritative as the diplomats helped contribute to a sudden effort by Hitler to unify the party and state in the administration of foreign Germans.

BOHLE'S APPOINTMENT AT THE *Wilhelmstrasse*

Surprising the diplomatic world on 30 January 1937, Hitler promoted Bohle to the Foreign Ministry and named him "Chief of the Auslands-Organisation in the Auswärtiges Amt."[71] Although the appointment was partly the outgrowth of the conflict over Bernard's status in Austria, it was mainly the result of the feud centering around control of foreign Germans that had existed between the AO and AA since 1933. Following the Nazi seizure of power, they had clashed repeatedly over what Bohle termed the *Menschenführung* of Germans abroad, or the manipulation, administration, and education of foreign Germans in the tenets of National Socialism.

As part of the *Menschenführung* of foreign Germans, the AO had claimed the right to dominate the economic development, legal affairs, schools, emigration, and repatriation of Germans outside the Reich. But since this work was normally handled by the AA, the question of competency had arisen: where did the authority of the AA cease, and where did that of the AO begin? By 1937 an answer had become vital to German foreign affairs; the AO's role was developing rapidly in Spain and Austria, and serious difficulties were being caused by the lack of coordination between it and the AA in South Africa, the United States, the Netherlands, Switzerland, Australia, the Dutch East Indies, Venezuela, Sweden, and other countries. Neurath, having been challenged during the previous months by the Nazi leadership to admit Bohle to the AA, proposed to Hitler that the AO leader be promoted to the Ministry. He hoped that by placing Bohle in the Ministry, he (Neurath) could finally gain "a certain control over the Auslandsorganisation."[72]

Although Bohle later maintained that the NSDAP had done nothing to secure his admission to the AA, he thanked Hess profusely for his "understanding assistance" in the affair in a personal letter in December 1937. Still another factor in the promotion may have been the sudden death in June 1936 of Bülow, the powerful anti-Nazi State Secretary of the AA, which removed an influential barrier to the party's expansion into the Ministry.[73] The appointment was also encouraged by Himmler and the SS, because it would limit the AO to handling only *Auslandsdeutschen* and would leave to the VoMi matters relating to *Volksdeutschen*.[74] Another consideration in the promotion was that until 1937, the NSDAP had succeeded in placing no one in a ranking position in the AA who was a trained diplomat. Men like Neurath, Weizsäcker (who was not yet a Nazi member), and Mackensen were hardly hard-core "party men" whom the National Socialists wished to place in high government posts. As for Hitler's personal motives in naming Bohle, the picture is less clear. By now, with Ribbentrop having become his unofficial Foreign Minister and with the AO's expansion in Spain and Austria, he may have been considering using the AO to reorganize the Foreign Service, or (what was more likely) to capture its total loyalty by making the AO a bonafide competitor.

Although the commissioning of Bohle was interpreted by the foreign press as meaning that the AO was being incorporated wholesale into the Ministry,[75] the truth was that only its leader was taken into the AA. The AO remained a party institution and completely separate from the Ministry. Bohle was given an office and a small staff in the AA, Ministry funds were channeled through him to the AO, and he attended daily conferences of AA officials that dealt with foreign Germans and related affairs.

In the weeks that followed, while party members hailed Bohle as a potential successor to Neurath, the foreign press and several governments overestimated (partly because of Nazi propaganda) his authority in the AA and the meaning of his new position. *The Times* (London) called the appointment "the first spectacular incursion by the National-Socialist Party into the conservative sanctuary of the Foreign Office." Dodd, the American Ambassador, interpreted what had occurred similarly, and the reaction of his government was to see Bohle's new post as a major expansion of the NSDAP's influence over the *Wilhelmstrasse*.[76] In some quarters the reaction was even more extreme and incorrect. The London *Daily Telegraph* speculated that the new Secretary of State in the AA would be either Mackensen or Weizsäcker. But, the paper stressed, whoever was selected "will, it is thought, only be keeping the place warm for Herr Bohle." Then there was the complete inaccuracy of another London paper that contended Bohle had been "until recently head of the London Nazi group" and that his appointment "will mean changes in the London organization."[77]

There is little doubt that Bohle himself viewed his good fortune as confirmation from Hitler that the AO had full authority to direct and supervise German citizens outside Germany. For Bohle, this was the realization of his perennial desire to exert greater influence over policy dealing with foreign Germandom. But as he was to discover, his authority in the AA was restricted significantly, even in the area of administering Germans abroad. During 1937 and 1938, at the peak of the AO's power, it was able to achieve solely minor changes in the AA's personnel and to affect only the policy of the Cultural-Political Department of the Ministry. When Ribbentrop, Bohle's archrival, became Foreign Minister in February 1938, its authority was limited even more.

Bohle's jurisdiction in the AA was quickly defined. It was restricted to matters concerning German citizens abroad, such as arranging celebrations of party holidays; handling tension in Nazi locals; guiding relations among party leaders, their host governments, and German diplomats; organizing the party's negotiations with foreign governments over issues involving German nationals; advising *Auslandsdeutschen* on questions concerning citizenship; and influencing cultural policy by controlling foreign teachers and students.[78] Bohle also completed regulations with the Propaganda Ministry for sending party mail abroad by diplomatic pouch. In addition, he worked on establishing a secret "slush fund" from the AA for the AO. He requested 750,000 marks (roughly $200,000) in January 1938 to enable him to "be in the position, from case to case, to help without bureaucratic or budgetary restrictions if an individual crisis occurs . . . in which the demands of foreign Germandom and therefore the Reich are served by the dispatch of funds." But in one of his many frustrations in the AA, he received less than one-third of the amount.[79]

Capturing official control over German schools abroad and repatriating foreign Germans for labor and military purposes in Germany were of special interest to him. Beginning in March 1937 numerous functionaries in the Cultural-Political Department of the AA were purged, including the head of its School Section, Böhme, and the AO and Ministry of Education ensured (by working through SD reports on potential successors) that only "old reliable party comrades" replaced them. Bohle also ordered an immediate halt to the financial support of German missions abroad to "active Jewish or non-Aryan professors and other scientists."[80] Since Germany badly needed labor to supply Hitler's rearmament program, the AO's Repatriation Office worked through Bohle to supervise the return of German citizens to Germany. The Office concluded an agreement with the AA whereby it was granted total command over the re-emigration process. It had repatriation camps throughout Germany; a camp in Munich, for example, administered the return of 2,271 foreign Germans from 1936 to 1938.[81]

Bohle introduced himself in his new role to the diplomats in a bombastic circular to the missions on 1 March, and he implied that he wielded more authority than he actually possessed. He began by stressing that his appointment had been a "logical consequence" of the AO's history. In a statement that must have sounded ominous to the diplomats, he instructed them that the NSDAP intended to use his position to recreate the Third Reich outside Germany: "Just as the National Socialist party possesses the sole right to educate the people inside the Reich . . . so must the communities of German citizens abroad be led by foreign groups of the party and trained in the spirit of our state today." In appealing for the diplomats' cooperation, he informed them that he had given "strictest orders" to his "leaders of the party abroad" to observe the "authority of the official representatives of the Reich." Yet, he reminded the mission officials that the party expected them to return the compliment and "consider the special place of the party in the lives of Reich citizens."[82]

The diplomats were hardly overwhelmed with admiration for the new arrangement, and Bohle's instructions were not always executed faithfully. A month later he had to chastise them angrily for using incorrect designations for *Landesgruppenleiters* in official correspondence. To educate them, he demanded that as many as possible attend the fifth annual conference of the AO in Stuttgart (recently named by Hitler the "city of foreign Germandom") in September. The encroachment into the affairs of the missions was further illustrated when he requested that they allow *Landesgruppenleiters* to see their lists of Germans who had lost German citizenship, moved from one country to another, or emigrated from Germany to a foreign land. The information, he maintained, was absolutely necessary to help the AO "uncover quickly possible activity against National Socialist Germany" by Germans abroad.[83]

He also wasted little time in defining where the authority of mission leaders over *Auslandsdeutschen* stopped and the power of foreign party functionaries began. According to a directive he issued in October, the party leaders were to be consulted by the diplomats about many of the issues that he dealt with in Berlin, which included organizing German communities, planning party activities, and handling legal and cultural matters of German citizens.[84] Although some mission leaders deeply resented the order, their jurisdiction was curtailed only minimally, and the party's authority was restricted to German nationals.

Added to the directives that flooded the missions, Bohle made his presence in the AA felt in other ways. *Landesgruppenleiters* were given permission to use rooms in German embassies and consulates without paying rent (e.g., in Istanbul, Sofia, Brussels, New York, and Madrid).[85] In rare instances, party leaders were able to prevent foreign governments from sending diplomatic representatives to Germany who were suspected of being hostile to the Reich. Emil Prüfert, *Landesgruppenleiter* of Colombia beginning in 1935, torpedoed plans of the Colombian government in the fall of 1937 to send Jorge Soto del Corral as its Minister to Berlin.[86]

A more frequent practice was the party's use of Bohle's position in the AA to threaten and punish disobedient German nationals. When an elderly German pastor in Oslo, Günther, opposed cooperation of the local German colony with the Nazi local, Bohle ordered the German Legation in Norway to send the rebel to Germany where he faced imprisonment and loss of his pension. A favorite tactic was to deprive uncooperative party members of their German citizenship, which meant, in effect, that their membership and privilege of returning to Germany were automatically destroyed and that their relatives in Germany were placed under immediate surveillance (and sometimes arrest) by the Gestapo.[87] Nor was the AO above using Bohle's status to strengthen its pressure on German firms to release their business representatives abroad when they opposed National Socialism. Eduard Nagelsbach, an agent in Southwest Africa for the Otavi Mine and Railway Company in Berlin, was fired by the firm and forced to return to Germany for writing an article for a German newspaper attacking the AO.[88] The return of anti-Nazi elements to Germany was facilitated by the AO's Office for Harbor Control (*Hafendienstamt*). It placed undercover agents in many large seaports whose chief tasks were to observe the arrival and departure of German nationals, and in rare instances, to take into custody persons whose activity was hostile toward Germany and send them home aboard German ships for punishment. The head of the Harbor Control operation was an oldtimer in the AO, Kurt Wermke, described by Bohle as "a fanatical National Socialist" and who worked closely with the Gestapo and the intelligence section of the German War Ministry.[89]

Closely connected with the Harbor Control agents and *Landesgruppen* was the Nazi Seafarer Section. Its main responsibility was to organize German merchant and passenger ships into *Ortsgruppen* of the party; by 1937 there were 1,097 such "shipping locals" sailing the seas, often carrying (or smuggling) propaganda to *Landesgruppen* or cooperating with Harbor Control people. Most party leaders aboard the ships were given political training at the AO's School of Leaders for Seamen and Germans Abroad, formed in April 1934 in Altona. In turn, the leaders trained rank and file seamen on the ships in Nazi ideology, German labor law, sports, and social policy (in conjunction with the DAF). In the harbors of foreign countries, the DAF's Strength through Joy (*Kraft durch Freude*) groups, organized with the *Landesgruppen*, entertained the crews of German ships. The NSDAP emphasized that a sort of mystical bond tied the seamen to its foreign groups; the latter busily arranged trips for the visiting mariners to acquaint them with harbor towns and the interior of foreign countries.

But on the negative side, this did little to allay the mistrust of the party organizations by foreign governments. German ships were often searched by foreign officials who were looking for Nazi propaganda or agents being smuggled into their countries, and sporadically the seamen became public symbols of the antagonism Germany was generating abroad. In September 1935 a Nazi emblem was torn from the German liner *Bremen* by an angry crowd in New York. Several weeks later, when the ship docked again in the city, the crew saluted the swastika flag as it was hoisted above the pier. Raising their right arms stiffly, the seamen shouted a threefold "heil Hitler," listened to an impassioned speech by their captain, and ended their spectacle by singing *Deutschland über Alles* and the Horst Wessel song.

In some countries where party groups encountered hostility to their activities, the ships docked and permitted the groups to hold parties and celebrations on board. Children from German schools were often invited onto the ships for tours, "indoctrination sessions," and visits to the ships' bookstore (which always featured copies of *Mein Kampf*). In Germany the mariners were praised and glorified by the NSDAP. A "National Congress of Seamen" was held annually, and the party's leaders attempted to bolster the seafarers' morale and sense of importance by speaking at the conference. Goebbels, comparing them to diplomats, once remarked that while the latter were "envoys of their Empire," the seamen were "envoys of their people."[90]

Even the AO's Party Court in Berlin capitalized on Bohle's appointment. Not only did it begin a witch-hunt to remove Freemasons in party groups abroad and begin investigating the "Aryan descent" of spouses of foreign party leaders, but it increased its use of Gestapo files to issue judgments against disobedient Nazis. Such cooperation resulted in the return to Germany of a diplomat in Argentina, Arthur Koch, to be punished for selling military secrets to a foreign government.[91] The Court worked with Heydrich and the SD to punish the captain and first officer (who were Nazi members) of the German passenger ship *Milwaukee*. They were accused of being involved in a homosexual clique aboard the ship, of refusing to celebrate properly Hitler's birthday, and of tolerating jokes among the ship's crew about Göring and Ley.[92]

On occasion the AO was able to influence lower level Ministry appointments and to increase pressure on diplomats to join the NSDAP. Outside of forcing a few diplomats who were on leave or on vacation to submit speeches to the AA for approval before they were delivered abroad, thereby avoiding complaints from foreign party leaders who believed that they were not pro-Nazi enough,[93] Bohle tried to exert considerable authority in the approval of personnel changes in the Ministry. Party membership was one of several aspects in such matters. An appointment or promotion rested on favorable judgments of candidates from the Ministries of Interior and Finance (for affairs concerning rank and budget), the

Foreign Minister, and Hess's office (which received information on the candidates' "political reliability" from the AO). When the party had finally arrived at a decision, the candidate's name was sent to Hitler.[94] The AO's assessment of the diplomats rested significantly on reports received about the officials from *Landesgruppenleiters*. Bohle had initially enlisted the reports in February 1934, and by 1937 he possessed an extensive file on most of the Foreign Service.[95]

During 1937 several AO leaders were appointed to offices in the AA as aides to Bohle or as bureaucrats in the School Section of the Cultural-Political Department. Commissioned *Legationssekretär* ("legation secretaries") were Fischer; Ehrich, who became head of Bohle's office in the Ministry; Burbach; and Karl Klingenfuss, a leader of the AO's Cultural Office, who was moved into the Cultural-Political Department. In addition, Kohn was named Consul General, and Fritz-Gebhardt von Hahn and Peter Bachmann were made attaches.[96]

Simultaneously a handful of *Landesgruppenleiters* were commissioned as secondary diplomats and attached to German missions. What the AA had hoped to avoid began to occur on a modest scale: party positions were united with diplomatic offices, and the claim by the Ministry to foreign governments that it was acting as an independent arm of the German government was blemished. Included in the appointments were Bernard, Consul General in Salzburg, named *Landesgruppenleiter* for Austria; Carl Dedering, *Landesgruppenleiter* of Peru, named Consul in Lima; Ettel, party leader in Italy, named Legation Counselor in Rome; Butting, head of the party's cover organization in the Netherlands, named attache in The Hague; Tiemann, party member and Consul General in Hankow, named Consul in Batavia; Bene, former party chief in England, named Consul General in Milan; Walter Pausch, member of Bohle's personal staff, named Legation Secretary in Tokyo; Georg Böhme, *Ortsgruppenleiter* in Davos, named "Administrator of the German Consulate in Davos"; Carl Burgam, *Landesgruppenleiter* of Poland, named Vice Consul in Warsaw; Wilhelm Rodde, named party leader in Canada and Consul in Winnipeg; Stiller, party leader in South Africa, named Legation Counselor in Capetown; and Wilhelm Graeb, party chief in Hungary, named Consul. The AO's only significant appointment occurred in November 1937 when the founder of the party in Guatemala, Langmann, was named Minister to Uruguay.[97] Probably more often, Bohle's candidates for the AA were rejected by Neurath and Mackensen. In the autumn of 1937 he failed to have Friedrich Willis, a cofounder of the *Ortsgruppe* Rome and an AO official, placed in the Ministry.[98]

Party leaders who entered the Ministry reflected the influence of the SS on the AO. Not only had the AO lost its authority in *Volksdeutsch* affairs to the VoMi, but a large number of its officials were SS officers: Ettel, Walter Hewel (an old friend of Hitler and Hess and a former party leader in the Dutch East Indies), Lehne (head of a new AO office, the *Amt für Erzieher*, or "Office for Educators"), Heinrich Hammersen (Bohle's adjutant), Rudolf Tesmann (Bohle's personal adviser), Schnaus (in charge of the AO's Inspection Office), Ruberg (chief of the AO's *Stabsamt*, or "Staff Office"), Butting, Friedrich Haus (Foreign Commissioner of the AO for South America), and Rodde. Bohle himself was promoted by Himmler in April 1937 to SS *Gruppenführer* ("major general"), and soon thereafter, he renounced his British citizenship.[99]

The AO also involved itself in the cloak and dagger business of having career diplomats dismissed from their posts. While such instances were not extensive, a few officials were released (or transferred to other posts in the AA) for the slightest opposition to the NSDAP—either they made an ill-conceived remark about the party or they behaved in a manner unbecoming a "Nazi diplomat"—or because of hostile reports against them sent to Bohle by *Landesgruppenleiters*. Wilhelm Erythropel, mission chief in Cuba, was recalled to Berlin because of his opposition to local Nazi functionaries. A similar fate befell the anti-Nazi Vice Consul in Batavia, Kleiber, who was accused by the party in the Dutch East Indies of keeping a mistress and thereby creating a public "scandal." Another example was the removal of the German Minister to Ireland, Schroetter, because he was criticized by the *Ortsgruppenleiter* in Dublin. A further instance was the transfer of Georg Vogel from the Embassy in London to Czechoslovakia; he was attacked by Otto Karlowa, the new *Landesgruppenleiter* of England, for not defending vigorously enough to British authorities a German caught stealing.[100]

Mission officials could also be removed on racial grounds. Wilhelm Haas, Legation Secretary and chief of the Trade Department of the German Embassy in Tokyo, was "retired" by the AA in April 1937 through pressure from the AO and *Landesgruppenleiter* of Japan, Hillmann. Not only was Haas's wife a Jewess, but he refused to offer his "wholehearted support of the National Socialist ideology." Furthermore, when he tried to land a job with I. G. Farben in Japan, Hillmann blocked his efforts, and it was only in 1939 that he was permitted to go to work for the firm in northern China.[101]

Although the AO was unable to exercise significant power in personnel affairs of the AA, it was hardly surprising that greater pressure was placed on Ministry officials to join the NSDAP. Ernst Woermann, the Embassy Counselor for Ribbentrop (who had been appointed Ambassador to England in August 1936), applied for party membership at the encouragement of Karlowa. Other ranking diplomats who joined the party were Otto von Erdmannsdorff and Faupel. Bohle also concluded an agreement with Goebbels, whereby Nazi members working in *Wilhelmstrasse* 74 would belong to the AO's membership rolls instead of those of the Berlin *Gau*. The pact was later expanded when the AO created an *Ortsgruppe Auswärtiges Amt*, which administered party members in the Foreign Service who lived outside Germany.[102]

The peak of the AO's authority in this regard appears to have developed in 1938. Woermann was finally accepted by the party and issued his membership card, and a month after Bohle approached Weizsäcker (the choice of Ribbentrop, named Foreign Minister in February, as Secretary of State) about joining, he too had received a card. The Ambassador to Brazil, Karl Ritter, was accepted (especially pleasing Bohle, since his groups in Brazil were under a serious attack by the Vargas regime and badly needed Ritter's support), and the AO suggested to Ribbentrop that the new Ambassador to Japan, Major Ott, be admitted. Mission leaders who entered the party were Hans Völckers (Cuba), Cecil von Renthe-Fink (Denmark), Papen (Turkey), Hans Carl Büsing (Paraguay), Otto Köcher (Switzerland), and Eduard Hempel (Ireland). In May Hitler ordered the *Ortsgruppe Auswärtiges Amt* dissolved and that future acceptance of diplomats be decided on by an agreement between Bohle and Ribbentrop.[103]

While Bohle subsequently used his share of such authority to approve the enrolling of other diplomats (e.g., Diego von Bergen and Dieckhoff), he was adamant in blocking membership for officials who were the least suspect. Freiherr von Mentzingen, a Vice Consul in Istanbul, was blackballed because he was too openly Catholic and had been educated in a Jesuit school. Membership for the Senior Counselor and Deputy Director of the AA's Cultural Policy Department, Fritz von Twardowski, was delayed because he had a brother in the United States who was allegedly "an enemy of Germany." Apparently, Bohle's work earned him top marks with the Nazi hierarchy; on his birthday in July 1938 he received telegrams and greetings from Hitler, Hess, Himmler, and Göring. But his job with the AA was nowhere near completion. Only one-third of its ninety-two higher officials in Berlin were party members, and 881 of its 2,665 employees had entered the NSDAP or declared their intention to do so.[104]

Bohle's promotion to the AA and his jockeying for power in the Ministry marked the height of the authority in the government of the AO and its groups outside Germany. He enjoyed for a brief time access to Hitler (which was always a mark of influence) to discuss important matters regarding foreign Germans. On at least one occasion he was asked by Hitler to report with Hess to the Führer on the party's development in Austria.[105] Hitler also apparently persisted in viewing the AO as a counterweight to the AA; in June 1939 he threatened in confidential circles to discuss with Bohle the intervention against mission officials abroad who received foreign visits from German warships "too stiffly and formally." According to the Chancellor, "Here and there the AOrg. of the Party [AO] must intercede when a block-headed Ambassador makes nonsense."[106]

Yet, as shown above, the extent of the AO's influence on the AA was minimal—in policy-making, personnel decisions, and affairs involving foreign missions. Perhaps the greatest threat the AO posed to the Ministry was psychological in nature: most diplomats ascribed to it an authority it never possessed. This, much more than any practical power it wielded, gave the strongest competition the party was to offer the Foreign Ministry. Except for petty quarrels among foreign party officials and diplomats and pressure exerted on the diplomats to join the party, the AA and its apparatus remained intact. But the image such difficulties projected to foreign governments was that the Ministry had been nazified.[107] In 1939 and 1940 Bohle was mentioned in the foreign press as a potential successor to Ribbentrop, an assertion based purely on myth and one that infuriated the Foreign Minister.

Myths seemed to surround the AO and its organizations abroad. Public opinion and foreign governments, particularly in the Western Hemisphere, believed honestly (but erroneously) that the groups formed a massive Nazi conspiracy or "fifth column" that threatened world security. On the other hand, the AO continued to function according to the legend that foreign Germans were as eager to become Nazi followers as Germans at home. Adding fuel to this view were Bohle's promotion to the AA, several partial successes of *Landesgruppen* in Spain and Austria, and misleading reports sent to Germany by party leaders that portrayed a far too favorable situation for their work. But beginning in 1938 and 1939, whatever hopes the AO entertained about becoming a vital agency in foreign affairs turned to disappointment. As the list of nations banning the noisy and visible *Landesgruppen* became longer, Berlin finally acknowledged that pushing the Nazi doctrines of race and power onto foreign Germans was a failure. The outlawing of the party abroad also undermined Bohle's position in the AA, an erosion that was accelerated by Ribbentrop's being commissioned Foreign Minister and by his strengthening of the Ministry against rivals like the party.

5

THE THREAT OF WAR AND THE FOREIGN REACTION AGAINST THE PARTY GROUPS ABROAD, 1937-1939

Following Hitler's meeting with his advisers in November 1937, in which he coldly outlined his intention to secure through any means *Lebensraum* in Austria and Czechoslovakia, Europe unknowingly found itself on a collision course with Germany. A series of political crises, perpetuated by the German government and NSDAP, developed in Europe, bringing on the destructive Second World War in September 1939. In each crisis—the *Anschluss* of Austria, the destruction of Czechoslovakia, the ban of the Nazis from Latin America and elsewhere, and the attack on Poland—the Nazi party was almost as deeply involved as the German government and army.

While the foothold of the party in the Foreign Service rested significantly on Bohle's position in the AA, it also depended on the organization of the AO in Berlin and its several hundred groups outside Germany. By June 1937 the AO was administering 29,099 Nazi members around the world and 22,469 German seamen.[1] Although the numbers were unimpressive (they represented barely five percent of the German nationals living abroad), the NSDAP had made gains in membership since 1933 in several countries that had tried to crush its indigenous groups: Southwest Africa, the Netherlands, Switzerland, Austria, and the United States. According to a statistical analysis by the AO, the social composition of its groups was not radically different from the largely young, middle-class party membership inside Germany. An overwhelming majority of the foreign members were males (90 percent), under thirty-eight years old (54 percent), and engaged in some type of business activity (32.5 percent) or other middle class profession.[2]

TABLE II
Countries With the Largest
Number of Nazi Members June 1937

Country	Members	German Citizens
Brazil	2,903	75,000
Netherlands	1,925	75,000
Austria	1,678	44,000
Argentina	1,500	42,600
Poland	1,379	6,500
Switzerland	1,364	120,000
Southwest Africa	1,127	13,000
Italy	1,076	9,500
Czechoslovakia	1,006	32,000
Chile	985	5,300
China	700	5,000
Tanganyika	688	2,140
Netherlands East Indies	682	3,000
United States	569	

Source: AO, "Parteimitglieder, Stand 30.6. 1937," T-120/78/60145-60148. The membership figures include an undetermined number of *Volksdeutschen* and persons with dual citizenship.

Although Bohle was extremely proud of his office in the AA, he spent most of his time at the AO, where a staff of eight hundred department leaders, bureaucrats, clerks, and secretaries were employed. Most AO leaders had lived abroad as businessmen, teachers, engineers, or officers. The largest percentage of department chiefs was under forty years of age, and many spoke or read several languages, a fact that was always a source of pride for Bohle. Another fact that pleased him was that most of his subordinates, who had been Evangelical in religion before 1933, had declared themselves to be non-Christians (*gottgläubig*).[3]

The leaders of the principal offices (*Hauptstellenleiter*) in the *Zentrale* in Berlin included Tesmann, who succeeded Ehrich as Bohle's personal adviser; Hammersen and Willy Gohert, Bohle's adjutants; Hess, Deputy *Gauleiter*; and Ruberg, leader of the Staff Office. In addition, eight regional departments (*Länderämter*), each guided by a veteran resident of the region, were responsible for the development of *Landesgruppen* assigned to the departments. The central office was further divided into twenty-four special departments whose heads held the rank of *Gauamtsleiter* and boasted of having substantial foreign experience. The Seafarer Section was headed by Wermke, a one-time merchant in Guatemala, and other departments led by persons who had lived abroad included the Foreign Trade Office (Wilhelm Bisse and Hess), Personnel Office (Reitzenstein), Inspection Office (Schnaus), Relief Committee for Spanish-Germans (Hellermann), DAF (Ruberg), Office for Technicians (Hermann Bohle), *Amt für Beamte* ("Office for Civil Servants," Georg Winkelmann, a former official in the *Ortsgruppe* Madrid), and Office for Educators (Lehne).[4]

THE *Landesgruppen*:
ORGANIZATIONS AGAINST THE JEWS

Beyond the Berlin headquarters the AO was comprised of roughly forty-nine *Landesgruppen* in nearly every corner of the world. The *Landesgruppe* served as a national organization that administered *Kreis* ("regional") groups, *Ortsgruppen*, *Stützpunkte*, and *Zellen* of the NSDAP in its country. (See Appendix II.) Bohle was a strict adherent to the *Führerprinzip* in his relations with the *Landesgruppenleiters*; they were to obey his directives like robots and demand the same unstinting obedience from their subordinates. Each *Landesgruppenleiter* was carefully chosen for his post by Bohle and confirmed by Hitler. In turn, the *Landesgruppenleiter* appointed (with Bohle's confirmation) the administrators who supervised the various offices in his organization and other party leaders (e.g., *Ortsgruppenleiters*) in his country. A large percentage of local and subordinate leaders were German merchants, owners of businesses, and teachers.[5]

By 1937 and 1938 the *Landesgruppenleiter* corps had become fairly stabilized, and most of them were veteran Nazis (whose longevity in the party had allegedly proven their loyalty to Hitler) drawn by Bohle from the educated business and professional middle classes. (See Table III.) Often, they worked full-time at their jobs, which involved building a network of locals and cells in their countries, recruiting party members, disseminating propaganda, and handling problems of foreign Germans. Some were well paid for their work; in 1939 the party leaders of England, Palestine, Hungary, Paraguay, Bulgaria, Australia, Norway, Colombia, Italy, and Spain earned as much as several thousand dollars.[6]

Most *Landesgruppen* had numerous departments and offices. An example was the party organization in the Union of South Africa, which administered 336 members through several local affiliates.

Concealing its activities wherever possible from the authorities, the *Landesgruppe* maintained an undercover headquarters in Capetown, and it employed officials to handle the party's treasury, membership records, indoctrination work, press, radio, films, archive for phonograph records, local economic affairs, harbor service, DAF, Winter Relief collections, and welfare work. Although the *Landesgruppen* were responsible for most of their propaganda, the AO sent them Nazi films (e.g., *Triumph of the Will*) and short wave radio sets that could receive broadcasts from Germany.[7] The usual materials, like pamphlets, brochures, books and swastika banners, were also sent from Berlin.

TABLE III

Landesgruppenleiters*

of the Auslands-Organisation 1937-1940

Country	Landesgruppenleiter	Date Entered NSDAP	Profession
Angola	Hans Kisker	Oct. 1930	Farmer
Argentina	Fritz Küster	Mar. 1932	Merchant
	Alfred Müller	July 1931	Merchant
Australia	Ladendorff	—	Unemployed
Austria	Hans Bernard	—	Consul (AA)
Belgium	Adolf Schulze	May 1933	Railroad Official
Bolivia	Ernst Wendler	—	Minister (AA)
Brazil	Hans-Henning von Cossel	May 1931	Businessman
Bulgaria	Joseph Drechsel	Jan. 1931	Professor
Canada	Wilhelm Rodde	Oct. 1932	Consul (AA)
	Otto Janssen	—	—
Chile	Karl Hübner	Apr. 1932	Railroad Official
China	Siegfried Lahrmann	Sept. 1930	Merchant
Colombia	Emil Prüfert	Aug. 1931	Owner, German Firm
Czechoslovakia	Stechele	—	—
Protectorate	Richard Ziessig	—	—
Denmark	Frielitz	May 1928	Press Attache (AA)

* According to Jacobsen, *Nationalsozialistische Aussenpolitik*, p. 664, 89.5 percent of the AO's rank and file membership joined the NSDAP after January 1933; but 83.9 percent of the LGL (whose entry dates are known) were members before 1933.

	Ernst Schäfer	Oct. 1930	Merchant
Egypt	Krahn	—	Engineer
England	Otto Karlowa	Apr. 1933	Interpreter (AA)
Finland	Wilhelm Jahre	Apr. 1934	Chief Clerk
France	Rudolf Schleier	—	Wine Merchant
	Emil Ehrich	Nov. 1930	AO, AA
Greece	Walther Wrede	Jan. 1934	Archaeologist
Guatemala	Gerhard Hentschke	Nov. 1931	Merchant
Hungary	Wilhelm Graeb	June 1933	Consul (AA)
Iran	Erwin Ettel	Mar. 1932	Legation Counselor (AA)
Italy	Ettel	—	—
	Ehrich	—	—
Japan	Rudolf Hillmann	July 1933	Merchant
Kenya/Uganda	Karl Hubl	—	—
Latvia	Henry Esp	July 1932	Engineer
Luxemburg	Heinrich Diehl	—	Doctor
Manchuria	Hanns von Kirschbaum	June 1934	Director, German Firm
Mexico	Wilhelm Wirtz	May 1931	Merchant
Netherlands	Otto Butting	Mar. 1932	Doctor, Attache (AA)
Netherlands East Indies	Otto Jaissle	May 1934	Businessman
Norway	Karl Spanaus	—	—
Palestine	Cornelius Schwarz	May 1933	Clerk
Paraguay	Rainer Behrens	June 1934	Bank Clerk
Peru	Carl Dedering	Apr. 1932	Consul (AA)
Poland	Carl Burgam	—	Vice Consul (AA)
	Ewald Krummer	—	Legation Counselor (AA)
Portugal	Julius Claussen	—	—
Rumania	Artur Konradi	Dec. 1931	Engineer
Southwest Africa	Michael Neuendorf	—	Sheep Farmer
Spain	Hans Thomsen	May 1933	Radio Operator, Navy
Sweden	Wilhelm Stengel	—	Engineer
Switzerland	Sigismund von Bibra	May 1933	Legation Secretary (AA)

Tanganyika		—	—
Turkey	Viktor Friede	—	—
Union of			
South Africa	Helmuth Kirchner	—	Editor (?)
United States	Frederick Mensing	—	Shipping Agent
	Friedhelm Draeger	—	Vice Consul (AA)
Uruguay	Julius Dalldorf	—	Businessman
Venezuela	Arnold Margerie	June 1933	Merchant
Yugoslavia	—	—	—

Source: DAI, "Anschriften der Landesgruppenleiter der AO. der NSDAP," 14 June 1940, T-81/350/5078482-5078483; issues of the AO's *Mitteilungsblatt*, 1937-1940; Bohle's discussion of the LGL, Bohle Interrogation, M-679/1/0092-0101; U.S. War Dept., *Nazi Party Membership Records*, passim; and biographical material from BDC and PA files.

Although Bohle denied it, an unofficial task of the *Landesgruppen* was to involve themselves subtly in the internal affairs of their country, hoping thereby to further German aims abroad. As noted previously, this intervention took several forms, but much of it centered around their following a doggedly anti-Semitic policy. Aside from their usual anti-Jewish propaganda and political activities, the groups' economic policies were highly anti-Semitic in nature and aimed at smashing the alleged "world Jewish conspiracy" against Germany.

Such practices extended even to Palestine, where the AO and *Landesgruppe* Palestine fought against the formation of a Jewish national home there, and against the transfer into the country of Jewish property from Germany by the *Haavara* (Hebrew for Transfer) Company. Beginning in 1933 the Nazi government had introduced measures that aided the emigration of German Jews to Palestine and permitted them to take a portion of their property with them. The *Haavara* organization, in agreement with the German government, received a monopoly on the shipping of German goods to Palestine. But when the British government began considering in the summer of 1937 the partition of Palestine and formation of a Jewish state there, the German government and NSDAP quickly opposed the idea.

A key reason for the opposition was the roughly two thousand German citizens living in colonies in Jerusalem, Jaffa, Haifa, Sarona, Wilhelma, Waldheim, and Bethlehem. It was feared that if

Palestine was divided, German settlements would fall within the borders of the Jewish state. The *Landesgruppe* Palestine, which controlled most of the colonies, discouraged the *Auslandsdeutschen* from returning to Germany and ordered them not to sell their land to Jews. The group, led by an elderly Jaffa clerk, Cornelius Schwarz, fought the planned partition by enflaming the local Arab-Jewish conflict with propaganda, and aiding Arab guerilla bands that attacked Jews.

Although the AA had opposed the creation of a Jewish state in Palestine before it became a serious British proposal, German hostility mounted rapidly in the fall of 1937. The AO's Foreign Trade Office, the *Landesgruppe*, and the German Consul General in Jerusalem demanded that Germany ban Jewish emigration and the transfer of Jewish property to Palestine. According to the party, failure to prohibit such practices would alienate the Arabs from Germany and contribute to the formation of a Jewish state (Palestine had accepted over one-third of the Jews who had left Germany since 1933) with German money, skills, and knowledge acquired by Jews in Germany. The AO also maintained that Germany must keep the Jews dispersed and prevent the creation of a Jewish state that would surely become another center of power for "international Jewry." But several ministries in the German government argued against the party, noting that if German Jews could not emigrate to Palestine, Hitler's order that Germany must become *Judenrein* ("pure of Jews") would never be achieved. In the end, there was no final decision regarding *Haavara* and Palestine, mainly because the British dropped the partition plan in 1938 and seriously limited Jewish migration to Palestine.[8]

Using the *Landesgruppen*, the AO persisted in trying to undermine Jewish economic influence abroad and stimulate German trade, which were not always compatible goals. Under the direction of Göring's Four-Year-Plan, the AO's Foreign Trade Office employed 244 agents or *Wirtschaftsstellenleiter*, who were attached to the *Landesgruppen*; their principal job was to gather information on Jewish businesses abroad and German firms hiring Jews. The *Wirtschaftsstellenleiter* in Buenos Aires, Volberg, supplied the German Economic Ministry and the German Embassy in Argentina with lists of banks, businesses, and individuals suspected of being Jewish, and these were boycotted by the Germans. The AO also succeeded in capturing control over the propaganda of German firms abroad; I. G. Farben, among other companies, harmonized its

public relations policy with the Foreign Trade Office. By 1939 the
Office had amassed records on roughly 110,000 foreign German
and Jewish businesses and German commercial representatives.[9]

The Office had also tried since 1933 to have foreign workers of
Farben and other companies dismissed for being "non-Aryan" or
failing to be fanatical National Socialists. Initially, Farben re-
sisted such pressures and retained its non-Aryan employees by playing off the AO against the APA and other agencies. Farben chiefs
argued that the employees were valuable to German foreign trade
and that they brought Germany foreign currency that was essential
to the rearmament program. But during 1937 the struggle was resolved in favor of the AO; a number of foreign representatives
were dismissed by Farben.[10]

Similar dismissals occurred in other German firms. The leader of
the *Ortsgruppe* Shanghai, Alfred Kroeger, helped secure the removal
of the Jew, Rudolf Herz, from the Agfa China Company. A Chilean
citizen of German descent, who represented Krupp in Chile and
employed a Jew, was threatened by the *Landesgruppe* Chile with
the loss of his privilege to represent Krupp if he did not dismiss
the Jew. By 1938 and 1939 an undetermined number of Jews had
lost their positions in German firms abroad, and Jewish refugees
from Germany were denied jobs in foreign German companies because of the party's pressure.[11] But again, by arranging for the
ousting of such persons, many with commercial contacts abroad,
the AO undercut attempts by the AA and other German agencies
to increase Germany's trade.

ANTI-COMINTERN POLITICS AND CRITICISM
OF THE NAZINTERN

Another key activity of the *Landesgruppen* was their campaign
against Communism, which formed a small part of Germany's
Anti-Comintern policy that took official form with the agreements
at the end of 1936 with Japan and Italy. While the Germans sought
to balance their Far Eastern interests by expanding their commercial and military involvement in China, they also began negotiations with Japan that led to the Anti-Comintern pact in November.
Once it had been signed, Germany found itself caught in the
dilemma of maintaining friendly relations with both China and
Japan (which were archenemies) and receiving from each what
benefitted Germany. But when the Sino-Japanese war broke out in

July 1937, Hitler was forced to choose between the two countries, and he supported Japan.

Although there were only twelve hundred German citizens and slightly over two hundred party members in Japan, Bohle firmly believed that the *Landesgruppe* Japan could do a great deal to foster German-Japanese trade and cement political relations between the two nations. Much of its leadership was comprised of German businessmen and included a Legation Secretary at the German Embassy in Tokyo, Pausch. He was Bohle's contact inside the Embassy, and in addition to his spying on the other diplomats, he was probably responsible for the removal of Haas, the Legation Secretary and expert on German-Japanese trade, who was a Jew.[12]

The work of the *Landesgruppe* was hardly the type that stimulated Japanese admiration for their new allies. It sponsored anti-Communist propaganda meetings for the German colony, such as a noisy reception in Tokyo harbor for the visiting German cruiser *Emden* which attracted the Ambassador, Herbert von Dirksen, and six hundred guests. The *Landesgruppenleiter*, Rudolf Hillmann, also built a thriving HJ group in the German schools in Tokyo and Yokohama.[13] But the bulk of the party's time was spent harassing Dirksen and the Embassy staff and keeping German travelers to Japan under tight surveillance. Although Germany and Japan were allies, the Nazis never forgot that the Japanese were racially different from the Germans, and therefore Germans in Japan were not allowed by the NSDAP to associate freely with the natives.[14]

Bohle and Himmler also spied on the Embassy staff. They combined to have inserted in the Embassy special "police attaches," who were allegedly to serve on the German commission that was supervising the Japanese execution of the Anti-Comintern pact. While they made life uncomfortable for Embassy workers who were not National Socialists, Dirksen was angered on several occasions by the meddling of the *Landesgruppe* into the Embassy's cultural and economic affairs. Hillmann greatly embarrassed the Germans among Japanese government circles by publicly questioning the honesty of a German armaments salesman who had been sent by Berlin to sell airplanes to Japan.[15]

Another problem arising from Germany's pro-Japanese policy was the resentment it provoked among Germans and party members in China. Many Germans there found themselves objects of government persecution because of the German-Japanese friendship. When

Siegfried Lahrmann, the *Landesgruppenleiter* of China, criticized Germany, Bohle commanded him to support Hitler's policy at all costs and reminded him that he was responsible for representing it to the NSDAP in China. He instructed Lahrmann, "Personal sympathies toward the Chinese and material losses of our own racial comrades [in China] must under no circumstances be placed before the necessities of the great policy of the Führer."[16]

Thus Bohle's dream that the party in Japan could strengthen German-Japanese ties was torpedoed by the *Landesgruppe's* trivial propaganda and surveillance antics, and the AO faced difficulties with unhappy Germans in China. But such troubles did not appear to hurt significantly the party's status with the Tokyo regime. When negotiations between Germany and Japan took place in the winter of 1937 and 1938 concerning the former German colonial possessions in the Pacific, Samoa and New Guinea, the Japanese unofficially contacted the AO. Apparently, Japan hoped to purchase the former German islands to prepare the way for their incorporation into Japan's planned empire in the Far East. When Ribbentrop led the Japanese to believe that Germany did not want to discuss the question on an official basis, the Japanese naval attache in Berlin visited Menche, head of the AO's Far Eastern Department, and discussed Japan's aims. Menche and Bohle told Ribbentrop, who ordered Menche to exercise the "greatest reservation" toward the attache. With Hitler having raised again in 1937 Germany's claims to her former colonies overseas (claims that were aimed primarily at England and territories in Africa), the German government did not want to compromise its demands by a sale of its former Pacific possessions to Japan. Despite their alliance against Communism, Germany and Japan had conflicting interests in colonial policy.[17]

If German policy toward Japan was directed at the danger allegedly posed by the Russians and Communism, the Nazis themselves experienced mounting public opposition in 1937 to several of their party branches abroad that foreshadowed the mass foreign attack on the groups in 1938 and 1939. The hostility occurred for two reasons: Hitler's aggressive foreign policy and his sharpening of demands for *Lebensraum* in Austria and eastern Europe, and Bohle's brazen insistence that his foreign leaders be placed on an equal basis with Germany's diplomats.

Bohle greatly intensified foreign suspicion of his leaders abroad by asserting in an interview with the *Berliner Tageblatt* in August 1937 that the "party organization in another country has a character similar to the German [diplomatic] representation."[18] This incredible claim resulted in part from his anger over the expulsion of several German journalists from England. In retaliation the Germans expelled the Berlin correspondent for the London *Times*, which only increased the already tense relations between Germany and England over Hitler's renewed demand that Germany's former colonies in Africa and German minorities in eastern Europe be united with the Reich.

Bowing to the pressure, Bohle had ordered a halt to the public operation of the *Landesgruppe* England in early August. Because of the expulsions, the organization and its new leader, Karlowa, had attracted attention from the British.[19] But Bohle's extreme statement demanding foreign protection for his officials abroad brought the German government a storm of criticism from the British, American, and European press. The sharpest denunciation came from Winston Churchill, who called the AO the "Nazintern" (i.e., the Nazi International, comparing it to the Comintern), warned that police should supervise NSDAP groups abroad tightly, and demanded that their leaders be expelled from foreign countries. He also threatened an investigation by Parliament of the AO and its penetration of England.[20] While his comparison was hardly an accurate one, it nevertheless served to increase the mythical view developing in the Western democracies that Nazi affiliates abroad formed a gigantic organization that threatened world security.

The wave of criticism had other foreign repercussions. When party groups in Hungary were accused of distributing propaganda among Hungarian-Germans, the Hungarian government refused to permit the upgrading of the *Ortsgruppe* Budapest to a *Landesgruppe*. The sour publicity stalking the AO was also employed by the United States government. A conflict between Dodd and his charge d'affaires, Prentiss Gilbert, was quickly suppressed in the German and American press when State Department officials (including Hull) reminded the press about Bohle's "recent" statements and the increased operation of Nazi groups abroad.[21]

But the strong reaction against the AO did little to daunt its belligerency. At its fifth annual Congress in Stuttgart in late August Bohle suggested that the party be allowed to send "cultural attaches" to German missions abroad, and Hess and Goebbels echoed the demand. Apparently, Hitler approved fully; he sent Bohle a telegram expressing "best wishes for your further work for Germandom abroad and the racial community of all Germans."[22] Such hard-line tactics, however, scarcely blunted the foreign outcry. Churchill noted repeatedly that the AO had become a major drawback to friendly Anglo-German relations and again hinted that he would call for an investigation by Parliament.

Ribbentrop and the German Embassy in London deeply resented this obvious burden on their diplomacy to win concessions from the British on the former German colonies in Africa and German demands in eastern Europe. The situation became so unbearable that Ribbentrop asked his government to respond to Churchill's attacks by sending Bohle to England to talk with the British leader. Such a trip had been planned since the summer, and before Bohle departed for England, Bene, his former party leader there, warned him not to repeat "the Rosenberg affair in London," which "would not be welcome in many circles." On 1 October 1937 Bohle and Churchill conversed privately for more than an hour at the latter's London residence, emerging with smiles and a friendly handshake.[23]

That evening Bohle addressed a Harvest Festival rally given by the *Landesgruppe* for the local German colony. A carefully selected audience of twelve hundred Germans attended the rally; seeking to reassure British leaders that the AO posed no threat to English democracy, he refused to allow British citizens to attend. After a "slight misunderstanding" at the meeting when Ribbentrop prematurely introduced him (a mix-up that seemed symbolic of the inability of the two to get along), a brief discussion was held at the platform, a band played several songs, and Karlowa spoke briefly.

Finally, it was Bohle's turn to speak. He began by denouncing foreigners who called his party members abroad "Nazi agitators" and "Gestapo agents," and he indicated his displeasure at being referred to in the foreign press as "chief of the Nazintern" or "chief of a devilish espionage organization." He flatly denied that his groups outside Germany intervened in the affairs of their host countries, and he stressed instead that they were "envoys of good will" and of Hitler, "a defender of peace, of peace for Germany and of peace for the world."[24] When he finished, the celebration closed with loud renditions of *Deutschland über Alles*, the Horst Wessel Song, and *God Save the King*. During the anthem the audience gave the Hitler salute, and many ended it with a threefold shout of "Sieg heil."

Although the visit was generally well received by the Western press[25] and persuaded Churchill to drop his opposition, Bohle's position had been seriously undermined in the AA and in his own government. His aggressive remarks in August had apparently been his own, without the approval of his superiors in the AA or the party. Consequently, because they damaged efforts by Ribbentrop to negotiate with England on several important issues, the statements were deeply resented by Neurath, Ribbentrop, and others in the AA. But while the diplomats complained about Bohle to Hitler, party leaders like Hess and Himmler rushed to his defense, and in keeping with the frequent Nazi policy of promoting loyal officials regardless of their blunderous actions, Hitler suddenly appointed him to the post of State Secretary in the AA. Hess in particular supported his underling and was primarily responsible for protecting him and securing his new title. Bohle was not ungrateful; he privately praised and thanked Hess, noting, "Through your intercession with the Führer, I am cloaked with the highest honor of the Third Reich."[26]

Neurath, hoping for the "removal of a few troubles" concerning Bohle's position in the Ministry, announced the promotion in a circular to mission officials and to other government agencies at the end of December.[27] Although the appointment was interpreted abroad as meaning that Bohle had become the second ranking diplomat in Germany and that he was the peer of Mackensen, this was hardly correct. His new title did not give him the official rank of Secretary of State *of* the AA, which would have made him a Deputy Foreign Minister, but it granted him instead the title of Secretary of State *in* the Ministry. Consequently, while he was permitted to make decisions regarding foreign Germans that were independent of Neurath and were at the ministerial level in the AA, he had substantially less power than his new title seemed to indicate. His rank, in fact, was comparable to a department chief in the AA, and his role in the Ministry was barely changed.[28] Yet, propaganda announcing his rank simply added fuel to the foreign notion that Bohle and the party were moving closer to capturing complete control of the Ministry.

Bohle, for his part, was firmly persuaded that his trip to London had been a "success" for the AO. But if he believed that he had avoided making a disastrous impression (à la Rosenberg in 1933), he had not convinced the British government. In December 1937 and during April of the following year, debates were held in Parliament that focused squarely on Nazi propaganda in England, the

Ortsgruppe London, and his visit. Calling Nazi groups in England "pretty formidable organisations," an angry member of the House of Commons argued, "It is the responsibility of the Home Office and the Government to put an end at once to this interference on the part of the German Government with people in this country . . . . Everybody knows that agents are here and that they are active."[29]

The AA also informed Hess that Bohle's use in his speeches of terms like *Auslandsdeutsche, Reichsdeutsche,* and *Volksdeutsche* was causing confusion among foreign governments and trouble for the Ministry. In a meeting among Mackensen, Hess, and Bohle, the latter was reminded that he should only use *Auslandsdeutsche* to mean "German citizens abroad" and that *Volksdeutsche* referred to ethnic Germans who possessed foreign citizenship.[30] While the NSDAP was instructed on the decision, there was no announcement to foreign governments, and the AO's "game of rhetoric" continued; so, unfortunately, did the difficulty the game caused for diplomacy.

AUSTRIA AND THE SOUTH TIROL

The hostility toward the AO and erosion of Bohle's position in high government circles were heightened by Germany's aggressiveness toward Austria and by the resulting *Anschluss* in March 1938. Hitler's Axis agreement with Mussolini, England's complacency and her appeasement of Germany, and the Austro-German agreements of July and November 1936 had seriously weakened Austria and opened the door to a renewed wave of Nazi interference there. While the German government steadfastly maintained that German Nazis were not active in Austria, the AO, SS, and Gestapo were pursuing another policy—pushing for the *Anschluss* and secretly supporting the militant Leopold faction in the illegal Austrian Nazi movement.

Bernard, still working through the League of German Citizens in Austria, spread *Anschluss* propaganda that viciously attacked the Schuschnigg government. A camouflaged (and armed) SA unit was formed in the League's *Turnerriege* ("Gymnastics Club") in Vienna, and SS men from Germany aided the unit's organization and engaged in espionage for the Gestapo. The *Turnerriege* held military exercises for former German front soldiers and trained them in "changes in war techniques" and new weapons. Similar groups were created in Salzburg, Linz, St. Pölten, Graz, Völkermarkt, and Bregenz.[31]

This activity, however, was closely followed by the Austrian police, who raided a secret office of the NSDAP in Vienna and seized evidence that revealed extensive contacts between the German and Austrian Nazis. Austro-German relations were further strained by a clash between the German colony and a detachment of Austrian troops in Pinkafeld, a village in the province of Styria. The conflict involved the right of Germans to fly the Reich flag on national holidays, and while Papen de-emphasized the incident to Hitler, the AO gave him a highly emotional report which argued that the affair had gravely insulted the entire German community in Austria.[32] The AO's account was obviously the type of report Hitler wished to receive, particularly since it gave him further **ammunition for annexing Austria and "protecting" the 6.5 million** German-Austrians there.

The incident also worsened relations between Papen and Bohle, who argued over the Minister's membership in the *Kulturbund*, a "cultural association" in Vienna led by Jews and opposed to union with Germany. These and other difficulties that arose with the split in the leadership of the Austrian Nazis between the activist Leopold and gradualist Seyss-Inquart factions, prompted Hitler in July 1937 to name a special Commissioner, Wilhelm Keppler, to handle Austrian affairs. Keppler's appointment was also the result of the growing influence in Austro-German relations of Göring and Himmler, who now sought to expand their personal power by taking over control of the Reich's policy in Austria. Through Keppler, the SS and SD pushed the evolutionary approach toward the *Anschluss*, which stressed the infiltration of the Austrian government with dedicated Nazis, and undermined Leopold's radical faction in the Austrian NSDAP.[33]

While Keppler's appointment meant a defeat for Bohle's pro-Leopold stance and may have caused him to begin rethinking his policy in Austria, it did not stop the AO's work there. The Austrian police observed AO agents in Vienna operating through the League of German Citizens to spy on German tourists in Austria. It was also learned that the League was sending Austrian HJ boys to Germany for training in propaganda activities, espionage, and opposing the Schuschnigg regime.[34] In addition, older Germans in Vienna were rounded up by the League when they failed to display the swastika flag outside their homes on national holidays; they were told that they were not being loyal to the Fatherland and that their names were being recorded in Germany so that punishments could be handed out when the *Anschluss* came. The AO also co-ordinated the youth club of the League, stressing to the young people the weaknesses of the Weimar Republic, Schuschnigg government, and Catholic Church.

An economic group in the League placed representatives on the executive committee of the German-Austrian Chamber of Commerce and removed Austrian firms from trade with Germany that did not have a favorable "national or racial view" in the Nazi sense. Another aspect of the group's work was infiltrating Austrian businesses with AO agents who could increase German influence in them. Jewish businesses were blacklisted in German newspapers, and Germans were ordered not to trade with such firms or with German and Austrian shops that did business with Jews. The AO's leaders also continued to harass Papen, quibbling with him over such petty things as the seating of party officials at diplomatic receptions.[35]

When the Austrian government protested the AO's ties to the Austrian Nazis, Bohle denied the connection. Traveling at the end of January 1938 to Budapest to confer with the Hungarian government about its approval for the AO to operate a *Landesgruppe* in the country, he gave a major speech that was designed to allay the world's fears about his organization. Addressing the Hungarian Society for Foreign Policy, he maintained that the AO distinguished fully between *Volksdeutschen* and *Auslandsdeutschen*, and that it had nothing to do with the former. He also argued that the NSDAP's groups outside Germany "never and under no circumstances intervene in the internal political relations of foreign states," and that "our groups [abroad] are also not diplomatic or consular representatives."[36]

His statements were aimed not only at luring the Austrians into a false sense of security, but they were an obvious retraction of his blatant assertions of several months earlier. This may also have been part of a move by Bohle away from the radical Austrian Nazi, Leopold (despised by Hitler because of his unwillingness to follow orders from Berlin), toward Seyss-Inquart, whom Bohle had previously opposed. Against the propaganda and subversive circles among the Austrian Nazis, Seyss-Inquart had contacts (through Keppler and Papen) with Hitler, Göring, and Himmler; since mid-

1936 he had worked as a special mediator between the Schuschnigg
government and the national opposition. His aim (and that of his
superiors in Germany) was to legalize the NSDAP by infiltrating
the government with persons who appeared to be moderate nationals and who would push the regime toward accepting the
Anschluss. At the end of 1937, however, Schuschnigg took him into
the government, hoping thereby to divide the pro-*Anschluss* movement while simultaneously cracking down on the illegal Austrian
Nazis.

These steps helped Hitler to conclude that the time was suddenly
ripe to annex Austria. His final preparations began on 4 February
1938, when he removed his military leaders for disagreeing with
him over the Austrian conquest. He also replaced Neurath as Foreign
Minister with Ribbentrop and made several other diplomatic
changes, including recalling Papen from Vienna (and sending him
to Turkey in April 1939).[37] Bohle must have winced at learning
of Ribbentrop's appointment. The two had been bitter enemies,
and Ribbentrop's pretentious attitude seemed far more oriented
toward the career bureaucracy in the AA than toward the NSDAP.
Not only did he want to avoid a feud with the diplomats, but he
disdained the thought of having Bohle, a party rival, in the AA.
Not surprisingly, he named Weizsäcker his Secretary of State,
quickly passing over Bohle, the person many Nazis believed should
have received the post.

Bohle, for his part, believed that Ribbentrop viewed him as a
serious threat. While it is highly dubious that Ribbentrop had a
great fear of his subordinate, Bohle claimed later that Ribbentrop
was envious of his knowledge of the English and angry about
rumors in the foreign press that he wished to become Foreign
Minister. His intense dislike of his new boss also centered around
Ribbentrop's arrogant personality, "We always used to say that he
sort of thought himself, 'Jesus Christ,' that ist [sic], he always gave
that sort of impression."[38] Ribbentrop, on the other hand, despised
even the sight of Bohle in the halls at the *Wilhelmstrasse*. The
two rarely met personally, and after making an appointment, it
took Bohle five weeks to see the Foreign Minister.

The AO leader's demise and subsequent withdrawal from activity in the AA did not become evident for some time. As noted
earlier, he retained partial authority over admitting diplomats to the
NSDAP. A few days after Ribbentrop's appointment, the AO was
able to push through the AA a decree requiring Germans residing

abroad longer than three months to report to their nearest German mission (or risk losing their citizenship). Furthermore, Bohle was still allowed to meet periodically with Hitler, as he did with his father and son on the Führer's birthday.[39]

As the *Anschluss* grew nearer and rumors spread of pending action by Germany, Bernard and his agents in the League of German Citizens in Austria became increasingly brazen in their speeches to Nazi members and German citizens. League meetings became so inflammatory in their demands for a German takeover, in fact, that Bohle was forced to direct Bernard in mid-February 1938 not to cause "internal altercations" that would provoke the Austrian government and attract foreign attention to the delicate Austrian situation.[40] Hitler, following his browbeating of Schuschnigg at Berchtesgaden, forced the Austrian Chancellor to resign on 11 March; that night German troops began occupying Austria, and the *Anschluss* suddenly became a reality.

Ironically, Bohle's dedicated effort in Austria and the absorption of the country into Germany spelled doom for the AO there. Soon after Hitler named Joseph Bürckel the new Commissioner for the NSDAP in Austria, the AO's organization there was dismantled and submerged into seven party districts, each ruled by a *Gauleiter*. Bernard was "retired" and presented by Hitler with the NSDAP's Golden Badge "in recognition of his service to the movement." About the only remaining task for the AO in Austria was its being commissioned by Hitler to enroll in the party Austrian Nazi members in foreign countries and to prepare them for participation in the Greater German plebescite on 10 April 1938 to approve the *Anschluss*.[41]

Losing the administration of the NSDAP in Austria was a hint of what was to come; it was also the first indication of the vulnerability of Bohle's personal position and of the institutional orientation of his organization. From its creation the AO had been a partially successful tool for the NSDAP in spying on German mission officials, spreading propaganda abroad, mobilizing some Germans for the Third Reich, and meddling in the political and economic affairs of other nations. Yet it was unable to handle what was to become the party's most crucial task once Hitler actually began his conquest of Europe: cementing the party's control of the thousands of Germans employed in Nazi-occupied Europe as party functionaries, businessmen, and employees.

Another factor undermining the AO was Germany's rearmament

program, which expanded sharply after 1936. Because of the subsequent labor shortage in German industry, the government, SS, AO, and Gestapo began a concerted effort to repatriate Germans abroad back into Germany. Consequently, the number of Nazi members and German nationals abroad decreased rather significantly, a fact that greatly alarmed Bohle. As the campaign unfolded, the Gestapo examined closely the "political and philosophical reliability" of *Auslandsdeutschen* who returned to Germany through the AO's repatriation camps. Its camp in Munich alone repatriated 3,097 Germans during 1938 and 1939, most being Austrians and Germans from the South Tirol.[42]

Despite the Axis agreement between Rome and Berlin and the personal friendship of Hitler and Mussolini, the NSDAP's operation in the South Tirol was deeply resented by the Italians. Nor had Bohle's efforts, beginning in October 1936 with his trip to Rome to visit with Mussolini and install a new *Landesgruppenleiter*, Ettel, helped to foster Italo-German affection.[43] Despite an agreement among Germany, Austria, and Italy in March 1934 to cooperate on the Tirolean question and despite Italy's granting of several concessions to German schools in the region, tension among German-Austrians and Italians continued. In addition to the VDA's agents in the South Tirol, the AO's groups in Bozen, Meran, and Milan were busy spreading anti-Italian propaganda among local Germans and Austrians. Much of this occurred without Hitler's knowledge and support, and it contributed significantly to the general Fascist mistrust of the Third Reich.[44]

Whatever favors the Italians granted in the Tirol were lost during 1935 in the outcry, stimulated by the *Landesgruppe* Italy, VDA, and DAI, over the drafting of Austrians and Germans from the *Alto Adige* to fight for Italy in Ethiopia. As a solution to the unhappy situation, the Fascist government planned to resettle Tirolean peasant families in Ethiopia, but the project was dumped because of opposition from the Tirol, Catholic Church, and German government. The *Anschluss* of Austria merely inflamed feelings in the Tirol on both sides. It had stimulated gross rumors, started by Nazi party groups in Salzburg, Linz, and Innsbruck that Italy was planning to give the Tirol as a gift to Germany (an idea also encouraged by Mussolini's visit to Germany in September 1937). On the other hand, during the spring of 1938 the Italians made known their wish to resolve the problem by hinting to Berlin that Germans there could be transferred to Germany.

But during the high-level discussions on the Italian suggestion,[45] the NSDAP worked at cross-purposes with its government by continuing through the *Landesgruppe* Italy and VDA to encourage reckless pro-German demonstrations in the Tirol and clashes between Germans and the Fascist police. Not only was the AO shipping Austrians and Germans from the Tirol to Germany, but its branches in Bozen and Meran and the German Consul General in Milan, Bene, distributed relief money to elderly and unemployed Austrians and disseminated propaganda that attacked Italy's control of the Tirol. In Bozen a large gathering of Germans sponsored by the *Ortsgruppe* to celebrate Hitler's birthday was disrupted by Fascist party members, and order was restored only by the police. A young German in nearby Cortsch, who made the mistake of hollering "heil Hitler" to a passing auto that sported a swastika emblem, was beaten and shot by angry Fascists. Bene reported to Berlin in April that the situation had worsened considerably, and he complained that the Fascist prefect of Bozen, Giuseppe Mastromattei, was "an industrious hater of Germans."[46]

Such problems may have been partly responsible for Hitler's visit in early May 1938 to Rome and for his discussions with Mussolini. Prior to the trip the AO helped to tighten security for Hitler's entourage by supervising the travel of Germans to Italy, and it arranged for Ettel to stand in the highest possible position in the reception line of the diplomatic corps in Rome. On the latter there was vigorous disagreement between the AO and AA, which was finally settled by Ribbentrop.[47] Although Hitler was mainly concerned with showing to the world his solid alliance with the Duce after the conquest of Austria and with reciprocating Mussolini's visit to Germany, Bohle accompanied him (as did most of the NSDAP's leadership), and one of his speeches was to a large rally of Germans in the Basilica Maxentius.[48]

The highly celebrated visit brought cold comfort to the Italians, and troubles in the Tirol persisted. Although the Axis agreement gained increasing strength over the Sudeten crisis and Munich Conference in September 1938, the Tirol remained an area of tension between Germany and Italy. During the early months of 1939 discussions were held among the AA, VoMi, AO, and Bene about transferring Germans in the South Tirol to Germany. Already the number of Germans wishing to return to Germany was greater than the AO's Repatriation Office in Munich could handle.[49]

In March Hitler ordered Himmler to prepare for the repatriation of thirty thousand South Tiroleans, but before the SS chief could execute the directive, an argument over a German protest march occurred in June in Bozen between the prefect, Mastromattei, and Nazi *Ortsgruppenleiter*, Kauffmann. The affair soon came to the attention of Mussolini, and his resentment forced Hitler to intervene by commanding Kauffmann to return to Germany and Bohle to stop the *Landesgruppe* Italy's provocative activities. The AO also circulated an order from Bormann prohibiting propaganda by party organizations that might aggravate the situation.[50]

At the end of June discussions in Berlin among a German delegation (headed by Himmler and including Bohle) and a group from Italy produced a plan whereby persons of German descent in the Tirol would vote in a plebescite on whether or not they wished to be transferred to Germany. After the conferences, Bene assembled in Bozen and Meran over two hundred leaders from Nazi *Ortsgruppen* in the Tirol, to instruct them on the resettlement proposal. In December, following a formal Italo-German agreement, the plebescite was held, which revealed that ninety percent of the Germans in the Tirol wished to live in Germany.

Much to the anger of the Italians, the *Ortsgruppen* tried to persuade the largest possible number of Germans to move to Germany. Ignoring Bormann's earlier directive, the groups deliberately distorted the terms of the agreement and spread propaganda that played skillfully on such vital issues to local Germans as Pan Germanism, resentment toward Italy, and the prospect of material advantages in going to Germany. Above all, the NSDAP hoped for a mass exodus, creating the impression of a popular vote of loyalty to the Reich on the part of all Germans living abroad. While many Germans in the Tirol were sent to Germany at the end of 1939, only 74,500 of them had been transferred by the summer of 1943, when Hitler exploited the war situation and Mussolini's overthrow to annex the Tirol.[51]

The question of the South Tirol was a barometer of Italo-German relations in the 1930s. It was a constant and principal source of friction between Germany and Italy, which was greatly exacerbated by the Nazi party and its organizations in Italy. Yet, German policy toward the Tirol illustrated not only the sharp conflict between the Axis allies, but between different agencies of the Nazi regime. Despite Hitler's friendship with Mussolini and his declarations that Germany had no claims to the Tirol and despite attempts by the AA to find a suitable agreement with the Italians regarding the region, the party refused to stay out of the matter. Revealing its dearth of diplomatic sense and its stubborn view that all Germans abroad must be united into a worldwide *Volksgemeinschaft*, the party was willing even to undermine the Axis agreement with its agitation and propaganda in the Tirol.

Ironically, it was toward Italy, Hitler's most valued ally, that German foreign policy particularly revealed its characteristic dualism and lack of coordination between the government and NSDAP. Nevertheless, the world was led to believe by German and Italian propaganda that the Axis was a powerful alliance that stood ready to bring the triumph of fascism to Europe and the globe. One can only guess whether Hitler was totally ignorant of the NSDAP's work in the Tirol or whether he knew about it and did not care. It was only when the party threatened Germany's friendship with Italy as he was about to go to war that he finally intervened and halted the *Landesgruppe*'s shenanigans in the Tirol.

THE DEBACLE IN THE UNITED STATES AND LATIN AMERICA

As Germany's aggressiveness increased in 1938—first with the *Anschluss* and later the Sudeten crisis—angry reactions to the Nazi party groups abroad mounted. In January the AO was forced by complaints from the Minister-President of Rumania, who contacted Hitler, to stop sending propaganda packets to the Iron Guard, the Rumanian fascist organization. The government of Iran tried to curtail local Nazi affiliates by requiring foreign citizens to sign a pledge not to become "politically" active. Propaganda antics of *Ortsgruppen* in Singapore and Toronto were attacked by local newspapers, which erroneously estimated the size of the AO as running "into millions here and abroad," and predicted that Bohle was soon to become German Foreign Minister. Switzerland, Latvia, and the Union of South Africa announced measures suppressing local Nazi organizations and civil rights of German nationals.[52]

The portrait of the party groups outside Germany as representing a massive organization (or Nazintern) rigidly controlling millions of Germans around the world became increasingly popular in the United States. Among other things, it offered a useful tool that helped liberal leaders and opponents of Nazism in America to arouse further American opinion against Germany. By the end of 1937 the AO was withdrawing what was left of its meager structure in the United States. Mensing had been removed in July when the AO's

Party Court and Nazi members in New York discovered that his wife was part Jewish. He was replaced by one who had led the attack on him, Draeger, the Vice Consul in New York, who supervised membership details and gathered party documents that were kept for protection in the Consulate General.[53]

Bohle, finally admitting in October that Germandom in the United States involved mainly *Volksdeutschen* and not German citizens, suggested to Hess and Neurath that the SS and VoMi take control of party activities in America. He also reorganized the party's leadership there by relying less on Draeger and more on the other German mission officials.[54] But organizational changes were scarcely what concerned the Americans about the NSDAP operating in the United States; instead, they were bothered by Germany's ties to the boisterous and pro-Nazi German American *Bund*, led by Kuhn.

During January and early February 1938 meetings among representatives from the AA, AO, VoMi, and Ministry of Propaganda produced a decision to sever completely Germany's ties to the *Bund*. On 1 March an edict was issued which directed German nationals in America to leave the group, ordered it to stop using NSDAP insignia, and informed Kuhn that should he venture a trip to Germany, he would be received only by the VoMi and would be forbidden to discuss the *Bund* publicly.[55] The reasons for the sharp break with Kuhn were numerous. One was the contempt toward the *Bund* of the German Ambassador to the United States, Dieckhoff (who replaced Luther in March 1937). In countless dispatches to the AA, he warned about the disastrous effects the group and Germany's *Deutschtum* policy were having on American opinion. The split was further stimulated by the investigation of the *Bund's* finances and "un-American" activities by several states, the Federal Bureau of Investigation, and a Congressional Committee headed by the heir to Dickstein, Martin Dies. Following the *Anschluss*, moreover, a new wave of hostility was reported to the AA by Dieckhoff.[56]

Kuhn was horrified at the March edict. To appeal personally against it, he visited Germany, where Fritz Wiedemann (acting for the VoMi) lectured him and commanded him to halt his group's provocative behavior. Anticipating that he would not obey the March directive or Wiedemann, the AO, VoMi, and AA ordered the German consuls in America to undermine Kuhn (while he was still in Germany) by instructing *Auslandsdeutschen* to withdraw from the *Bund*. Germany also stopped all support of the group, except for sending it a limited supply of Nazi literature. After March 1938 the Germans channeled their money and isolationist propaganda through the American Embassy, consulates, German Library of Information, German Railroads Information Office, Transocean News Service, and American Fellowship Forum to a host of Nazi front organizations, isolationist groups, and private individuals working for the German cause.[57]

The Germans were correct about Kuhn; he refused to comply with Wiedemann's command to temper his conduct. But what made German-American relations more critical was the negative reaction of America to the Nazi pogrom against German Jews on the night of 9-10 November 1938, provoked by the murder of embassy official Ernst vom Rath in Paris. The night of broken glass (*Kristallnacht*) was condemned publicly by Roosevelt; shortly thereafter he recalled the American Ambassador from Berlin, and Germany countered by recalling Dieckhoff. American authorities also discovered that German seamen docking at East Coast harbors were engaging in espionage and kidnapping disobedient German-Americans and shipping them to Germany. Gissibl, who had emigrated to Germany and entered the Propaganda Ministry, was discovered in February 1939 advertising in Canada and the United States for Germans with strong ties to the Fatherland to migrate to Germany to help solve the labor shortage. He had also formed, with Bohle's reluctant consent, the *Kameradschaft USA*, a German group for former Nazi members in the United States.[58]

The early months of 1939 marked the beginning of the end for the *Bund* and Kuhn. In January the Dies Committee issued a preliminary report, claiming in sensational fashion that "unless checked immediately, an American Nazi force may cause great unrest and serious repercussions in the United States." The noisy and inconsequential *Bund* (which had less than twenty-five thousand members) was seen as a dangerous Nazi fifth column; as a force (among many) in the deterioration of German-American relations, it was this exciting myth, not the more mundane reality, to which most Americans reacted. But the *Bund* craved the publicity and limelight, and on 20 February it held a large pro-American rally in Madison Square Garden to celebrate George Washington's birthday and compare him to Hitler.

The meeting elicited a storm in the American press against the group, as many journals and newspapers raised serious questions concerning allowing it to continue.[59] The uproar over what Americans believed was a Nazi conspiracy "to instill in the American citizen of German descent a consciousness of the German 'race' and a feeling of allegiance toward the German Reich," finally succeeded in driving the NSDAP out of the United States entirely. In March the AO dissolved its department which handled party affairs in North America, and although Bohle retained contact with Draeger and other consuls until 1941, they were used chiefly for the VoMi and, when the war began, to suppress party members discussing publicly Germany's war aims.[60] However, when Kuhn was suddenly arrested in May 1939 and convicted for embezzling $14,500 from his beloved *Bund*, even the VoMi halted work in the United States.[61] But the damage had been done. The antagonism generated by the confusing German policy toward America and by the NSDAP's adamant refusal to disassociate itself totally from groups like the *Bund* during the 1930s, helped to lay a firm foundation for America's later entry into the war against Germany.

Another element alienating the United States was Germany's continued commercial and political penetration of Latin America. An example was Mexico, where the German government stressed stronger political and economic ties with the Mexican regime, but where the *Landesgruppe* Mexico helped to create a native fascist movement that was hostile to the government, the *Union Nacional Sinarquista* ("National Assembly of the Enemies of Anarchism"). The founders of the right-wing movement, which dedicated itself to fighting Jews and Communists, were Hermann Schreiter, a member of the *Landesgruppe*, and José Urquiza, who had fought for Franco's army in Spain.[62] Except for an attack on the NSDAP by the Guatemalan government and the Venezuelan authorities, party affiliates in Latin America had enjoyed since 1933 considerable freedom to pursue their activities.

But beginning in 1937 and 1938 the Latin Americans reversed sharply their friendly policy toward Germany and its *Landesgruppen*, and in several major states party organizations were banned and their leaders arrested. The clampdown resulted from a combination of forces. Politically the Nazis were undercut by the growing strength of left-wing elements in several countries (e.g., in Mexico and Chile) and by the intervention of Germany in the Spanish Civil War, which impressed on many South Americans the potential danger of German expansion. The *Anschluss* and Sudeten crisis, bound with the noisy and undisguised activity of the AO in

Latin America, reinforced the feeling that the Nazis represented a threat to the South Americans.

Following the Buenos Aires Conference in December 1936, there was also growing pressure placed by the United States on the Latin American nations to force them into a more pro-American and anti-German policy. American aims were helped substantially by the gradual decline of the World Depression, which expanded the economic dependence of most Latin American countries on the United States and robbed fascist groups (like the Nazis) of a portion of their lower-middle-class supporters in Latin America. Yet, while such factors prompted several South American nations to outlaw Nazi *Landesgruppen* and other fascist organizations, none broke off official relations with Germany. What apparently saved Berlin in this respect was Germany's strong trade relations with Latin America, which provided the latter with a market for its raw materials and a source for purchasing armaments and manufactured goods. Such ties also enabled the South Americans to play off the United States and Germany against one another, a policy that generally benefitted the Latin Americans.[63]

Hints of what was about to happen in Latin America came in several of the lesser countries. Anti-Nazi feeling in Chile on the part of the government and the Catholic Church forced the *Landesgruppe* Chile to lessen its support of the native Chilean National Socialist party and to camouflage its activities among *Volksdeutschen* in a new organization, the Colony of Reich Citizens (*Reichsdeutsche Kolonie*). The Nazi-infested *Jugendbund* was dissolved by the authorities, and in September 1938 they threatened to outlaw the NSDAP when it was implicated in a coup against the government.[64] The party's pseudo-withdrawal was also forced in Bolivia, where it created a cover group called the Association of Reich Citizens. In Colombia the *Landesgruppenleiter*, Prüfert, was encouraged by police harassment to move the party's offices in Barranquilla into the German Consulate.[65] Max Reichle, a Nazi member, was imprisoned in Honduras for supplying weapons to a group of generals trying to lead an insurrection against the government. Even in Uruguay, a party stronghold, the friendship that had developed between the *Landesgruppenleiter*, Julius Dalldorf, and the army began dissolving, and the NSDAP was criticized for its control of the German-Uruguayan Youth League.[66]

But the most serious blow to German relations with Latin America came with the ban of the NSDAP in Brazil, where the party had its largest *Landesgruppe* and where German penetration of the government, army, native fascist movements, and economy had been noticeable. American pressure on Brazil against the growing German presence had resulted in February 1937 in the AA ordering its missions in Latin America to activate local Nazi organizations as combatants against Yankee propaganda. On 10 November, however, Vargas suddenly destroyed the constitution and increased his already dictatorial authority over the government. With the aid of the army, he eliminated every real or potential opposition to his rule, and while he had suppressed the Communists since 1935, he now turned against right-wing movements like the Integralists, which were banned in December.

The government also implemented a series of measures to suppress Nazi and Fascist party groups and to expand its policy, begun several years earlier, of promoting a more extensive assimilation of foreign elements into society. Already in May 1937 the *Landesgruppenleiter*, Cossel, had been accused of subversion in the Brazilian Congress by a leftist deputy, Cafe Filho, who demanded an investigation of the party's influence on German-Brazilian youth. Filho's argument received more support when a conflict over leadership of the *Ortsgruppe* Porto Alegre became public and involved both Germans and Brazilians. The new measures hit the Nazis first in southern Brazil, where German schools were ordered to use only the Portuguese and Spanish languages in classrooms, German youth groups were submerged into Brazilian clubs, offices of Nazi *Ortsgruppen* were raided by police, and party leaders were arrested.[67]

Despite repeated assurances by the Brazilian authorities to Cossel and the German Ambassador, Ritter, the NSDAP would not be outlawed, the states of Rio Grande do Sul, Paraná, and Santa Catarina prohibited the party in March 1938. This anti-Nazi tide was impressed personally on Bohle. When his wife visited Brazil to recover from an illness, Ritter warned him, "If your wife travels further to São Paulo, then she will become exhausted with the unavoidable [anti-German] agitation. Rio is also much more interesting and pretty than São Paulo."

The AO halted party mail sent from Germany to Brazil, but on 18 April a presidential decree banned all foreign political activities. Ritter was shocked and angrily protested the law, but with little success.[68] As he informed the AA, Vargas's measures had been prompted by fear of potential political rivals, pressure from the

United States, and the government's belief that the German set- tlements in the south were a serious threat to national security. To these he could have added the influence of Brazilian army planners, who felt threatened by Nazi agents and their propaganda and were determined to force the assimilation of the German and other foreign colonies. Such suspicions were heightened even more when the Integralists, supported by a few naval units, tried to over- throw Vargas on the night of 10-11 May. The uprising, however, was crushed. Rumors circulated that Germans had participated in the fiasco, and in the days that followed, arrests of National So- cialists were made in São Paulo.

Vargas, when pressed by Ritter for proof of Nazi ties to the plot, arrested one of Cossel's key advisers in the *Landesgruppe*, a *Volksdeutsche* named Federico Colin Kopp. A day later Kopp al- legedly committed suicide, but Ritter was told by the police that he had been deeply involved in the conspiracy and that a large cache of documents dealing with the *coup* had been confiscated from him. Kopp was a high official in a pro-German, pro-Integralist, and *Volksdeutsch*-oriented political group called the *Federação 25 de Julho* ("Society of 25 July," formed in 1935 to commemorate the day on which the first German settlers had arrived a century earlier in São Leopoldo). Ritter learned further that Kopp and others were planning another Integralist insurrection in the southern states, with the aim of creating a large state whose government would be friendly to Germany and located in São Paulo.[69]

While Bohle should not have been surprised at what had hap- pened to his prize party organization, he was apparently stunned enough to issue a directive in May through the German missions to the *Landesgruppenleiters* in Latin America. He ordered an im- mediate cessation of "any visible activity" (e.g., parades or public meetings) by Nazi groups and the "separation [of German citizens] from Volksdeutschen" (i.e., the removal of *Volksdeutschen* and Ger- mans with dual citizenship from the party and resignation of German nationals from *Volksdeutsch* political groups). He also commanded the party leaders to begin the "formation of associations of Reich citizens" that could function as cover groups for the party.[70]

But again, as in countless instances before, the authorities recog- nized the nature of the new organizations, and they were not willing to tolerate them. More Germans, particularly editors of the *Deutsche Morgen* in São Paulo, were arrested and jailed, a press campaign against the Nazis ensued, and the police refused to give the German Embassy information on the Germans imprisoned. Bohle, reacting to the pressure, called Cossel to Berlin for discussions with Hess, Ribbentrop, and other officials of the AA. It was decided that the leading party officials in Brazil, to protect themselves and to ensure their freedom to guide the party's underground operations, should be attached to German missions. Cossel returned to Brazil to become the "cultural adviser" to the Embassy, and in the weeks that followed, other party agents were inserted as attaches in the consulates.[71]

Bohle also posed to his government the possibility of reprisals for the arrest of Germans in Brazil; he suggested to Himmler that the SS and police imprison Brazilians in Germany. But this radical idea was quickly vetoed by the AA, which argued that it would destroy completely German-Brazilian relations. The German tactic of infiltrating the missions failed to thwart the Brazilian government; soon the consulates and the Embassy became targets of the authorities. In September 1938 Ritter was declared *persona non grata* because of his aggressive behavior and front activities for the NSDAP; he was recalled to Germany, not to be replaced. The AO remained in contact with Cossel through the Embassy, poured money for propaganda purposes into German newspapers, and encouraged Germans in southern Brazil to migrate to Germany.[72] But the heyday of the NSDAP in Brazil was over.

The crisis in Brazil was viewed with great alarm in the AA, and particularly among German mission chiefs in South America. At the end of July 1938, Ritter, Wilhelm Schoen, Langmann, and Thermann met in Montevideo to discuss the situation. They generally agreed with Bohle's command in May to the *Landesgruppenleiters* ordering the separation of *Auslandsdeutschen* from *Volksdeutschen* in party affairs and the elimination of public activity by the party. They also discussed the issue of Germans in Latin America holding dual citizenship and the strain which the policy (encouraged by the AO) was now placing on German-Latin American relations. Bohle, in a surprising move to support their wishes and reaffirm his May directive, commanded his party leaders abroad not to recruit Germans with dual nationality and not to permit *Volksdeutschen* to remain in the party.[73] The orders represented a major shift in German policy in Latin America. Above all, the AA (and to a lesser extent the AO) wanted to ensure Germany's economic position in Latin America and to preserve the neutrality of the latter in the event of war in Europe. In August Thermann informed the AA that he and his colleagues in Brazil, Chile, and Uruguay were convinced that Germany could not combat the United States politically in South America and that she would have to confine herself to cultivating economic and cultural relations.[74]

But when it came to Argentina, the second largest haven for German citizens and Nazi members abroad, the AO refused to cooperate with the AA. Although there were rumblings among Argentine leaders about following Brazil's example, Bohle was determined not to withdraw in Argentina. As elsewhere, it was not his tactic to compromise or to avoid difficulties, but to encourage them in a mindless fashion. After the catastrophe in Brazil, his position and that of the AO in Germany scarcely needed the embarrassment of an official ban of the party in Argentina. But his refusal to retreat was to bring himself and Germany another disaster equally damaging as that in Brazil.

Even before the Brazilian move, the Justo government in Argentina had become suspicious of German policy; while it did not believe that Germany posed a direct threat to Latin America, it began worrying about Germany's role in the Spanish Civil War, in the growing ideological polarization of the world, and in the rise of extremist ideas in South America. Argentines were also progressively alarmed by the loud and visible activities of the *Landesgruppe* Argentina, which held large youth rallies and nationalist parades with marchers in SA uniforms. In October 1937 the police closed the meeting hall of the Nazi *Stützpunkt* in Eldorado.

While the left-wing press attacked the German annexation of Austria, the *Landesgruppe* did its best to attract more adverse publicity. On 10 April 1938 a party rally in the Luna Park hall in Buenos Aires, attended by twenty thousand persons, ended in violence. Anti-German demonstrations occurred outside, swastika flags were trampled, and windows of nearby German businesses were smashed. When police intervened to restore order, many Nazis and demonstrators were hurt, two persons died, and fifty-one were arrested. The *Argentinisches Tageblatt* gleefully described the fracas, and two weeks later, the government banned the displaying of foreign flags and issued new directives that instructed German schools to fly the Argentine flag, buy maps of Argentina, and offer classes that emphasized national heroes. Then came the startling news from Brazil of the Integralist coup and the arrest of a number of Brazilian Nazis.[75]

The *Landesgruppe* also had internal problems. One of its strongest

supporters, the *Deutsche La Plata Zeitung*, was on the brink of
bankruptcy and close to suspending publication for weeks at a
time, and the *Landesgruppe* was riddled with petty conflicts. The
main quarrel involved the deputy *Landesgruppenleiter*, Alfred
Müller, and Ludwig Rauenbusch, the party court arbitrator. They
had criticized the doctor attached to the German Embassy, Röhmer,
for alleged negligence in examining Germans wishing to migrate to
Germany to serve in the army or Labor Service. They also attacked
Röhmer for not being a Nazi member and for retaining the post of
chairman of the *Deutsche Volksbund*. Röhmer threatened to split
the German community in Buenos Aires by exposing the attack
on him to the press and by taking Müller and Rauenbusch to court
to protect his "honor." The argument thus endangered the *Landesgruppe* by calling its internal discord to the attention of the
Argentine authorities.

Bohle, wishing to avoid such troubles and hoping to continue
the AO's work in Argentina partly through the *Volksbund* (thereby violating his May directive of 1938), ordered a halt to the attack
on Röhmer and the formation of a cover organization, the Association of Reich Citizens, in Argentina. He also persuaded the AA to
replace Röhmer in the Embassy, and he removed the *Landesgruppenleiter*, Küster, who had attracted the suspicion of the authorities
and who was unwilling to cooperate with the *Volksbund*. But such
changes hardly brought peace to the *Landesgruppe*; it quarreled
with Thermann and the Embassy over separating *Volksdeutschen*
from German citizens in party organizations, and it disliked the idea
of forming an Association of Reich Citizens to camouflage its
activities.[76]

Bohle's hardnosed decision not to follow his May directive and
to continue the NSDAP's work through the *Volksbund* brought
sharp disapproval from the AA. Thermann argued that there must be
a total organizational separation of Germans from *Volksdeutschen*
and that the NSDAP must extricate itself completely from the
Volksbund. Bohle responded by sending a representative from the
AO to Buenos Aires to confer with the Ambassador, and later he
and Thermann met at the party rally in Nuremberg. The result was
a compromise, albeit in the AO's favor. Bohle agreed that *Volksdeutschen* and Germans with dual citizenship should be removed
from the NSDAP, but he refused to stop infiltrating the *Volksbund*.
He was also unwilling to pull teachers who were German nationals
out of local *Volksdeutsch* schools. He even moved to make Ther-

mann and the Embassy more cooperative; to the Embassy staff, he added Klingenfuss, who was to serve as Legation Secretary and *Landesgruppenleiter*, and another party man and former official in the *Landesgruppe*, Sanstede, as Press Attache. In addition, he pushed the AA to appoint Brandt, a one-time party leader in Argentina, as a consul in the Embassy.[77]

The Argentine reaction to the Czech crisis and the Munich Conference in September was extremely cynical; few people believed that England and France could avoid war by appeasing Hitler. Amidst stricter measures from the government regarding German schools in Argentina and following the *Kristallnacht*, the *Landesgruppe* drafted a plan which it believed would benefit both Germany and its racial comrades in Latin America. The plan called for the exchange of German Jews for German settlers in Argentina and southern Brazil. But while the project would have helped rid Germany of its remaining Jews and would have brought valuable industrial and farm labor to Germany, the Argentines refused to consider the exchange.

By the beginning of 1939 the Germans were experiencing in Argentina heavy political and economic opposition from the United States, which stressed the alleged threat to South America of a German invasion. German propaganda, which countered with attacks on Roosevelt and with accusations of "Pan Americanism" against the United States, was poorly organized to meet the American challenge. The greatest problem was the complete lack of coordination among the host of German agencies in Argentina (including the *Landesgruppe*, *Volksbund*, and missions) that were distributing propaganda. The net effect on Argentine press and radio was extremely small.[78]

The NSDAP was finally thrown out of Argentina in the spring of 1939, when Müller was arrested and hauled before a court in Buenos Aires for allegedly planning espionage operations and a program for Germany's annexation of Patagonia. The evidence against him was his signature on a supposed despatch from the German Embassy to the NSDAP's Colonial Policy Office. Although he was eventually acquitted of the charges, public opinion was aroused further against Germany, and the government issued a report detailing the activities of the *Landesgruppe* and suggesting that it be suppressed. Müller, on his release, tried in incredible fashion to unify the *Landesgruppe* behind him by publishing a forged letter in *Der Trommler* from President Roosevelt congratulating him on his acquittal. On 15 May the government responded by outlawing all foreign political groups.[79]

Bohle's reaction was hardly unique; he ordered the creation of an underground *Landesgruppe* with headquarters in the Embassy, promoted Müller to *Landesgruppenleiter*, and arranged for German threats of reprisals against Argentine citizens in Germany. But Ribbentrop had seen enough of the AO's injurious meddling into German affairs in Latin America. Extremely irritated, he was unwilling to allow the *Landesgruppe* to work in the Embassy, he demanded a report from the AO justifying its continued presence in Argentina, and he called for a showdown meeting of leaders from the AO, AA, VoMi, and German missions in Latin America.[80]

The result was the Ibero-American Conference held in Berlin in mid-June, which met amidst the worst foreign attack on the party groups in their brief history. In addition to their expulsion from Brazil and Argentina, they were banned during the summer from Guatemala and Honduras, the press adviser to the *Landesgruppe* Chile was deported for distributing anti-Semitic literature, and party officials were under heavy pressure to leave Iraq, Costa Rica, Australia, and the Philippines.[81] The Conference was significant not only for the impressive array of diplomats and foreign party officials who were present, but for the sharp criticism expressed by both sides against one another. Rarely was the Nazi party so openly attacked inside Germany during the Third Reich as it was by the mission leaders from South America at the meeting. Thermann, Schoen, and even Langmann, a veteran official of the AO, presented scathing indictments of the AO's refusal in Latin America to distinguish fully between German citizens and persons of German descent and the party's unwillingness to obey the commands of the mission leaders.

Bohle, in defending the AO at the meeting, responded by noting that friction between the *Landesgruppen* and foreign governments was inevitable, and he denied that his officials in South America had not agreed or complied with the commands of the mission chiefs. He passionately defended the AO's foreign propaganda, recruitment policies, assigning of party leaders to missions for protection, and anti-Semitic work. Following his adamant stand, Weizsäcker, representing Ribbentrop, tried to summarize the results of the Conference by glossing over the fundamental differences that had been expressed and stressing that they were not as divergent as they appeared.[82]

Although the Conference failed to solve the grave issue confronting both sides (i.e., the interference of the party in foreign policy) and the conflict was allowed to smolder further, Ribbentrop's calling Bohle on the carpet to defend the AO's policies reflected the Foreign Minister's disgust with the AO and his anger at its leader. The Conference also signaled an abrupt end to the AO's attempted penetration of the AA. After July 1939 Ribbentrop closed the Ministry's doors tightly to the AO by permitting only a trickle of AO officials to become diplomats.[83] In this respect, any hope the NSDAP harbored of infiltrating the AA on a large scale was dashed (except, perhaps, for functionaries being chosen from what was left of the *Dienststelle Ribbentrop*), and Ribbentrop's personal vendetta against Bohle, which was to reach its peak in 1941, was unfolding.

PARTY GROUPS IN EASTERN EUROPE: PREPARATIONS FOR GERMAN EXPANSION

Hardly had the party and AA approached a partial compromise over Latin America than the Czechoslovakian crisis reached its peak. At the Munich Conference on 29-30 September 1938, the Western democracies appeased Hitler a final time by permitting the Germans to occupy the bordering Czech territory of the Sudetenland. Hitler's claim to the land was based on the fact that its population was predominantly German and that the democratic Czech government was allegedly persecuting the Sudeten Germans. While the SS, VoMi, VDA, and AA had been the principal German agencies agitating in the Sudetenland for its return to Germany and supporting Henlein's Sudeten German party with money and propaganda,[84] the AO had also been active. Hoping to organize the roughly thirty thousand German citizens and one thousand party members in Czechoslovakia for the same goal, it had constructed an undercover organization in the country since 1933.

During 1935 and 1936 the AA had tried without success to persuade the Czech government to legalize the NSDAP.[85] Several *Ortsgruppen* were led by German consuls in Czechoslovakia, such as Lierau in Reichenberg, who was deeply involved in Nazi penetration of Sudeten German schools and cultural programs with the AA, Propaganda Ministry, and German Legation in Prague. Lierau smuggled propaganda to Henlein's movement, staunchly supported the radicals in the Sudeten German party who demanded union with Germany, and undermined the moderate wing of the party that concerned itself with the protection and unity of the German minority. The objective was to radicalize the movement and Sudeten German community and bring massive pressure against the Republican government of Eduard Beneš. The *Ortsgruppen* also held "indoctrination sessions" to train party members in such tasks, and the locals drafted lists of Germans and Czechs who were hostile to Germany.[86] This work did not go unnoticed by the government, and at the beginning of 1937 numerous Germans were arrested and deported from the country.[87]

Reacting to the expulsions, the German government renewed its pressure on Prague to legalize the NSDAP, and when Beneš refused, the AO, AA, and Reich Ministry of the Interior began planning reprisals against Czech nationals in Germany (e.g., imprisoning them and confiscating their property). Although Bohle had a cordial discussion in November with the Czech Minister to Berlin, Vojtech Mastny, about legalizing the party, the German government soon began the ugly reprisals at the urging of the AO and SS. The countermeasures brought Bohle into a sharp conflict with Ernst Eisenlohr, German Minister in Prague, who demanded they be stopped. Eisenlohr also enraged Bohle when he reported to the AA that Beneš sincerely desired to improve the situation of the Sudeten Germans and that German pressure on the Czech government could only arouse fear and hatred in Prague; this, he claimed, would work to the detriment of the German minority. Eisenlohr's warning (which was repeated on several occasions) fell on deaf ears, except for Bohle, who complained about him to Ribbentrop with the hope of having the Minister dismissed. In a lengthy memo to Ribbentrop of 1 April 1938, he argued that Eisenlohr was too friendly with Beneš, that the Minister had done nothing to further Germany's cause in the Czech press, and that he had opposed the reprisals. But apparently Bohle's fury was ignored, as were Eisenlohr's warnings, because the Minister remained at his post until September.[88]

The final stage of the Czech crisis began following the *Anschluss* and Henlein's secret visit to Berlin at the end of March; at that time he received directions from Hitler to step up his attack on the Czech government and to bring chaos to Czech politics. The NSDAP groups in the Sudetenland contributed to the intense emotional atmosphere by helping party, SA, and SS outposts on the Czech-Austrian border plant rumors that German troops would soon march into Czechoslovakia. But if the groups engaged in rumor-mongering, they refused to be a part to arming the special fighting units of Sudeten Germans that were formed at the beginning of April; consequently, the units turned for weapons to SS formations inside the German border. At the end of May, amidst increasing rumors of German troop movements toward the Czech border that produced a sudden diplomatic crisis, Hitler ordered the German army to prepare to attack Czechoslovakia on 1 October. In the days that followed, an invasion was forestalled only by appeasement at the Munich Conference.[89]

The incorporation of the Sudetenland into Germany in October 1938 paved the way for the complete destruction of Czechoslovakia the following March. Although Bohle dissolved the party organization in the Sudetenland, his groups were allowed to operate freely in the remainder of the Czech state, and a special committee was formed in the AO to assist the German government in redrawing (according to the Munich Agreement) Czech frontiers so that all Germans who wished could become a part of the Third Reich.[90] Ribbentrop and the AA widely publicized the NSDAP's activities in the rump Czech state, aiming thereby at concealing a vital railroad pact between the Germans and Czechs in January 1939 that permitted the passage of German troops through Czech territory. The publicity was also directed at deflecting attention away from reports that Hitler was planning another surprise for Europe in mid-February or early March. On 15 March the rumors sadly turned to fact; Germany occupied the remainder of Czechoslovakia and created the German Protectorate of Bohemia and Moravia and the "protected" state of Slovakia. A week later the Nazis seized Memel, a German city given to Lithuania after World War I. Hitler proudly announced to Memel Germans when he arrived on 23 March, "I bring you back into that homeland which you have not forgotten and which has never forgotten you."[91]

Already in February Bohle had reorganized the party groups in Bohemia and Moravia and named Richard Ziessig, a well-paid *Landesgruppenleiter* (1300 marks per month), to rule them. But on the heels of the creation of the Reich Protectorate, Hitler issued a decree directing that it be divided into four rigidly policed party districts, each with its own *Gauleiter* to administer the NSDAP's organization and German citizens. Subsequently, Bohle relieved his officials throughout Czechoslovakia from their positions, and as with Austria, he and the AO found themselves sacrificed to Hitler's plans for expansion.

The disappearance of Czechoslovakia as a free nation suddenly awakened the Western democracies and the world to the fact that Hitler's demands for *Lebensraum* could not be satisfied. Neville Chamberlain, the British Prime Minister, inaugurated a sharp change in England's foreign policy: a wide and binding commitment would be undertaken in eastern Europe, and especially toward Poland and Rumania.[92] Nazi party groups in Rumania, led by Konradi, had erected such close ties with the native fascist Iron Guard and agitated so aggressively (with Pan German propaganda) among the large *Volksdeutsch* minority that the king of Rumania asked Hitler to recall Konradi. The latter's agents spied on Rumanian officials and the German Ambassador, Wilhelm Fabrizius, and Konradi carried on a personal campaign to discredit anti-Nazi churches among the Germans.[93]

But even before the Czech crisis had ended, some Europeans had tried singlehandedly to avenge Hitler's brutality. On the morning of 7 November 1938 a third-rate German Embassy official in Paris, Ernst vom Rath, was shot to death by Herschel Grünspan, a young Polish-German Jew, whose family had been driven from Germany by Nazi anti-Semitism. Hitler used the murder as a pretext for the riot against German Jews (the *Kristallnacht*) two days later, and Bohle exploited it for propaganda purposes by arguing at Rath's funeral that the diplomat had been the "victim of Jewish-Bolshevist murderous schemes abroad."[94]

As Bohle discovered, however, the anti-Jewish riot hurt Germany's prestige abroad and brought a flood of protest telegrams from foreign Germans to the AO. Yet he ruthlessly ordered his officials in Berlin to boycott Jewish businesses, and acting on orders from Göring and the Four-Year-Plan, the AO collected information from its groups abroad on damages done to foreign Germans because of the riot. Not surprisingly, the material was used as justification for the further persecution of the German Jews.[95]

The anxiety building in Europe by the late spring of 1939 and the determination of England and France to stand firm against further German aggression were illustrated by the suppression of the Nazi *Landesgruppen* in both countries. The *Landesgruppe* France, with its headquarters in Paris and local groups in cities like

Marseilles, Nice, Bordeaux, Lyons, Le Havre, and Lille, was officially dissolved by a French law limiting foreign political organizations. The German Ambassador, Welczeck, and the new *Landesgruppenleiter* of France, Ehrich (who had replaced Rudolf Schleier
in July 1938), quickly camouflaged the party within a German cultural association in Paris called the *Deutsche Gemeinschaft* ("German Community"). In addition, the twelve leading officials of the
party in Britain (including Karlowa) were expelled.[96]

These setbacks more than overshadowed the wave of publicity
in Germany that was showered on the AO for its participation in
the Spanish Civil War, which had recently ended with Franco's
victory. The AO gave a hero's welcome in Berlin to the Condor
Legion, to which the Spanish Ambassador to Germany and leaders
of the Falange were invited. Franco later awarded his government's
highest medal of honor to Bohle and several other Nazi leaders
for their role in the war.[97] But the success in Spain was not enough
to compensate for the AO's fiascos in the Americas and elsewhere.
Considerable authority over foreign Germans (and even over the
AO) had passed by mid-1939 to Himmler's SS, and particularly
to the VoMi. In addition to using party officials abroad as intelligence
agents to spy on mission leaders and foreign Germans suspected
of being unfaithful to Germany, the SS undercut the NSDAP's
activity among foreign Germans by developing *Volksdeutsch* political groups around the world administered by the VoMi.[98]

The most important of these groups were in Yugoslavia, Latvia,
Lithuania, Memel, Poland, Rumania, Czechoslovakia, Slovakia,
Hungary, and the Carpathian-Ukraine region, where the SS hoped to
use the large German minorities as pawns in Hitler's military expansion for *Lebensraum*. Similar groups had been created in Belgium, Denmark, and France (Alsace-Lorraine), and the VoMi had
contacts (thanks in part to the AO) with *Volksdeutsch* leagues in
Argentina, Chile, Paraguay, Canada, Southwest Africa, Australia,
the Netherlands East Indies, and the United States. Bohle, except
for quarreling with the leader of the VoMi, Werner Lorenz, over his
criticism of the competency of AO officials (such as Klingenfuss),
did nothing to challenge his rival.[99]

Another area where the VoMi had asserted its power over foreign
Germandom involved the resettlement in Germany of Germans
abroad. By the spring of 1939 Germany needed at least 800,000
more laborers to ensure the succes of its rearmament program. Consequently, the VoMi, AO, AA, and German police were ordered

into high gear to encourage Germans abroad to return home. Sometimes, the campaign included the use of force, blackmail, and extortion against the Germans. The AO informed a German professor in Istanbul that his Reich citizenship would be revoked if he did not persuade his son (who lived in the United States) to return to Germany for duty in the Labor Service and army. In July the role of the *Landesgruppenleiters* was increased in decisions regarding which *Auslandsdeutschen* were to be deprived of their nationality.[100]

While the Germans were busy repatriating their countrymen, Hitler pushed Europe nearer to war by securing Germany's eastern frontier through the signing of a nonaggression pact on 24 August with his archenemy, Russia. According to the agreement, eastern Europe from the Baltic Sea to Rumania was to be divided between Germany and the Soviet Union; but above all, Hitler had made full preparations for invading Poland, conquering the western half of the country, and returning to Germany the roughly one million *Volksdeutschen* there. The pact was absolutely necessary to his plans, because it ensured him the neutrality of Russia during the attack and the isolation of Poland.

The Nazis, employing their usual combination of propaganda and political pressure, had controlled the Danzig government since May 1933.[101] Hitler's justification for invading Poland lay not only in his demands for uniting Danzig with Germany, but for the return of the Polish Corridor to Germany and for a halt to the alleged persecution by the Poles of the *Volksdeutsch* minority. When World War II began, the AA published documents, which, according to Ribbentrop, revealed "Poland's systematic campaign of extermination against Germans in Poland and Danzig" and established clearly "the irrefutable and proven fact that England, and England alone is responsible for the war" because it supported Poland.[102]

Such claims were untrue,[103] but while Hitler publicly grieved over the alleged ill-treatment of Germans in Poland, the NSDAP, AA, and VoMi contributed to inflaming internal divisions and hatreds among Poles and Germans. As noted previously, party groups had existed in Poland since 1931, working amidst minority organizations like the Polish-sanctioned *Deutsche Vereinigung* and the pro-Nazi *Jungdeutsche Partei*; by June 1937 the *Landesgruppe* Poland administered 6,500 German citizens and 1,400 Nazi members. Large regional affiliates of the *Landesgruppe* existed in Warsaw, Thorn, Posen, and Kattowitz. Under the supervision of Burgam, the party leader and Vice Consul at the German Embassy in Warsaw, the party distributed radical literature to arouse German emotions against the Poles, and it encouraged *Volksdeutsch* enthusiasm for union with Germany by dominating German schools and pastors.[104]

The party's leaders in Poland were often trained functionaries imported for periods of time from Germany, which was observed by the Polish government and resulted at the end of 1937 in the deporting of Germans and canceling of passports of suspected party officials. The *Landesgruppe* responded by asking the AO to have reprisal measures initiated against Poles in Germany.[105] After the conquest of Czechoslovakia in March 1939 and Bohle's naming of a new *Landesgruppenleiter*, Ewald Krummer, the NSDAP expanded its work. Party leaders were attached to consulates for protection, and the *Landesgruppe's* attention turned toward organizing a system for protecting Germans when the Reich invaded Poland.[106]

Following 23 May, as Hitler instructed his generals that war with Poland was "inevitable," the army began distributing through the *Landesgruppe* material on protection from gas attacks and air raids to the Germans. Provisions were also made to keep German refugees fleeing to Germany from blocking Polish streets and roads that were to be used by German troops, and the *Landesgruppe*, AO, and German police constructed "receiving camps" on the Polish-German border to administer the refugees. During July and August the system started to operate as Germans were evacuated. But when some of them wished to return to Poland, the Poles disapproved, suspecting that the refugees had been schooled in espionage, propaganda, and sabotage activities. The Polish authorities also uncovered a training center of this nature, conducted by the *Jungdeutsche Partei*, in Kattowitz and other districts.[107]

Another task was to prepare for the occupying of vital political and economic positions in Poland with "tested party comrades from the Old Reich" who would enter Poland after the invasion. Lists detailing such posts were drafted, and arrangements were made for officials in the *Landesgruppe* to govern Germans who remained in Poland until new party, police, and government institutions could be established by the Nazis to rule the country. These and other projects were financed by the AO and AA, which funneled money to the *Landesgruppe* through the Embassy in Warsaw.[108]

Germans in Poland were also to participate in the invasion. To aid the advancing German army, they were to avoid being mobilized in the Polish military, and instead join the Reich's forces; prevent the Poles from destroying bridges and highways; and sabotage "Polish rear communications." They were further directed to paralyze the movement of Polish troops by blocking roads, employing terror, circulating false information about German troop movements, spreading panic among Polish civilians, and starting fires. When the Germans attacked, such spies "commanded key positions in the communications as well as in other fields."[109]

Bohle, too, did his part to hasten the destruction of Poland. On 21 August, addressing a gathering of lawyers in Danzig, he became one of Hitler's propaganda mouthpieces on Poland by accusing the Poles (with material gathered by the AA and cleared through Weizsäcker) of committing intolerable excesses against Germans which could not go unchallenged by Germany. He mentioned nothing of his political and propaganda organization in Poland, which was feverishly preparing for the German attack. Hardly had he returned to Germany when the Nazi-Soviet pact was announced, and he was ordered by the AA to command the *Landesgruppe* Poland to "destroy without delay all party documents." At all costs, when the invasion came, there was to be no evidence left that could incriminate Germany. Two days later Reich citizens in Poland, England, and France were directed to find the "quickest way" to Germany, and arrangements were made between the Italian government and *Landesgruppe* Italy to permit the free transportation of Germans to the German border.[110] The calamity was about to begin, and ironically, in light of what the war was to bring Germany, Bohle argued that the *Auslandsdeutschen* "stand loyal and determined behind the Reich" and that they were not foreign troublemakers because they had "everything to lose by war."[111]

6

WAR IS "A PATRIOTIC DUTY TAKEN FOR GRANTED," 1939-1945

Early on the morning of 1 September 1939, Germany invaded Poland; World War II had begun. It was to be the most destructive conflict in history and the most debasing event ever to confront the human spirit. Two days later, England and France tried to save Poland by declaring war on Germany, but soon Poland lay conquered and divided by Germany and Russia. Hitler's war machine turned toward western Europe in the spring of 1940, smashing Norway, Denmark, Holland, Belgium, Luxemburg, and France. The Nazi armies appeared unstoppable.

Wherever Germans marched in Europe they were greeted as saviors by the small Nazi party groups and by Germans who were sympathetic to the Fatherland. Germans abroad often found their lives changed dramatically by the war; they were asked to make great sacrifices of life and property, tolerate persecution from foreign authorities, and give up much of their freedom to wartime directives of the NSDAP. After a meeting in Berlin in October 1939 of *Landesgruppenleiters* from Europe, foreign Germans were instructed that they must engage in "propaganda activity for the German cause" and "counterespionage." "As always," they were told, "it is of decisive importance to know where the enemy stands and what he does."[1]

The most pressing tasks facing the AO were evacuating Germans in Poland and the Baltic states who were threatened by Russia's advance into eastern Europe, and supervising Russian and German seamen who were shipping goods and war materiel between their nations as a by-product of the Nazi-Soviet agreement. When Russian ships and crews began docking in German harbors and vice versa, Bohle and the Seafarer Section were at a loss as to how to react to the Communists. After seeking advice from Count Friedrich von der Schulenberg, the German ambassador to Russia, they gave strict orders to German seamen not to mix with their Soviet counterparts or to enter seamens' clubs in Russian harbors, because they were "propaganda places for Bolshevism."

Yet Bohle could not resist the temptation to seek control of the large number of German officials who were entering Russia in conjunction with the Nazi-Soviet pact. Since the AO had been unable to find a viable pretext for building an NSDAP organization in Russia, he now saw a key opportunity to form a German community in Moscow according to "principles of the party." Apparently, his only contact in Russia was the naval attache at the German Embassy in Moscow, Baumbach, who sent him reports on other German diplomats in the Soviet Union. Consequently, the AO argued to Hess that it must administer the visas to Russian-bound officials to ensure "their suitability for party work" there and to recall the "unsuitable elements" (i.e., nonparty members) from Russia. But while Bohle was secretly conspiring to send agents to Russia, he publicly courted the Soviets (in keeping with Hitler's policy at the moment) by thanking them for treating German seamen well while they were in Russian ports.[2]

In anticipation of the Soviet takeover of the Baltic states and Finland, the AO (along with other agencies like the VoMi) hurriedly evacuated Germans from both regions. The project was well executed. Rescue ships sailed from Danzig to harbors in Estonia and Latvia, where German mission officials secured the free departure of Germans and their property. Helping the mission leaders were special commissions, comprised of functionaries from the AO and VoMi. These decided which Germans should be allowed to emigrate and what property should be left behind. In charge of transporting the Germans out of Lithuania was Stegmann, *Ortsgruppenleiter* of Kaunas, who shipped several thousand Germans (including *Volksdeutschen*) out of the country through Eydtkau to Königsberg. To guide the evacuation of Germans in Finland, Bohle sent Ehrich; the last ship loaded with refugees to leave Helsinki sailed on 6 December, two days after the Russian invasion and beginning of the "winter war." A large number of Baltic Germans, once they were processed through receiving camps operated by the VoMi and AO, were resettled in Poland.[3]

Resettling and recruiting foreign Germans for the war effort quickly turned into a brutal business, because the Germans and other nationalities became helpless pawns in the game of power that was unfolding. Nazi members abroad came under particularly close surveillance, and some, like Cornelius Schwarz, the *Landesgruppenleiter* of Palestine, and fifty members of the party in Cuba, were imprisoned. Bohle immediately demanded reports from German missions regarding the treatment of *Auslandsdeutschen* by foreign authorities, and these were used by the AO to push for reprisal measures against foreign citizens in Germany.

The AO, in fact, became the chief agency in Germany for ordering reprisals against citizens of enemy and neutral nations. As German citizens were threatened with expulsion from Hungary, the AO and SS, rejecting a more conciliatory policy advocated by the German Embassy in Budapest, drafted lists of Hungarian nationals in Germany who were to be imprisoned.[4] Following the imprisonment by Egypt of officials of the *Landesgruppe* (including the *Ortsgruppenleiter* of Port Said, Bernard Rensinghoff), who worked as camouflaged bureaucrats in German consulates, Germany retaliated by banning the departure of Egyptian citizens and detaining personnel of the Egyptian Legation.

But the AO was not satisfied. During 1941, responding to a report that Germans were still in prison in Egypt, Bohle proposed to Weizsäcker that Egyptians in occupied France be arrested, and he compiled a list of 283 candidates in Paris available for the retaliation. Reflecting his closed mind on the issue of reprisals, he maintained in a short wave broadcast to foreign Germans in December 1941, "It is contrary to the German nature to make war on civilian persons and against women and children, and to confiscate and destroy their goods and property." Eventually, German citizens moving to Germany were required to have in their possession special "political judgments" signed by their *Landesgruppenleiter*, which enabled German authorities to decide which returnees could be trusted to work in sensitive war industries.[5]

The war also brought to the surface the old enmity between the AO and AA, and it provided Ribbentrop with an opportunity to persuade Hitler to make a firm decision on the authority of the AA and AO in matters concerning foreign Germans. Already on 3 Sep-

tember Hitler issued a decree whereby offices of the state and party
abroad were placed under the strict jurisdiction of the German
mission chiefs. While some mission leaders quickly demanded a
declaration of loyalty from their *Landesgruppenleiters*,[6] the party
leaders lodged complaints against their superiors by continuing to
file monthly reports with the AO. Some diplomats took advantage
of the new decree to ban party work, as Papen did in Turkey.[7]

Ribbentrop himself sniped at Bohle's position. He ordered the
AO not to dispatch regular circulars to its leaders abroad, because
valuable information might be intercepted by the enemy, and he
demanded that *Landesgruppenleiters* be approved by himself or
Weizsäcker. By the beginning of 1940 Bohle quietly admitted that
"a change in my position" in the AA was "creeping in." His orders
to diplomatic missions, in contrast to his directives in 1937 and
1938, now dealt with mundane items such as the duty of diplomats
and foreign party leaders to give aid to needy Germans and to
collect for the Winter Relief program.[8]

Ribbentrop also moved to capture sole control of wartime propaganda distributed abroad, a job coveted especially by Bohle, Goebbels, and agencies in the SS and police. As Bohle met in Berlin with
Landesgruppenleiters from Europe on 7 September 1939 to discuss
propaganda, Hitler issued another decree which granted the AA
(and thereby Ribbentrop) the authority to clear for distribution all
foreign propaganda from government and party organizations. The
decree shocked Bohle and angered Goebbels, but it reflected Ribbentrop's great favor with Hitler (which declined as the war pro-
gressed and as military decisions overrode diplomacy) and the
Foreign Minister's emphasis on propaganda as a tool of foreign policy and war.

Since the NSDAP considered its brand of fanatical propaganda
vital to the control of Germans outside Germany, it was almost
inevitable that a bitter quarrel would ensue. Goebbels, Bohle, and
the *Landesgruppenleiters* complained vigorously that "not enough
quick and driving propaganda" was processed through the AA,
and that the Ministry, with its more subtle and sophisticated material, should have no authority over the party's propaganda sent
to foreign Germans and party branches. In August 1940 the party
leaders allied against Ribbentrop by coordinating their foreign
propaganda through a new Reich Propaganda Office for Foreign
Countries (*Reichspropagandaamt Ausland*, or RPA), whose chief
was an AO movie producer from Uruguay, Felix Schmidt-Decker.[9]

The RPA plunged into its work as though the AA never existed. Drawing liberally on the resources of the Propaganda Ministry and NSDAP, it used every instrument known to the Nazis to flood Germans and party groups abroad with political information—party speakers, brochures, books, films, phonograph records, film projectors, radio receivers, pictures, calendars, newspapers, and swastika flags.[10] Much of the RPA's propaganda, which was oriented toward the European party groups, focused on Germany's alleged war aims. The *Landesgruppe* Italy, receiving material from the RPA, instructed its subordinate leaders to stress to local Germans that the Western Powers had wanted the war for a long time to gain the "removal of the Führer and his movement" from Germany, the "disarmament and pauperization of the German people," and the "recovery of a situation whereby Germany will be the plaything of foreign powers." The Germans were also told that Hitler's foreign policy, on the contrary, was designed solely "to secure the vital rights of Germans" against foreign attack, and that Germans were "to confide blindly in the Führer and to follow him without hesitation." Foreign Germans were also forbidden to "second guess" Hitler among themselves and foreigners, " 'Armchair war aims politics' only present our enemies with the opportunity to impute to us views and objectives that must call forth to the end the mistrust of other peoples in our policy."[11]

The one-sided and blatant propaganda of the party and the formation of the RPA aroused such antagonism from Ribbentrop that he demanded a showdown with Bohle. At a meeting of their staffs in early December 1940, Ribbentrop spoke for three hours, bitterly denouncing Bohle and declaring that there was only one AA in Germany and not two. He insisted that the reports which Bohle received from his *Landesgruppenleiters* be channeled to the AO through the AA. Another matter discussed was limiting Bohle's remaining authority over promotions and appointments in the Ministry; although the AO's power was minimal (except on the issue of party membership for diplomats), Ribbentrop believed otherwise, and he detested even its smallest input. After the meeting, Bohle appeared "very seldom" at his office in the *Wilhelmstrasse*, and he asked Hess to support him and to insist to Hitler that the AO remain controlled by the party and not by the AA.[12]

Although the war had not yet engulfed all of Europe, the party groups outside Germany at the beginning of 1940 were already feeling the effects of the conflict. Party members and Germans were imprisoned in enemy nations such as France, England, Belgium, Sweden, South Africa, and Southwest Africa. The office of the *Landesgruppe* Uruguay was bombed, prompting the AO to dissolve its organizations there and in Paraguay, and place their underground development in the hands of German mission chiefs (e.g., Langmann). Most of the major party organizations in Latin America, therefore, had been banned or officially dissolved by mid-1940.[13]

But if an *Auslandsdeutsche* managed to avoid prison or persecution by a foreign government, he was hardly a free person. His activities were supervised from Germany by directives from Bohle, which were issued through German missions. He was strictly prohibited, for instance, from associating with his foreign or non-German friends abroad, and he was forbidden to discuss Germany's territorial annexations in the war.[14] The *Landesgruppen* played an equally vital role. Like the NSDAP inside Germany, they dominated their members and other Germans through a combination of threats to harm relatives in Germany and propaganda. Propaganda was used by the *Stützpunkt* Kunming in China in February 1940 to silence defeatism and discontent among local Germans; party officials in Switzerland were commanded by the *Landesgruppe* to ensure that "every German racial comrade" acted as "a mirror of the invincible strength of Germany."[15]

Nazi members, if they disobeyed their party leader or were suspected of being unwilling to give themselves body and soul to Germany's cause, were subject to expulsion from the NSDAP by the AO's Party Court. Unfortunately, when a foreign member was expelled, he lost much more than his party membership. He automatically lost his German citizenship and contact with relatives and friends in Germany, because members who refused to cooperate actively in the war violated, in Bormann's words, "the interests of the party" and the state, and they were "to be punished by the Party Courts."[16]

In most respects, however, party work outside Germany was carried on in a normal fashion. Agents abroad representing the AO's Foreign Trade Office camouflaged foreign subsidiaries of I. G. Farben and other German firms to prevent them from being closed down. *Landesgruppenleiters* prohibited German citizens abroad from buying in Jewish stores; Viktor Friede, the Commissioner for Questions on Reich Citizens in Turkey, sent a blacklist of such stores to the German Embassy in Ankara, and he asked the Embassy to inform German nationals in Turkey accordingly.[17]

The party organization that maintained the most ordinary life was the *Landesgruppe* Spain. Its leader was Hans Thomsen, a well-traveled naval officer, who mixed liberally in politics and espionage. Eberhard von Stohrer, the German Ambassador in Madrid, who was allegedly sympathetic to the Nazis, complained loudly of the "frequently incorrect information" collected by the *Landesgruppe* about himself and other political figures in Spain and sent to Berlin.[18] But the central conflict separating Stohrer and the AA from the *Landesgruppe* was the question of Spain's entry into the war. Following Franco's refusal to join in a proposed German-Spanish assault against the British stronghold at Gibraltar at the beginning of 1941, the Germans became divided over their policy toward Spain. The AA and Stohrer favored Germany's continuing to trade its military, political, and economic support of Spain for the latter's raw materials and bases for German submarines. However, Thomsen and the *Landesgruppe* insisted on drawing Spain into the war, and to this end Thomsen discussed in 1940 and 1941 with a circle of discontented Falangists and military officers possible German aid to overthrow Franco and create a military dictatorship.

The peak of the conspiracy came in the spring of 1941, when Thomsen and Bernhardt met with the anti-Franco colonel, Antonio Aranda Mata, and a representative from an opposition group led by the general Emilio Tarduchy. Thomsen further arranged (without the knowledge of the German Embassy in Madrid) for Spanish leaders to visit Germany and confer with Goebbels, Ley, and other party officials. The *Landesgruppenleiter* also pushed for the formation of the Blue Division, a Spanish unit comprised of fanatical Falangists who fought alongside the German army against Russia. At the end of 1941, Thomsen spent two months on the eastern front, apparently with the Division. The anti-Franco machinations eventually came to nothing, mainly because Hitler did not support them actively (fearing their failure and accepting Spanish neutrality more than the forced entry of Spain into the war) and because Franco arrested or exiled the ranking conspirators.[19]

INVASIONS, INTELLIGENCE WORK, AND THE "NEW ORDER"

On 9 April 1940 Hitler suddenly ended the uneasy *Sitzkrieg* ("phony war") in western Europe by conquering Norway and Denmark; a month later his armies blitzed the Netherlands, Belgium, Luxemburg, and France. On 17 June one of the world's most powerful nations, France, requested an armistice from him, and soon the Nazis occupied Paris and northern France while the German puppet government of Vichy ruled the south. As Hitler tried to bomb England into submission in the ensuing months, he halted his armies on the continent to give his administrators in the newly conquered lands time to consolidate Nazi power. Plans for the "New Order," designed by Germany to exploit Europe economically and politically, began to unfold. A year later Hitler expanded the war to southeastern Europe and Russia, a move which added to the New Order but also proved to be Germany's downfall and his own destruction.

The *Landesgruppen* in Norway and the Netherlands contributed to the German invasions of both countries. Bohle later noted that aiding advancing German troops was considered by the NSDAP to be "a patriotic duty taken for granted."[20] In Norway the *Landesgruppe* helped to camouflage the landing of German troops. Coordinating efforts with the Seafarer Section and German High Command, it concealed for several days prior to the attack on 9 April the presence of German troops aboard German freighters docked in Norwegian harbors. Already in September 1939 the *Landesgruppe* (on orders from Berlin) had increased its staff sharply; Karl Spanaus, its leader, recruited Germans who were highly familiar with the culture, language, and geography of Norway. Other Germans, like Hans Wilhelm Scheidt, a correspondent in Oslo for the *Völkischer Beobachter*, were sent from Germany to Norway to work with the party. The aim was to furnish the German army with information on possible targets of attack along the Norwegian coast. The increased staff also spread pro-Nazi propaganda among Norwegians.[21]

As in Poland, the party in Norway assisted the invading German troops by providing officers with translators and lists of foreigners and anti-German Norwegian leaders who were to be arrested. Within hours the Gestapo began mass arrests and deportations, many of whose victims were identified by the *Landesgruppe* and included Germans who had fled to Scandinavia after 1933 and supported from there the German resistance to Hitler inside the Reich. In Oslo, when a rumor gripped the city on 9-10 April that an English air attack was imminent to repel the Germans, the party feverishly squashed the report in the streets and prevented panic that would have slowed the work of the German troops. Once the army had arrested several hundred English and French in Norway (and Denmark), Bohle urged Ribbentrop to exchange them for Germans being held prisoners by the British.[22]

But the shabby espionage of the *Landesgruppe* Netherlands gave the Dutch ample warning of the invasion of their country. A few days after the attack on Norway police in The Hague discovered a thick envelope lying in a street. It contained photocopies of highly classified Dutch military documents that were being sent through the mail by Otto Butting, the *Landesgruppenleiter* of the Netherlands and member of the German Legation, to the AO. Similarly, the Nazi *Ortsgruppenleiter* in Amersfoort, Sommer, was arrested on charges of espionage.

When the Dutch government presented the envelope and Sommer's case to the perplexed German Minister in The Hague, the latter received an admission from Butting that he had used the party organization in the Netherlands to construct a large "military espionage net." When he was asked why he did not send the documents by diplomatic pouch to Germany, he replied that German military intelligence (*Abwehr*) distrusted the AA and forbade him to do so. Both the Dutch and German Minister demanded that Butting leave the country, and he was quickly recalled to Germany. News of the embarrassing episode reached Ribbentrop, who personally directed Bohle to inform the Dutch government that Butting had acted completely on his own, that Bohle was furious over Butting's insubordination, and that the AO was recalling him to Berlin for punishment. But when he returned to Germany, Bohle rewarded his loyalty (and incompetency) by treating him as a hero and appointing him (with Ribbentrop's approval) the party leader for Italy. Yet Butting was not finished in Holland. Following the German conquest of the Netherlands in mid-May, he returned to The Hague under a cover name and sneaked into the Dutch archives to destroy incriminating documents against him. He was quickly expelled by the German army.[23]

At the end of May Bohle tried to strenthen the *Landesgruppe* by dispatching Ruberg to Holland to administer the roughly two thousand party members and 75,000 German nationals there. Ruberg's aim was to establish his authority and make the *Landesgruppe* the supreme civilian agency for Germans.[24] But instead of capturing control of the police and securing the cooperation of the German military authorities for his mission, he concerned himself with petty matters like rationing gasoline to his party groups and conferring medals of honor on German mothers. The AO soon proved itself sadly incapable of converting its well-developed *Landesgruppe* (which had over 102 *Ortsgruppen*) into a structure that could effectively control the thousands of Germans in the Netherlands who were party and government officials, businessmen, and police personnel. Furthermore, Ruberg was rivalled for leadership of the party by Bormann, who sent a special "political commissioner" to Holland, Fritz Schmidt, and by Seyss-Inquart, Hitler's Reich Commissioner for the Occupied Netherlands.

In short, Ruberg failed to transform his propaganda-oriented organization, which was designed to recruit and activate members for the NSDAP, into an institution that could firmly consolidate the party's total control over Germans. Bohle, fearing the *Landesgruppe* would be removed from the AO and placed under Seyss-Inquart, visited the latter in The Hague on 4 June; apparently he even considered turning to Hitler to prevent the loss of his Dutch operation. But he was hardly a match for his powerful superiors. To attain the full integration of government and party activities in the Netherlands, Hess, Bormann, and Himmler created in October 1940 a new regional organization for the country called the *Arbeitsbereich* Netherlands, which was an "activity sphere" of the NSDAP that replaced the *Landesgruppe*. In charge of the *Arbeitsbereich* was Seyss-Inquart, who was presented with the *Landesgruppe* by Bohle in a festive ceremony at the end of October. About the only consolation for the AO was the naming of Bene to the Reich Commissioner's staff and the promotion of Ruberg (who was highly embittered at what had happened) in the SS.[25]

Along with the removal of the AO from the Netherlands, an *Arbeitsbereich* was formed in Poland, and the AO found itself being supplanted in Norway by the Nazi Commissioner, Joseph Terboven, who reduced the authority of the *Landesgruppe* to nothing. A bit later, after Germany's invasion of Russia, a third *Arbeitsbereich* was organized in the Baltic region and the Ukraine under Rosenberg, Commissioner for the Occupied Eastern Territories.[26] Party leaders in the Baltic states, like Henry Esp in Latvia, were recalled by the AO and sent elsewhere in Europe; Esp, for example, became *Landesgruppenleiter* in Hungary.

By the end of 1940 the AO's activity abroad had been limited significantly—the major *Landesgruppen* in Latin America had been dissolved or banned, and the AO had been removed from a large chunk of Europe (including England). Bohle obviously had little choice but to accept the dramatic curtailment of his organization.

He understood that the *Arbeitsbereiche* had been a product of power politics in the Nazi hierarchy. They were directly subordinate to the Deputy Führer's office (especially Bormann), and with Hess's favor with Hitler having already slipped noticeably, Bormann and Himmler pushed for the creation of the *Arbeitsbereiche* and scrambled to control them.[27]

Despite the loss of the *Landesgruppen*, Bohle appeared undaunted. He arranged for the imprisonment of Dutch leaders as a reprisal for the arrest of Germans in the Netherlands East Indies, and he became increasingly involved with Germany's foreign intelligence work. Before the *Landesgruppe* Netherlands was dissolved, it carefully drafted lists of several hundred prominent Dutch, many of whom were arrested by Seyss-Inquart and deported in July to Nazi concentration camps at Buchenwald and Ravensbrück. When Seyss-Inquart allegedly refused to carry out Hitler's order to arrest ten Dutch for every German interned in the East Indies, Bohle protested to Hess and demanded an "eye for an eye" and a "sharp retaliation."[28]

Eventually Seyss-Inquart sent several hundred more Dutch prisoners to Buchenwald. Yet, when many of them died, he made numerous appeals to Bohle for the release of those that remained alive. In August 1942, following the freeing of the Germans in the Dutch East Indies, 220 of the "Buchenwald hostages" were returned to the Netherlands. There the prisoners remained captive, but they were granted leaves to see their families and were allegedly treated more humanely. At the end of the war Seyss-Inquart estimated that roughly one hundred were still behind bars.[29]

As Hitler organized for a massive air attack on England during the late summer of 1940, the AO leadership anticipated (as did most Nazi officials) a quick German victory. Once Bohle received confirmation from Weizsäcker that the German government was making "preparations for the annihilation of England," he and Alfred Hess drafted a set of guidelines for the AO's participation in future peace agreements. Although the English successfully defended themselves in the "Battle of Britain" and the directives were never implemented, they are nevertheless interesting because they revealed the AO's aims in conquered lands. They also specifically defined the types of persecution which the Nazis believed foreign Germans had received since World War I. In agreements with both enemy and neutral countries, the AO intended to secure the indemnification of foreign Germans for economic and physical damages caused by the war, removal of discrimination against Germans, complete freedom of Germans to join the NSDAP, protection of Germans against hostile propaganda, equality of work for Germans, abolition of special tax systems aimed at foreigners, and establishment of most-favored-nation treatment in trade for Germany.[30]

By the beginning of 1941 there was evidence that the AO was expanding its intelligence activities abroad and that foreign intelligence sections of the SD and *Abwehr* were using more of the AO's agents in the *Landesgruppen*. Although Hitler heatedly denied to the foreign press during the war that Germany engaged in fifth column work abroad, nothing could have been further from the truth. But while many foreigners correctly disbelieved him, the same persons were convinced erroneously that the German espionage groups "had been built into a single consistent plan and one centralised system of organization, in which all wires were pulled by one man: the Führer."[31] The lack of truth in this view was illustrated by the AO's relationship to the SD and *Abwehr*, which produced a picture of the administrative chaos that characterized the Third Reich.

No agreements were concluded by the AO with the rival agencies,[32] and the absence of a formal understanding invited sharp disagreement among them and resulted in the use of the AO by the others. Bohle complained personally to Himmler in November 1942 that the *Abwehr* had been employing thirty-six *Ortsgruppenleiters* in Switzerland without his knowledge.[33] Antagonism between the *Abwehr* and AO had surfaced in June 1938, when a prominent Nazi member in Copenhagen revealed publicly the identity of one of the *Abwehr's* key agents in Denmark, and the army demanded that the member be recalled to Germany and tried for treason. The party's main criticism of the agent was his alleged friendship with a half Jew.[34] When the war began the quarreling increased. In December 1939, Canaris, chief of the *Abwehr*, attacked Bohle for disrupting the army's intelligence network in Rumania; the *Landesgruppe* there had destroyed the cover of several *Abwehr* spies who had assisted the army in sabotaging Rumanian oil deliveries to Britain. Still other disagreements arose over the Butting affair in the Netherlands and the AO sending secret agents to Yugoslavia, who competed with army intelligence.[35]

In Turkey officials of the *Landesgruppe* and *Abwehr* "were always getting in each other's way," and they so rivaled one another "that they denounced each other's agents to the Turkish police." *Abwehr* agents eventually discovered that their work was better concealed if they dropped their Nazi membership and disassociated themselves from the *Landesgruppen.* The exceptions were in Canada, where the AO had agents with code names serving simultaneously with military intelligence, and in Chile, where the undercover *Landesgruppe* gave protection to *Abwehr* men.[36] Conflicts also arose between the AO and SD, particularly when the Security Service used party leaders without Bohle's knowledge. The party organizations abroad also clashed with the SD and German Security Police (*Sicherheitspolizei*) over political authority; the *Landesgruppe* France fought with the police over which possessed the power to withdraw Reich citizenship from German Jews in Occupied France.[37]

In a few instances the AO's spy work was successful. In Belgium the *Landesgruppe* assisted the German army in separating the "doubtful opportunists" from the "reliable men" in Flemish and Dutch political groups which the Germans planned to use in reconstructing the government of the country. AO agents infiltrated the Hungarian political movement, the National Front, to keep its pro-Nazi activities under the guidance of persons of German descent.[38] Throughout the war the docility to Germany of Balkan countries like Hungary, Rumania, and Bulgaria was fostered in part through the organizing of German minorities and other political forces in each country by the VoMi, SS, and to a lesser extent, the AO. The penetration of southeastern Europe was also the first step toward Hitler's completing what was to become the Nazi New Order on the continent.

An example of the AO's subversion in southeastern Europe was its work in Rumania. Since 1937 the *Landesgruppe* Rumania and its leader, Konradi, had supplied propaganda to the Rumanian Iron Guard, hoping to strengthen local fascists against the government and encourage them toward a pro-German policy. Konradi had been active for the NSDAP since 1930 and had formed the *Landesgruppe* singlehandedly. He had used his positions as Commercial Attache in the German Mission in Bucharest and Secretary of the Rumanian-German Chamber of Commerce to build by 1939 an organization that included twenty *Ortsgruppen* and 250 Nazi members. Three German consular officials were local leaders: Hans Turiek (Cernowitz), Friedrich Roth (Craiova), and Ludwig Tomoor (Timosoara).

But the aim of the party was not solely to strengthen the position of the Iron Guard; it was also to persuade the German minority in Rumania (approximately 800,000 persons) that the country should become a base for German raw materials. Propaganda in the summer of 1939 stressed the "right" of Germans to *Lebensraum* in eastern Europe and the obligation of the minority to support Hitler's foreign policy at all costs. Along with the VoMi, APA, and DAF, the *Landesgruppe* cultivated ties to the Rumanian *Volksdeutsch* leader, Fabritius, whose political organizations claimed control over the minority. Konradi and his party affiliates also drafted and sent to Berlin lists of Rumanian officials and Germans who were allegedly anti-National Socialist. Their names were compiled into a kind of "Brown Book" to be used later in the war by the Nazis in imprisoning and removing from the Rumanian government persons who had been hostile to Germany.[39]

With the outbreak of the war the party's pressure increased, particularly its work with the Iron Guard. Hitler's pseudo-legal control over Rumania was greatly expanded in September 1940, when the Rumanian Defense Minister and protector of the Iron Guard, Jon Antonescu, was named Prime Minister by the king. Bohle, believing that he saw an opportunity to raise his prestige with Hitler, the Guard, and the new Antonescu regime, visited Bucharest on 30 November and discussed further AO activity with Horia Sima, leader of the Guard. But his dreams were quickly dashed when Hitler suddenly decided to support Antonescu and to strengthen the Prime Minister's authority by aiding the crushing of the nationalist and unruly Guard. The puppet Antonescu responded by forcing the abdication of the king, suppressing a revolt of the Guard, and allying Rumania with the Axis powers. Revealing that Hitler had been correct in supporting Antonescu over the Rumanian fascists, the Prime Minister led his country into Germany's war against Russia in June 1941. Several months later Bohle suffered another setback when Konradi and other *Landesgruppe* officials who had close ties to the Guard were expelled from the country.[40]

The AO was also involved in Greece, Hungary, and Yugoslavia. When Hitler expanded the war into southeastern Europe and into Russia in the spring and summer of 1941, the *Landesgruppen* in the Balkans played a conspicuous role. As German troops entered Athens on 27 April the *Landesgruppe* Greece, headed by an archaeologist, Walther Wrede, assisted the army by supplying it with interpreters and guides and introducing German officers to cooperative Greek leaders.[41] During the lightning campaign in Greece and Yugoslavia, the *Landesgruppe* Hungary and its leader Esp helped to administer German troops moving through the country to the front. Its women's auxiliary established special "welcoming stations" for the soldiers, and the women visited the wounded in Hungarian hospitals, distributing among them "care packages" of cigarettes and chocolate. The German army estimated that the *Landesgruppe* contacted over 100,000 soldiers, and as a reward, Esp and his staff were presented with a military decoration.[42]

Simultaneously the Nazis brutally conquered Yugoslavia, which refused to become a German satellite and thereby threatened the German advance into Russia. By mid-April 1941 the Germans had destroyed the old-Serbian-controlled government and created a Nazi puppet state, Croatia, which was occupied jointly by the Germans in the northeast and Italians in the west, and was torn by a bloody civil war among Croats, Serbs, Turks, Bosnians, *Volksdeutschen*, and Communists. The approximately 250,000 *Volksdeutschen* and 3,300 German citizens in Croatia supported fully the government and the nationalist organization which formed the basis for it, the Ustasha movement. The Germans received large sums of money from the AA and VoMi, and they were administered by the VoMi through a political structure called the *Deutsche Volksgruppe in Kroatien* ("German Racial Group in Croatia"), led by Branimir Altgayer.[43]

When the new state was formed, the AO created a *Landesgruppe* Croatia, headed by Rudolf Empting. Although the group was not extraordinarily large, its activities represented one aspect of Nazi policy in southeastern Europe. Its work illustrated the NSDAP's efforts to pursue the German policy of controlling the countries of southern and eastern Europe by tying them to Germany economically, organizing their German minorities, influencing local political parties that were pro-German, and playing on internal divisions between peoples and classes in each country.[44]

Empting's personal activities in Croatia were designed to establish ties to the government, and in this respect his role was almost as vital to Germany as that of the German Minister in Zagreb, Siegfried Kasche. Empting and Kasche visited one another regularly, and Empting met frequently with the Croatian Prime Minister and military commanders. The *Landesgruppe*'s political operations had one objective—to assist Germany in controlling Croatia. The NSDAP flooded persons of German descent and Croatians with propaganda against the rising Communist resistance movement under Tito, fed the Croatian press pro-Nazi political and economic reports, presented free records of German songs to radio stations, and offered German language courses in local schools. The *Landesgruppe* operated its own school in Zagreb, trained teachers for *Volksdeutsch* schools, and persuaded the Croatian Ministry of Education to institute a series of "racial-biological courses" for teachers, professors, and doctors.

The party also supported efforts to construct a National Socialist movement among the Croatians, and it assisted the Ustasha in organizing the latter's leadership in a way similar to the NSDAP's *Führerprinzip*. Hitler Youth clubs in the *Landesgruppe* contributed directly to the German war effort. Like German youth in other eastern European countries, *Volksdeutsch* youth in Croatia and Serbia were used for espionage and recruited for SS and German army units. Many HJ members became officers in the army, and other HJ boys were drafted into a special SS division called "Prinz Eugen." It was formed early in 1942 and was the first of many foreign divisions that were established in the SS during the war.

The Nazis also did their utmost to preserve Germany's economic domination of Croatia. Croatia and Hungary had to be retained in the German fold because of their large deposits of minerals for industrial production and building jet aircraft. The *Landesgruppe's* commercial adviser was Hans Gerlach, an I. G. Farben agent and president of the local German Chamber of Commerce. In association with the AO's Foreign Trade Office, he counseled Germans on forming new businesses, expelling Jews from German and Croatian firms, occupying administrative committees and boards of control of corporations, and supplying replacements for German business representatives recalled to Germany. The *Landesgruppe* also purged non-German elements from the *Volksdeutsch* business community, and Empting and Kasche presented a portrait of Hitler to the Croatian Chamber of Labor to celebrate the sending of the 100,000th Croatian worker to Germany in June 1942.[45]

Empting was one of Bohle's more perceptive leaders in Europe, and he filed regular political reports that were passed by the AO to the SS and SD. His report of July 1942 discussed the growing desertion of Croatian soldiers to Tito's Communist resistance and the Croatian army's lack of control over large partisan groups that had been formed. He also stressed the "often sharp cross-purposes of Italo-German interests in Croatia," the protection by Italian troops of the Serbians (and Jews) from the government (and Germans), and the refusal of the Italians to battle insurrectionary groups of Communists and other partisans. This information led in the fall of 1942 to a new German offensive to repress the Communists and another partisan group, the Chetniks.[46]

The *Landesgruppe*'s varied activities and its efforts to acquire Croatian labor for Germany represented one aspect of Nazi plans to establish a New Order in southern and eastern Europe. While the New Order was eventually to include all of Europe, its creation was planned during the war by a host of state, private and party agencies in Germany: the SS, party Chancellery, AO, AA, Ministry of Economics, *Reichsbank*, and numerous German corporate organizations. It was based on Hitler's idea that struggle is the natural form of relations between states and peoples and that only subordination of the weaker to the stronger assures a degree of stability. The Nazi agencies were agreed on the basic objectives of the New Order—the establishment of the greatest possible German influence and power over the nations of Europe.

Politically the goal was to subject Europe to varying degrees of German control; economically, the objective was to interweave the economies of Europe, place them under German domination, and use them to develop the German standard of living to its highest possible point.[47] As a small part of this massive plan, the *Landesgruppe* Croatia spread propaganda, attempted to influence the Croatian government, established an educational campaign among Croatian-Germans, recruited for the SS, infiltrated German "advisory" personnel into local professional and economic organizations, and submitted regular intelligence reports to Berlin. In each respect, its work was a microcosm of the New Order's development and of the Nazi party's contribution to it.

HESS'S FLIGHT AND BOHLE'S ALLIANCE WITH HIMMLER AND RIBBENTROP

On 10 May 1941 a decisive pillar supporting the NSDAP groups abroad and the career of the *Gauleiter* and State Secretary in the AA, Bohle, suddenly dissolved. Hess, Hitler's blindly loyal deputy and Bohle's party superior and close friend, suddenly rocked the Nazi world by flying to Scotland to seek out the Duke of Hamilton about negotiations for a peace between England and Germany. His flight, which was in part a result of his desire to achieve a dramatic coup and end his loss of influence with Hitler to Himmler and Bormann, was unwittingly assisted by Bohle. One October evening in 1940 the AO leader was summoned to Hess's office, where he pledged Bohle to the strictest secrecy in translating a letter into English that he was preparing for the Duke. Bohle, hardly dreaming that Hess was contemplating something as bizarre as a flight to England, believed that he was planning to meet the Duke in Switzerland.

Bohle was called to Hess's office on three other occasions until the letter was completed in January 1941. While Bohle noted that the letter pleaded for the ceasing of hostilities between Germany and England, he also saw that Hess portrayed to the Duke the horrors which further German bombings would bring to the British and that Hess clearly expressed his belief that Hitler would defeat England. Hess had also mentioned in the letter that he was writing "at the suggestion of Dr. Haushofer." But that was all Bohle knew of the strange affair until he received the shocking news that Hess had landed in Scotland. Hitler, who may have known of Hess's mission beforehand and encouraged it to rid himself of his deputy and to test the English reaction to a peace feeler,[48] acted dumbfounded and called his government and party leaders to the Obersalzburg on 13 May. When they, including Bohle, had assembled, Bormann (who immediately succeeded Hess and was appointed the head of the party Chancellery) read a letter that Hess had left for Hitler.

Hitler then addressed the audience and angrily informed his listeners that he wanted absolutely no further interference by "unauthorized" persons or agencies into his foreign policy. A few minutes later Bohle was asked if he knew anything about the flight in advance, and when he sheepishly related that he had helped Hess translate the letter to the Duke of Hamilton, Hitler shouted: "What in the hell do you mean? How was it possible that you helped him to do this?" A sudden fear gripped Bohle, he noted later, as he envisioned himself being condemned to a concentration camp. At the end of the meeting, however, he quickly approached Hitler and tried to explain his behavior. He told Hitler that he had acted in accord with the *Führerprinzip* when he assisted Hess, who was (he reminded the Nazi leader) Bohle's superior and who had been appointed by the Führer. Whether or not the explanation impressed Hitler it is difficult to know. Although Bohle was interrogated by Heydrich two days later, and he laid much of the blame for Hess's flight on Haushofer and his son Albrecht (the latter having worked for the *Dienststelle Ribbentrop* and having been denounced in 1938 as "politically unreliable" and a defeatist), he remained a free man.[49]

But although he avoided internment in a concentration camp and was allowed to remain in his party and government offices, his power was gone. Alfred Hess, his Deputy *Gauleiter*, was stripped of his office and placed under continual surveillance by the police. Bohle's little empire, which was already crumbling when the war began, was fully destroyed by the war and by Hess's peace mission. Like many Nazi leaders, he found himself a victim of the war that he had believed was absolutely necessary to save Germany from Judaism and Bolshevism. Having been disgraced before Hitler and the other Nazi leaders, he became a figurehead whose future rested on the whims of Bormann, Himmler, and Ribbentrop. After the Hess affair he saw Hitler personally on only one occasion before the war's end, and none of his efforts to send political reports from *Landesgruppenleiters* to Hitler received the slightest attention.[50]

No one grasped the meaning of what had happened better than Ribbentrop. Anxious to apply the *coup de grace* to his old enemy, he went to Hitler on 9 June and requested that the AO be placed directly under his leadership. He admitted that "distinct differences" separated himself and Bohle and that consequently, "the Foreign Minister must also be the Chief of the Auslandsorganisation." He further maintained that the "suitable" German mission chiefs abroad must also serve as leaders of the foreign party organizations. He noted, for example, that "old party comrades" like Kasche, Manfred von Killinger, and Dietrich von Jagow, whom Ribbentrop had commissioned German ministers in southeastern Europe, could "also take over the leadership of the Landesgruppen" of the AO.[51]

The issue was finally settled when Hitler and Ribbentrop met on 28 July, and Hitler decided against the recommendation. A loud quarrel, which had been brewing since their earlier disagreement over Germany's war with Russia, ensued between them. The invasion of Russia, which Ribbentrop had strenuously opposed, had begun at Hitler's command in mid-June. The heated dispute on the twenty-eighth was significant because it marked the beginning of Ribbentrop's decline with Hitler, and it had the effect, in Hitler's eyes, of dealing a further blow to the reputation of the AA.

The dissension also saved Bohle. Although Hitler agreed to remove Bohle from his position as State Secretary in the AA, he decided that "any further changes in the Auslandsorganisation, as the Foreign Minister wishes them, will in no instance be carried out." Holding firmly to the NSDAP's traditional view that only the party could be responsible for the *Menschenführung*, he noted that "the task of the Foreign Minister and his apparatus is foreign policy, and the organization and administration of foreign Germans is the task of the Auslandsorganisation of the NSDAP, and this job may in no case be supervised by officials of the Auswärtiges Amt."[52]

Ribbentrop's failure to bring the AO under his control was also a classic illustration of Hitler's fondness for the competing authorities of the party and the state in his regime. It reflected, too, Bormann's decisive influence on Hitler, his dislike of Ribbentrop, and his desire to retain full authority over the AO. Bormann informed Ribbentrop of Hitler's decision at the beginning of August, saying that the AO was not to involve itself with "foreign policy affairs" in the future and that Ribbentrop should give Bormann "immediate communication" if "you have any complaints against the Auslandsorganisation."[53]

Bohle, reacting to his pending demotion, petitioned the head of Hitler's Reich Chancellery, Lammers, maintaining that it would be intolerable for him to be retired from his offices and pleading with Lammers to persuade Hitler to let him retain his post as Secretary of State. His pathetic zeal for keeping his titles, and his deep sense of personal disgrace at possibly losing them, were not uncommon feelings among Nazi leaders. He later remarked, "It is a rather funny thing, but you are hardly considered a real human being in Germany unless you have some sort of title by which you can be addressed."[54]

Bohle's request was successful, mainly because Hitler did not want to make a visible change in the AA that might appear to be a sign of weakness or hesitation on his part. What, for example, would the world (and especially Germans abroad) believe if the notorious leader of the Nazi party's foreign groups were suddenly removed? He guessed that many foreigners would be convinced that Germany was softening her aggressive foreign policy and that the NSDAP was losing its alleged power over the Ministry. With the Nazis ruling most of Europe and achieving startling successes in Russia by the fall of 1941, such ideas could only undermine Germany's position by giving the enemy hope. Lammers instructed

Bohle that his position as State Secretary had been dissolved, but that he could continue using the "official designation of Secretary of State" in public and that Hitler would decide at the end of the war if he should be returned to the AA. His future relationship with the AA, Lammers continued, would be governed by Ribbentrop.[55]

The Foreign Minister, aided by his Undersecretary of State in the AA, Martin Luther, immediately informed the Reich mission leaders abroad of the changes, and he cut back drastically Bohle's staff in the AA. Another power seized from the AO was its authority to approve and to supervise official trips abroad by Nazi leaders: this was placed in the hands of the party Chancellery and AA.[56] Ribbentrop also settled the nagging question of who controlled foreign propaganda, the party (i.e., Goebbels and Bohle) or the AA. While he permitted the AO and Propaganda Ministry to continue operating the *Reichspropagandaamt Ausland*, he also ruthlessly squelched efforts by Goebbels and Bohle to influence German propaganda aimed at the United States, against which Germany declared war in December 1941.[57] About all that Goebbels and Bohle could do was to console one another by exchanging reports and secretly denouncing Ribbentrop and the AA as "not fitted to conduct propaganda abroad."[58]

Still another function that had become important to the AO and that was snatched from it following the Hess affair was Germany's administration of its former colonies in Africa, which Hitler fully expected to recover from England during the war. On 2 May 1941 Hitler officially announced plans for the creation of a new Reich Colonial Ministry, whose leadership appeared to be destined for either Bohle, Epp, or Philip Bouhler (leader of the Führer's Chancellery and supreme censor of the NSDAP). Hess's flight quickly eliminated Bohle.[59] Yet a further indication of the AO's waning authority was the low number of its officials joining the AA or promoted within the Ministry in 1940 and 1941. While there is no evidence that Bohle lost his share of power in admitting diplomats to the NSDAP, there were only six changes involving AO personnel and the AA.[60]

Slowly, following the deterioration of the *Landesgruppen* outside Europe and the continuation of difficulties between the AO and Ribbentrop, Canaris, Bormann, and the mission chiefs abroad, Bohle began late in 1942 to attempt a political comeback by currying Himmler's favor and making his peace with Ribbentrop. Except for

Chile and Argentina, most of the Latin American countries had broken off diplomatic relations with Germany, and the AO's activities there had dwindled to nothing.[61] Even relations between the *Landesgruppe* Japan and the Japanese became strained, which was probably an offshoot of the general antagonism between Germany and her ally during the war.

Although the *Landesgruppe* Manchuria contributed money, collected from its Winter Relief program, to the Japanese army in March 1942, the Japanese were unimpressed. Reflecting the tense relationship between the allies, the *Landesgruppe* Japan and movements of local Germans were severely restricted by the government; merely the presence of a German political organization seemed to contribute to the hostile atmosphere. Bohle, hoping to offset the mistrust and suspicion surrounding the *Landesgruppe*, appointed a new party leader, Franz Joseph Spahn, at the beginning of 1943.[62]

Bohle was also harassed throughout the summer of 1942 by a quarrel between the German Ambassador to Turkey, Papen, and Friede, the party leader in Turkey. When Friede claimed that Papen should either be shot or placed in a concentration camp for being lukewarm toward National Socialism, Papen responded by banning Friede from the Embassy. Matters were complicated because the Ambassador also became embroiled in a conflict with Ribbentrop's brother-in-law, and the Foreign Minister sent Papen several threatening telegrams. The squabble was resolved when Friede left Turkey, and Ribbentrop pleaded with Papen to do his best to work with Bohle. But in a frustrating moment for Papen, Friede was rewarded for his "heroic" service abroad with a war medal from Hitler.[63]

About the only bright spot for Bohle in relations between his leaders abroad and mission officials was Ettel, Germany's envoy to Iran during the first years of the war. Next to the veteran German Minister to Iraq, Fritz Grobba, the former *Landesgruppenleiter* of Colombia and Italy was the most active German diplomat in the Near East during the war. He arranged for German arms shipments to Iraq, which aided the Iraqi rebellion against the British in the spring of 1941, and he organized an espionage network among Germans in Iran that allegedly endangered Russian security and British oil interests there. When a conflict developed between himself and Grobba, he secured Grobba's transfer to Paris by accusing him of not being anti-Jewish enough.[64] Following the occupation of

Iran in August 1941 by British and Russian troops to force the expulsion of the German colony, Ettel was recalled to Berlin to become Bohle's contact with Ribbentrop and the AA. But compared to his previous posts, he found himself only a "letter carrier between the Foreign Ministry and the AO," and at the end of 1943 he left the AA and entered the *Waffen*-SS ("Combat SS").[65]

Another factor that pushed Bohle toward allying himself with Himmler and seeking to befriend Ribbentrop was the discovery that Canaris and the *Abwehr* had organized a spy network inside the AO. In a move that brought greater chaos to German intelligence abroad, the *Abwehr* inserted inside the *Landesgruppen* agents who sent classified reports on the work of foreign party leaders to Heinz Cohrs, the AO's contact with the *Abwehr*. Although Cohrs was nominally an AO official, his loyalties lay with the army; through his efforts, amazingly enough, two German intelligence services spied on one another, and Cohrs operated as a sort of "double agent."[66]

Also undermining the *Landesgruppen* was an order by Bormann in June 1942. The directive reinforced Hitler's earlier decree that had subordinated party leaders abroad to German mission chiefs. Among other things, the *Landesgruppenleiters* were commanded to refrain entirely from intervening in German foreign policy, to submit their political reports to mission leaders for forwarding to Berlin, to secure the mission chiefs' permission before instituting party measures that might have "foreign political repercussions," and to subordinate the party's foreign propaganda to the AA.[67] As a consequence of the order, the authority of the *Landesgruppen* dwindled to nothing; after a decade of confusion and conflict among mission chiefs and foreign party leaders, the former finally reigned supreme. But the thrust toward a firm subordination of the NSDAP to the AA was almost a decade late, as the party had contributed significantly since 1933 to the Nazis' destroying friendly relations between Germany and many countries.

The AO's reaction, for a change, was to carry out the directive. Bohle correctly noted that it was issued by the party Chancellery, which was the highest authority in the NSDAP and which acted for Hitler, and not by the AA, which had issued most previous commands limiting the AO. Disobeying Bormann would have placed Bohle in an extremely vulnerable position, particularly since Bormann exercised a decisive influence on Hitler and since disobedience meant violating the *Führerprinzip*.

Bohle even went a step further. He tried to mend his strife-torn relationship with the AA by proposing to Ribbentrop in April 1943 that the mission leaders and *Landesgruppen* cooperate in a new campaign of propaganda and intelligence to counter the "ever-increasing enemy propaganda" in "the neutral European countries." Ribbentrop, who was grasping the potential meaning of the dramatic reverses suffered by Germany at Stalingrad and El Alamein several months earlier, grabbed the olive branch without hesitation. At the end of June the AO and AA formed a special Foreign Information Service (*Auslandsinformationsdienst*) in the Ministry, whose objective was to use the *Landesgruppen* and foreign Germans in a massive "whispering campaign" (*Flusterinformation*) or a subtle spreading of propaganda through rumor and gossip.[68]

Ribbentrop's sudden willingness to collaborate with the AO was also the result of Bohle's effort to resurrect himself through an alliance with Himmler and to re-establish himself with Hitler. Before the agreement between the AO and AA was reached, he had pleaded for Himmler's assistance in acquiring the support of the AA for the *Reichspropagandaamt Ausland*. Foreign Germans, he told Himmler, "are our best propagandists outside the borders of the Reich, because their national experience, knowledge of language, and their tie to the people where they reside enable them to understand what must be done." When Bormann stopped reading Bohle's political reports from the *Landesgruppenleiters* and they were no longer forwarded to Hitler, the AO sent them to Himmler.[69]

An accord with the SS was also noticeable at other levels. Not only were a growing number of SS officers dispatched as leaders to *Landesgruppen* (e.g., to Ecuador and Turkey), but the party organizations in eastern Europe (e.g., Hungary and Croatia) were involved extensively in drafting *Volksdeutschen* into the *Waffen*-SS to bolster Germany's military effort and in naturalizing the new recruits as German nationals.[70] The groups also contributed to the destruction of the Jews being carried out by the SS in eastern Europe. Ludwig Kohlhammer, *Landesgruppenleiter* of Rumania, and his counterpart in Slovakia, Kurt Rudershausen, gave orders to their *Ortsgruppen* to assist the SS and AA in "aryanizing" Jewish businesses, forcing German firms to release Jewish employees, and drafting blacklists of Jewish or German-Jewish firms that were off limits to German buyers. Still another popular anti-Semitic venture undertaken jointly by the *Landesgruppen* and SS was the practice of removing Aryan children from Jewish or half-Jewish families.[71] Thus, while the AO never involved itself in the Nazi extermination of the Jews, through its foreign affiliates it contributed its share towards removing Jews from the economic and political life of several southeastern European states.

Finally, Bohle's tie to Himmler was designed to counter his servitude to Bormann. By 1943 he had become convinced of the enormous power of both Bormann and Himmler, and he believed that they were responsible for the acts of brutality and terrorism that now appeared to rule his country. Although he was aware of foreign labor in massive numbers in Germany and had heard "by rumor" or "from other sources" that "large numbers [of Russian prisoners of war] died of starvation," he never visited factories or plants that used such workers. He also knew of the lynching of Allied flyers, mainly from Goebbels's newspaper articles glorifying the killings.

While he knew, furthermore, that European Jews were being deported to the occupied territories in the east, he believed that they were being shipped to labor camps and used in road construction or in manufacturing war equipment. Above all, he apparently knew nothing of the "Final Solution" (i.e., the extermination of the Jews) or the conferences regarding it held among party, SS, and police functionaries. His knowledge about deportation came primarily from rumors and "general Party and State information;" the party Chancellery and SS were extremely careful to keep him and similar officials uninformed, particularly because the horror that was occurring in the east might leak through the AO to foreign countries.

It was only after the collapse of the Third Reich that Bohle was to learn about Auschwitz for the first time, and until then, he testified at the Nuremberg trials, he had believed that Theresienstadt had been merely "a kind of town reserved for Jews of old age." Did Hitler know what was happening? Bohle thought not:

. . . I was firmly convinced that Hitler himself was so absorbed by his tremendous duties, as Supreme Commander of the Armed Forces, that he simply had to neglect his other duties; and I thought that Bormann especially, and possibly Himmler, were taking advantage of this almost total seclusion of Hitler, in order to form Germany slowly but surely into a terroristic state; and it was the hope that I and many others had that at the close of the war Hitler would use the iron broom.[72]

THE MYTH OF VICTORY

The brutal concept that annihiliating the Jews would bring Germany closer to freedom and victory proved to be illusory. By the early months of 1943 the war was weighing down heavily on Germany, and the initiative was shifting to the side of the democracies and Russia. In January several hundred thousand German troops surrendered at Stalingrad, thereby sealing Germany's fate in the Soviet Union, and with large American assistance, the Allies expelled the Germans from North Africa and began attacking Italy and southeastern Europe. Waves of Allied bombers hit German cities, and the Reich "situation reports" of the SD began to note the "deepest excitement" among the people and a sense of defeatism.[73]

A similar feeling engulfed Germans living and working in occupied Europe. *Landesgruppen* in the conquered countries were forced to focus their entire attention on propaganda to buoy the morale of foreign Germans and on relief measures for Germans ravaged by Allied bombing. The *Landesgruppe* France, which had fifty-four *Ortsgruppen* and filled Paris "with representatives of the party," was faced with administering both German civilians in France and French laborers in local German-dominated industries.[74] The party and DAF collaborated with the Reich's Commissioner for Labor Supply, Fritz Sauckel, in acquiring and increasing French labor by transferring peacetime businesses into war industries and flooding French industrial plants with propaganda.

In France, as in most of the conquered territories, hundreds of Germans worked as labor managers, engineers, and special technicians to operate factories and armaments industries. Factories in the hands of German management were run by iron-fisted workers' delegates (*Betriebsobmänner*), who were responsible to the DAF and party and whose function was to exploit ruthlessly workers for the sake of production. While Nazi propaganda stressed that such factories were decorated by the DAF in Germany's "war efficiency competition" and that the factories operated with great "cooperation between local [French] workers and the Germans," the opposite was more correct. Few French workers voluntarily labored for Nazi managers to the point where there was (as the AO claimed) "almost no friction."

The party in France also collected food and clothing for dispatch to bombed-out areas of western Germany, distributed ration cards and gas masks to German workers, and protected Germans from air raids. In a short wave broadcast to Asia, the RPA leader, Schmidt-Decker, lauded the *Landesgruppe* for its collection of clothes for the needy in Germany, boasting that "even French people contributed voluntarily."[75] By December 1943 the loss of qualified party leaders in the war forced the *Landesgruppe* to draft German soldiers occupying France to serve during their free time in party offices, and because of heavy Allied air assaults and repeated bombing alarms, the *Ortsgruppe* Paris-Boulogne found it impossible to hold party meetings.[76]

The *Landesgruppe* Belgium also searched for methods to increase production of local Flemish and Belgian workers. To free mothers and fathers to work longer hours for German factories, the party established kindergartens and day-care centers, and several thousand Flemish children were sent to Germany for propaganda and schooling purposes.[77] All *Landesgruppen* in Europe, however, spent the greater part of their time distributing propaganda among Germans and foreigners. It had the unenviable task of explaining away Germany's deteriorating situation and of transforming military defeats into moral victories. The *Landesgruppe* Italy tried to counter Marshal Badoglio's overthrow of Mussolini and bombing raids on Hamburg and Berlin in the summer of 1943 by emphasizing that Germany was winning once again in Russia, that Germany would firmly resist the Allies in Sicily, and that German armaments production would soon be ready to unleash "new German weapons" that would destroy the enemy.[78]

In France the *Landesgruppe* argued that Germans must fight the war to the bitterest end because it was a racial conflict, pitting the "Jewish race and its allies against western culture and civilization." Party radio broadcasts from Paris stressed the evil "alliance between Jew-ridden high capitalism of England and the USA and the exponents of 'world revolution,' Moscow."[79] But as the war continued to deteriorate for Germany, efforts to persuade the people to believe the propaganda became more difficult. In May 1943 the *Landesgruppe* Belgium informed the RPA that many Germans no longer respected Germany and that propaganda could do little to remedy the situation. Still, the *Landesgruppenleiters* of Europe were frequently called to Berlin for special discussions with Bohle and Goebbels on the value of propaganda. In a meeting in January 1944 Goebbels warned them that the coming year would be "a year of difficult battles, but also of greater decisions and success-es."[80] As 1944 dragged on and the war entered its final phase, propaganda of the *Landesgruppen* clutched at anything that would spur exhausted Germans and foreigners to greater sacrifices.

Although the Allies had landed at Normandy in June and were moving rapidly toward Paris, the *Landesgruppe* France told Ger-mans that the war had become a Jewish "attack on the nerves" and that a "general mobilization of heart" was needed to continue the conflict. Allegedly, the party continued, the war had displayed the "inferiority of the philosophical position of Bolshevism," be-cause Stalin was being forced to unite Communism, Russian na-tionalism, and Greek Orthodox Catholicism to save his "reign of terror."[81] It mattered little to the NSDAP that the Russians had broken through the eastern front and were advancing speedily toward Germany.

In some respects the last months of the war brought a perverted and carnival-like atmosphere to the work of the *Landesgruppe* France. As Hitler's Fortress Europe crumbled around France, the party busily arranged for symphony concerts in Paris, speakers at rallies, flowers and choirs to celebrate Hitler's birthday, and propaganda that worshiped the Führer. Few in the party seemed to realize (or to care) that such activities were now totally frivolous and could hardly halt the advancing Allies.[82]

A similar air of fantasy developed among Germans in eastern Europe. There Bohle contributed to their illusions by speaking to the *Landesgruppe* Slovakia in Bratislava in April, and assuring his audience that Hitler would still save Germany from Communism and "the danger from the east." Claiming that "over 50,000 Auslandsdeutschen" had returned to Germany since 1939 to enter the German army, he dwelled on his often repeated idea about the "eternal value of race and of blood" that must be protected among the world's Germans. Then, to spur his listeners to fight on, he warned, prophetically, "Today we recognize that the struggle of the Führer can only end with the production of a massive and powerful German Reich, or, if success will remain denied to him, with the annihilation of the Reich and the obliteration of our na-tion."[83] For several months prior to his address, the *Landesgruppe* Bulgaria had been evacuating Germans from Sofia, and the rescue effort could only be continued because of a subsidy from the AO.[84]

A striking illustration of the disillusionment in Germany with Hitler and the war was the plot to assassinate him on 20 July 1944.

Because of the numerous officials from the AA who were implicated with the army in the affair, many in the Ministry were quickly dismissed from their posts or arrested. Hitler and the NSDAP viewed the conspiracy as final confirmation of their age-old suspicions about the AA; it had clearly revealed itself to be subversive, anti-National Socialist, and "reactionary" in spirit. Goebbels took particular delight in the shattered prestige of the AA and demanded full control over Germany's foreign propaganda—a coveted prize that had heretofore eluded him. He even went so far as to declare to Hitler that the AA lacked the proper "moral qualities" to operate foreign propaganda, as, he maintained, the involvement of several of its leading members in the assassination plot had shown!

As an indication of Bohle's success in establishing himself in Himmler's favor by the end of 1944, the AO was asked by the SS and police chief to draft lists of "politically unreliable" diplomats who were to be purged. The SD compiled similar records. Eventually, after negotiations among the SD, AO, and Personnel Director of the AA, Schröder, the lists were reduced.[85] Bohle also reported to Himmler that 625 of the 690 higher officials in the AA still considered themselves Christians. To the AO leader, who frequently proclaimed the incompatibility of the party and Church and who urged that his party officials abroad leave the Church, the figures spoke for themselves. They were solid proof, he said, of the "inner rejection" of National Socialism by most of the Ministry; there was little doubt that he was accurate.[86]

Just as the war was closing for the *Landesgruppen* and Germans in Europe who had supported Hitler, it began to end rapidly for Bohle and the AO *Zentrale* in Berlin. A tragic symbol was the sinking by a Russian submarine in the Baltic Sea of the huge German passenger ship *Wilhelm Gustloff*, named for the Nazi leader slain in Switzerland. Over 8,000 German refugees from East Prussia, frantic to escape the Russians, had boarded the ship at Danzig and perished in this greatest of all sea disasters. Because of massive Allied bombing of Berlin, the AO's offices and Bohle's family were moved to Bad Schandau, a town southeast of the capital on the German-Czech border. Bohle saw Hitler for the final time in February 1945. Two months later Hitler was dead, a victim of suicide as the Russians advanced to within a few blocks of his bunker beneath the Reich Chancellery in Berlin.

But Bohle was kept well informed about the powerful advance of the Russians from the east by his *Landesgruppenleiter* for Croatia,

Empting, who had fled for safety to Vienna following the Communist conquest of his country. In a report from Empting (which Bohle forwarded to Bormann) at the beginning of March 1945, he noted that the Austrian capital was swamped with refugees from Hungary and other southeastern states who were fleeing the Russians. Bohle, determined to fulfill his functions to the bitter end, complained to Bormann about the "public nuisance" which these uninvited "southeastern friends" had become for Germans in Vienna. Even outside Europe, what was left of the AO's leadership blindly clung to the hope that Germany would reverse the military situation. In Tokyo the party leader, Spahn, attacked the naval attache at the German Embassy for his alleged defeatism.[87]

After ordering two of his aides to burn the AO's records in the Czech mountains, Bohle destroyed his identification papers to avoid capture by the Russians, whom he feared and hated. On 2 May he fled in an army plane across the Russian lines to Flensburg, home of the provisional German government. There, for the last time, he saw Himmler, who insisted on being a part of the Flensburg regime. But Bohle and the leaders of the new government realized the folly of negotiating with the Allies through a ministry that included the notorious SS chief. When Bohle tried to reason with Himmler in a brief discussion on 4 May, Himmler retorted, "Give me half an hour's talk with General Eisenhower, and I'll come to terms with him because he needs me as the element of order in Germany." As Bohle laughed at the statement, Himmler met him with a chilling stare and walked away.[88] Finally, on the afternoon of 23 May, Bohle surrendered to the American Third Army at Falkenau on the Czech border. Among his belongings were a diplomatic passport from Flensburg and a phial of poison.[89] The passport and poison were symbolic of the alternatives that were now presented to the Nazis in their hour of defeat. Bohle chose to live.

7

EPILOGUE: PLEADING GUILTY
AT NUREMBERG

With the fall of the curtain on the brutal war and the liberation of Europe from Hitler's barbarism, the Nazi leadership and (as many Germans believed) the German nation went on trial before the International Tribunal at Nuremberg. In various ways the AO, Nazis in party organizations outside Germany, and foreign Germans were also placed on trial. They were represented before the Tribunal by their political whip for twelve years, Bohle, who was tried as a war criminal. The verdict on each remained inconclusive, which was not necessarily the result of their being judged by the Allies as having done nothing wrong in Hitler's system, but because their activities were dwarfed by the hideous war crimes of other Germans.

Another factor was Bohle's plea of guilty at Nuremberg and his receiving a light prison sentence for his role as helmsman of the AO. The fact that the AO was a secondary agency in German politics also tended to obscure its role in Nazi foreign policy; the masses of captured AA files, which contained large numbers of AO documents, were not yet completely examined and made available to the Nuremberg judges. Nevertheless, the Allied prosecution produced evidence linking the AO to Rudolf Hess, the AA, the destruction of Austria, and Nazi anti-Semitic policies. The Tribunal revealed how the AO collaborated in Hitler's aggressive policy, pushing Germany into a corner from whence it could assert its claims to world power only through war.

Bohle, following his surrender, was taken with Göring, Ribbentrop, and other Nazi leaders to the Allied prison camp at Mondorf-les-Bains in Luxemburg, where he remained until the beginning of the Nuremberg trials in November. He was quickly indicted as a war criminal and interrogated numerous times.[1] Immediately, it became apparent that he was far less belligerent toward his captors than the other Nazi leaders, and that he was even willing to admit he and his cohorts had committed some serious mistakes in following Hitler blindly. Before the Tribunal began trying the twenty-one major war criminals, he expressed the opinion to interrogators that Germany had lost the war because ninety-five percent of the National Socialist leaders had no knowledge of the world outside Germany or of foreign attitudes and ideas. The history of the Nazi party groups abroad supported his contention. On the other hand, he possessed as much exposure to foreign attitudes and cultures as any National Socialist, but the experience had hardly controlled his incredible claims to leadership of Germans in foreign countries or prompted him to stop the thoughtless work of his party groups abroad.

He also sought to take the burden of guilt off foreign Germans by arguing that they had been "very disciplined, and they always did what I advised them" (which was less than correct). He acknowledged that what he had told foreign Germans had often been erroneous, that he had misdirected the AO, and that he was "ready to admit I made mistakes."[2] Still, he adamantly defended the AO against allegations that it had assisted Hitler's expansion for *Lebensraum* and that it had engaged in espionage. At the end of March 1946 he was called at Nuremberg to testify on behalf of his former boss, Hess, who had been in an English jail cell since his flight in 1941. Responding to charges from the Allied prosecution that Hess had used him to erect and control the AO as an instrument for fifth column activities, he maintained (as he had done in London in 1937 and Budapest in 1938) that the AO had an "undisputable legality" around the world. The banning of the NSDAP from numerous countries and the attack on party members in many neutral lands during the war had apparently done little to change his mind.

He also argued that Germans abroad "would certainly be the last people who would let themselves be misused as warmongers or as conspirators against the peace." A bit later he added flatly, "There is no basis whatsoever for applying the term 'Fifth Column' to the Auslands-Organisation of the NSDAP."[3] Evidently he was more concerned with protecting Hess and himself than with discussing the extent to which the AO had collaborated with the AA and SS in politicizing German minorities in eastern Europe and assisting with the invasions of Poland, Norway, Denmark, and the Netherlands. He also chose to ignore the AO's role in the subversion, support of native fascist groups, and the anti-Communist campaign of the German government in Latin America.

Several of his former enemies in the Nazi hierarchy were unwilling to defend him at Nuremberg. Papen claimed to interrogators that it was "well known" that Bohle had ambitions during the war of becoming Germany's Foreign Minister or Minister of Colonies. Ribbentrop portrayed Bohle similarly, "He was young, capable and anxious to disseminate the National Socialist ideology." In his memoirs, which were published after his execution in 1946, Ribbentrop noted that Bohle had been a "favorite child" of Hess and that the AO "had given me very grave difficulties abroad, especially in the first years of my activity as Foreign Minister."[4]

On the heels of the major trial that was completed in October 1946, other trials were held against leading Nazi figures and German industrialists accused of supporting Hitler. Among them was Bohle, who was tried beginning in November 1947 with Weizsäcker, Woermann, Lammers, Keppler, and sixteen other officials in the so-called "Ministries Case," or the *United States of America v. Ernst von Weizsäcker et al.* The defendants were arraigned in December, and each (including Bohle) entered a plea of "not guilty." But much to the amazement of most of the people associated with the trial, Bohle changed his plea to "guilty" on 27 March 1948—the first and only Nazi leader to do so. In a statement released to the press, he noted, "The Nuremberg courts and courts in the American and British zones have handed down verdicts of *Guilty* for subordinates of mine, hence it would be irresponsible on my part to plead 'Not Guilty' and thereby shift the burden to others."[5]

He was indicted on several counts: planning, initiating, and waging aggressive war (count I); conspiracy to commit crimes against peace (II); atrocities against German citizens prior to the war (IV); atrocities against civilian populations (V); plunder and spoliation (VI); and membership in the SS, which the Tribunal considered a criminal organization because of its persecution of the Jews, operation of the extermination camps, and waging of war (VIII). According to his plea in March Bohle requested that counts I, II, and VI be withdrawn against him and that he be allowed to plead guilty to counts V and VIII (count IV was dropped against all defendants so charged in the trial).[6]

Inasmuch as he was the first at Nuremberg to plead guilty, the decision was not made lightly, and it was greeted with hostility by his former cohorts who had categorically denied any wrongdoing. Elisabeth Gombel, his defense counselor whom he greatly admired and later married, may have urged him to enter a guilty plea because she believed that the prosecution possessed a solid case against him. The attorney obviously felt a strong attachment to her client. In requesting favors from the Tribunal for him, she praised his "record of conduct" in prison, and she argued that his "general reputation" was "deserving of confidence" of the Court and that she was prepared "to accept any personal responsibility desired" for his activities outside the Tribunal or prison.[7]

Several other factors weighed heavily on his decision to plead guilty; among them were his declining health while in prison since 1945, his pro-Western attitude, and his apparently sincere belief that he and others in the Nazi leadership had been wrong to follow Hitler. The move was also encouraged by the prosecution, however, which reluctantly agreed to plea bargain with him. Before he pleaded guilty and during the prosecution's presentation of its case against him, a conference was held among Gombel, counsel for the prosecution, and members of the Tribunal, whereupon Bohle proposed to change his plea in exchange for "the withdrawal of certain charges on the part of the Prosecution." The Tribunal instructed the prosecution to examine the proposal and "to draw up a stipulation in the nature of a bill of particulars setting out the specific acts to which the defendant [Bohle] would plead guilty and the charges which the Prosecution would withdraw."

But arriving at such "a stipulation" proved "to be impossible." Nevertheless, a misunderstanding occurred between Bohle's counsel and the prosecution, which led the latter on 27 May 1948 to recommend that the Tribunal accept his change of plea. In a carefully worded statement that was probably designed to protect the prosecution against potential accusations that it had made a deal with a Nazi war criminal, the prosecution explained its position to the Tribunal:

> It has never been the policy of the Prosecution before any of the Nurnberg Tribunals to agree to dismiss charges appearing to the Prosecution to be well founded in return for a plea of guilty in response to other charges. However, it appears that during the conferences referred to above certain representations were made by members of the Prosecu-

tion staff on the basis of which counsel for the defendant Bohle may have been led to assume that the Prosecution would agree to dismiss Counts I, II and VI of the Indictment, and may have filed his plea of guilty on the basis of that assumption. Solely for that reason, and in order that the rights of the Defendant Bohle shall not be prejudiced in any manner by representations made by the Prosecution, the Prosecution herewith respectfully moves that the name of the defendant Bohle be withdrawn from Counts I, II and VI of the Indictment. The Prosecution will continue to press the charges set forth against the defendant Bohle in Counts V and VIII of the Indictment.[8]

Thus, either by accident or by design, during the negotiations the prosecution gave Bohle the impression that if he pleaded guilty, several charges against him would be dropped; when he entered his new plea, this was what occurred.[9] Yet, the prosecution expressed the desire to continue pressing for a conviction of him on counts V and VIII. Before the Tribunal could act on his plea and on the prosecution's motion, however, he filed still another plea on 1 June 1948, maintaining his guilt under count VIII and withdrawing his guilty plea under count V. Three days later the Tribunal ordered that the charges against him on counts I, II, and VI be dropped and that his most recent plea be accepted.

The effort by the prosecution to convict him on count V failed. Gombel, who recognized that the prosecution's case rested on the fact that Bohle had held high offices in several Nazi party organizations, claimed in her opening defense statement on 23 July 1948 the he was "for this very reason alone already burdened with criminal guilt" in the eyes of his accusers. But she cautioned the Tribunal not to assume that such reasoning was valid, maintaining that the Court would be committing the same mistake as the National Socialists had made. Noting that the Nazis had engaged in "reducing life . . . to a few typical and radically simplified facts," she compared Bohle's being "categorized" as a criminal merely because he was a Nazi leader to the Nazis refusing to consider the Jews as individuals and instead lumping them together into a massive group. The lawyer argued that "it is this collective way of thinking in its extreme which ultimately prompted criminal brains to plan and carry out the ghastly program known as the 'Final Solution of the Jewish Question.' " The defense, she therefore maintained, "takes the position that the words 'National Socialist' and 'Criminal' are not necessarily and *ipso facto* synonymous."[10]

Bohle buttressed her appeal when he took the witness stand on his own behalf. Following testimony regarding his childhood, professonal and party career, and knowledge (or lack thereof) of foreign labor and the Jewish persecution during the war, he made an apologia that was almost unheard of at Nuremberg. When asked about what had happened to the Jews, he responded:

> Retrospectively, I think that it was undoubtedly one of the most traggic [sic] and fundamental mistakes of all of us who held leading positions, no matter in what walk of life, to disregard or close our eyes to a development which ultimately led to such ghastly conditions. I believe that many of us who have no inmate [sic] anti-Jewish feelings should today frankly admit that the persecution of the Jews in Germany was not only, as we have seen, a terrible political error, but . . . that this persecution was an insult to human dignity and to the general honesty of character for which the Germans formerly were known.[11]

When questioned about his personal responsibility for the German catastrophe, he declared his readiness to accept his share of the guilt and expressed a deep desire to help return his defeated and war-torn people to a position of moral and cultural respectability in the world:

> We know that a low estimate of human life and carelessness to human misery is not and never has been a trait of the German character, and for that very reason I think that we should frankly admit the atrocities that have been committed and that have defiled the German name in the world . . . . And I think it is my firm conviction that the world will regain its belief in our national honesty, only if we ourselves are honest and straightforward in our confessions and thereafter also in our will to make amends. I think we leading men have this responsibility, not only to the victims of these crimes but just as much to the German people, as such, who, with or without our participation, were misled and misguided and are today, without any fault of their own, outlawed in the world.[12]

There seems little reason to believe that his admission was not sincere or that he was offering a self-justifying apologia in the hope that self-accusation would be his best defense. While his remarks and guilty plea may have pleased his judges at Nuremberg, his behavior hardly made him popular with his own countrymen. But if he was basically an honest man wishing to clear his conscience by admitting his role in Hitler's system, he was also guilty of seeking to whitewash the German people. By hinting that the Germans had been "misled and misguided," he was shifting the responsibility for the evils of Nazism away from the people onto a gang of criminals. Like Hitler and most other Nazis, he was a human puzzle and one who failed to acknowledge the entire truth. His worshiping of the German race remained with him, and it continued to be a veil between himself and reality.

Several weeks later the Tribunal agreed to Bohle's plea at the beginning of June. His sentence, which was administered in April 1949, was five years in prison; in comparison, three defendants in the Ministries Case received twenty or more years in prison, five received ten or more years, and several others received seven years. According to the judgment, "Bohle's acts" as head of the Nazi party groups outside Germany (and especially his depriving German Jews of their livelihood) were "reprehensible from a moral stand-point," but in the Tribunal's view, they "do not come within the scope of either count five of the indictment or of the crimes defined by the London Charter and Control Council Law No. 10."[13]

By the end of the trial Bohle was a sick and broken man whose life had become a testament to the tragedy of the war for numerous German leaders and their families. His father had died during the war, and property which the family owned in Berlin, the Rhineland, and Hanover could not be sold for enough money to support Bohle's sisters and his son.[14] Having been in jail since the summer of 1945, he was granted an early parole from Landsberg prison in December 1949. He quickly withdrew to Hamburg, hoping to resume the commercial activities in which he had been engaged before the Nazis had rescued him from obscurity in 1931. But he found that he was anathema to most German firms; some refused to hire him because he had been a Nazi leader and tried at Nuremberg, while others disliked his being the only official to plead guilty. In March 1951 he was finally given a job by the South African Research Society, and except for a letter to the editor of *Die Zeit* two years later contending (inaccurately) that the AA had included many Nazis and that Hess and the NSDAP had nothing to do with his appointment to the Ministry, his public life was finished. While on a business venture to Düsseldorf he died of a heart attack on 9 November 1960, the thirty-seventh anniversary of the Hitler *Putsch* in Munich.[15]

With his capture and Germany's defeat came the destruction of the remaining Nazi party groups outside Germany that had not been dismantled during the war. In some countries, like Switzerland, party leaders were investigated, their homes searched, and many were expelled. By 1945 the party's total membership abroad had increased only minimally since 1937, as the war had encouraged few foreign Germans to join the NSDAP and Hitler.[16] The groups abroad and the AO had found impossible their task of forcing the world to accept their ideology and leadership.

In assessing the importance of the foreign party groups in German foreign policy, historians have differed greatly. Some, like Louis de Jong and the former German diplomat, Erich Kordt, have argued that the "practical significance" of the AO "has been vastly overestimated," while several American historians have asserted that the organization had "considerable power." Horst Kühne, the East German scholar, has also argued that the "Auslandsorganisation of the NSDAP was the sharpest weapon which the German imperialists had ever possessed abroad."[17] Perhaps Hans-Adolf Jacobsen and Paul Seabury were more correct, however, in stressing that the AO was primarily an "auxiliary instrument" in Germany's foreign policy, far less significant than the AA but similar to the VoMi, APA, DAI, VDA, and *Dienststelle Ribbentrop*.[18]

Judged purely by the sheer numbers in its affiliates abroad, the AO was of little consequence; yet, measuring it solely by numbers does not present an accurate picture of its impact on foreign Germans, the AA, and foreign public opinion. Nor would it reveal the incredibly aggressive foreign policy advocated by the Nazi party. As illustrated by the history of the AO, the party was totally unrestrained, uncompromising, and without any sense of international law (except where it served the party's interests). Hitler, in contrast to the super-radical views of his movement on foreign affairs, appears almost cautious and conservative, particularly before 1939.

Figures also cannot explain the problems and dilemmas created for Germans abroad by the pressure (e.g., threats, reprisals, blackmail, and withdrawal of German citizenship) exerted on them by Nazi groups to support Hitler. The small party groups outside Germany, with their raucous and mindless activities and their public declarations of loyalty to Germany, exercised a far greater influence on foreign opinion than their membership figures justified. As late as March 1948 *The New York Times* maintained in sensational fashion that Bohle was "once chief of the Nazi spy ring in the United States."[19] But except for several Latin American states, where *Landesgruppen* infiltrated military and government circles on a limited scale and established close ties to native fascist movements whose goal was to overthrow their governments, the groups posed no danger to the world's security. While organized nicely after 1931 according to a theoretical framework in Hamburg, Munich, and Berlin, most *Landesgruppen* were disorganized, undisciplined, and rendered even more ineffective by factionalism and conflict.

Yet, particularly in the United States, England, and other western nations (some of whom outlawed the Nazis), popular opinion genuinely viewed the groups as a part of a monolithic political system that directly threatened the freedom of foreign nations. In this respect, the AO's work often led to recurrent conflicts with the AA's efforts to maintain normal diplomatic relations abroad. Many diplomats in the AA appear to have held the view, sincere but erroneous, that the AO was a powerful rival of the Ministry, when in fact it was not. While the AO failed in 1937 and 1938 to place a large number of National Socialists in the AA and while it fell far short of imposing its will on the Ministry, even Ribbentrop seemed to fear it as a serious competitor. This was particularly true during the war, when his prestige with Hitler declined, his daring diplomacy was superceded by military decisions, and his confidence was shaken. But in diplomacy Bohle and his subleaders were their own worst enemies. He represented the archetypal party diplomat; disdaining the regular diplomatic virtues of cooperation and compromise, he was loud, demanding, bombastic, and dominated by a totalitarian mind-set that knew only a blind loyalty to Hitler and Germany.

German foreign policy was guided by decrees from Hitler and Ribbentrop, but the execution and enforcement of them depended on the everyday work of the AA and other agencies like the AO. In short, the AO converted Hitler's wishes and Nazi ideology regarding foreign Germans into policy. But again the significance of the AO must not be overemphasized. Although it had authority in enforcing and even determining the extent of directives that dealt with foreign Germans, it was a second-echelon institution, which had little positive effect on decision-making in foreign policy. It merely received the major decisions from above and transformed them into political and economic activity.

Viewed solely by itself, the AO was one of many organizations competing for political power in Hitler's totalitarian system. It also

represented a means by which ambitious men like Bohle could further their own political careers. Even the *Landesgruppenleiters*,
many of them exercising party functions long distances from Germany, acted like "little Hitlers" and ruled their groups in a semi-
feudal, authoritarian manner. In a number of instances, they clashed
with German mission officials, but while such conflicts centered
around *how* Nazi influence should be expanded abroad, they rarely
involved the issue of whether or not the goal of expansion was correct. In the latter, unfortunately for the AA, there was frequent
agreement, which helps to explain the friendly relations among
some diplomats and party officials. The history of the AO further
illustrated the freedom of institutions in the Third Reich to operate
as they pleased until they interfered with the interests of their
competitors and such meddling came to the attention of Hitler or
his key leaders. The AO enjoyed considerable freedom until it
threatened in 1937 and 1938 to disrupt the regular diplomatic work
of the AA and to destroy completely Germany's relations with several countries.

As with the entire National Socialist system in Germany, the seed
of failure for the party organizations abroad lay in their totalitarian
nature and in the substance of their mission. Germans outside the
Reich and foreigners were generally unimpressed with the Nazi
obsession with the mythical division of Jew and German and the
Darwinian view of life and politics. The party's groups were never
able to overcome a fatal weakness—the belief that the world could
be conquered by the principles of race and power. The idea that
foreign Germans must be guided and supervised by the NSDAP
just as Germans at home was another form of Nazi imperialism,
and the demand rested on the party leaders' highly deficient knowledge about foreign cultures and international law. The Nazis operated according to assumptions about foreign relations that were un-
believably naive—no modern foreign policy can survive very long the
alienation of world opinion or the total lack of consideration of
such a policy's consequences.

Nor can a successful foreign policy be based entirely on the
premise that what works at home will produce comparable results in
other nations. The NSDAP tried to nazify Germans abroad and
foreign citizens by using the same tactics Hitler had exploited to
conquer Germany: propaganda, extortion, blackmail, reprisals,
persecution of Jews and non-Aryans, wearing of Nazi uniforms, and
parading boisterously with swastika flags. Neither Bohle nor his

Landesgruppenleiters heeded the advice of Hermann Rauschning, the Nazi leader in Danzig who abandoned Hitler, when he remarked in 1934 that "outside the Reich only a National Socialism adapted to the particular conditions of Germandom in the country in question was possible."[20]

The foreign party groups, while contributing to Germany's poor image abroad and to the German war effort, illustrated that the German concept of nationality was far more ethnic in nature than political. Although Nazi leaders like Bohle claimed otherwise, they made no distinction between German citizens and *Volksdeutschen* in their schemes to mobilize world Germandom for Hitler. But in this respect, Hitler had set the example for his underlings by advancing the idea in *Mein Kampf* that "once a German, always a German," and that it mattered little whether Germans lived inside or outside Germany.[21] In his view what was of worldwide significance was their preservation through his leadership and through their loyalty to the Nazi community of blood and race.

Despite the success of the Soviet Union in building a totalitarian state, Germany's defeat and Hitler's destruction were examples of the failure of totalitarianism, and particularly of the Gestapo, SS, concentration camps, and Nazi party's racism. To these one may add the unsuccessful (and less notorious) party groups in foreign countries. In view of their relentless work to carry the Third Reich to foreign Germans, it was ironical that Hitler could remark while "table-talking" at his military headquarters in May 1942, "I am firmly opposed to any attempt to export National Socialism. If other countries are determined to preserve their democratic systems and thus rush to their ruin, so much the better for us."[22] As with much that he discussed or undertook, his theory failed completely to resemble reality.

APPENDIX I
Diagram of the Auslands-Organisation January 1945
NSDAP Party Chancellery, Martin Bormann

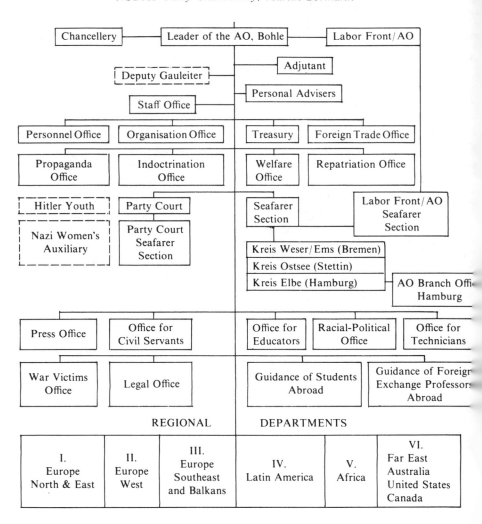

Source: Bohle Interrogation, M-679/1/0187, which noted: "This diagram is valid as of January, 1945, and was corrected and approved by Ernst Wilhelm Bohle on September 8, 1945, before W. W. Blancke."

The Auslands-Organisation and the Nazi Party Groups
in Foreign Countries 1935-1945

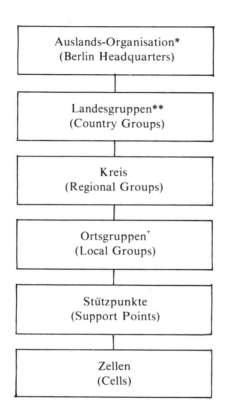

* For a diagram of the AO offices in Berlin, see Appendix I.

** Between 1937 and 1940 there were forty-nine *Landesgruppen*, or country groups, around the world; there were thirty-seven in 1934.

+ The number of *Ortsgruppen* in a country group varied with the size of the German population administered by the country group. In July 1940, for example, there were 102 *Ortsgruppen* in the *Landesgruppe* Netherlands; in April 1936 the *Landesgruppe* Spain had nearly fifty *Ortsgruppen* and *Stützpunkte*; and in the spring of 1933 there were six *Ortsgruppen* in the United States.

APPENDIX III
Major Newspapers of the Auslands-Organisation (1937)

Argentina	*Der Trommler*, Buenos Aires
Brazil	*Deutsche Morgen*, São Paulo
	Fürs Dritte Reich, Porto Alegre
Chile	*Westküsten Beobachter*, Santiago
Paraguay	*Deutsche Warte*, Asuncion
Uruguay	*Deutsche Wacht*, Montevideo
Costa Rica	*Mitteilungsblatt der Ortsgruppe San Jose de Costa Rica*
Guatemala	*NS.-Pionier*, Guatemala
Mexico	*NS.-Herold*, Mexico City
China	*Ostasiatischer Beobachter*, Shanghai
Netherlands East Indies	*Deutsche Wacht*, Batavia
Australia	*Die Brücke*, Sydney
Kenya-Uganda	*Ostafrika-Warte*, Kitale
Portuguese West Africa	*Rundbrief* of the *Landkreis* Angola
Italy	*Italien Beobachter*, Rome

Source: Jacobsen, *Nationalsozialistische Aussenpolitik*, p. 655; an extensive list of German language newspapers worldwide that were pro-Nazi or influenced directly by the Germans, is in *Das Braune Netz*, pp. 33-38.

NOTES

PREFACE

1. For a lengthy list of books published in the 1930s and 1940s warning of the danger, see the Library of Congress, *The Nazi State, War Crimes and War Criminals*, compiled by Helen F. Conover for the U.S. Chief of Counsel for the Prosecution of Axis Criminality (Washington, D.C.: U.S. Government Printing Office, 1945). Even a recent scholarly work has exaggerated the strength of the groups. Note Louis L. Snyder, *Encyclopedia of the Third Reich* (New York: McGraw-Hill, 1976), p. 14, which claims the Nazi party "had some 60,000 members in 1939" in Argentina.

2. The party agency in Germany assigned the task of directing the foreign affiliates was the Foreign Organization (*Auslands-Organisation*, or AO). Its administrative history and place in German foreign policy are surveyed by Hans-Adolf Jacobsen, *Nationalsozialistische Aussenpolitik, 1933-1938* (Frankfurt/Main: Alfred Metzner, 1968), pp. 90-160, 495-598. My study is intended to complement his pioneering work, especially by stressing the history of the AO's groups in foreign countries, linking their activities more closely with the fortunes of the AO, and dealing with the period after 1938. About the only monograph focusing mainly on German Nazis outside Germany, at least to my knowledge, is Herbert S. Levine, *Hitler's Free City: A History of the Nazi Party in Danzig, 1925-39* (Chicago: University of Chicago Press, 1973). In this connection, Mussolini's Fascist party also had foreign affiliates and agents; Alan Cassels, *Mussolini's Early Diplomacy* (Princeton, N.J.: Princeton University Press, 1970), pp. 97, 141, 173-74, 190, 196-98, 353-54.

3. One could not agree more with the statement by Klaus Hildebrand, "Hitler's War Aims," a review article in the *Journal of Modern History*, 48 (1976), 524, "that studies on the foreign policy of a nation-state, seen within the context of the international state system, remain one of the indispensable tasks of historiography."

4. See, for example, Gerhard L. Weinberg, *The Foreign Policy of Hitler's Germany: Diplomatic Revolution in Europe, 1933-36* (Chicago: University of Chicago Press, 1970).

CHAPTER 1

1. Edmond Taylor, Edgar Snow, and Eliot Janeway, *Smash Hitler's International: The Strategy of a Political Offensive Against the Axis* (New York: Greystone Press, 1941), pp. 6, 28-30.

2. Klaus Hildebrand, *The Foreign Policy of the Third Reich*, trans. Anthony Fothergill (Berkeley: University of California Press, 1973), pp. 12-19; Otto Strasser, *Mein Kampf: Eine politische Autobiografie* (Frankfurt/Main: Heinrich Heine Verlag, 1969), pp. 58-69; and Reinhard Kühnl, *Die nationalsozialistische Linke, 1925-1930* (Meisenheim/Glan: Hain, 1966).

3. Adolf Hitler, *Mein Kampf* (2 vols.; Munich: F. Eher, 1943), particularly vol. 2; Gerhard L. Weinberg, ed., *Hitlers zweites Buch: Ein Dokument aus dem Jahr 1928* (Stuttgart: Deutsche Verlags-Anstalt, 1961); Henry Ashby Turner, Jr., "Hitler's Secret Pamphlet for Industrialists, 1927," *Journal of Modern History*, 40 (1968), 348-74; Karl Lange, "Der Terminus 'Lebensraum' in Hitlers 'Mein Kampf'," *Vierteljahrshefte für Zeitgeschichte*, 13 (1965), 426-38; and Karl Heinz Ritschel, *Diplomatie um Südtirol: Politische Hintergründe eines europäischen Versagens* (Stuttgart: Seewald, 1966), pp. 127-39.

4. Hitler's grandiose aims, most of them formulated by 1933, are discussed in an extensive literature that includes Hugh Redwald Trevor-Roper, "Hitlers Kriegsziele," *Vierteljahrshefte für Zeitgeschichte*, 8 (1960), 121-33; Eberhard Jäckel, *Hitlers Weltanschauung: Entwurf einer Herrschaft* (Tübingen: R. Wunderlich, 1969), pp. 29-58; Axel Kuhn, *Hitlers aussenpolitisches Programm: Entstehung und Entwicklung, 1919-1939* (Stuttgart: Klett, 1970), pp. 104-41; Gerhard L. Weinberg, "Hitler's Image of the United States," *American Historical Review*, 69 (1964), 1006-22; Holger H. Herwig, "Prelude to *Weltblitzkrieg*: Germany's Naval Policy toward the United States of America, 1939-1941," *Journal of Modern History*, 43 (1971), 649-55; and Hildebrand, *Foreign Policy of the Third Reich*, pp. 21-22.

5. Jacobsen, *Nationalsozialistische Aussenpolitik*, pp. 54-160, 197-319; and *Das Braune Netz: Wie Hitlers Agenten im Auslande Arbeiten und den Krieg Vorbereiten* (Paris: Éditions du Carrefour, 1935), pp. 15-74.

6. Christopher Thorne, *The Approach of War, 1938-1939* (London: Macmillan, 1971), pp. xiii, 27; Paul Seabury, *The Wilhelmstrasse: A Study of German Diplomats Under the Nazi Regime* (Berkeley and Los Angeles: University of California Press, 1954), p. 33; Ernst L. Presseisen, *Germany and Japan: A Study in Totalitarian Diplomacy, 1933-1941* (The Hague: Nijhoff, 1958), p. 60; and Jacobsen, *Nationalsozialistische Aussenpolitik*, pp. 34-45.

7. Bohle to Franz Schwarz (NSDAP Treasurer), 8 Oct. 1941, BDC/PK/*Artur Konradi.*

8. Illustrated by Weinberg, who also discusses the role of Hitler's "personal diplomats" like Rosenberg, Kurt Ludecke, and Ernst Hanfstaengl (in the 1920s) and Ribbentrop, Ferdinand Heye, and Johannes Bernhardt (after 1933); *Foreign Policy of Hitler's Germany*, pp. 10, 126-31, 175-76, 215, 272-73, 288-92, 342-43. See also, Franz von Papen, *Memoirs*, trans. Brian Connell (New York: Dutton, 1953), p. 340; and Ulrich von Hassell, *The von Hassell Diaries, 1938-1944* (London: H. Hamilton, 1948), p. 26.

9. Heinz Paechter et al., eds., *Nazi-Deutsch: A Glossary of Contemporary German Usage* (New York: Frederick Ungar, 1944), pp. 19, 51, 62. Such terms as

Auslandsdeutsche are often misinterpreted, as by Ronald M. Smelser, "The Betrayal of a Myth: National Socialism and the Financing of Middle Class Socialism in the Sudetenland," *Central European History*, V (1972), 256-57. The most accurate estimates of Germans outside the Reich are in Wilhelm Winkler, *Statistisches Handbuch für das gesamten Deutschtums* (Berlin: Verlag Deutsche Rundschau, 1927), p. 25; he defined Germans as persons who spoke the German language and felt themselves culturally attached to Germany (p. 1).

10. *Reichsstelle für das Auswanderungswesen*, ed., *Die hauptsachlichsten deutschen Vereinigungen, Kirchen, Schulen und sonstige deutsche Einrichtungen im Auslande* (Berlin: Zentralverlag, 1932).

11. Hans Luther, *Politiker ohne Partei: Erinnerungen* (Stuttgart: Deutsche Verlags-Anstalt, 1960), p. 399; Friedrich von Prittwitz und Gaffron, *Zwischen Petersburg und Washington: Ein Diplomatenleben* (Munich: Isar Verlag, 1952), p. 166; and Papen, *Memoirs*, p. 355.

12. Kurt Bloch, *German Interests and Policies in the Far East* (New York: Institute of Pacific Relations, 1940), pp. 6, 10; Lukasz Hirszowicz, *The Third Reich and the Arab East* (London: Routledge and Kegan Paul, 1966), p. 15; Carole Fink, "Defender of Minorities: Germany in the League of Nations, 1926-1933," *Central European History*, V (1972), 330-57; and Christoph M. Kimmich, *Germany and the League of Nations* (Chicago: University of Chicago Press, 1976), pp. 131-49.

13. Sander A. Diamond, *The Nazi Movement in the United States, 1924-1941* (Ithaca, N.Y.: Cornell University Press, 1974), pp. 85-86.

14. Jacobsen, *Nationalsozialistische Aussenpolitik*, pp. 197-252; Arthur L. Smith, Jr., *The Deutschtum of Nazi Germany and the United States* (The Hague: Nijhoff, 1965), pp. 4-9, 15-19; and Diamond, *The Nazi Movement in the United States*, pp. 48-54. The German word *völkisch* refers to extreme right-wing groups in German politics that rejected Western democracy and liberalism and tried to construct a new political system for Germany based on racial, rather than legal, similarities among the German people.

15. See the copy of Bohle's speech to Germans in Norway, "Kriegserntedank in Oslo," 7 Oct. 1942, WL/PC5/211A2 (Nazi Foreign Propaganda: Germans Abroad); and Rudolf Hess, *Reden* (Berlin: Zentralverlag der NSDAP, 1938), p. 34.

16. Bohle to Kurt Daluege, 17 June 1936, BDC/PK/*Ernst Wilhelm Bohle*.

17. Waldemar Damer, *Unsere Brüder jenseits der Grenzen* (Berlin, n.d.), p. 6. Hitler rarely spoke solely to the foreign Germans, but in Nuremberg at the party rally in Sept. 1935, he addressed AO leaders from abroad; Norman H. Baynes, ed., *The Speeches of Adolf Hitler: April 1922-August 1939* (2 vols.; London: Oxford University Press, 1942), II:1252-53.

18. *Nationalsozialistische Partei-Korrespondenz: Pressedienst der NSDAP* (hereafter *NSPK*), 296 (19 Dec. 1936), a, of which complete issues through 1944 are in the LC; and "Die Auslandsdeutschen sind Nationalsozialisten," *Wir Deutsche in der Welt, 1935*, edited by the *Verband Deutscher Vereine im Ausland* (Berlin, 1935), pp. 19-30.

19. The AO's activities in these countries were investigated by the Nuremberg tribunals; see the Nuremberg documents, NA/Case No. 11 (*United States v. Ernst von Weizsäcker et al.*)/RG 238 (Collection of World War II War Crimes Records [Nuremberg]); and chapters 2-6 above.

20. Cordell Hull, *The Memoirs of Cordell Hull* (2 vols.; New York: Macmillan, 1948), I:602; and Dodd to Secretary of State, 16 Nov. 1934, *Foreign Relations of*

the United States, 1934 (hereafter *FRUS*; Washington, D.C.: U.S. Government Printing Office, 1951–), II:255.

21. Gottfried Feder, *Was will Adolf Hitler? Das Programm der N.S.D.A.P.* (5th ed.; Munich: F. Eher, 1932), pp. 3-4; and *NSDAP Mitgliedsbuch* (Munich: F. Eher, 1927), p. 4, BDC/PK/*Franz von Pfeffer*.

22. The most useful studies on the origins of the NSDAP and on the *Putsch* are Werner Maser, *Die Frühgeschichte der NSDAP: Hitlers Weg bis 1924* (Frankfurt/Main: Athenäum Verlag, 1965); Georg Franz-Willing, *Die Hitlerbewegung: Der Ursprung, 1919-1922* (Hamburg: R.v. Decker, 1962); and Harold J. Gordon, *Hitler and the Beer Hall Putsch* (Princeton, N.J.: Princeton University Press, 1972).

23. The literature here is vast, but the best works are Weinberg, *Foreign Policy of Hitler's Germany*, pp. 1-24; Hildebrand, *Foreign Policy of the Third Reich*, pp. 12-24; Jäckel, *Hitlers Weltanschauung*, pp. 29-58; and Kuhn, *Hitlers aussenpolitisches Programm*, pp. 104-41.

24. Hitler, *Mein Kampf*, II:439.

25. Weinberg, *Hitlers zweites Buch*, p. 79.

26. See the copy of Bohle's speech on Reich radio, "Reichsprogramm, 20.4.44.," WL/PC5/211A2; and Nitz Volker, *Unser Grenz- und Auslanddeutschtum* (Munich: F. Eher, 1931), pp. 5-6.

27. Baynes, *Speeches*, II:1061-62.

28. Hitler's awareness of the supposed ill treatment of foreign Germans is noted by the French Ambassador to Germany, Andre Francois-Poncet, *Botschafter in Berlin, 1931-1938* (3rd ed.; Berlin/Mainz: F. Kupferberg, 1962), p. 162. On the Nazi belief about the disloyalty of foreign Germans during the war, see the NSDAP's official propaganda organ, *Völkischer Beobachter* (hereafter *VB*), 9 Sept. 1934.

29. See, for example, the AO's "information sheet" for its foreign groups, *Mitteilungsblatt der Leitung der Auslands-Organisation der Nationalsozialistischen Deutschen Arbeiterpartei* (hereafter *Mitteilungsblatt*), 46 (Feb. 1937), 11, copies of which are scattered in the LC and IfZ (1937-1939) and BDC (1940-1942); and "Direct Examination [of Bohle]," 23 July 1948, "Official Court Transcript," Case 11/RG 238. The conscious effort to project the image of Hitler as the "superhuman" Führer is discussed by Ernest K. Bramsted, *Goebbels and National Socialist Propaganda, 1925-1945* (East Lansing, Mich.: Michigan State University Press, 1965), pp. 197-233.

30. Austrian *Vaterländischer Schutzbund* to SA leadership Munich, 7 Apr. 1927, Stanford University, Hoover Institution, NSDAP *Hauptarchiv* Microfilm Collection (hereafter HA)/Roll 34/Folder 642; *Nationalsozialistisches Jahrbuch, 1927*, edited by *Hauptparteileitung* NSDAP (Munich: Eher Verlag, 1927), pp. 90-91; and the useful summary of the early party in Austria, Radomir Luza, *Austro-German Relations in the Anschluss Era* (Princeton, N.J.: Princeton University Press, 1975), pp. 19-22.

31. Weinberg, *Foreign Policy of Hitler's Germany*, pp. 3-9.

32. Dietrich Orlow, *The History of the Nazi Party: 1919-1933* (Pittsburgh: University of Pittsburgh Press, 1969), pp. 133-64.

33. Wolfgang Schäfer, *NSDAP: Entwicklung und Struktur der Staatspartei des Dritten Reiches* (Hanover: Norddeutsche Verlagsanstalt, 1956), p. 12; *Nationalsozialistisches Jahrbuch, 1929*, edited by *Reichsleitung* NSDAP (Munich: Eher Verlag, 1929), p. 144; and Weinberg, *Foreign Policy of Hitler's Germany*, pp. 9-12.

34. AO to DAI, 5 May 1934, NA/Microcopy T-81 (Records of the National Socialist German Labor Party)/Roll 404/Frames 5147585-5147586.

35. Heinz Sanke, ed., *Der deutsche Faschismus in Lateinamerika, 1933-1943* ([East] Berlin: Humboldt Universität, 1966), pp. 9-22; Hans-Jürgen Schröder, *Deutschland und die Vereinigten Staaten, 1933-1939: Wirtschaft und Politik in der Entwicklung des Deutsch-Amerikanischen Gegensatzes* (Wiesbaden: F. Steiner, 1970), pp. 9-33; and the unpublished Ph.D. dissertation, William Newton Simonson, "Nazi Infiltration in South America, 1933-1945," (Fletcher School of Law and Diplomacy, 1964), pp. 45-74.

36. NSDAP RL to Hamburg GL, 21 Feb. 1931, T-81/147/0185888; and Franz Reitzenstein, "Bericht ueber die Taetigkeit des ehemaligen Standartenfuehrers Bruno Fricke im Hohenau bzw. Obligado," n.d., NA/Microcopy T-580 (Captured German Records Filmed at Berlin)/Roll 57/Folder 296a. On Asanger and Künze, see "Fünfzehn Jahre der AO," *Hamburger Fremdenblatt*, 3 July 1943; and Nazi short wave broadcast, "[Radio] Zeesen . . . , 11.7.43," WL/PC5/211A2.

37. Blumenau O.Gr. to RL, 10 Apr. 1931, T-580/57/296a.

38. Diamond, *The Nazi Movement in the United States*, pp. 28-29; Kuhn, *Hitlers aussenpolitisches Programm*, pp. 131-36; and Weinberg, "Hitler's Image of the United States," pp. 1007-09.

39. C. E. Dale, *Amerikanisches Auskunftsbuch* (Union Hill, N.J., 1923); F. Eiselmeier, *Das Deutschtum in Angloamerika* (Brandenburg [Havel]: Deutscher Schutzbundverlag, 1926); and Arnold A. Offner, *American Appeasement: United States Foreign Policy and Germany, 1933-1938* (Cambridge, Mass.: Harvard University Press, 1969), pp. 2-3. The WL possesses a large collection of such pamphlets and propaganda pieces, dealing with Germandom in all parts of the world.

40. Kurt Ludecke, *I Knew Hitler: The Story of a Nazi Who Escaped the Blood Purge* (New York: Scribner's, 1937), pp. 192-201. Ford did not contribute to the party; Diamond, *The Nazi Movement in the United States*, pp. 96-97; and Ph.D. dissertation, Dieter Dedeke, "Das Dritte Reich und die Vereinigten Staaten von Amerika, 1933-1937: Ein Beitrag zur Geschichte der deutsch-amerikanischen Beziehungen" (Free University of Berlin, 1969), pp. 49-55.

41. Diamond, *The Nazi Movement in the United States*, pp. 86-92, 360.

42. Hitler to Teutonia, 26 May 1926, T-81/144/0183166; Diamond, *The Nazi Movement in the United States*, pp. 92-95; Smith, *Deutschtum of Nazi Germany*, pp. 61-62; Jacobsen, *Nationalsozialistische Aussenpolitik*, p. 528; and Dedeke, "Das Dritte Reich und die Vereinigten Staaten," pp. 45-49.

43. "Politischer Lebenslauf des Pg. Klausfeldner . . . . ," n.d., T-81/140/0177791; and Diamond, *The Nazi Movement in the United States*, pp. 114-15. On the Free Corps, see Robert G. L. Waite, *Vanguard of Nazism: The Free Corps Movement in Postwar Germany, 1918-1923* (New York: Norton, 1969).

44. Schneider, "Erlebnisse aus der Kampfzeit," 31 Dec. 1936, HA/27B/531. On Teutonia's membership figures and Spanknöbel, see Diamond, *The Nazi Movement in the United States*, pp. 95, 99-100. Ironically, Diamond's thorough study does not mention Schneider and his organization, except in a footnote.

45. NSDAP Propaganda Dept. (Himmler) to Teutonia, 24 Sept. 1930, HA/35/695.

46. NSDAP Propaganda Dept. to party group in Southwest Africa, 31 Dec. 1930, HA/34/657.

47. RL to Hamburg GL, 21 Feb. 1931, T-81/147/0185888. Parts of this study dealing with the Far East were presented by the author in a paper, entitled "Nazi Party Activities in the Far East," to the American Historical Association Annual Meeting, Washington, D.C., 29 Dec. 1976.

CHAPTER 2

1. *The New York Times* (hereafter *NYT*), 15 Sept. 1930. *The Times* (London), 16 Sept. 1930, called the election a "painful surprise."

2. Nazi member in Putna, Rumania to RL, 16 Sept. 1930, HA/35/685.

3. Grothe, "Personalfragebogen für die Anlegen der SA-Personalakte," 15 Feb. 1938, BDC/SA/ *Willy Grothe*; Bohle to Philip Bouhler, 3 Apr. 1937, Nuremberg Document 1973-NG, Case 11/RG238, recommending Grothe for the party's Golden Badge of Honor; and Arthur L. Smith, Jr., "Hitler's *Gau Ausland*," *Political Studies*, 14 (1966), 90-92.

4. Bohle to Hermann Sack, 22 Apr. 1937, PA/ *Büro des Chefs der Auslandsorganisation* (hereafter *Chef* AO)/Folder 47 (*Gauleiter Bohle* [*Persönliche Korrespondenz*]); and Bohle's essay, "Die Auslandsorganisation der NSDAP," in Wilhelm Kube, ed., *Almanach der nationalsozialistischen Revolution* (Berlin: Brunnen Verlag, 1934), p. 90. Jacobsen, *Nationalsozialistische Aussenpolitik*, p. 91, contends that Strasser approached Nieland about heading the new Dept.; this seems to ignore, however, Nieland's personal ambition and Bohle's repeated assertion of Grothe's role in the formation of the *Abteilung*. See also, Hans-Adolf Jacobsen, "Die Gruendung der Auslandsabteilung der NSDAP (1931-1933)," in *Gedenkschrift fuer Martin Goehring* (Wiesbaden: Steiner, 1968), pp. 353-55.

5. Ludecke, *I Knew Hitler*, p. 410; and Strasser's command, "Anordnung," 28 Apr. 1931, BDC/PK/ *Hans Nieland*.

6. Ludecke, *I Knew Hitler*, p. 320.

7. Jacobsen, *Nationalsozialistische Aussenpolitik*, p. 91. Nieland's role in the Hamburg party leadership is discussed by Albert Krebs, *Tendenzen und Gestalten der NSDAP: Erinnerungen an die Frühzeit der Partei* (Stuttgart: Deutsche Verlags-Anstalt, 1959), pp. 73, 101, 115; and Nieland, "Lebenslauf," 22 Dec. 1937, BDC/ RuSHA/ *Hans Nieland*.

8. Nieland, "Rundverfügung Nr. 1," 1 June 1931, T-580/54/292; and Strasser, "Anordnung," 28 Apr. 1931, BDC/PK/ *Hans Nieland*.

9. Nieland, "Rundverfügung Nr. 1," 1 June 1931, T-580/54/292.

10. Ibid., and Nieland to Strasser, 9 Nov. 1931. The advisers are in Jacobsen, *Nationalsozialistische Aussenpolitik*, p. 92.

11. Nieland, "Dienstanweisung Nr. 1," 28 Sept. 1931, T-580/54/292. The Dept. was extremely small compared to the average party organization in Germany; compare, for example, *Führer zum Gautag der Nationalsozialistischen Deutschen Arbeiter-Partei am 21. und 22. Februar 1931 in der Stadt Braunschweig*, in the BDC.

12. Louis de Jong, *The German Fifth Column in the Second World War*, trans. C. M. Geyl (Chicago: University of Chicago Press, 1956), p. 278; Jacobsen, *Nationalsozialistische Aussenpolitik*, p. 115; and Bohle Interrogation, NA/Microcopy M-679 (Records of the Department of State Special Interrogation Mission to Germany, 1945-1946)/Roll 1/Frame 0073.

13. Nieland to Strasser, 24 July 1931; copies of the letters in T-580/54/292; and Jacobsen, *Nationalsozialistische Aussenpolitik*, p. 94.

14. *Auslands-Abteilung* to ROL, 15 Aug. 1931, T-580/54/292.

15. Strasser, "Anordnung," 3 Feb. 1932, T-580/55/292; Strasser to Nieland, 3 June 1931; and *Auslands-Abteilung* to Strasser, 10 Aug. 1931, T-580/54/292.

16. Edouard Calic, ed., *Unmasked: Two Confidential Interviews with Hitler in 1931*, trans. Richard Barry (London: Chatto and Windus, 1971), p. 42.

17. A good summary of party law is Hans Frank, *Neues deutsches Recht*, Vol. II of *Hier spricht das neue Deutschland!* (Munich: F. Eher, 1934), in the IfZ.

18. Sanke, *Der deutsche Faschismus in Lateinamerika*, p. 22; and Simonson, "Nazi Infiltration," pp. 2-9.

19. Arnold Ebel, *Das Dritte Reich und Argentinien: Die diplomatischen Beziehungen unter besonderer Berücksichtigung der Handelspolitik (1933-1939)* (Cologne: Boehlau Verlag, 1971), pp. 12-20, 23-30; AO to DAI, 5 May 1934, T-81/404/5147585; *NSPK*, 105 (7 May 1936), a; Sanke, *Der deutsche Faschismus in Lateinamerika*, pp. 81, 85; and Klaus Kannapin, "Deutschland und Argentinien von 1933 bis 1945," *Wissenschaftliche Zeitschrift der Universität Rostock*, 14 (1965), 110-11.

20. A good history of the O. Gr. São Paulo is Cossel to Gottfried Richter, 24 May 1933, T-580/57/296a. A short biography of Cossel is "Aufzeichnung für den Herrn Reichsaussenminister," 20 June 1938, NA/Microcopy T-120 (Records of the German Foreign Office Received by the Department of State)/Roll 225/Frame 170980.

21. A biography of Reitzenstein is in AO, "Franz Reitzenstein," n.d., BDC/PK/ *Franz Reitzenstein*; born in July 1879 in Annaburg, he was one of the first foreign Germans to join the NSDAP (July 1929). See also, AO to DAI, 5 May 1934, T-81/404/5147585.

22. AO, "Karl Hübner," 30 July 1942, BDC/MF/*Karl Hübner*; the booklet by the AO, *Auslands-Organisation der N.S.D.A.P.: Arbeitstagung der Politischen Leiter in Erlangen vom 6.-9. September 1935* (hereafter *Auslands-Organisation der N.S.D.A.P.*), p. 40, a copy of which is in the BA; and *Mitteilungsblatt*, 2 (Feb. 1939), 1-2.

23. *Auslands-Abteilung* to Strasser, 10 Aug. 1931, T-580/54/292; Diamond, *The Nazi Movement in the United States*, p. 98; and Ludecke, *I Knew Hitler*, pp. 319-20. Party members in the new O.Gr. erroneously called their local the *Gauleitung-USA*. A *Gau* was a party "district," the largest territorial administrative unit of the NSDAP, not a local.

24. RL to Hamburg GL, 21 Feb. 1931, T-81/147/0185888. Diamond, *The Nazi Movement in the United States*, does not mention Krinn, except in a footnote on p. 99, where Krinn's name is misspelled.

25. Nieland to Kappe, 17 June 1931, T-580/57/296a.

26. Ibid., Ludecke to Nieland, 21 Oct. 1931; and "Der deutsche Weltkampf und Nord-Amerika," *Vorposten: Nachrichten der deutschen Freiheitsbewegung in den Vereinigten Staaten*, 1 July 1931. On Ludecke's friendship with Hitler, note Weinberg, *Foreign Policy of Hitler's Germany*, pp. 10-11; and Walter Werner Pese, "Hitler und Italien, 1920-1926," *Vierteljahrshefte für Zeitgeschichte*, 3 (1955), 117-18.

27. Nieland to ROL, 31 July 1931, T-580/57/296a; Ludecke, *I Knew Hitler*, p. 325; and Diamond, *The Nazi Movement in the United States*, p. 100. According to Diamond, Manger was appointed later in 1932, and he does not mention Manger as leader of the O.Gr. New York.

28. Orlow discusses the "totalitarian mind-set," *The Nazi Party: 1919-1933*, pp. 3-5. See also, Donald M. McKale, *The Nazi Party Courts: Hitler's Management*

of Conflict in His Movement, 1921-1945 (Lawrence, Kansas: University Press of Kansas, 1974), p. 6.

29. German Legation Berne to AA, 6 Jan. 1932, T-120/3365/E598034-E598038; and unpublished Ph.D. dissertation by Günter Lachmann, "Der Nationalsozialismus in der Schweiz, 1931-1945: Ein Beitrag zur Geschichte der Auslandsorganisation der NSDAP" (Free University of Berlin, 1962), p. 23.

30. See the newspaper clipping, T-120/3132/E510485.

31. ROL to J. A. Sprenger, 19 Jan. 1931, T-580/58/298.

32. Mario Toscano, *Alto Adige-South Tyrol: Italy's Frontier with the German World*, ed. George A. Carbone (Baltimore: Johns Hopkins University Press, 1975), pp. 15-17, 21; Conrad F. Latour, *Südtirol und die Achse Berlin-Rom, 1938-1945* (Stuttgart: Deutsche Verlags-Anstalt, 1962), pp. 11-13, 14-18, 20; and Elizabeth Wiskemann, *The Rome-Berlin Axis: A History of the Relations Between Hitler and Mussolini* (New York: Oxford University Press, 1949), p. 23.

33. Alan Cassels, "Mussolini and German Nationalism, 1922-25," *Journal of Modern History*, 35 (1963), 151-57.

34. Frank to Hitler, 10 Aug. 1926, BDC/PK/*Hans Frank*; Hitler, *Mein Kampf*, II:699, 705, 709, 755-58; Toscano, *Alto Adige-South Tyrol*, p. 28; Ritschel, *Diplomatie um Südtirol*, pp. 127-39; Pese, "Hitler und Italien, 1920-1926," pp. 113, 117-18; and Erhard Klöss, ed., *Reden des Führers: Politik und Propaganda Adolf Hitlers* (Munich: Deutscher Taschenbuch Verlag, 1967), p. 251.

35. *Auslands-Abteilung* to ROL, 4 Nov. 1931, T-580/58/298.

36. "Nationalsozialisten in Rom," *Münchener Telegramm-Zeitung*, 24 Nov. 1931; and "Wie sie lügen!" *VB*, 27 Nov. 1931.

37. "Gründungsdaten der Auslandsgliederungen," Dec. 1937, T-580/55/293.

38. Bene was born in Sept. 1884 in Kloster-Altenberg/Wetzlar Lahn and entered the SS in Dec. 1939; "Otto Bene," 13 Feb. 1944, BDC/RuSHA/*Otto Bene*; *Who's Who in Germany and Austria* (London: British Ministry of Economic Warfare, 1945), p. 11; and [World Committee for the Victims of German Fascism] *The Brown Network: The Activities of the Nazis in Foreign Countries* (New York: Knight Publications, 1936), p. 133.

39. For the vital role which personality and charisma played in the NSDAP, see Joseph Nyomarkay, *Charisma and Factionalism in the Nazi Party* (Minneapolis, Minn.: University of Minnesota Press, 1967), pp. 3-5; and Walter C. Langer, *The Mind of Adolf Hitler: The Secret Wartime Report* (New York: New American Library, 1973), pp. 49-66. On the *Führerprinzip* and its theory, see Wolfgang Horn, *Führerideologie und Parteiorganisation in der NSDAP (1919-1933)* (Düsseldorf: Droste Verlag, 1972), passim; Hess to Walter Hewel, 30 Mar. 1927, in Gerhard L. Weinberg, "National Socialist Organization and Foreign Policy Aims in 1927," *Journal of Modern History*, 36 (1964), 428-34; and Konrad Heiden, *Adolf Hitler: Das Zeitalter der Verantwortungslosigkeit* (Zurich: Europa-Verlag, 1936), pp. 121-25.

40. Bohle to Bouhler, 3 Apr. 1937, Nuremberg Document 1973-NG, Case 11/RG 238; and "Bernhard Ruberg," 13 Feb. 1944, BDC/RuSHA/*Bernhard Ruberg*.

41. Meyer-Donner, "Bericht. Betr.: Reise/Schweden," 25 Dec. 1931; and Nieland to Göring, 29 Dec. 1931, T-580/56/296.

42. *Auslands-Abteilung* to ROL, 23 Jan. 1932, T-580/55/292; and Buch to W. R. Köhler, 11 Nov. 1931, BDC/OPG/*Walter Buch*.

43. Strasser, "Anordnung," 3 Feb. 1932, T-580/55/292; and Nieland's bitter complaint to Strasser, 15 Feb. 1932, T-580/58/298. On the Austrian situation, see

Bruce F. Pauley, *Hahnenschwanz und Hakenkreuz: Steirischer Heimatschutz und österreichischer Nationalsozialismus, 1918-1934* (Vienna: Europa-Verlag, 1972), pp. 107-30; Jürgen Gehl, *Austria, Germany, and the Anschluss, 1931-1938* (London: Oxford University Press, 1963), p. 48; and Ernst Nolte, *Die faschistischen Bewegungen* (2nd ed.; Munich: Deutscher Taschenbuch Verlag, 1969), pp. 252-57.

44. Gustloff to Heinrich Sack (LGL Spain), 27 Mar. 1932; and Gustloff to Schwarz, 8 Mar. 1932, HA/35/687.

45. *NYT*, 10 June 1932.

46. See a copy of "Auslands-Ausweis" in T-580/54/292.

47. Ibid., "Satzung des Bundes der Freunde der Hitler-Bewegung," 14 June 1932; and Jacobsen, *Nationalsozialistische Aussenpolitik*, p. 93.

48. Bohle to Goebbels, 3 Oct. 1934, BDC/KK/*Franz Hasenöhrl*; Hasenöhrl, "Lebenslauf," n.d., BDC/PK/*Franz Hasenöhrl*; and Hasenöhrl to Stüpu. Harbin, 4 Mar. 1933, T-580/57/296a.

49. Concerning German interests in China, note Bloch, *German Interests and Policies in the Far East*, pp. 1-21; Herbert von Dirksen, *Moskau-Tokio-London: Erinnerungen und Betrachtungen zu 20 Jahren deutscher Aussenpolitik, 1919-1939* (Stuttgart: Kohlhammer, 1949), pp. 154-55; and *Wir Deutsche in der Welt, 1938*, edited by *Verband Deutscher Vereine im Ausland* (Berlin, 1938), pp. 75-86.

50. "Werden und Wirken der Landesgruppe Union von Südafrika, der Auslands-Organisation der NSDAP.," 4 Dec. 1937, T-120/239/174844-174846; Hellmut Kirchner, *Hermann Bohle: Leben, Kämpfen und Denken eines Auslandsdeutschen* (Berlin: Junker und Dünnhaupt, n.d.), pp. 7-61, 72-73, 82; Heinrich Stuebel, "Die Entwicklung des Nationalsozialismus in Südwestafrika," *Vierteljahrshefte für Zeitgeschichte*, 1 (1953), 170-72; and Heinz Tillmann, "Tätigkeit und Ziele der Fünften Kolonne in Südafrika während der zweiten Weltkrieges," *Zeitschrift für Geschichtswissenschaft, Sonderheft* (1961), 182-86.

51. O.Gr., "Monatsbericht Maerz 1932," T-580/59/301.

52. Ibid., *Auslands-Abteilung*, "Rundverfügung für die Niederlande," 7 May 1932; Patzig, "Rundschreiben No. 5/32 vom 12.5.32;" and Nieland to ROL, 17 June 1932. On Mussert's movement, formed in 1931, note his "12 Jahre NSB aus der Vogelperspektive," 11 Dec. 1943, HA/34/678; and Konrad Kwiet, "Zur Geschichte der Mussert-Bewegung," *Vierteljahrshefte für Zeitgeschichte*, 18 (1970), 164-76. See also, VB, 1 June 1932; and pamphlet by Georg Angler, *Adolf Hitler en de door hem opgerichte Nationaal Socialistische Duitsche Arbeiderspartij* (n.p., 1932), pp. 19-21, in the BDC.

53. Thiele to Strasser, 4 May 1932; Karl Kaufmann to Strasser, 6 Jan. 1932; Strasser to Schwarz, 29 Feb. 1932; Reinhold to Buch, 31 Mar. 1932, T-580/54/291; *Wir Deutsche in der Welt, 1938*, p. 24; and "Die NSBO 'Seeschiffahrt' der Auslandsorganisation angeschlossen," *Hansa*, 71 (2 June 1934), 844.

54. Thiele to Strasser, 2 Dec. 1932, 31 May 1932, T-580/54/291. See also, *Hamburger Fremdenblatt*, 2 Mar. 1942.

55. "Gründungsdaten der Auslandsgliederungen," Dec. 1937, T-580/55/293; Kube, *Almanach*, p. 92; and Jacobsen, *Nationalsozialistische Aussenpolitik*, p. 91.

56. Diamond, *The Nazi Movement in the United States*, pp. 100-01.

57. As an example, see Gissibl to Schneider, 26 Feb. 1932, HA/27B/531. Note further, Smith, *Deutschtum of Nazi Germany*, p. 68; Bohle Interrogation, 13 Nov. 1945, RG 238; O. John Rogge, *The Official German Report: Nazi Penetration, 1924-1942, Pan-Arabism, 1939-Today* (New York: Yoseleff, 1961), p. 17; and

Auslands-Abteilung, "Vereinigte Staaten von Nord-Amerika," 1932, T-580/55/293. Contrary to Diamond, *The Nazi Movement in the United States*, pp. 99-102, Gissibl and Spanknöbel did not remain close friends until the spring of 1933 (here, note Dedeke, "Das Dritte Reich und die Vereinigten Staaten," pp. 66-68). Also, Diamond's contention (p. 99) that the various branches across the United States were formed by June 1931 appears unfounded; Nieland had not yet confirmed Manger as leader of the O.Gr. New York and contact man for America. It is also difficult to believe his assertion because his evidence in note 29 (i.e., Schneider, "Ortsgruppe Chicago," 1932-1935, T-81/140/185886) does not exist as cited. Furthermore, as the letter above from Gissibl to Schneider reveals, he is incorrect (pp. 100-01) in stating that Teutonia was dissolved late in 1932.

58. *NYT*, 4 Apr. 1932.

59. Ludecke, *I Knew Hitler*, p. 411; and Schneider, "Erlebnisse aus der Kampfzeit," 31 Dec. 1936, HA/27B/531. Estimates of Nazi members in America varied from 60 to 200 in late 1932; Jacobsen, *Nationalsozialistische Aussenpolitik*, p. 529; and Diamond, *The Nazi Movement in the United States*, pp. 95, 100.

60. James V. Compton, *The Swastika and the Eagle: Hitler, the United States, and the Origins of World War II* (Boston: Houghton Mifflin, 1967), pp. 66-67, which deals chiefly with such claims after 1933.

61. Reiner to Strasser, 7 Aug. 1932; Reich Press Office to ROL, 12 Sept. 1932, T-580/56/296; Bohle to Meiss, 28 Dec. 1932; Nieland to ROL, 1 Aug. 1932; and Nieland to Georg Normund (one of the rebels in Windhoek), 23 July 1932, T-580/57/296a.

62. "Erwin Ettel," 13 Feb. 1944; and Ettel, "Kurzer Lebenslauf und bisherige pol. Tätigkeit," 18 Dec. 1937, BDC/RuSHA/*Erwin Ettel*.

63. For instance, Dietrich Orlow, *The Nazis in the Balkans: A Case Study of Totalitarian Politics* (Pittsburgh: University of Pittsburgh Press, 1968); Reinhard Bollmus, *Das Amt Rosenberg und seine Gegner: Zum Machtkampf im nationalsozialistischen Herrschaftssystem* (Stuttgart: Deutsche Verlags-Anstalt, 1970); Nyomarkay, *Charisma and Factionalism*; and McKale, *Nazi Party Courts*.

64. Nieland to ROL, 7 Mar. 1932, T-580/55/292; and Martin Broszat, *Der Staat Hitlers: Grundlegung und Entwicklung seiner inneren Verfassung* (Munich: Deutscher Taschenbuch Verlag, 1969), p. 74.

65. Bohle Interrogation, 13 Nov. 1945, RG 238. The Nieland-Wagner squabble was finally settled by the NSDAP's Supreme Court, *Reichs-Uschla*; Wagner to the Court, 4 Oct. 1932, BDC/OPG/*Joseph Wagner*.

66. Strasser to Nieland, 6 Dec. 1932, T-580/55/292; and on the reforms, Orlow, *The Nazi Party: 1919-1933*, pp. 258-65.

67. Strasser, "Anordnung Nr. 13," 21 Nov. 1932, T-580/54/291; and Nieland to ROL, 3 Sept. 1932, T-580/55/292, pushing Strasser to promote him to the rank of GL.

68. PO to *Gau Ausland*, 4 Jan. 1933; and ROL to *Gau Ausland*, 25 Oct. 1932, T-580/57/296a.

69. ROL to Reich party treasurer, 12 July 1932, T-81/133/166632, refusing admission of the German national, Wilhelm Hein, to the party branch in Santiago, Chile; and *Gau Ausland* to Strasser's Private Secretariat, 4 Nov. 1932, T-580/55/292.

70. The *Reichs-Uschla*, for example, dissolved the O.Gr. Meran in the Tirol; PO to the Court, 21 Feb. 1933, BA/NS 22 (*Reichsorganisationsleiter der NSDAP*)/Box 337/*Ordner* 877. See also, LGL Italy to PO, 29 Jan. 1933; and "Bericht zu

den Vorgängen in Italien [Betr. wandernde Pgg. in Italien]," 27 Jan. 1932, T-580/ 58/298. The documents reveal that as early as Sept. 1931, party groups in Meran, Milan, Florence, and Venice were having difficulties with unemployed Nazis from Germany seeking to live off the Italian affiliates. Later, during the war, Bohle tried to strengthen the Rome-Berlin Axis by stressing to the Italians that SA men fleeing Germany in 1932 were welcomed into Italy with open arms by their "comrades" in the Fascist movement; see the typed manuscript published in an Italian paper in Oct. 1940, "Kampfkameradschaft," T-120/124/119412.

71. LGL Italy, "Rundschreiben 18," 3 Feb. 1933, T-580/58/298.

72. As, for instance, in the expulsion of F. Krais from France; *Auslands-Abteilung* to ROL, 8 Mar. 1932, T-580/55/292.

73. A case in point being the Austrian diplomat, Hanns von Winter, who sent political reports during 1932 from Paris and Moscow to the GL for Austria, Alfred Frauenfeld; Winter to AO, 3 Feb. 1939, T-81/147/0187080-0187081.

74. The figures are taken from AO, "Parteimitglieder, Stand 30.6.1937," T-120/78/60148; and Jacobsen, *Nationalsozialistische Aussenpolitik*, p. 137.

75. *Diplomaticus* (pseud.), *Diplomatie und Hakenkreuz: Kämpfe und Erlebnisse eines Journalisten* (Berlin: Buch- und Tiefdruck-Gesellschaft, 1934), p. 158.

CHAPTER 3

1. As, for example, Kurt Kuhn, Ogrl. of Panama, "Deutsche Landsleute!" 23 Mar. 1933, T-580/57/296a. The seizure of power and unfriendly foreign reaction are studied best by Karl Dietrich Bracher, Wolfgang Sauer, and Gerhard Schulz, *Die nationalsozialistische Machtergreifung: Studien zur Errichtung des totalitären Herrschaftssystems in Deutschland, 1933/34* (2nd ed.; Cologne: Westdeutscher Verlag, 1962), and Weinberg, *Foreign Policy of Hitler's Germany*, pp. 38-39.

2. On the APA, see Jacobsen, *Nationalsozialistische Aussenpolitik*, pp. 45-89; Günter Schubert, *Anfänge nationalsozialistischer Aussenpolitik* (Cologne: Verlag Wissenschaft und Politik, 1963), pp. 220-38; Erich Kordt, *Wahn und Wirklichkeit: Die Aussenpolitik des Dritten Reiches* (Stuttgart: Union Deutsche Verlagsgesellschaft, 1948), p. 98; and "Dr. Hans Nieland," 13 Feb. 1944, BDC/RuSHA/*Hans Nieland*, showing that Nieland entered the SS in 1934 and became Lord Mayor of Dresden in World War II.

3. Ley, "Anordnung Nr. 26/33," 2 June 1933, T-580/54/291.

4. Hess, *Reden*, pp. 106-07; and his essay, "Wie wird der Man beschaffen sein, der Deutschland wieder zur Höhe führt?" HA/35/689.

5. Bella Fromm, *Blood and Banquets: A Berlin Social Diary* (New York: Harper, 1942), p. 252 (the entry for 22 Aug. 1937).

6. "Direct Examination [of Bohle]," 23 July 1948, "Official Court Transcript," Case 11/RG 238; Bohle Interrogation, M-679/1/0102; Bohle, "Lebenslauf," Apr. 1933, T-580/55/293; *Das Deutsche Führerlexikon, 1934/1935* (Berlin: Stollberg, 1935), p. 65; Z.A.B. Zeman, *Nazi Propaganda* (London: Oxford University Press, 1964), p. 67; and Bohle to Otto Karlowa, 17 Sept. 1937, PA/*Chef* AO/Folder 47.

7. SS personnel file on Bohle, 13 Feb. 1944, Nuremberg Document 2057-NG, Case 11/RG 238; and Bohle Interrogation, M-679/1/0144.

8. Bohle Interrogation, 25 Oct. 1945, RG 238; and Bohle Interrogation, M-679/ 1/0075.

9. Bohle Interrogation, M-679/1/0104-0108; Vicco v. Bülow-Schwante, "Eides-

stattliche Versicherung," 21 Apr. 1948, Nuremberg Document 38 (Defense Exhibit Bohle), Case 11/RG 238; and *Wir Deutsche in der Welt, 1936,* edited by *Verband Deutscher Vereine im Ausland* (Berlin, 1936), p. 20.

10. "Direct Examination [of Bohle]," 23 July 1948, "Official Court Transcript," Case 11/RG 238; Hassell, *Diaries,* p. 183 (the entry for 13 July 1941); and Nolte, *Die faschistischen Bewegungen,* which shows that Bohle's views fitted well into the European fascist *Weltanschauung.*

11. Bohle Interrogation, 25 Oct. 1945, RG 238.

12. Bohle to Schmeer, 4 Apr. 1933, T-580/55/293.

13. Weinberg, *Foreign Policy of Hitler's Germany,* pp. 34-35, 165; and Lord Vansittart, *The Mist Procession: The Autobiography of Lord Vansittart* (London: Hutchinson, 1958), p. 475.

14. Bohle to Ley, 8 July 1933; Schwarz to ROL, 14 July 1933; PO, "Ernennung," 8 May 1933, T-580/55/293; and Jacobsen, *Nationalsozialistische Aussenpolitik,* p. 100.

15. Bohle, "Zukunftsaufgaben der Auslands-Abteilung der NSDAP," 31 Aug. 1933; Hess, "Verfügung!" 3 Oct. 1933, T-580/55/293; *VB,* 8 Sept. 1934; Bohle, "Rundschreiben! An sämtliche Auslandsgruppen der N.S.D.A.P.," 3 Oct. 1933, WL/Document Collection No. 585 (The Nazi Party in Spain); and "N.S.-Ortsgruppenleiter aus dem Auslande beim Führer," *VB,* 6 July 1933. A partial list of the foreign groups and their leaders is in Jacobsen, *Nationalsozialistische Aussenpolitik,* pp. 651-54. In Nov. 1933 Bohle became a member of the *Reichstag,* which had already been "coordinated" by the Nazis; *Das Deutsche Führerlexikon,* p. 65.

16. Hess, "Anordnung," 17 Feb. 1934, *Verordnungsblatt der Reichsleitung der Nationalsozialistischen Deutschen Arbeiter-Partei* (hereafter *VOBl*), 66 (Feb. 1934), 145.

17. Hess, "Anordnung," 16 Mar. 1934; PO, "Anordnung Nr. 21/34," 15 June 1934, T-580/54/291; and Kube, *Almanach,* p. 93.

18. "3000 auslandsdeutsche Parteigenossen erleben Nürnberg," *VB,* 8 Sept. 1934; Jacobsen, *Nationalsozialistische Aussenpolitik,* p. 145; and *NYT,* 22 Feb. 1934.

19. Bohle to DAI, 1 June 1934, T-81/404/5147555.

20. "Der Landesgruppenleiter," *NSPK,* 288 (10 Dec. 1936), 1-3; and Bohle Interrogation, M-679/1/0159-0161.

21. "Abschrift. Rundlauf. Neu-Organisation der A.O.," 30 May 1934, T-580/55/293.

22. Bohle Interrogation, M-679/1/0162.

23. Bohle to Goebbels, 3 Oct. 1934, BDC/KK/*Franz Hasenöhrl*; Burbach, "Richtlinien fuer die Durchfuehrung der Sammlung fuer das Winterhilfswerk der Reichsregierung gegen Hunger und Kaelte," 22 Sept. 1933, WL/585; and Ebel, *Das Dritte Reich und Argentinien,* pp. 246-47.

24. See the Nazi publication, Otto Gauweiler, *Rechtseinrichtungen und Rechtsaufgaben der Bewegung* (Munich: F. Eher, 1939), pp. 71-76.

25. As Bohle did, for instance, with the party leader in Dublin, Colonel Brase; AO to AA, 1 June 1934, T-120/1176/477890-477891.

26. Franz Thierfelder, *Die wirtschaftliche Bedeutung des Auslanddeutschtums* (Stuttgart: F. Enke, 1934), pp. 11-23.

27. A sample of the material gathered is O.Gr. Madrid, "Rundschreiben Nr. 9," 26 July 1935, WL/585; see also, *Auslands-Organisation der N.S.D.A.P.,* pp. 40-41.

28. "Directives for the Cooperation between the Economic Offices of the NSDAP

Abroad and the German Chambers of Commerce Abroad," 7 July 1934, Nuremberg Document 14141-NI, Case 11/RG 238; and Hess, *Reden*, pp. 34-38.

29. Relevant documents are in the DZA; Sanke, *Der deutsche Faschismus in Lateinamerika*, p. 62.

30. See the Nuremberg Documents, I. G. Farben-Bayer to Heinrich Homann, 10 Aug. 1934, 6492-NI; letters from Farben representatives in Argentina, 5, 14 June and 6, 12 Nov. 1935, 4613-NI; and Heinrich Gattineau (head of Farben's Political Economy Dept.), "Affidavit," 13 Mar. 1947, 4833-NI, all in Case 11/RG 238. Further, note Ebel, *Das Dritte Reich und Argentinien*, pp. 230-34.

31. AO to *Gutehoffnungshütte*, 21 June 1934; *Gutehoffnungshütte* to AA, 18 Aug. 1934; and AO to AA, 12 Apr. 1935, T-120/357/264971-264972, 264969-264970, 264988, respectively.

32. Horst Kühne, "Die Fünfte Kolonne des faschistischen deutschen Imperialismus in Südwestafrika (1933-1939)," *Zeitschrift für Geschichtswissenschaft*, 8 (1960), 774; AO to DAI, 13, 14 Aug. 1935; and AO to DAI, 13 Mar. 1936, T-81/404/5146688-5146689, 5146683, 5148153, respectively. On the removal of Jews from firms in the Netherlands, see LGL Netherlands to APA, 12 May 1933, T-580/59/301. See further, Hans Harnisch (a German industrialist from Argentina), "Affidavit," 20 Aug. 1947, Nuremberg Document, 2548-NG, Case 11/RG 238.

33. AO to O.Gr. Madrid, 7 Feb. 1935 ("Betr. Handelsabkommen zwischen Uruguay und Spanien."); on Falk, "Protokoll ueber eine Aussprache bei der Landes-Gruppenleitung Spanien ueber die AEG IBERICA de Electricidad am 9. und 10. November 1935," WL/585; and Franz Spielhagen (pseud.), *Spione und Verschwörer in Spanien: Nach offiziellen nationalsozialistischen Dokumenten* (Paris: Éditions du Carrefour, 1936), pp. 103-18.

34. An example is "Angola—Rundbriefe der Ortsgruppenleitung, Nr. 3, August 1934," HA/35/684. On the reorganization of the *Uschla* and creation of the party court system, note Reichs-Uschla, "Uschla Rundschreiben Nr. 11, 9 Dezember 1933," BA/*Sammlung Schumacher* (hereafter *Slg. Schu.*)/*Ordner* 380 (*Oberstes Parteigericht*); and McKale, *Nazi Party Courts*, pp. 117-18. For official directives on the *Uschla* in foreign groups, see Kraneck, "Rundschreiben an sämtliche der Auslands-Abteilung unterstehenden Dienststellen," 28 Nov. 1933 ("Betr. Untersuchungs- und Schlichtungs-Ausschüsse."), WL/585.

35. Kraneck, "Rundschreiben," 18 Jan. 1934 ("Betr.: Die Stellung der Auslandsdeutschen zu den Rassefragen."), WL/585; AO Party Court, "Beschluss," 20 Feb. 1935; and the Court to LGL Brazil, 9 July 1938, T-81/146/0185569, 0185589.

36. Wagner, "Denkschrift," n.d., T-81/57/60087-600140.

37. Gestapo to AA, 13 Oct. 1934, investigating accusations that Erich Dahle, party leader for northern Brazil, was associating too much with "English circles," T-120/1176/477925; AO to DAI, 18 Apr. 1934, T-81/404/5147610; AA, "Auszug aus einem Brief des Botschafters Grafen Welczeck vom 8. Januar 1935 an Staatssekretär von Bülow," T-120/357/264954; and AO to NSDAP's Accounting Office, 12 Apr. 1935, T-580/385/58.

38. AA to missions and consulates, 31 May 1934, T-120/1129/460143-460145; and Karl Haushofer, "Versuch . . . soweit sie von hier aus überschaubar scheint," n.d., NA/Microcopy T-82 (Records of Nazi Cultural and Research Institutions and Records Pertaining to Axis Relations and Interests in the Far East)/Roll 149/Frames 0286363-0286364, discussing Goebbels's cooperation with Bohle.

39. Strölin Interrogation, M-679/3/1245; Kipphan, *Deutsche Propaganda in den*

Vereinigten Staaten, 1933-1941 (Heidelberg: C. Winter, 1971) pp. 36-44; and Carl Peterson and Otto Scheel, eds., *Handwörterbuch des Grenz- und Ausland-Deutschtums* (5 vols.; Breslau: F. Hirt, 1934-1935).

40. Hans-Adolf Jacobsen, ed., *Hans Steinacher: Bundesleiter des VDA, 1933-1937 (Erinnerungen und Dokumente)* (Boppard/Rhine: Boldt, 1970), pp. 149-52.

41. Zeberer, "Rundschreiben an sämtliche Landesgruppen, Ortsgruppen und Stützpunkte im Ausland," 22 Sept. 1933 ("Betr.: HJ-Gruppen."), WL/585; *Arbeitsbericht für das Jahr 1934 der Abteilung "Ausland" in der Reichsjugendführung* (n.p., n.d.), pp. 73-128, in the LC; Bohle to PO, 30 June 1933, T-580/55/293; Schirach Interrogation, International Military Tribunal, *Trial of the Major War Criminals* (hereafter *TMWC*; Nuremberg, 1947-1949), XIV:524; and *NSPK*, 170 (24 July 1935), a.

42. "Record of a Decision by the Deputy Führer," 27 Oct. 1933, *Documents on German Foreign Policy*, Series C (hereafter *DGFP*; Washington, D.C.: U.S. Government Printing Office, 1957-), Vol. II, Document No. 31; Bohle Interrogation, 9 Nov. 1945, RG 238; Jacobsen, *Steinacher*, pp. 35-36; and MacAlister Brown, "The Third Reich's Mobilization of the German Fifth Columns in Eastern Europe," *Journal of Central European Affairs*, 19 (1959), 130.

43. Ronald M. Smelser, *The Sudeten Problem, 1933-1938: Volkstumspolitik and the Formulation of Nazi Foreign Policy* (Middletown, Conn.: Wesleyan University Press, 1975), pp. 71-79, 89-90, 95, 100-03, 113-17, 120-21, 136-37; German Minister in Czechoslovakia to AA, 10 Oct. 1933, *DGFP*, C, I, No. 488; and Jacobsen, *Nationalsozialistische Aussenpolitik*, p. 128, 517.

44. Jacobsen, *Nationalsozialistische Aussenpolitik*, pp. 584-96; and Polish Ministry of Information, ed., *The German Fifth Column in Poland* (London: Hutchinson and Co., 1940), pp. 37, 44-45.

45. Although considerable material is available in the T-175 (Records of the Leader of the SS and Chief of the German Police), T-81, and T-580 microfilm collections on the SS and *Volksdeutsche* in eastern Europe, little has survived on the AO's early role in Bulgaria, Rumania (see pp. 173-74), and Hungary. For an introductory view of what was happening there in 1933 and 1934, see "Schwaebisch-Deutscher Kulturbund: Voelkisch kulturelle Organisation der Deutschen in Jugoslawien," n.d., BDC/*Slg. Schu.*/Ordner 299 (*Jugoslawien*); "Politische Parteien der Deutschen in Rumänien," n.d., BDC/*Slg. Schu.*/Ordner 309 (*Rumänien*); and "Anschriften-Liste," 1933 (?), BDC/*Slg. Schu.*/Ordner 293 (*Auslandsorganisation ab 1933*). Also, note *NYT*, 5 July 1934.

46. Jacobsen, *Steinacher*, pp. 162-65; AA, "Notiz," 12 July 1934, T-120/1176/477918-477919; AA, Minute, 19 Mar. 1934; AA to various government departments, 17 Nov., 20 Dec. 1933, *DGFP*, C, II, Nos. 330, 74, 140, respectively.

47. Gerhard to German Consulate General Montreal, 4 Nov. 1935, T-120/1129/460409; and Jacobsen, *Steinacher*, pp. 212-16, 289-90.

48. Bene to Bohle, 25 Nov. 1937, PA/*Chef* AO/Folder 47; and Jacobsen, *Nationalsozialistische Aussenpolitik*, pp. 246-49.

49. Ehrich, "Affidavit," 21 May 1948, Nuremberg Document 39 (Defense Exhibit Bohle), Case 11/RG 238; and Bohle Interrogation, M-679/1/0111-0112.

50. Kordt, *Wahn und Wirklichkeit*, p. 98; H. R. Trevor-Roper, ed., *Hitler's Secret Conversations, 1941-1944*, trans. Norman Cameron and R. H. Stevens (New York: New American Library, 1961), p. 387 (the entry for 6 Apr. 1942); and Andreas

Hillgruber, ed., *Henry Picker: Hitlers Tischgespräche im Führerhauptquartier, 1941-1942* (Munich: Deutsche Taschenbuch Verlag, 1968), pp. 180 (the entry for 7 June 1942), 224 (the entry for 6 July 1942).

51. Leonidas Hill, "The Wilhelmstrasse," *Political Science Quarterly*, 82 (1967), 546-70; and Jacobsen, *Nationalsozialistische Aussenpolitik*, p. 466.

52. Hencke, "Das Auswaertige Amt und die Auslandsorganisation," a memo written after the war, M-679/2/0489-0492; and Bohle, "Rundschreiben Folge 55/34," 28 Feb. 1934, WL/585. On the perennial attitude of the Nazis toward Freemasons, see *Gau Uschla* Westphalia South to Frederick Hesseldieck, 11 June 1933, and other materials in BDC/*Slg. Schu./Ordner* 2671 (*Religiöse Gemeinschaften*); and Helmuth Reinke to *Uschla*, 11 Nov. 1928, Werner Jochmann, ed., *Nationalsozialismus und Revolution: Ursprung und Geschichte der NSDAP in Hamburg, 1922-33* (*Dokumente*) (Frankfurt/Main: Europäische Verlagsanstalt, 1963), p. 275.

53. Halbekann to *Gau Ausland*, 20 Mar. 1933; LGL Southwest Africa to *Gau Ausland*, 21 Mar. 1933; Meiss to *Gau Ausland*, 28 Mar. 1933, T-580/57/296a; LGL South Africa to Hess, 16 Mar. 1933, T-580/58/298; Patzig to Dept. for Germans Abroad, 3 May 1933, T-580/59/301; and *Deutsche Shanghai Zeitung*, 17 Mar. 1933.

54. Jacobsen, *Nationalsozialistische Aussenpolitik*, pp. 36-37, 43, 103-05, who appears to emphasize the cooperation of the diplomats with party leaders abroad; he deals little with the personal and political nature of the conflict between them.

55. Bohle and Grünau, "Vereinbarung dem Auswärtigen-Amt und der Auslands-Abteilung der N.S.D.A.P. über den Eintritt von Angehörigen des Auswärtigen Dienstes in die Nationalsozialistische Deutsche Arbeiterpartei," 20 Dec. 1933, WL/585.

56. Bohle to Ernst Eisenlohr, 16 Aug. 1934, Nuremberg Document 3521-NG, Case 11/RG 238; Wagner, "Denkschrift," n.d., T-81/57/60087-60094; and report by LG Chile, "Auslands-Organisation Gauobmann des NSLB," 29 Aug. 1934, T-81/404/5147379.

57. "50 Jahre Deutsche Schule Rustschuk," *Die Deutsche Schule im Auslande: Monatsschrift für deutsche Erziehung im Schule und Familie*, 12 (1933), 395-96; DAI, "Uebersicht über die Zahl der deutschen Auslandschulen und ihrer Schüler für das Schuljahr 1934/35 nach Ländern geordnet," Jan. 1936, T-81/350/5079211-5079212; and regarding the cooperation of party groups abroad and NSLB, Ehrich, "Rundschreiben. An alle bisherigen Mitglieder des NS. Lehrerbundes im Ausland. An alle Landesgruppen, Ortsgruppen und Stützpunkte der NSDAP im Ausland.," 10 Mar. 1934, WL/585.

58. "Rede des Ortsgruppenleiters Pg. Behnke auf der Ortsgruppentagung über deutsches Schulwesen am 24. November 1934 in Habana, Kuba.," BDC/MF/*Walter Lehne*; "Sitzung der Arbeitsgemeinschaft des NSLB Schulgruppe La Paz—Freitag dem 9. Februar 1934.," T-580/382/52; Wilhelm Henss (a high school instructor from Hessen and father of the idea that the NSDAP should seize control of the German schools) to NSLB, 8 Aug. 1933; NSLB to Reich Ministry of Interior, 27 Sept. 1933; and NSLB to German school in Blumenau, 16 Sept. 1933, T-580/399/89.

59. LG Bolivia, *Tag der Arbeit, 1934: Dia del Trabajo* (n.p., 1934); Tokyo-Yokohama German Community, "Mitglieder-Verzeichnis: Partei-Organisationen," Jan. 1938, T-82/85/0245188-0245190; NSDAP Organization Office to Bohle, 30 June 1933, complaining about difficulties in Athens, T-580/56/296; the closing of the

school in Guatemala in May 1934, described in Jacobsen, *Nationalsozialistische Aussenpolitik*, p. 129; and "Conference . . . in the Foreign Ministry, on December 14, 1933, at 11:00 A.M.," *DGFP*, C, II, No. 140.

60. Memo by Reich Office Manager NSLB, 17 Jan. 1935, T-580/382/52.

61. NSLB (Foreign Dept.) to the League, 30 Nov. 1933, T-580/399/89; and AO to AA, 5 Jan. 1935 ("*Betr. Neue Lehrer für Lima.*"), T-580/385/58.

62. Ehrich to NSLB, 19 July 1934, enclosing a Memo on Stieve by the APA, "Abschrift! Aufzeichnung," 16 July 1934, T-580/399/91; and Donald M. McKale, "Hitlerism for Export! The Nazi Attempt to Control Schools and Youth Clubs Outside Germany," *Journal of European Studies*, 5 (1975), 244.

63. Bohle to Goebbels, 3 Oct. 1934, BDC/KK/*Franz Hasenöhrl*. The assertion of Jacobsen, *Nationalsozialistische Aussenpolitik*, p. 106, that Goebbels was a major opponent of the AO may not be correct; certainly after 1938 he allied with Bohle to halt Ribbentrop's increasing control over propaganda sent abroad (see pp. 201-02, 221 above). Prüfer became personnel chief in the AA in Apr. 1936; see Jacobsen, p. 469.

64. Hencke, "Das Auswaertige Amt . . . . ," M-679/2/0490; and Hans Kroll, *Lebenserinnerungen eines Botschafters* (Cologne: Kiepenheur und Witsch, 1968), p. 72.

65. *Auslands-Abteilung* to RL, 24 Oct. 1933, BDC/*Ordner Diplomaten*; and Zuchristian to AO, 2 May 1934 ("Streng Vertraulich!"), WL/585. For diplomats who joined the party, note Jacobsen, *Nationalsozialistische Aussenpolitik*, pp. 627-32.

66. Zuchristian to his party groups, 15 Mar. 1934, *Der Gruppe das Deutsche-Anarcho-Syndikalisten*, eds., *Schwarzrotbuch: Dokumente über den Hitler-imperialismus* (Barcelona: Asy-Verlag, 1937), pp. 73-74; and Bohle, "An alle Auslandskommissäre, Landesgruppen-, Ortsgruppen- und Stützpunktleiter im Ausland," 30 Apr. 1934, WL/585.

67. O.Gr. Mexico City to *Auslands-Abteilung*, 22 Apr. 1933; and LGL Southwest Africa to *Gau Ausland*, 21 Mar. 1933, T-580/57/296a.

68. Ibid., Cossel to Richter, 24 May 1933.

69. Schröder, *Deutschland und die Vereinigten Staaten*, pp. 221-35, 238-39. Stanley E. Hilton, *Brazil and the Great Powers, 1930-1939: The Politics of Trade Rivalry* (Austin, Texas: University of Texas Press, 1975), pp. 141-46, dates America's "urgent concern" from 1936.

70. According to Hermann Rauschning, *The Voice of Destruction* (New York: G. P. Putnam's Sons, 1940), pp. 61-63. The German settlements, their importance for German-Brazilian trade, and Japanese influx are discussed in Käte Harms-Baltzer, *Die Nationalisierung der deutschen Einwanderer und ihrer Nachkommen in Brasilien als Problem der deutsch-brasilianischen Beziehungen, 1930-1938* (Berlin: Colloquium Verlag, 1970), pp. 8-14, 24; and Hilton, *Brazil and the Great Powers*, pp. 41-43, 63, 84-85.

71. Cossel to *Auslands-Abteilung*, 23 Mar. 1933, T-580/57/296a.

72. "Conference . . . in the Foreign Ministry, on December 14, 1933, at 11:00 A.M.," *DGFP*, C, II, No. 140; and "Abschrift: Franz Wolf," n.d., T-580/57/296a.

73. As portrayed by Harms-Baltzer, *Die Nationalisierung der deutschen Einwanderer*, pp. 21-30; Meiss to *Gau Ausland*, 28 Mar. 1933; and PO, "Vollmacht," 30 June 1933, T-580/57/296a.

74. O.Gr. Porto Alegre, "Protokoll ueber den Sprechabend am 15.3.1933," 16 Mar. 1933, T-580/57/296a; and *Der Kompass* (Curitiba), 26 Sept. 1933.

75. LG Chile to *Gau Ausland*, 9 Mar. 1933; German Legation La Paz to AA, 9 Nov. 1933; and German Legation La Paz to AA, 15 Nov. 1933, T-580/57/296a.

76. German Legation in Uruguay to AA, 13 Dec. 1933 ("Betrifft: Zwistigkeiten innerhalb der Deutschen Kolonie Montevideo"), T-120/1129/460102-460104.

77. Ebel, *Das Dritte Reich und Argentinien*, pp. 79-105; and Bohle to Schmeer, 8 Apr. 1933, T-580/57/296a. On the school controversy, see Thilde Deckner to Dr. Boye, n.d., HA/34/660; and regarding the close economic ties between Germany and Argentina, note Kannapin, "Deutschland und Argentinien von 1933 bis 1945," pp. 111-12. The *Tageblatt*'s battles with the LG and Thermann are detailed in Peter Bussemeyer, *50 Jahre Argentinisches Tageblatt: Werden und Aufstieg einer Auslanddeutschen Zeitung* (n.p., n.d.), pp. 97-99, 112, 128-29, 135-36, 144-45.

78. Ebel, *Das Dritte Reich und Argentinien*, pp. 219-25, 237, 241-42, 244; this is the best study of any of the foreign NSDAP organizations. Regarding Brandt and Röhmer, see the pamphlet by Enrique Jürges, *Hakenkreuz am Rio de La Plata vor und hinter den Kulissen* (n.p., n.d.), pp. 7, 13, which is anti-Nazi and in the WL.

79. German Legation for Central America and Panama to AA, 16 Nov. 1933, T-120/1129/460091-460092; Jacobsen, *Nationalsozialistische Aussenpolitik*, p. 129; Sanke, *Der deutsche Faschismus in Lateinamerika*, p. 149; and "Walter Lehne," n.d., BDC/RuSHA/*Walter Lehne*.

80. *NYT*, 30 July, 22 Oct., 13 Nov., 1933.

81. Bohle Interrogation, 19 July 1945, NA/RG 165 (United States War Department [Shuster] Mission); and Luther, *Politiker ohne Partei*, p. 421.

82. Weinberg, *Foreign Policy of Hitler's Germany*, pp. 136-43; Offner, *American Appeasement*, pp. 59-61; and Moshe Gottlieb, "The Anti-Nazi Boycott Movement in the United States: An Ideological and Sociological Appreciation," *Jewish Social Studies*, 35 (1973), 198-227. These generally refute the unpublished dissertation by Daniel Shepherd Day, "American Opinion of German National Socialism, 1933-1937," (University of California, Los Angeles, 1958), pp. 12-78.

83. Dr. Stichel to Schmeer, 3 Apr. 1933, T-580/57/296a; and Diamond, *The Nazi Movement in the United States*, pp. 108, 110-11.

84. Bohle Interrogation, 9 Nov. 1945, RG 238.

85. Spanknöbel, "An alle Ortsgr. u. Stützpunkte der NSDAP—Lagru. USA.," 12 Apr. 1933; and Schneider, "Erlebnisse aus der Kampfzeit," 31 Dec. 1936, HA/27B/531.

86. Suggested by "Anschriften-Liste," 1933 (?), BDC/*Slg. Schu.*/*Ordner* 293. Schmeer, Memo, 28 May 1933, T-580/57/296a, implies that the Friends was already in existence in May, which is the opinion of Diamond, *The Nazi Movement in the United States*, p. 113. Rogge, *Official German Report*, p. 17, maintains it was formed in July; Geoffrey S. Smith, *To Save A Nation: American Countersubversives, the New Deal, and the Coming of World War II* (New York: Basic Books, 1973), p. 89, argues that it was created in April; and Smith, *Deutschtum of Nazi Germany*, p. 72, says it was founded in June.

87. Diamond, *The Nazi Movement in the United States*, pp. 113-15, 117; Klaus Kipphan, *Deutsche Propaganda in den Vereinigten Staaten*, pp. 61-77; and Smith, *To Save a Nation*, p. 89. A readable summary of the Friends is Leland V. Bell, *In Hitler's Shadow: The Anatomy of American Nazism* (Port Washington, N.Y.: Kennikat, 1973), pp. 7-19.

88. Telegram, PO to Spanknöbel, 23 Sept. 1933, T-580/57/296a; Rogge, *Official German Report*, pp. 18-20; Diamond, *The Nazi Movement in the United States*,

pp. 121-22; Smith, *To Save a Nation*, p. 90; and Dedeke, "Das Dritte Reich und die Vereinigten Staaten," pp. 70-76.

89. Bohle Interrogation, 13 Nov. 1945, RG 238; Kipphan, *Deutsche Propaganda in den Vereinigten Staaten*, p. 59; and U.S. House of Representatives, *Investigation of Nazi Propaganda Activities and Investigation of Certain Other Propaganda Activities: Hearings Before the House Special Committee on Un-American Activities, 73 Cong., 2nd Sess.* (2 pts.; Washington, D.C.; U.S. Government Printing Office, 1934), II:485.

90. Dr. Fuehr (AA), Memo, 16 Oct. 1933, *DGFP*, C, II, No. 5; and Alton Frye, *Nazi Germany and the American Hemisphere, 1933-1941* (New Haven, Conn.: Yale University Press, 1967), p. 40.

91. Rogge, *Official German Report*, pp. 20-21; Diamond, *The Nazi Movement in the United States*, pp. 123-25; Smith, *To Save a Nation*, p. 90; Dedeke, "Das Dritte Reich und die Vereinigten Staaten," p. 77; and "Quarrelsome Nazi Propagandist," *Manchester Guardian*, 26 Oct. 1933.

92. *NYT*, 7 Feb. 1934; and Hull, Memo, 27 Jan. 1934, *FRUS*, 1934, II:529.

93. Hasenöhrl to Stüpu. Harbin, 4 Mar. 1933; Kurt Wermke, "Warnung an Alle!" 9 Oct. 1933, T-580/57/296a; and Weinberg, *Foreign Policy of Hitler's Germany*, pp. 75, 80-81. One count listed only seventeen party members in Russia; U.S. War Department, *Nazi Party Membership Records Submitted by the War Department to the Subcommittee on War Mobilization of the Committee on Military Affairs, United States Senate* (Washington, D.C.: U.S. Government Printing Office, 1946), p. 624. These published records of AO members are available in the Manuscript Division of the LC.

94. LG China, "Rundschreiben," 2 Mar. 1933, T-580/57/296a; and *Deutsche Shanghai Zeitung*, 17 Mar. 1933. On Sino-German relations in 1933 and 1934, see Bloch, *German Interests and Policies in the Far East*, pp. 5-30; Weinberg, *Foreign Policy of Hitler's Germany*, pp. 121-26; Offner, *American Appeasement*, p. 163; Presseisen, *Germany and Japan*, pp. 41-42; and Billie K. Walsh, "The German Military Mission in China, 1928-38," *Journal of Modern History*, 46 (1974), 503-07.

95. Hillmann was born in Apr. 1886 in Ost Zellerfeld; AO, 'Rudolf Hillmann," 30 July 1942, BDC/MF/ *Rudolf Hillmann*. See also, Hasenöhrl to GL Hamburg, 25 Feb. 1933, T-580/57/296a; and PO to Bernard Eichinger, 6 June 1934, T-580/382/53. On the party's interest in Japan and its opposition to the AA, German army, and German business (which disliked competing with cheap Japanese goods), note Theo Sommer, *Deutschland und Japan zwischen den Mächten, 1935-1940: Vom Antikominternpakt zum Dreimächtepakt* (Tübingen: Mohr, 1962), pp. 18-23; Presseisen, *Germany and Japan*, pp. 3-6, 9-32, 41-45; and Karl Drechsler, *Deutschland-China-Japan, 1933-1939: Das Dilemma der deutschen Fernostpolitik* ([East] Berlin: Akademie-Verlag, 1964), pp. 9-26.

96. As shown by Presseisen, *Germany and Japan*, pp. 60-62, 79; Weinberg, *Foreign Policy of Hitler's Germany*, pp. 126-31; Karl Ritter, Memo, 8 June 1934, *DGFP*, C, II, No. 889; and Dirksen, *Moskau-Tokio-London*, pp. 159-60. On Kirschbaum, see AO, "Hanns Günther von Kirschbaum," n.d., BDC/MF/*Hanns von Kirschbaum*.

97. AO to DAI, 22 June 1934, T-81/404/5147516; R. Groth (Batavia) to Heinz Krahn, 8 Oct. 1933, HA/35/680; German Consulate General Bombay to AA, 20 Feb. 1934, T-120/1176/477865-477866; and Bloch, *German Interests and Policies in the Far East*, pp. 53-57.

98. O.Gr. Cairo to *Gau Ausland*, 24 Mar. 1933; Bohle to Schmeer, 14 June

1933, T-580/57/296a; and Hirszowicz, *The Third Reich and the Arab East*, pp. 15-16, 18-19.

99.   O.Gr. Cairo to *Gau Ausland*, 22 Mar. 1933, T-580/57/296a; and Jacobsen, *Nationalsozialistische Aussenpolitik*, pp. 114-15.

100.   Schröder to AO, 19 Nov. 1934; German Legation Cairo to AA, 26 Nov. 1934 ("Betrifft: Neubildung der Deutschen Kolonie Kairos nach dem Führerprinzip"); and German Consulate Alexandria to AA, 24 Nov. 1934, T-120/1176/477964-477965, 477963, 477959-477962, respectively.

101.   *Brown Network*, pp. 135-36.

102.   Hitler's remark is in "Minutes of the Conference of Heads of Departments, Wednesday, May 24, 1933, at 5:00 p.m.," *DGFP*, C, I, No. 483. Revealing on the foreign impact of Germany's anti-Semitism is the AA Memo, 19 Aug. 1935, *DGFP*, C, IV, No. 266.

103.   His use of propaganda as a means to achieve his foreign policy aims is discussed by Schubert, *Anfänge nationalsozialistischer Aussenpolitik*, pp. 82-90.

104.   *Gau Ausland*, "An alle Landesgruppen-, Ortsgruppen- und Stützpunktleiter im europäischen Ausland.," 30 Mar. 1933, T-580/55/293.

105.   German Mission Berne to AA, 20 July 1933, WL/Document Collection No. 506 (Nazi Propaganda).

106.   *Landesvertrauensmann* Denmark to Dept., 2 Mar. 1933, T-580/56/296.

107.   German Legation Dublin to AA, 17 Dec. 1935, T-120/1129/460186-460187; German Legation Dublin to AA, 17 May 1934; and AO (Bohle) to AA, 8 June 1934, T-120/1176/477885-477886, 477893-477894. See also, O.Gr. London to *Gau Ausland*, 26 Apr. 1933; and Bohle to Schmeer, 2 May 1933, T-580/56/296. On Hoesch's anti-Nazi views, see Erich Kordt, *Nicht aus den Akten . . . Die Wilhelmstrasse in Frieden und Krieg: Erlebnisse, Begegnungen und Eindrücke, 1928-1945* (Stuttgart: Deutsche Verlags-Anstalt, 1950), pp. 147-48.

108.   AA to its missions, 30 June 1934, *DGFP*, C, III, No. 48; and articles on each colony in *Nachrichtenblatt des Verbandes Deutscher Kolonien in den Niederlanden*, 82 (Oct. 1934), 5-10. Also, note German Consulate Rotterdam to AA, 19 May 1934, T-120/1176/477888-477889; "Deutsche Kolonie. Unter Führung der N.S.D.A.P.," 13 May 1933; O.Gr. The Hague to RL, 3 May 1933; Patzig to Dept. for Germans Abroad, 3 May 1933; and Patzig, "An die Ortsgruppenleiter, Stützpunktleiter und Blockleiter der N.S.D.A.P. in den Niederlanden," 15 May 1933, T-580/59/301.

109.   *Brown Network*, pp. 140-43; Patzig to PO, 9 May 1933, T-580/59/301; and *Das Braune Netz*, pp. 190-91.

110.   O.Gr. Sofia to RL, 2 May 1933; and O.Gr. Athens to *Gau Ausland*, 28 Mar. 1933, T-580/56/296. Note also, Hans Zomak-Spengler (Antwerp) to Heinz Schaeper, 25 Aug. 1933, HA/34/662; and German Consulate Albania to AA, 21 Apr. 1934, T-120/1176/477883.

111.   Brand, "Rundschreiben 21," 18 Feb. 1933, T-580/58/298.

112.   D. C. Watt, "The Rome-Berlin Axis, 1936-1940: Myth and Reality," *Review of Politics*, 22 (1960), 525-27; and PO to *Reichs-Uschla*, 21 Feb. 1933, BA/NS 22/Box 337/Ordner 877. In July 1933 Bohle sent the head of the AO's Press and Propaganda Office, Hans Zeberer, to Italy to reorganize the Italian groups; Bohle to Schmeer, 8 July 1933; "An die Ortsgruppen in Italien," 30 Mar. 1933; and Brand, "Rundschreiben 22," 12 Mar. 1933, T-580/58/298. For the number of groups in Italy, see "Anschriften der Ortsgruppen und Stützpunkte in Italien," 1933, BDC/Slg. Schu./Ordner 298 (*Italien NSDAP*).

113.   Luza, *Austro-German Relations*, pp. 18-25; Gehl, *Austria, Germany and*

the Anschluss, p. 48, and first chapters; *Die Erhebung der österreichischen Nationalsozialisten im Juli 1934 (Akten der Historischen Kommission des Reichsführers SS)* (Frankfurt/Main: Europa-Verlag, 1965), pp. 291-300; and documents relating to the NSDAP in Austria before 1933 in BDC/*Slg. Schu./Ordner* 302 (*Österreich*).

114. "Personalbogen," 20 Jan. 1939, BDC/OPG/*Richard Koderle*; and Jens Petersen, *Hitler-Mussolini: Die Entstehung der Achse Berlin-Rom, 1933-1936* (Tübingen: Niemeyer, 1973), p. 311. Koderle was born in 1889 and entered the NSDAP in Dec. 1931.

115. On Papen, see Bruce F. Pauley, *The Habsburg Legacy, 1867-1939* (New York: Holt, Rinehart and Winston, 1972), pp. 137-38; and Ulrich Eichstädt, *Von Dollfuss zu Hitler. Geschichte des Anschlusses Österreichs, 1933-1938* (Wiesbaden: Steiner, 1955), pp. 58-59, 72-79, 161-62, which maintains erroneously that the AO first moved into Austria at the end of 1936. Note, on Bohle's expanding authority, Hess, "Anordnung 85/35," 29 Apr. 1935; Bohle to Schwarz, 9 Oct. 1934; Bohle to Hess, 8 Dec. 1934, BDC/*Slg. Schu./Ordner* 303 (*Österreich: Mitgliedswesen NSDAP, Hilfswerk, Kampfring*); Bohle, "Aufzeichnung," 18 Feb. 1937, PA/*Chef AO/*Folder 24 (*Österreich*); and Zeberer, "Folge 65/34," 8 Mar. 1934, WL/585. On the Dollfuss murder, see Gehl, *Austria, Germany, and the Anschluss*, pp. 87-102; Weinberg, *Foreign Policy of Hitler's Germany*, pp. 90-106; and Eichstädt, pp. 50-61.

116. AO (Bohle) to AA, 7 Dec. 1934, T-120/357/264944-264945; AA to its missions and consulates, 18 Feb. 1935, T-120/1176/477978-477979; and Hess to Frauenfeld, 21 Aug. 1934, *DGFP*, C, III, No. 173.

117. Butting, "Tätigkeit in der Auslands-Organisation der NSDAP," n.d. (1942?), BDC/PK/*Otto Butting*; AO to Schwarz, 20 June 1935, BDC/PK/*Richard Koderle*; *Bundeskanzleramt* Austria (hereafter BKA), " 'Bund der Reichsdeutschen in Oesterreich.' Neuorganisation, Winterhilfe.," 9 Nov. 1935; BKA, "Abschrift eines Berichtes d. Bundespolizeidirektion Wien, 16.1.36, Pr.Z. IV-201/7, an das Bundeskanzleramt, Staatspolizeiliches Bureau."; and BKA, " 'Bund der Reichsdeutschen' in Vorarlberg; Ausschluss aller nichtreichsdeutschen Mitglieder, Reorganisation," 22 Jan. 1936, PA/*Chef* AO/Folder 26 (*Österreich: Erledigte Akten des Chefs A.O. betr. Österreich*). Butting entered the NSDAP in March 1932 and was born in Cross/Oder in Apr. 1898.

118. LGL Spain to Dept. for Germans Abroad, 9 May 1933, T-580/56/296; *Brown Network*, pp. 104, 110; and *Jahrbuch der Auslands-Organisation der NSDAP, 1942* (Berlin, 1943), p. 21. On Köster's anti-Nazi views, see Kordt, *Nicht aus den Akten*, pp. 147-48.

119. *Schwarzrotbuch*, pp. 68, 143-52; O.Gr. Madrid, "Anordnung gültig für sämtliche Pgg. der O.-G. Madrid," 1934, WL/585; and German Embassy Spain to AA, 30 May 1933, WL/506.

120. Spielhagen, *Spione und Verschwörer*, pp. 18-20, 36-38, 44-47, 89-90, 120-26, 128, 133-37, containing documents seized by the Spanish government in a raid on the headquarters of the LG Spain in mid-1936.

121. See, for instance, Zuchristian to AO, 2 May 1934 ("Streng vertraulich!"), WL/585.

122. For example, *Manchester Guardian*, 26 July 1934. Also, note "Abschrift," 28 Aug. 1933; Schlichting to Zuchristian, 11 Feb. 1934, WL/585; and Spielhagen, *Spione und Verschwörer*, pp. 89-90, 120-26, 128-37.

CHAPTER 4

1. Weinberg, *Foreign Policy of Hitler's Germany*; Hildebrand, *Foreign Policy of the Third Reich*, pp. 38-60; Bracher, Sauer, and Schulz, *Die nationalsozialistische Machtergreifung*, pp. 220-61; and famous Hossbach Memo, 10 Nov. 1937, *DGFP*, Series D (Washington, D.C.: U.S. Government Printing Office, 1949-), Vol. I, Document No. 19.

2. *VB*, 22 Mar. 1935; and *NSPK*, 208 (6 Sept. 1935), 3-5.

3. Emil Ehrich, *Die Auslands-Organisation der NSDAP* (Berlin: Junker und Dünnhaupt, 1937), p. 16; and Jacobsen, *Nationalsozialistische Aussenpolitik*, p. 109, on the meeting with Hitler.

4. Sanke, *Der deutsche Faschismus in Lateinamerika*, pp. 25, 114; Ebel, *Das Dritte Reich und Argentinien*, pp. 270-71; and on the LG's role, LG Brazil to Bohle, 23 Dec. 1937 ("Betr. Interesse der brasilianischen Regierung an der Taetigkeit der Anti-Komintern."), T-120/225/170852. On the Communist uprising, see Frank D. McCann, Jr., *The Brazilian-American Alliance, 1937-1945* (Princeton, N.J.: Princeton University Press, 1973), p. 29. The figures for the rallies, probably exaggerated, are Nazi estimates; *NSPK*, 101 (2 May 1935), a.

5. See the Minister's report, "Vertraulich! Politisches," early 1935, T-120/1129/460217-460220; Sanke, *Der deutsche Faschismus in Lateinamerika*, pp. 24-25; and McCann, *Brazilian-American Alliance*, pp. 30-31, 84-85. According to Hilton, *Brazil and the Great Powers*, pp. 110-31, the Brazilian military had a powerful influence on its government's political and economic policies. He also notes (p. 175) the Nazi fear of Integralism as a competitor.

6. German Consulate for Paraná to AA, 9 May 1935, T-120/357/264989-264998; and AO to DAI, 6 Jan. 1936, T-81/404/5148308.

7. See McCann's estimate of the danger, *Brazilian-American Alliance*, p. 134; and Sanke, *Der deutsche Faschismus in Lateinamerika*, pp. 24-25.

8. Kannapin, "Deutschland und Argentinien von 1933 bis 1945," pp. 114-15; Ebel, *Das Dritte Reich und Argentinien*, pp. 161-65, 230-35, 240; Sanke, *Der deutsche Faschismus in Lateinamerika*, pp. 23, 83-84, 87-88; and on Küster, "Fritz Küster," n.d., BDC/KK/*Fritz Küster.*

9. Schröder, *Deutschland und die Vereinigten Staaten*, pp. 239-40, 242-43, 246-47, 253-55, 257-61; Offner, *American Appeasement*, pp. 167-69, which overemphasizes the success of the Buenos Aires Conference of 1936 for the United States; and Sanke, *Der deutsche Faschismus in Lateinamerika*, p. 63, citing documents in the DZA on Catholic and left-wing opposition to Nazism. Also on the opposition, see Jürges, *Hakenkreuz am Rio de La Plata*, pp. 5-6; and Kannapin, "Deutschland und Argentinien von 1933 bis 1945," p. 114.

10. Telegram, Luther to AA, 11 Feb. 1934; and Luther to AA, 20 Apr. 1934 ("Subject: Attitude of the State Department toward the NSDAP organization in the U.S."), *DGFP*, C, II, Nos. 248, 410.

11. Smith, *To Save a Nation*, pp. 90-91; "Memorandum by the Secretary of State," 23 Mar. 1934, *FRUS*, 1934, II:516-20; *NYT*, 21 Mar. 1934; Robert Dallek, *Democrat and Diplomat: The Life of William E. Dodd* (New York: Oxford University Press, 1968), p. 225; Offner, *American Appeasement*, p. 82; Weinberg, *Foreign Policy of Hitler's Germany*, pp. 149-50; and Kipphan, *Deutsche Propaganda in den Vereinigten Staaten*, pp. 75-77.

12. Diamond, *The Nazi Movement in the United States*, pp. 134-40, 142, 145-

46, 149-53; and Kipphan, *Deutsche Propaganda in den Vereinigten Staaten*, pp. 103-33.

13. Luther to U.S. Secretary of State, 20 Feb. 1934, *FRUS*, 1934, II:532; Luther to AA, 20 Apr. 1934, T-580/57/296a; Offner, *American Appeasement*, p. 85; Kipphan, *Deutsche Propaganda in den Vereinigten Staaten*, p. 59; and Diamond, *The Nazi Movement in the United States*, p. 160.

14. DAI to AO, 17 Sept. 1934; and Ehrich to DAI, 4 Sept. 1934, expressing doubts about Borchers, T-81/404/5147384-5147387, 5147396-5147397.

15. Heinrich Lammers (head of Hitler's Reich Chancellery) to AA, 3 Dec. 1934; Lammers to Neurath, 2 Nov. 1934, *DGFP*, C, III, Nos. 572, 570; and Diamond, *The Nazi Movement in the United States*, pp. 169-71.

16. Smith, *Deutschtum of Nazi Germany*, p. 96; Gienanth's tie to the AO, AO to DAI, 27 Mar. 1935, T-81/404/5146945-5146946; and on the same roll, frames 5146843, 5146888, 5147008-5147009, respectively, AO to DAI, 26 Feb., 29 Apr., 17 May 1935.

17. Diamond, *The Nazi Movement in the United States*, pp. 132-33; AO to NSDAP Reich Treasury, 11 Mar. 1935, T-81/146/0185108-0185109; "Parteigenossen in U.S.A., welches aus der NSDAP austraten, um in Bunde 'Freunde des neuen Deutschland' weiterhin tätig sein zu können," n.d., T-81/147/0185890; and Kipphan, *Deutsche Propaganda in den Vereinigten Staaten*, p. 68.

18. German Charge d'Affaires in America (Leitner) to AA, 31 July 1935, *DGFP*, C, IV, No. 237; Smith, *To Save a Nation*, p. 92; and Weinberg, *Foreign Policy of Hitler's Germany*, pp. 150-51.

19. Jacobsen, *Nationalsozialistische Aussenpolitik*, p. 541; Diamond, *The Nazi Movement in the United States*, pp. 172-76, 185, 190; and Kipphan, *Deutsche Propaganda in den Vereinigten Staaten*, p. 63.

20. Bell, *In Hitler's Shadow*, p. 15; Frye, *Nazi Germany*, p. 63; Jacobsen, *Nationalsozialistische Aussenpolitik*, pp. 541-42; Diamond, *The Nazi Movement in the United States*, pp. 191-92; and Smith, *To Save a Nation*, p. 93.

21. Diamond, *The Nazi Movement in the United States*, pp. 205, 211-13, 217, 219, 222, 227-45; Jacobsen, *Nationalsozialistische Aussenpolitik*, pp. 541-42; and Kipphan, *Deutsche Propaganda in den Vereinigten Staaten*, pp. 78-83, 91-95; and Smith, *To Save a Nation*, pp. 94-95. See further, Memo, Ernst von Weizsäcker (acting head of the AA's Political Dept. and former German Minister to Switzerland), 2 Oct. 1937, *DGFP*, D, I, No. 411.

22. Strempel Interrogation, 14 Feb. 1946, Nuremberg Document 3800-PS, *TMWC*, 33:165-66; Borchers Interrogation, M-679/1/0196; and on the *Bund*'s income, Diamond, *The Nazi Movement in the United States*, pp. 206, 228.

23. Weinberg, *Foreign Policy of Hitler's Germany*, pp. 152-57; Diamond, *The Nazi Movement in the United States*, pp. 206-09, 255-57; William E. Dodd, Jr., and Martha Dodd, eds., *Ambassador Dodd's Diary, 1933-1938* (New York: Harcourt, Brace and Company, 1941), p. 340 (the entry for 14 Aug. 1936); Offner, *American Appeasement*, p. 85; and Compton, *The Swastika and the Eagle*, pp. 58-59, which maintains incorrectly that America was not disturbed over Hitler's foreign policy until 1937.

24. See, as an example, speeches of Hess and Hitler at the party rally in Nuremberg in 1935, "Appel des Führers an die Auslandsdeutschen," *VB*, 14 Sept. 1935; and Kube, *Almanach*, p. 96.

25. AO, "Notiz für Pg. Langmann . . . . ," 12 Feb. 1935, T-580/385/58; AO

to Strölin, 3 Apr. 1935, T-81/404/5146934; and AO to Reich leadership of the NSLB, 29 Nov. 1934, T-580/382/53.

26. "Auslandsdeutsche Jugend in München," *VB*, 17 Aug. 1935; list of books in NSLB to German school in Barcelona, 16 Apr. 1936, T-580/399/91; and Otfried Dankelmann, "Aus der Praxis auswärtiger Kulturpolitik des deutschen Imperialismus, 1933-1945," *Zeitschrift für Geschichtswissenschaft*, 6 (1972), 722-23. Further, see McKale, "Hitlerism for Export!", pp. 246-47.

27. AO to DAI, 10 Dec. 1935, T-81/404/5148353-5148354.

28. For instance, "A very strong Nazi Organization in City," *The Standard* (Montreal), 31 Mar. 1934; German Consulate General for Canada to Gerhard, 26 Feb. 1934, T-120/1176/477868-477878; and German Consulate Manila to AA, 26 Aug. 1935, T-120/1129/460245.

29. Schacht to Hitler, 19 Mar. 1935; Schnee to Hitler, 20 Mar. 1935, *DGFP*, C, III, Nos. 544, 549; Klaus Hildebrand, *Vom Reich zum Weltreich: Hitler, NSDAP und koloniale Frage, 1919-1945* (Munich: Wilhelm Fink Verlag, 1969), pp. 43-56, 113-18, 288-89, 373-90; Schäfer, *NSDAP*, pp. 53-54; and Weinberg, *Foreign Policy of Hitler's Germany*, p. 278.

30. Benjamin Bennett, *Hitler Over Africa* (London: T. Werner Laurie, 1939), pp. 17, 19, 21-23, 27-35, 157-67, 176, which includes an appendix of German documents seized by the police at the Nazi local in Windhoek in July 1934; Stuebel, "Die Entwicklung des Nationalsozialismus in Südwestafrika," p. 173; Kühne, "Die Fünfte Kolonne des faschistischen deutschen Imperialismus in Südwestafrika," pp. 776-81; and "Quotations from Documents Seized by the Attorney- General at Windhoek," and other material in *The Anti-Jewish Movement in South Africa* (n.p., n.d.), pp. 5-11, 21, in the WL.

31. Otto Pfafferott (Tsumeb) to Herbert Seller, 10 Oct. 1934, HA/34/657; AO (E. W. Bohle) to AA, 21 June 1934, T-120/1176/477907; Bennett, *Hitler Over Africa*, pp. 19-20, 168-69; and Kirchner, *Hermann Bohle*, pp. 78-79.

32. Bennett, *Hitler Over Africa*, pp. 157-97; "Nazis Outlawed in Africa," *NYT*, 30 Oct. 1934; Stuebel, "Die Entwicklung des Nationalsozialismus in Südwestafrika," pp. 173-74; Kühne, "Die Fünfte Kolonne des faschistischen deutschen Imperialismus in Südwestafrika," pp. 781-82; and Jacobsen, *Nationalsozialistische Aussenpolitik*, pp. 568-69.

33. Neurath to Hess, 19 Sept. 1934, T-120/352/263877.

34. Hess to Neurath, 21 Feb. 1935, ibid., 263883-263884; Menche, "Personalfragebogen für die Anlegung der SA-Personalakte," 3 Nov. 1937, BDC/SA/*Heinz Menche*; and AO, "Lebenslauf des Friedrich Franz Erbgrossherzog von Mecklenburg," n.d., PA/*Chef* AO/Folder 42 (*Beamte des Auswärtigen Amts*).

35. Kirchner, *Herman Bohle*, p. 109; *NSPK*, 298 (21 Dec. 1935), a; "Botschafter Ribbentrop besucht die A.O.," *NSPK*, 152 (3 July 1935), b; Ribbentrop to AO (Bohle), 3 July 1935, T-120/352/263898-263900; Hildebrand, *Vom Reich zum Weltreich*, p. 361; Kordt, *Wahn und Wirklichkeit*, pp. 96-97; and Smelser, *Sudeten Problem*, pp. 124-25.

36. Brown, "The Third Reich's Mobilization," p. 131; and AA, Memo, 11 Oct. 1935, *DGFP*, C, IV, No. 347. A brief history of the origins and rise of the VoMi is in Smelser, *Sudeten Problem*, pp. 128, 188-89; and Hans Buchheim, Martin Broszat, Hans-Adolf Jacobsen, and Helmut Krausnick, *Die SS—Das Herrschaftsinstrument, Befehl und Gehorsam*, Vol. 1 of *Anatomie des SS-Staates* (Freiburg: Walter-Verlag, 1965), pp. 229-31.

37. For example, "SS Ernennungen" and "SS Beforderungen," *Mitteilungsblatt*, 53 (Nov. 1937), 1; and on Bohle's appointment to the SS, "Eidesstattliche Erklärung," 9 Apr. 1948, by Karl Wolff, Nuremberg Document 30 (Defense Exhibit Bohle), Case 11/RG 238. On Himmler's espionage plans, note Roger Manvell and Heinrich Fraenkel, *Himmler* (New York: Putnam, 1965), p. 55.

38. Concerning the status of the party in Czechoslovakia, see German Legation in Prague to AA, 27 Mar. 1936, T-120/3555/E672328; Smelser, *Sudeten Problem*, pp. 136-37, 158-61; circular of the RL to AO, APA, AA, and Propaganda Ministry, 11 Mar. 1935; German Minister in Czechoslovakia to AA, 5 Feb. 1935, *DGFP*, C, III, Nos. 525, 482; and regarding the AO's role there in 1937 and 1938, see pp. 153-56 above. On Rumania, note the unsigned AA Memo, 7 July 1936, *DGFP*, C, V, No. 440. See, moreover, AO to Hans Hinkel, 23 Mar. 1936 ("Betr. Pressehetze in Niederl.-Indien gegen die N.S.D.A.P."), T-580/59/301; "Nasty Nazis in Melbourne," *Melbourne Truth*, 5 Dec. 1936; German Consulate General Sydney to AA, 12 Mar. 1936 ("Inh. Australische Regierung droht mit Aktion gegen Parteiorganisation."); German Legation for Venezuela to AA, 29 Aug. 1936; and Costa Rica Consulate in Westphalia to AA, 25 Apr. 1936, T-120/347/260029-260032, 260048-260049, 260037, respectively.

39. Lachmann, "Der Nationalsozialismus in der Schweiz," pp. 25-26, 34-36, 38-40.

40. Daniel Bourgeois, *Le Troisème Reich et la Suisse, 1933-1941* (Neuchâtel [Switzerland]: Éditions de la Baconnière, 1974), pp. 53-57; Lachmann, "Der Nationalsozialismus in der Schweiz," pp. 37-40, 46-48, 50-54; *Das Braune Netz*, pp. 333-56; *The Times* (London), 20 Aug. 1935, on a German professor and leader of the O.Gr. Berne, Porzig, dismissed from the local university; and Jacobsen, *Nationalsozialistische Aussenpolitik*, pp. 513-15.

41. Telegram, German Consulate Berne to AA, 4 Feb. 1936, T-120/3132/E510454; and Ernst von Weizsäcker, *Memoirs of Ernst von Weizsäcker*, trans. John Andrews (London: Gollancz, 1951), p. 94. On Frankfurter's trial (he was sentenced to eighteen years in prison, which the Nazis considered no punishment at all), see T-120/3365/E598051-E598142; Bourgeois, *Le Troisème Reich*, pp. 59-60, 63-65; Lachmann, "Der Nationalsozialismus in der Schweiz," pp. 66-67; and Jacobsen, *Nationalsozialistische Aussenpolitik*, pp. 514-17.

42. Baynes, *Speeches*, II:1264-65; German Consulate General Zurich to AA, 12 Feb. 1936, T-120/3132/E510466-E510468; letter (author unidentified) to State Secretary in Reich Ministry of Finance, 2 Oct. 1936, HA/35/687; and Lachmann, "Der Nationalsozialismus in der Schweiz," p. 56.

43. *VB*, 22 Feb., 25/26 Dec. 1936; Weizsäcker to Bibra (German Charge d'Affaires transferred to Berne), 26 Oct. 1936, *DGFP*, C, III, No. 627; *Mitteilungsblatt*, 46 (Feb. 1937), 8-9; *Wir Deutsche in der Welt, 1938*, pp. 48-49; and Lachmann, "Der Nationalsozialismus in der Schweiz," p. 56.

44. Weizsäcker, *Memoirs*, pp. 94-95; and the Minister's report discussed in Lachmann, "Der Nationalsozialismus in der Schweiz," pp. 62-64. According to Bourgeois, *Le Troisème Reich*, p. 34, the LG claimed to have sufficient evidence to send Weizsäcker to a concentration camp.

45. *NYT*, 27 Feb. 1936; Jacobsen, *Nationalsozialistische Aussenpolitik*, pp. 518-19; Bülow to Neurath, 6 Feb. 1936, T-120/3589/E680949-E680950, dealing with Sweden; and on the Dutch situation, Woermann, "Aufzeichnung," 26 June 1936, T-120/347/260042-260043. Regarding Switzerland, see Bruno Grimm, *Gau Schweiz?*

Dokumente über die nationalsozialistische Umtriebe in der Schweiz (Berne: Unionsdruckerei Bern, 1939), pp. 43, 94; and AO to Kuske, 26 July 1937, T-120/2828/E446173. A solid piece of research on the party's history there after 1936 is Lachmann, "Der Nationalsozialismus in der Schweiz." The party was again legalized in Oct. 1940, *Mitteilungsblatt*, 8 (Dec. 1940), 10; and Bourgeois, *Le Troisème Reich*, pp. 194-95.

46. Spielhagen, *Spione und Verschwörer*, pp. 25-26; *The Times* (London, 29 Feb. 1936); and Jacobsen, *Nationalsozialistische Aussenpolitik*, pp. 518-19.

47. Lammers to Neurath, 19 Mar. 1936, Nuremberg Document 4030-PS, Case 11/RG 238.

48. Bohle, "Vorschlag für die Schaffung der Einheit von Partei und Staat in der Bearbeitung des Auslandsdeutschtums," 26 Feb. 1936, T-120/1624/E000057-E000065; and on the discussions, Jacobsen, *Nationalsozialistische Aussenpolitik*, pp. 122-27.

49. Hepp Interrogation, M-679/2/0549-0550; and Jacobsen, *Nationalsozialistische Aussenpolitik*, pp. 627-32. Pressure by the party on government agencies was hardly uncommon; see E. N. Peterson, *The Limits of Hitler's Power* (Princeton, N.J.: Princeton University Press, 1969), passim; Kroll, *Lebenserinnerungen*, pp. 72-73; and Dirksen, *Moskau-Tokio-London*, p. 183.

50. Bene to Gustav Moshack (DAI), 26 Mar. 1936, T-81/404/5148136; and Bohle Interrogation, M-679/1/0078. An example of the information collected on diplomats was Ehrich's Memo, 6 Oct. 1936, concerning Prinze zu Wied, German Minister in Sweden, who was accused of being pro-Jewish and friendly to Freemasonry, T-120/1418/D565549-565550. See also, Bohle's role in pushing the AA to release the German Minister to Venezuela, Count Tattenbach; Bohle to Hitler's Adjutant, Fritz Wiedemann, 18 June 1936, T-120/178/14100-14101.

51. Neurath, "Affidavit," 19 Sept. 1946, Nuremberg Document 163-NG, Case 11/RG 238; and Weizsäcker, *Memoirs*, p. 95.

52. Glen T. Harper, *German Economic Policy in Spain during the Spanish Civil War, 1936-1939* (The Hague: Mouton, 1967), p. 13; and Bernhardt, "Bericht Presse," 5 May 1935, WL/585.

53. *Schwarzrotbuch*, pp. 297-315; and Spielhagen, *Spione und Verschwörer*, pp. 32-33.

54. The details are recounted in Weinberg, *Foreign Policy of Hitler's Germany*, pp. 288-89; and Manfred Merkes, *Die deutsche Politik gegenüber dem spanischen Bürgerkrieg, 1936-1939* (Bonn: Röhrscheid, 1961), pp. 19-20. Although Weinberg implies that the AA was not consulted, there is evidence to suggest that Neurath discussed the issue with Hitler: Dieckhoff Interrogation, M-679/1/0257. Neither Burnett Bolloten, *The Grand Camouflage: The Spanish Civil War and Revolution, 1936-39* (New York: Praeger, 1968), nor Franz Borkenau, *The Spanish Cockpit: An Eye-Witness Account of the Political and Social Conflicts of the Spanish Civil War* (Ann Arbor, Mich.: University of Michigan Press, 1963), mention the NSDAP in Spain.

55. Consul at Tetuan to AA, 3 Aug. 1936, *DGFP*, D, III, No. 27.

56. Erich Raeder, *Vom 1935 bis Spandau, 1955*, Vol. II of *Mein Leben* (Tübingen-Neckar: F. Schlichtenmayer, 1956), pp. 79-81; *Mitteilungsblatt*, 46 (Feb. 1937), 4; AA to *Diplogerma* (German mission) Madrid, 4 Apr. 1936, T-120/3132/E510529; AO (*Personalamt*), "Personalbogen [Hellermann]," WL/585; AO Repatriation Office to its Munich affiliate, 23 Aug. 1937 ("Betrifft. Betreuung der Spanienflüchtlinge."),

PA/ *Chef* AO/Folder 47; and Marion Einhorn, *Die ökonomischen Hintergründe der Faschistischen deutschen Intervention in Spanien* ([East] Berlin: Akademie-Verlag, 1962), p. 62.

57. Some of the correspondence was published by Spielhagen, *Spione und Verschwörer*, passim; telegram, AA to German Embassy Rome, 26 Aug. 1936, T-120/1594/D682671; and Martha Dodd, *Through Embassy Eyes* (New York: Harcourt, Brace and Company, 1939), p. 248.

58. Bohle to Schwendemann, 11 Mar. 1937, PA/ *Chef* AO/Folder 42; Bohle to Faupel, 12 Mar. 1937, T-120/239/174284-174285; Merkes, *Die deutsche Politik*, pp. 68-70; and on Faupel's background, Harper, *German Economic Policy in Spain*, p. 28.

59. Faupel to AA, 7 Jan. 1937; and German Minister to Portugal to AA, 11 Sept. 1936, *DGFP*, D, III, Nos. 197, 80. On Bernhardt's role in Hisma, see Merkes, *Die deutsche Politik*, pp. 84-85, 89, 129, 131-32, 142-43, 148, 155-56, 158; and Harper, *German Economic Policy in Spain*, pp. 11-68.

60. Regarding the various factions in the Austrian NSDAP, see Luza, *Austro-German Relations*, pp. 27-34; and on the general situation, Weinberg, *Foreign Policy of Hitler's Germany*, pp. 270-71; Hildebrand, *Foreign Policy of the Third Reich*, p. 47; and Bohle Interrogation, M-679/1/0073.

61. *VB*, 12 Sept. 1936; and *NSPK*, 199 (27 Aug. 1936), a.

62. Weizsäcker, Memo, 7 Oct. 1936, *DGFP*, D, I, No. 167.

63. Weizsäcker, Memo, 11 Nov. 1936, Nuremberg Document 4152-NG, Case 11/RG 238; *NYT*, 26 Oct. 1936; and Eichstädt, *Von Dollfuss zu Hitler*, pp. 161-62.

64. AA to German Legation in Vienna, 12 Nov. 1936; "Protocol," 21 Nov. 1936, signed by Neurath and Schmidt, *DGFP*, D, I, Nos. 177, 182; and Wiskemann, *Rome-Berlin Axis*, p. 69. Bohle's rather vigorous role in such negotiations is not mentioned by Weinberg, *Foreign Policy of Hitler's Germany*; Gehl, *Austria, Germany and the Anschluss*; or Eichstädt, *Von Dollfuss zu Hitler*.

65. As, for instance, with the Nazi agent, Johannes Uwe; report of Austrian Security Office to Austrian Foreign Ministry, 7 Jan. 1937, Nuremberg Document 1985-NG, Case 11/RG 238. Note also, *Der Hochverratsprozess gegen Dr. Guido Schmidt vor dem Wiener Volksgericht* (Vienna: Österreichische Staatsdruckerei, 1947), p. 105, which contains valuable documents and testimony on the Austrian story.

66. "Foreign Organization NSDAP- Landesgruppe Austria," n.d., Nuremberg Document 1981-NG; and Austrian police report, 7 Jan. 1937, Nuremberg Document 1969-NG, Case 11/RG 238.

67. BKA, "Bund der Reichsdeutschen in Österreich: politische Tätigkeit," containing intelligence and police reports, Feb. 1936; and BKA, report, 2 Jan. 1937, PA/ *Chef* AO/Folder 26. The figures on the *Bund*'s membership are in Bohle, "Aufzeichnung," 18 Feb. 1937 ("Betr. Reichsdeutsche Landesgruppe Österreich der Auslands-Organisation der NSDAP."), PA/ *Chef* AO/Folder 24. Although Gehl, *Austria, Germany and the Anschluss,* does not mention the *Bund* or AO, it contains a discussion of the Austrian Legion (pp. 62, 103); the same is true of Luza, *Austro-German Relations*, p. 22.

68. AA, Memo, 25 Jan. 1937, T-120/356/264743-264744.

69. Which was first given a legal basis by the Nazi government's "Gesetz zur Sicherung der Einheit von Partei und Staat v. 1 Dezember 1933," *Reichsgesetzblatt*, edited by Reich Ministry of Interior (Berlin: Reichsverlagsamt, 1933), I:1016.

70.   Reich Treasury to AO Treasury, 22 Dec. 1936, PA/*Chef* AO/Folder 47, raising the subsidy to 150,000 marks (roughly $35,000) per year.

71.   Jacobsen, *Nationalsozialistische Aussenpolitik*, pp. 132-33; "Die Reichsdeutschen im Ausland," *Frankfurter Zeitung* (hereafter *FZ*), 3 Feb. 1937; and Hans Volz, ed., *Von der Grossmacht zur Weltmacht, 1937*, Vol. V of *Dokumente der deutschen Politik* (Berlin: Junker und Dünnhaupt, 1938), pp. 57-58.

72.   Contrary to Dodd, *Through Embassy Eyes*, p. 248, and Fromm, *Blood and Banquets*, p. 206 (the entry for 12 Oct. 1935), Neurath did not protest Bohle's appointment, but welcomed it; Neurath, "Affidavit," 19 Sept. 1946, Nuremberg Document 163-NG, Case 11/RG 238; and Kordt, *Wahn und Wirklichkeit*, p. 98. Neurath had felt since 1930 that the NSDAP gave the Reich a poor image abroad; Ernst Ziehm, *Aus Meiner Politischen Arbeit* (Marburg/Lahn: Johann Gottfried Herder-Institut, 1956), p. 187. The concept of *Menschenführung* is discussed by Hencke, "Das Auswaertige Amt . . . . ," M-679/2/0486-0487.

73.   Kordt, *Nicht aus den Akten*, pp. 147-48; and Bohle to Hess, 23 Dec. 1937, PA/*Chef* AO/Folder 47.

74.   Brown, "The Third Reich's Mobilization," pp. 131-32.

75.   "Nazis Create Office for Germans Abroad," *NYT*, 3 Feb. 1937.

76.   U.S. Department of State, *National Socialism: Basic Principles, Their Application by the Nazi Party's Foreign Organization, and the Use of Germans Abroad for Nazi Aims* (Washington: U.S. Government Printing Office, 1943), p. 95; Dallek, *Democrat and Diplomat*, p. 299; and "A Nazi Incursion," *The Times* (London), 3 Feb. 1937.

77.   "New Chief for London," *News Chronicle* (London), 4 Feb. 1937; and "Head of the 'Nazintern'," *Daily Telegraph* (London), 8 Mar. 1937.

78.   "Auswärtiges Amt, eing. 11 Februar 1937," T-120/727/264705-264707.

79.   Bohle, "Begründung für den Antrag betr. Schaffung eines Geheimfonds für den Chef der Auslands-Organisation im Auswärtigen Amt.," 21 Jan. 1938, T-120/78/59778-59779; and AA (Bohle) to German missions and consulates, 12 June 1937, T-120/64/51662-51665.

80.   Bohle to diplomatic and consular representatives abroad, 23 July 1937; Lehne (head of the AO's *Amt für Erzieher*, or "Office for Educators") to Bohle, 3 Mar. 1937; and AO, "Unterredung mit Herrn Reichsminister Rust in seinem Ministerium am 28. Oktober 1937," T-120/78/60168-60169, 60104, 60121, respectively. See also, SD report, 15 Oct. 1937, T-120/399/308517-308518.

81.   AO Repatriation Office Munich, "Passbuch I, Zwgst. München, 1936-1938," T-81/148/0167201-0167297; AO Repatriation Office, "Aktenvermerk," 15 May 1937; Bohle to German missions abroad, 3 May 1937; and AO Repatriation Office to Bohle, 27 Feb. 1937, T-120/78/59924-59926, 59889, 59892-59893, respectively.

82.   Bohle, "Runderlass AO 1.," 1 Mar. 1937, T-120/3131/E509623-E509627.

83.   AO to *Chef* AO, 9 July 1937, enclosing a Memo, 14 Aug. 1937, T-120/78/60171; Bohle, "Runderlass AO 3," 14 Apr. 1937; and Bohle, "Runderlass AO 4," 30 Apr. 1937, T-120/3131/E509631-E509632, E509640-E509641.

84.   Bohle, "Runderlass AO 6," 11 Oct. 1937, T-120/3131/E509651-E509654.

85.   Bohle Interrogation, *TMWC*, X:28; Reich Ministry of Finance to AA, 31 Dec. 1937; and Rudolf Tesmann to AO Treasury, 12 Oct. 1939, T-120/78/59882, 59883.

86.   AO, "Emil Prüfert," n.d., BDC/PK/*Emil Prüfert*; Esperstedt to Prüfert, 12 Sept. 1937; Prüfert to AO, 23 Sept. 1937; and LG Colombia to AO, 7 Nov. 1937

("*Betr.*: Neuer kolumbianischer Gesandter in Berlin."), T-120/103/110889, 110890, 110904, respectively.

87. AO to Fischer, 20 Dec. 1937 ("Betr.: Ausbürgerung Hippel."), T-120/78/ 60190-60191; Bohle to German Legation Oslo, 18 Nov. 1937, T-120/33/29213.

88. Telegram, Bohle to *Consugerma* (German Consulate) Windhoek, 23 Feb. 1937; and Bohle to Michael Neuendorf, 7 Apr. 1937, T-120/239/174737-174757.

89. Bohle to Himmler, 23 Mar. 1936, BDC/RuSHA/ *Kurt Wermke*. Examples of Germans sent to the Reich are in *Schwarzrotbuch*, pp. 121-22; and AO (Harbor Control) to LG Spain, 18 June 1936, WL/585.

90. Jacobsen, *Nationalsozialistische Aussenpolitik*, p. 145; *VB*, 25 May 1937, 25/26 Dec. 1937; Drechsel Interrogation, 29 Dec. 1934, U.S. House of Rep., *Investigation of Nazi Propaganda Activities*, II:446-48, 450, 453-56; "Bremen Hoists the Swastika Flag," *Daily Telegraph* (London), 18 Sept. 1935; and Ernest Hamburger, "A Peculiar Pattern of the Fifth Column—The Organization of the German Seamen," *Social Research*, 9 (1942), 498-503, 506-07, 509.

91. McKale, *Nazi Party Courts*, p. 142; and *Mitteilungsblatt*, 51 (Aug./Sept. 1937), 3.

92. Heydrich to the Court, 19 Mar. 1938, T-175/80/2600381-2600395.

93. As in the case of the former Ambassador to the United States, Luther, when he spoke in Batavia in early 1937; Luther, *Politiker ohne Partei*, p. 422.

94. Hencke, "Einfluss der Parteikanzlei auf Beamtenernennungen und auf aus-senpolitische Fragen," M-679/2/0484.

95. For instance, Zuchristian's report to the AO, 2 May 1934, WL/585. Very few of them have survived, at least to this author's knowledge.

96. *Mitteilungsblatt*, 45 (Jan. 1937), 3; 49 (May 1937), 2; 54 (Dec. 1937), 1.

97. Neurath, Memo, 25 Feb. 1937, *DGFP*, D, I, No. 212; Bohle to AO, 17 Aug. 1937, T-120/1382/D535587; and Jacobsen, *Nationalsozialistische Aussenpolitik*, pp. 474-76. Also, note *Mitteilungsblatt*, 48 (Apr. 1937), 3; 49 (May 1937), 2; 51 (Aug./ Sept. 1937), 1; 53 (Nov. 1937), 1; 54 (Dec. 1937), 1.

98. Funk to Mackensen, 27 Oct. 1937; and Memo, Mackensen, 1 Nov. 1937, PA/ *Chef* AO/ Folder 42.

99. SS personnel file on Bohle, 13 Feb. 1944, Nuremberg Document 2057-NG, Case 11/RG 238; Bohle to Lammers, 18 Aug. 1937, PA/ *Chef* AO/Folder 47; and *Mitteilungsblatt*, 45 (Jan. 1937, 3; 46 (Feb. 1937), 3; 51 (Aug./Sept. 1937), 1; 53 (Nov. 1937), 1.

100. Georg Vogel, *Diplomat unter Hitler und Adenauer* (Düsseldorf: Econ, 1969), pp. 45-47, 50-51; Ruberg to Ogrl. Dublin, 6 July 1937, T-120/2956/E471481-E471482; Jacobsen, *Nationalsozialistische Aussenpolitik*, p. 471; and Bohle to AO (*Amt* VIII), 17 Aug. 1937, T-120/1382/D535587.

101. Ehrich, "Bericht," 27 Feb. 1937, T-120/368/281487-281488; Haas, "Affi-davit," 2 Mar. 1948, Nuremberg Document 13 (Defense Exhibit Bohle), Case 11/RG 238; Hermann Lüdtke to Ehrich, 17 June 1938 ("Betr. Förster und Haas. IG Farben"), PA/ *Chef* AO/ Folder 42.

102. AO to *Chef* AO, 29 June 1937 and 12 May 1937, PA/ *Chef* AO/ Folder 42; *VB*, 1 Dec. 1937; and Memo to officials, employees, and workers in the AA in Berlin, 30 Apr. 1937, T-120/3968/E044100.

103. Hitler, "Anordnung Nr. 62/38," 23 May 1938, BDC/ *Slg. Schu./ Ordner* 378 (*Partei-Mitgliedswesen: Sonderfälle*); Bohle to Ribbentrop, 20 June 1938, PA/ *Chef* AO/Folder 41 (*Beamte: Allgemeines*); Woermann to Bohle, 25 Apr. 1938;

Leonhardt to *Chef* AO, 21 Apr. 1938 ("Betr. Aufnahme des Staatssekretärs Ernst Freiherr v. Weizsäcker . . . , in die Partei."), PA/*Chef* AO/Folder 42; Jacobsen, *Nationalsozialistische Aussenpolitik*, pp. 627-32; and Leonidas E. Hill, ed., *Die Weizsäcker-Papiere, 1933-1950* (Frankfurt/Main: Propylaen, 1974), p. 124.

104. The figures are taken from AO, "Parteimitglieder, Stand 30.6.1937," T-120/78/60148 (see Jacobsen, *Nationalsozialistische Aussenpolitik*, p. 663); and Seabury, *Wilhelmstrasse*, pp. 62-64. Also, note Tesmann to Ehrich, 2 Aug. 1938, PA/*Chef* AO/Folder 47; Bohle to Ribbentrop, 9 Sept. 1940, PA/*Chef* AO/Folder 41; Tesmann to Ehrich, 2 Aug. 1938; Bohle to Ogrl. AA, 28 Mar. 1938; and Bohle to Bergen, 21 Oct. 1939, PA/*Chef* AO/Folder 42.

105. Bohle to Reich Chancellery, 9 Feb. 1937, Nuremberg Document 2794-NG, Case 11/RG 238.

106. Quoted from Hildegard v. Kotze, ed., *Heeresadjutant bei Hitler, 1938-1943: Aufzeichnungen des Majors Engel* (Stuttgart: Deutsche Verlags-Anstalt, 1974), p. 49 (the entry for 18 June 1939).

107. For example, Bennett, *Hitler Over Africa*, p. 16, noted, "Most of the German Consular Service is supervised by Bohle and the Auslands Organisation . . . . Overseas German diplomats are members of the Nazi Party and expected to do all in their power to foster the movement in foreign lands . . . ."

CHAPTER 5

1. AO, "Stand der zahlenden Mitglieder lt. Reichsleitung der NSDAP," n.d. (probably 1942), T-580/59/301; and AO, "Parteimitglieder, Stand 30.6.1937," T-120/78/60148, which is in Jacobsen, *Nationalsozialistische Aussenpolitik*, pp. 661-64.

2. AO, "Erläuterung zur 1. statistischen Erhebung der AO.—Stichtag 30. Juni 1937."; and AO, "Parteimitglieder—Parteieintritt, Stand 30.6.1937," T-120/78/60144.

3. Jacobsen, *Nationalsozialistische Aussenpolitik*, pp. 110, 137. On the religion of major AO officials, see the biographical records in the BDC.

4. *Jahrbuch für Auswärtige Politik, 1938* (Berlin: Brückenverlag [A. Gross], 1938), pp. 284-86; and Ehrich, *Die Auslands-Organisation der NSDAP*, pp. 16-21.

5. Sanke, *Der deutsche Faschismus in Lateinamerika*, pp. 142-43, for the leadership in Colombia; and German Community Tokyo-Yokohama, "Mitglieder-Verzeichnis: Partei-Organisationen," Jan. 1938, T-82/85/0245188-0245190, 0245081-0245171, for the leadership in Japan. Also, note *Mitteilungsblatt*, 51 (Aug./Sept. 1937), 1-2; and Bohle's order to AO, 25 Nov. 1934, showing there were thirty seven LG at the time, *Schwarzrotbuch*, p. 19.

6. The figures, which ranged from 4,200 marks paid to the LGL Colombia and Bulgaria to 12,600 marks paid to the LGL Italy, are in Erwin Knörk to Bohle, 21 Feb. 1939, T-120/78/59783.

7. DAI, "Liste der 49 Geräte, die der Auslands-Organisation zur Verfügung gestellt wurden.," Aug. 1938, T-81/424/5171083-5171084; and Kirchner, "Werden und Wirken . . . ," 4 Dec. 1937, T-120/239/174859-174871.

8. Hirszowicz, *The Third Reich and the Arab East*, pp. 21-24, 26-33; Wilhelm Döhle to AA, 22 Mar. 1937, T-120/64/51604-51621; Ehrich, "Betr. Jüdischer Nationalstaat in Palestina und Kapitaltransferierung jüdischer Auswanderer nach Palestina (Haavara-Abkommen)," 5 June 1937, T-120/776/370143-370144; Döhle to AA, 13 July 1937, *DGFP*, D, V, No. 565; and *Reichsstelle für das Auswanderungs-*

wesen, "Betrifft. Auswanderung im Zweiten Kalendervierteljahr 1937," 30 Oct. 1937, PA/*Chef* AO/Folder 56 (*Volksdeutsche, Auswanderer, Rückwanderer, Doppelstaatler*). On Schwarz and the LG's other activities, see AO, "Cornelius Schwarz," n.d., BDC/PK/*Cornelius Schwarz.*

9. The figure is from Joachim Trotz, "Zur Tätigkeit der deutschen V. Kolonne in Lateinamerika von 1933-1945," *Wissenschaftliche Zeitschrift der Universität Rostock,* 14 (1965), 120. See also, "Affidavit," 4 Mar. 1947, by Georg von Schnitzler (member of executive board of Farben from 1925 to 1945), Nuremberg Document 5191-NI; Volberg, "Eidesstattliche Versicherung," 19 Apr. 1948, Nuremberg Document 1 (Defense Exhibit Bohle), Case 11/Rg 238; and Ebel, *Das Dritte Reich und Argentinien,* pp. 230-35.

10. Anton Reithinger, "Affidavit," 29 Jan. 1947, Nuremberg Document 3763-NI; and names of Jews and others removed from Farben offices, "Eidesstattliche Erklärung," 29 Apr. 1948, by Kurt Krüger (official in Farben's Control Office), Nuremberg Document 3 (Defense Exhibit Bohle), Case 11/RG 238.

11. Wilhelm von Schoen (German Minister to Chile, 1935-1944), "Affidavit," 22 Sept. 1947, Nuremberg Document 3402-NG; and Kroeger, "Eidesstattliche Erklaerung," 10 Apr. 1948, Nuremberg Document 5 (Defense Exhibit Bohle), Case 11/RG 238.

12. Bohle to Stohrer, 18 Jan. 1937, PA/*Chef* AO/Folder 47; on Haas, see pp. 116-17. Regarding Germany's Far Eastern policy, there is a vast literature that includes Sommer, *Deutschland und Japan zwischen den Mächten,* pp. 17-18, 25, 32-34, 43-81, 103-16; Presseisen, *Germany and Japan,* pp. 87-154; Bloch, *German Interests and Policies in the Far East,* pp. 30-43; Johanna Menzel Meskill, *Hitler and Japan: The Hollow Alliance* (New York: Atherton Press, 1966), pp. 4-5; Weinberg, *Foreign Policy of Hitler's Germany,* pp. 131-32, 342-48; Drechsler, *Deutschland-China-Japan,* pp. 41-61; and Walsh, "The German Military Mission in China," pp. 509-12.

13. *Chef* AO to Reich HJ, 13 Dec. 1937, T-120/49/39494-39495; and "Empfang für Kreuzer 'Emden' in Tokio," *NS-Dienst für auslandsdeutsche Blätter* (Berlin), No. 5/37. The LG may also have been involved in the effort by the German Embassy to spread anti-Semitic literature (e.g., Japanese translations of Nazi works) among the Japanese. See David Kranzler, *Japanese, Nazis and Jews: The Jewish Refugee Community of Shanghai, 1938-1945* (New York: Yeshiva University Press, 1976), pp. 205-08, 485-88.

14. Ehrich, "Aufzeichnung," 6 Mar. 1937, T-120/49/39552-39495, 39456. On the party's racial views toward Japan, see Presseisen, *Germany and Japan,* pp. 3-12; and Sommer, *Deutschland und Japan zwischen den Mächten,* p. 18.

15. AO to LGL Japan, 30 Apr. 1937; O.Gr. Tokyo-Yokohama to AO, 10 Mar. 1937; and Bohle to Himmler, 18 Mar. 1937, T-120/49/39465, 39457, 39459-39460, respectively.

16. Bohle to LGL Lahrmann, 18 June 1938, T-120/1624/D700694; and Sommer, *Deutschland und Japan zwischen den Mächten,* pp. 115-16.

17. "Aufzeichnung über eine Unterredung Amtsleiter VIII mit dem japanischen Marine-Attache Kapitän z.S. Kojima am 26.2 vormittags," 26 Feb. 1938, T-120/325/241912-241914. This document is printed and the negotiations are discussed in Gerhard L. Weinberg, "Deutsch-Japanische Verhandlungen über das Südseemandat, 1937-1938," *Vierteljahrshefte für Zeitgeschichte,* 4 (1956), 390-98; and Drechsler, *Deutschland-China-Japan,* p. 61.

18. "Die Ziele der Auslandsorganisation," *Berliner Tageblatt*, 21 Aug. 1937.

19. On Karlowa's background, see Bohle to Goebbels, 3 Oct. 1934, BDC/KK/ *Franz Hasenöhrl*; and "Otto Karlowa," n.d., BDC/MF/*Otto Karlowa*. Also, note telegram, Bohle to German Embassy London, 11 Aug. 1937, T-120/2719/E420197; and on the expulsions, *Aufklärungs-Ausschuss Hamburg-Bremen*, "Bericht unserer Vertrauensleute in England," 14 Aug. 1937, WL/506.

20. "Ren beskjed til Tyskland!" *Tidens Tegn*, 26 Aug. 1937; "Diplomatic Status Sought for Nazis," *NYT*, 23 Aug. 1937; and anti-AO article in the *Manchester Guardian* summarized in the German news agency publication, *Eigentum des Deutschen Nachrichtenbüros*, 236 (26 Aug. 1937, evening), 23.

21. Recounted in Nancy Harvison Hooker, ed., *The Moffat Papers: Selections from the Diplomatic Journals of Jay Pierrepont Moffat, 1919-1943* (Cambridge, Mass.: Harvard University Press, 1956), pp. 148-49 (the entries for 3-6 Sept. 1937); and Dallek, *Democrat and Diplomat*, pp. 312-13. See also, German Legation in Budapest to AA, 11 Oct. 1937, T-120/1454/D600741-D600742; and "Aufzeichnung für Pg. Tesmann," 10 Nov. 1937, T-120/368/281485-281486.

22. "Der Führer an Gauleiter Bohle," *Westdeutscher Beobachter* (Cologne), 31 Aug. 1937; "Dr. Goebbels antwortet dem Ausland," *Germania* (Berlin), 6 Sept. 1937; and Hess, *Reden*, pp. 264-65.

23. Bohle Interrogation, *TMWC*, X:13-14; and Bene to Bohle, 29 July 1937, PA/*Chef* AO/Folder 42.

24. "Rede des Gauleiters Bohle bei der Feier des Erntedankfestes der Deutschen Kolonie zu London vom 1 Oktober 1937.," Volz, *Von der Grossmacht zur Weltmacht, 1937*, pp. 76, 80, 83; and a rough translation of the address in U.S. Dept. of State, *National Socialism*, pp. 387-96. Also, note "What I Saw at the London Nazis' Secret Meeting," *Evening Standard* (London), 2 Oct. 1937.

25. *The Times* (London), 2 Oct. 1937; *NYT*, 2 Oct. 1937, which called the rally "no more exciting than a community meeting;" and *Evening Standard* (London), 2 Oct. 1937. Given the press coverage of the visit, it is curious that Bohle is not mentioned in Franklin Reid Gannon, *The British Press and Germany, 1936-1939* (London: Oxford University Press, 1971).

26. Bohle to Hess, 23 Dec. 1937, PA/*Chef* AO/Folder 47.

27. "Die Stellung des Chefs der Auslandsorganisation," *VB*, 23 Dec. 1937.

28. Hencke, "Das Auswaertige Amt . . . . ," M-679/2/0487; *NYT*, 23 Dec. 1937; and "Herr Bohle's New Rank," *The Times* (London), 22 Dec. 1937.

29. Great Britain, Parliamentary Debates, House of Commons, *Official Report* (London: H.M. Stationery Office, 1938), 334, 96 (Thurs., 14 Apr. 1938), 1406, and 330, 41 (Tues., 21 Dec. 1937), 1866-67.

30. Bohle to Strölin, 19 Oct. 1937, PA/*Chef* AO/Folder 47.

31. Report of the Austrian Security Police, 31 Mar. 1937, Nuremberg Document 1984-NG, Case 11/RG 238. Cogent summaries of the *Anschluss* are Gehl, *Austria, Germany and the Anschluss*, pp. 166-95; Hermann Mau and Helmut Krausnick, *Deutsche Geschichte der jüngsten Vergangenheit, 1933-1945* (Tübingen-Stuttgart: Casterman, 1964), pp. 99-106; and Offner, *American Appeasement*, pp. 226-29. On the SA and *Turnerriege*, see BKA, "Aufstellung von Turnerriegen im 'Bund der Reichsdeutschen'," 19 Feb. 1937, PA/*Chef* AO/Folder 26.

32. Papen, *Memoirs*, pp. 391-92; and Eichstädt, *Von Dollfuss zu Hitler*, pp. 170-71.

33. Luza, *Austro-German Relations*, pp. 34-39; "Österreich ["Papen Memoran-

dum"]," 15 Apr. 1947, *Der Hochverratsprozess*, p. 373; and Bohle to Papen, 13 Dec. 1937, PA/*Chef* AO/Folder 24.

34. Papen to AA, 8 Jan. 1938, *DGFP*, D, I, No. 275; and report of Austrian Security Police, 15 Sept. 1937, Nuremberg Document 1986-NG, Case 11/RG 238.

35. BKA, "Tätigkeit der Wirtschaftsgruppe des 'Bundes der Reichsdeutschen in Österreich'," 16 July 1937; BKA, "Tätigkeit der Landesgruppe Oesterreich der AO der NSDAP; Wechsel der Funktionäre," 28 May 1937, PA/*Chef* AO/Folder 26; Bohle to Papen, 16 Apr. 1937; and "Auszug aus einem Bericht des Deutschen Botschafters in Wien von 17.3.37 (Tgb. Nr. A. 1851.)," PA/*Chef* AO/Folder 24.

36. "Gauleiter Bohle über die Auslandsarbeit der NSDAP," *FZ*, 25 Jan. 1938; and Jacobsen, *Nationalsozialistische Aussenpolitik*, pp. 526-28.

37. On Seyss-Inquart's views and position and Bohle's antagonism toward him, see Wolfgang Rosar, *Deutsche Gemeinschaft: Seyss-Inquart und der Anschluss* (Vienna: Europa-Verlag, 1971), pp. 92, 98, 105, 123, 127, 142, 172, 336; Eichstädt, *Von Dollfuss zu Hitler*, pp. 178-79, 261-63, 325; and Luza, *Austro-German Relations*, pp. 38-39.

38. Bohle Interrogation, 11 Sept. 1945, RG 238; Seabury, *Wilhelmstrasse*, pp. 59-61, 181; Kordt, *Wahn und Wirklichkeit*, pp. 94-99; and Waclaw Jedrzejewicz, ed., *Diplomat in Berlin, 1933-1939: Papers and Memoirs of Josef Lipski, Ambassador of Poland* (New York: Columbia University Press, 1968), pp. 361-62.

39. See the picture in Kirchner, *Hermann Bohle*, p. 86; *FZ*, 11 Feb. 1938; and Bohle Interrogation, 25 Oct. 1945, RG 238.

40. Bohle to Bernard, 21 Feb. 1938, PA/*Chef* AO/Folder 24; Federal Police Vienna to State Secretary for Security (Austria), 8 Nov. 1937; and BKA, "Bund der Reichsdeutschen in Oesterreich; Monatsversammlung der Ortsgruppe Bregenz," 4 Jan. 1938, PA/*Chef* AO/Folder 26.

41. *VB*, 22 Mar. 1938; *NSPK*, 133 (10 June 1938), 1, and 121 (25 May 1938), 1-3; "Affidavit," 20 July 1947, by Wilhelm Schmitt, Nuremberg Document 2212-NG, Case 11/RG 238; and thorough account of the reorganization of the party in Austria, Luza, *Austro-German Relations*, pp. 57-94.

42. AO Repatriation Office Munich, "Passbuch II," 1938-1939, T-81/149/0167298-0167391; *Verfügungen/Anordnungen/Bekanntgaben*, edited by NSDAP, *Partei-Kanzlei* (Munich: F. Eher, 1943), III:192-93; Alan S. Milward, *The German Economy at War* (London: Athlone Press, 1965), chapter one; Memo, "Aussprache Götz mit Gauleiter Bohle," n.d., T-81/141/0178615-0178616; and SS to AO (Bohle), 14 Mar. 1938 ("Betrifft. Rückkehr deutschblütiger Emigranten in das Reichsgebiet."), T-120/78/59953-59955.

43. Bohle, "Zur Persönlichkeit des Landesgruppenleiters Italien, des Legationssekretärs Erwin Ettel . . . .," 26 Apr. 1937, T-120/124/118780-118781; and on Ettel's expansion of the LG Italy, "Neun Jahre NSDAP in Italien," *Italien Beobachter, Sonderausgabe: Führerbesuch* (May 1938), issues of which are in the LC.

44. Winfried Schmitz-Esser, "Hitler-Mussolini: Das Südtiroler-Abkommen von 1939," *Aussenpolitik*, 13 (1962) 399-401; Latour, *Südtirol und die Achse Berlin-Rom*, pp. 20-21; Ritschel, *Diplomatie um Südtirol*, pp. 139-40; and Wiskemann, *Rome-Berlin Axis*, p. 47. The general Italo-German rivalry over interests in Austria, Hungary, Yugoslavia, and the Balkans is discussed by Petersen, *Hitler-Mussolini*, pp. 207-31, 303-69.

45. Schmitz-Esser, "Hitler-Mussolini: Das Südtiroler-Abkommen von 1939," pp. 401-02; Latour, *Südtirol und die Achse Berlin-Rom*, pp. 22-25; Ritschel, *Diplomatie*

um *Südtirol*, pp. 141-46; and Wiskemann, *Rome-Berlin Axis*, pp. 105-06. The assertion by Jacobsen, *Nationalsozialistische Aussenpolitik*, p. 128, that the Axis agreement improved relations between the NSDAP and Fascist regime is not entirely correct.

46.   German Consulate General Milan to AA, 21 Apr. 1938; Bene, "Aktennotiz," 22 Apr. 1938; German Embassy Rome to AA, 22 Apr. 1938; German Consulate General Milan to AO, 17 Mar. 1938; Weizsäcker, "Vermerk," 17 Feb. 1938; German Consulate General Milan to AO, 22 Apr. 1938, T-120/124/119008-119011, 119020, 119021-119025, 118879-118880, 118865-118866, 118915-118918, respectively; and Latour, *Südtirol und die Achse Berlin-Rom*, pp. 22-25.

47.   "Aufzeichnung für Pg. Alfred Hess," 26 Apr. 1938; and Fischer, "Betr. Überwachung des Reiseverkehrs nach Italien in der Zeit vor und bei dem Führer-Besuch," 1 Mar. 1938, PA/*Chef* AO/Folder 82 (*Staatsbesuch*). The significance of the Tirol in Hitler's visit is underscored by Mario Toscano, *The Origins of the Pact of Steel* (Baltimore: Johns Hopkins University Press, 1967), pp. 10-13.

48.   Baynes, *Speeches*, II:1459; Heinrich Hoffmann, ed., *Hitler in Italien* (Munich: Verlag Heinrich Hoffman, 1938), pp. 30-31, showing pictures of Hitler speaking to the rally; and Heinrich Hansen, ed., *Der Schlüssel zum Frieden: Führertage in Italien* (Berlin, 1938).

49.   Bene to Bohle, 1 Nov. 1938, PA/*Chef* AO/Folder 56.

50.   AO, "Tagesbefehl Nr. 33/38," 8 June 1938, PA/*Chef* AO/Folder 41; and AO to *Chef* AO, 7 Sept. 1939 ("Entlassung des Pg. Kauffmann früher Bozen aus dem Konzentrationslager"); telegram, German Embassy Rome to AA, 24 June 1939; telegram, Bohle to *Diplogerma* Rome, 20 June 1939; Fischer, Memo, 22 June 1939 ("*Betr.* Fall des Ortsgruppenleiters Kauffmann in Bozen."), T-120/124/119156, 119130-119131, 119121, 119128-119129, respectively. The contention by Robert Koehl, *RKFDV: German Resettlement and Population Policy, 1939-1945* (Cambridge, Mass.: Harvard University Press, 1957), p. 45, that only the SS resettled persons from the South Tirol and the AO did not is incorrect. See also, Latour, *Südtirol und die Achse Berlin-Rom*, pp. 27, 29-30, 33-37; Ritschel, *Diplomatie um Südtirol*, pp. 160-66; and Wiskemann, *Rome-Berlin Axis*, pp. 147-48, 181.

51.   AA, "Deutsch-italienische Abkommen, Richtlinien und Briefwechsel vom 21. Oktober 1939.," T-120/124/119188-119220; Toscano, *Alto Adige-South Tyrol*, pp. 44-45, 49-50; Ritschel, *Diplomatie um Südtirol*, pp. 164-69, 174, 179; Latour, *Südtirol und die Achse Berlin-Rom*, pp. 36-41, 43, 51-52, 56-57, 59, 69-70, 103-24; Schmitz-Esser, "Hitler-Mussolini: Das Südtiroler-Abkommen von 1939," pp. 404-07; and Wiskemann, *Rome-Berlin Axis*, pp. 148-49, 181, 190, 313, 330-34.

52.   Union of South Africa Legation to Ribbentrop, 30 May 1938, T-120/239/174875; Esp (LGL Latvia) to Bohle, 10 Aug. 1938, T-120/103/110987-110988; Bibra to Bohle, 1 June 1938; Lammers to Neurath, 18 Jan. 1938 ("Betrifft. Eiserne Garde/Rumänien."), T-120/775/370101, 370012-370013; "Overseas Citizens Spread Reich Influence," *Singapore Free Press*, 8 Nov. 1938; *Daily Clarion* (Toronto), 4 Mar. 1938; and AO to *Chef* AO, 24 Mar. 1937, T-120/49/39627-39628.

53.   For instance, Gissibl's correspondence with Hitler, Hess, Rosenberg, and other German leaders; AO to German Consulate General New York, 31 May 1937, T-120/38/32705. On Mensing's removal, note "Aktennotiz für das Büro des Chefs der AO im AA z.Hd. von Pg. Dr. Ehrich," 7 July 1937, same roll, frame 32702; and Kipphan, *Deutsche Propaganda in den Vereinigten Staaten*, p. 59. Also, note *The German Reich and Americans of German Origin* (New York: Oxford University

Press, 1938), sponsored by such leaders as Felix Frankfurter, Henry L. Stimson, and James Byrne.

54. Bohle to Gyssling, 29 Jan. 1938; and Ehrich, "Die Aufzeichnung vom 11.10 37 über das Deutschtum in den Vereinigten Staaten trifft im grundsätzlichen die Auffassung von Gauleiter Bohle und der Leitung der AO.," T-120/38/32724, 32710.

55. Diamond, *The Nazi Movement in the United States*, pp. 293-96; and Frye, *Nazi Germany*, p. 87.

56. Dieckhoff to Weizsäcker, 22 Mar. 1938; Ribbentrop to Dieckhoff, 29 Mar. 1938, *DGFP*, D, I, Nos. 445, 446; Diamond, *The Nazi Movement in the United States*, pp. 280-91, 295, 303-04, 307-10; Smith, *Deutschtum of Nazi Germany*, p. 103; Smith, *To Save a Nation*, pp. 150-51; Kipphan, *Deutsche Propaganda in den Vereinigten Staaten*, pp. 95-99; and Compton, *The Swastika and the Eagle*, pp. 55-60, 63-65.

57. Diamond, *The Nazi Movement in the United States*, pp. 297-302; Kipphan, *Deutsche Propaganda in den Vereinigten Staaten*, pp. 86-87, 185-98; and Offner, *American Appeasement*, p. 85.

58. Arthur L. Smith, Jr., "The Kameradschaft USA," *Journal of Modern History*, 34 (1962), 398-408; Kipphan, *Deutsche Propaganda in den Vereinigten Staaten*, pp. 100-02; AO to Gissibl, 8 Feb. 1939, T-81/140/0177169-0177170; telegram, German Embassy Washington to AA, 29 May 1938, T-120/38/32779-32780; Dieckhoff to AA, 2 June 1938, *DGFP*, D, I, No. 455; and Diamond, *The Nazi Movement in the United States*, pp. 276-78, 310-12.

59. Diamond, *The Nazi Movement in the United States*, pp. 308-10, 323-24, 326-28; Kipphan, *Deutsche Propaganda in den Vereinigten Staaten*, pp. 95-99; and Smith, *To Save a Nation*, pp. 150-51.

60. German Consulate General New York to AA, 5 Apr. 1940, PA/*Chef* AO/ Folder 73 (*Erlasse A.O. 1/40, 2/40, 3/40, 4/40, 5/40, 6/40*); telegram, Bohle to Consulate General New York, 4 May 1939, T-120/38/32844; *Mitteilungsblatt*, 3 (Mar. 1939), 3; and *German Reich*, p. vi.

61. Covered exhaustively by Diamond, *The Nazi Movement in the United States*, pp. 329-37; Kipphan, *Deutsche Propaganda in den Vereinigten Staaten*, p. 88; Smith, *Deutschtum of Nazi Germany*, pp. 107-08; and Smith, *To Save a Nation*, pp. 153-55.

62. Sanke, *Der deutsche Faschismus in Lateinamerika*, p. 32.

63. Sanke, *Der deutsche Faschismus in Lateinamerika*, p. 26; Ebel, *Das Dritte Reich und Argentinien*, pp. 391-93; Schröder, *Deutschland und die Vereinigten Staaten*, pp. 246-61; and Offner, *American Appeasement*, pp. 167-71.

64. German Embassy Santiago to AA, 7 May, 1 June, 15 Oct. 1938; German Consulate General Valparaiso to AA, 4 July 1938, T-120/225/171263-171266, 171271-171274, 171298-171300, 171291-171292, respectively; Jacobsen, *National-sozialistische Aussenpolitik*, p. 566; and unpublished dissertation, Michael Potashnik, "*Nacismo*: National Socialism in Chile, 1932-1938" (University of California, Los Angeles, 1974).

65. Prüfert to AO, 4 Jan. 1938, T-120/103/110899; and telegram, German Mission La Paz to AA, 3 Oct. 1938, T-120/225/171224, 171231.

66. German Legation Montevideo to AA, 19 May 1938, T-120/1304/487011-487017; *VB*, 5 Jan. 1938; and AO Legal Office, "Strafdrohung gegen die Einmischung Reichsdeutscher in die Innere Politik Ausländischer Staaten.," 5 Oct. 1937, T-120/368/281492-281499.

67. Harms-Baltzer, *Die Nationalisierung der deutschen Einwanderer*, pp. 32-34, 42-49; Trotz, "Zur Tätigkeit der deutschen V. Kolonne in Lateinamerika von 1933-1945," p. 122; AO, "Vorgänge in Brasilien," Mar. 1938, T-120/225/170869-170871; Jacobsen, *Nationalsozialistische Aussenpolitik*, pp. 555-56; McCann, *Brazilian-American Alliance*, pp. 82, 90; and Hilton, *Brazil and the Great Powers*, pp. 148-51.

68. See the discussion of the law in Harms-Baltzer, *Die Nationalisierung der deutschen Einwanderer*, pp. 49-60; McCann, *Brazilian-American Alliance*, pp. 87-89; Bisse, "Tagesbefehl Nr. 12/38," 23 Mar. 1938, T-580/55/294; Sanke, *Der deutsche Faschismus in Lateinamerika*, p. 115; Ebel, *Das Dritte Reich und Argentinien*, pp. 274-79, 283-86; and German Embassy Rio de Janeiro (Ritter) to Bohle, 18 Mar. 1938, PA/*Chef* AO/Folder 42. Ritter's surprise is also noted by Hilton, *Brazil and the Great Powers*, p. 173.

69. Trotz, "Zur Tätigkeit der deutschen V. Kolonne in Lateinamerika von 1933-1945," p. 123; Harms-Baltzer, *Die Nationalisierung der deutschen Einwanderer*, pp. 63-72; Ebel, *Das Dritte Reich und Argentinien*, pp. 280-81, 315; Sanke, *Der deutsche Faschismus in Lateinamerika*, pp. 115-18; and Jacobsen, *Nationalsozialistische Aussenpolitik*, pp. 556, 561. McCann, *Brazilian-American Alliance*, pp. 81, 91-95, 100-01, estimates that 1600 Integralists and Germans were arrested, a third being in the various armed services. Hilton, *Brazil and the Great Powers*, pp. 173-75, maintains the Integralists "made the greatest headway in precisely those areas of heavy German settlement."

70. Telegram, Bohle to German missions in South and Central America, 18 May 1938, T-120/225/170914.

71. As, for example, the appointment of Herbert Schmidt as Commercial Attache to the Consulate General in São Paulo; German Consulate General São Paulo to AA, 5 Nov. 1938; and telegram, German Embassy Rio de Janeiro to AA, 18 May 1938, T-120/225/171021, 170916-170917. Also, note Frye, *Nazi Germany*, p. 107.

72. Harms-Baltzer, *Die Nationalisierung der deutschen Einwanderer*, pp. 67-68, 105-16; AO to APA, 9 Feb. 1939, T-81/12/Flash No. 1 (no frame numbers); AO to *Chef* AO, 12 Nov. 1938; and Woermann, Memo, 21 Sept. 1938, T-120/225/171106, 170996-170997. On Ritter, see McCann, *Brazilian-American Alliance*, pp. 103-04.

73. Bohle, "Anordnung Nr. 14" and "Anordnung Nr. 15," 25 Aug. 1938, T-120/320/241438-241441; Ebel, *Das Dritte Reich und Argentinien*, pp. 332-34; and "Aufzeichnung über die Zusammenkunft der deutschen Missionchefs in Argentinien, Brasilien, Chile and Uruguay in Montevideo am 28. und 29. Juli 1938," T-120/218/168208-168215.

74. Offner, *American Appeasement*, p. 170; and Sanke, *Der deutsche Faschismus in Lateinamerika*, p. 27.

75. Ebel, *Das Dritte Reich und Argentinien*, pp. 289-315; and Kannapin, "Deutschland und Argentinien von 1933 bis 1945," p. 114.

76. Ebel, *Das Dritte Reich und Argentinien*, pp. 335-36; "Abschied des Landesgruppenleiters Argentinien," *NSPK*, 195 (21 Aug. 1938), 6; Jürges, *Hakenkreuz am Rio de La Plata*, p. 10; AO, Memo, 26 July 1938, T-120/1304/487487-487488; AO to German Embassy Buenos Aires, 15 Sept. 1938; AO (Party Court) to *Chef* AO, 3 June 1938, T-120/218/168225, 168198-168200; and Frye, *Nazi Germany*, p. 103.

77. Sanke, *Der deutsche Faschismus in Lateinamerika*, pp. 88-92; Frye, *Nazi Germany*, pp. 110-12; an abstract of Bohle's conference with Thermann at Nuremberg, 13 Sept. 1938; Bohle, "Anordnung," 13 Oct. 1938, T-120/1304/487489-

487491, 487497; Klingenfuss's arrival in *Mitteilungsblatt*, 1 (Jan. 1939), 1; and on Brandt, "Hiermit Herrn Ministerialdirektor Prüfer überreicht.," 2 Mar. 1938, PA/ *Chef* AO/Folder 42.

78. As clearly shown by Ebel, *Das Dritte Reich und Argentinien*, pp. 391-401.

79. Ibid., pp. 401-10; Sanke, *Der deutsche Faschismus in Lateinamerika*, pp. 91-92; "Freispruch im 'Patagonien-Fall'," *FZ*, 28 June 1939; Simonson, "Nazi Infiltration," pp. 174-75; "Patagonia Document," German Embassy to Colonial Policy Office, 11 Jan. 1937, T-120/218/168590-168593; and Jürges, *Hakenkreuz am Rio de La Plata*, p. 11.

80. "Stellungnahme der AO der N.S.D.A.P. zu dem Fragebogen des Auswärtigen Amtes vom 4.5.39.," 17 May 1939, T-120/1304/487498-487505; AA to *Diplogerma* Buenos Aires, 21 Aug. 1939; telegram, German Embassy Buenos Aires to AA, 5 May 1939; and telegram, Bohle to *Diplogerma* Buenos Aires, 1 July 1939, T-120/218/ 168352, 168622, 168308, respectively.

81. See Frye, *Nazi Germany*, p. 114; German Legation for Central America and Panama to AA, 24 June 1939, T-120/352/264817; telegram, German Embassy Santiago to AA, 15 May 1939, T-120/225/171418; telegram, Fritz Grobba (German Minister to Iraq) to AA, 10 Apr. 1939, T-120/1400/D549033; AO to *Chef* AO, 12 June 1939, T-120/38/32869; and J. H. Becker (Tanuda) to Bohle, 29 Oct. 1938, PA/*Chef* AO/Folder 4 (*Australien*).

82. "Niederschrift über die erste Sitzung der Lateinamerika-Konferenz am 12. Juni 1939 im Auswärtigen Amt (Bundesratssaal).," T-120/64/51571-51584. The most comprehensive study of the conference is Ebel, *Das Dritte Reich und Argentinien*, pp. 418-23.

83. *Mitteilungsblatt*, nos. 4-12 (Apr./Dec. 1939), listing very few promotions to the AA; also, note AA, "Beamte: Monatliche Personalveränderungen," Apr. 1937- June 1940, PA/*Chef* AO/Folder 41.

84. Smelser, *Sudeten Problem*, chap. eight on the SS and SD; Johann Wolfgang Brügel, *Tschechen und Deutsche, 1918-1938* (Munich: Nymphenburger Verlagshandlung, 1967), pp. 246, 250-51, 259, 328, 361-62, 500-13; "Draft of Despatch by the Foreign Minister to the German Legation in Czechoslovakia, Enclosing a Memorandum by the Foreign Minister," 29 Mar. 1938; and two memos by VoMi, 3 June 1938, *DGFP*, D, II, Nos. 109, 237, 238, respectively.

85. German Legation Prague to AA, 27 Mar. 1936, T-120/3555/E672328.

86. German Consulate Reichenberg to AO, 1 Dec. 1937 ("26. Monatsbericht. Geheim und vertraulich."); and German Consulate Reichenberg to AO, 31 Dec. 1937 ("27. Monatsbericht. Vertraulich."), T-120/239/175050-175051, 175059-175061. Lierau was also one of Himmler's agents and apparently worked for both the SD and *Abwehr*; Smelser, *Sudeten Problem*, pp. 174-75, 181-82; and Brügel, *Tschechen und Deutsche*, pp. 292, 595.

87. *Chef* AO to AO, 24 Mar. 1937 ("Streng vertraulich! Betr. Haftfall des Pg. Urban."), T-120/239/174999.

88. Brügel, *Tschechen und Deutsche*, pp. 329-33, 335-36, 352-54, 371-72; Smelser, *Sudeten Problem*, p. 215; Bohle's Memo, "Aufzeichnung," 1 Apr. 1938; and Memo of the Mastny meeting, 30 Nov. 1937, T-120/239/175126-175131, 175046-175049.

89. Smelser, *Sudeten Problem*, pp. 217-20; Gerhard L. Weinberg, "The May Crisis, 1938," *Journal of Modern History*, 29 (1957), 213-25; Brügel, *Tschechen und Deutsche*, pp. 365-71, 500-13; telegram, German Legation Prague to AA, 1 Apr. 1938; and telegram, German Legation Prague to AA, 31 Mar. 1938, T-120/239/175089- 175090, 175086.

90. Bohle to German missions abroad, 14 Nov. 1938; AO, "Aktenvermerk," 6 Oct. 1938; Fischer, "Aufzeichnung für den Gauleiter," 3 Oct. 1938; Bohle's Memo to Ribbentrop, 5 Oct. 1938, T-120/402/304989-304990, 304734-304736, 304687-304688, 304689, respectively; and Brügel, *Tschechen und Deutsche*, pp. 513-21.

91. Baynes, *Speeches*, II:1588-89; Martin Broszat, "Die Memeldeutschen Organisationen und der Nationalsozialismus," *Vierteljahrshefte für Zeitgeschichte*, 5 (1957), 273-78; and Troutbeck (British Minister to Prague) to Viscount Halifax, 30 Jan. 1939, Great Britain, *Documents on British Foreign Policy, 1919-1939*, Third Series (hereafter *DBFP*, 3rd; London: H.M. Stationery Office, 1954), Vol. 4, pp. 56-57.

92. Thorne, *The Approach of War*, pp. 119-47, revealing Chamberlain's determination to resist by force further German expansion; Bohle, "Verfügung," 28 June 1939, *Mitteilungsblatt*, 6 (June 1939), 2; *Verfügung/Anordnungen/ Bekanntgabe*, III:245-47; and Tesmann to AO Treasury, 13 Feb. 1939, T-120/239/ 175194.

93. Nicholas M. Tagy-Talavera, *The Green Shirts and the Others: A History of Fascism in Hungary and Rumania* (Stanford: Hoover Institution Press, 1970), p. 301, maintains Konradi "was the most formidable Volksdeutsch leader besides Konrad Henlein in the *Südostraum*." For more details on Konradi and his activities, see pp. 173-74, above.

94. Bohle's oration is in Wolfgang Diewerge, *Anschlag gegen den Frieden* (Munich: Zentralverlag der NSDAP, 1939), pp. 57-59; and Raul Hilberg, *The Destruction of the European Jews* (Chicago: Quadrangle, 1961), pp. 22-23.

95. Fischer, "Aufzeichnung für den Staatssekretär und Chef der A.O. im A.A.," 18 Nov. 1938, T-120/776/370153; Bohle, "Tagesbefehl Nr. 82/38," 9 Dec. 1938, T-580/55/294; and "Auszug aus dem englischen Protokoll ueber die Vernehmung Graf von Rodern vor der IMT Kommission.," n.d., Nuremberg Document 27 (Defense Exhibit Bohle), Case 11/RG 238.

96. German Embassy Paris, "Memorandum," 2 June 1939; and Fischer, "Ausweisungen aus Grossbritannien," 8 July 1939, T-120/49/39607-39608, 39449-39450.

97. *Deutsches Wollen: Zeitschrift der Auslands-Organisation der NSDAP*, 7 (1 July 1939) 25; and *NYT*, 21 Oct. 1940. The *Deutsches Wollen* was the AO's first (and only) effort at publishing a major, illustrated magazine, but publication lasted only a year because of a lack of funds (all issues are in the LC).

98. As, for instance, the SD agent, Kienast, and Wilhelm Graeb, LGL and Consul in the Budapest Legation; Leon Poliakov and Josef Wulf, eds., *Das Dritte Reich und Seine Diener* (Berlin: Arani, 1956), p. 149.

99. Bohle to Lorenz, 22 May 1937, PA/*Chef* AO/Folder 47; "Politische Parteien der Deutschen in Rumänien," n.d., BDC/*Slg. Schu./Ordner* 309; DAI, "Die deutschen Volksgruppenführungen. Stand März 1939," T-81/350/5078859-5078862, listing twenty-six *Volksdeutsch* groups and their newspapers; and Brügel, *Tschechen und Deutsche*, p. 328.

100. Bohle to German missions and consulates, 10 July 1939 ("Betrifft: Beteiligung der Hoheitsträger bei Staatsangehörigkeitsfragen, insbesondere bei Ein- und Ausbürgerungen."), PA/*Chef* AO/Folder 71 (*Erlasse A.O. 1,2,3,4,5*); Fischer, Memo, 10 Mar. 1939 ("Betr. Ausbürgerung des Professors Dr. Kessler"), T-120/ 78/60211-60212; and labor figures and role of the AO, VoMi, and DAI in encouraging Germans to return home, Götz, "*Vertraulich!* Gedanken zur planmässigen Rückführung Reichsdeutscher und Volksdeutscher ins Reich," 16 May 1939, T-81/ 141/0178666-0178671.

101. Levine, *Hitler's Free City*; Carl J. Burckhardt, *Meiner Danziger Mission, 1937-1939* (2nd ed.; Munich: Callwey, 1960), pp. 81-125; Ziehm, *Aus Meiner Politischen Arbeit*, pp. 189-96; and Alan Bullock, *Hitler: A Study in Tyranny* (New York: Bantam Books, 1961), pp. 466-73.

102. German Foreign Office, *Documents on the Events Preceding the Outbreak of the War* (New York: German Library of Information, 1940), pp. lxi-lxii.

103. Richard Breyer, *Das Deutsche Reich und Poland, 1932-1937: Aussenpolitik und Volksgruppenfragen* (Würzburg: Holzner, 1955), pp. 270-72, revealing that the minority was well organized, fairly prosperous, had representatives in the Polish Diet and Senate in Warsaw, and had a system of German schools on a large scale.

104. According to Theodor Bierschenk, *Die Deutsche Volksgruppe in Polen, 1934-1939* (Würzburg: Holzner, 1954), pp. 32-33, "many Germans in Poland" were "enthused" about National Socialism in Germany. See also, LGL Poland to *Chef* AO, 23 July 1937; "Aufzeichnung," 11 Aug. 1937 ("Betr.: Oberschlesien. Ausweisung reichsdeutscher Geistlicher."), T-120/775/369833, 369840; and Jacobsen, *Nationalsozialistische Aussenpolitik*, pp. 593-96, on the role of the VoMi and AA.

105. LG Poland to AO, 14 Aug. 1937 ("Betr.: Ausweisungen von Reichsdeutschen im Soldauer Gebiet."); Mackeben (AA), Memo, 23 Nov. 1937 ("Betr. Ausweisung von Politischen Leitern aus Poln. O/S."), PA/*Chef* AO/Folder 23 (*Oberschlesien: Genfer Abkommen über Oberschlesien*); and LGL Poland to AA, 15 Oct. 1937, T-120/775/369841-369842.

106. On Krummer, note *Chef* AO, "Hiermit über Abteilung Pers. dem Herrn Reichsaussenminister mit der Bitte um wohlwollende Prüfung vorgelegt.," 24 Nov. 1939, PA/*Chef* AO/Folder 42.

107. For example, Philip V. Cannistraro, Edward D. Wynot, Jr., and Theodore P. Kovaleff, eds., *Poland and the Coming of the Second World War: The Diplomatic Papers of A. J. Drexel Biddle, Jr., United States Ambassador to Poland, 1937-1939* (Columbus, Ohio: Ohio State University Press, 1976), pp. 80-81 (the entry for 27 Aug. 1939), which estimates that 16-17,000 Germans were evacuated beginning in May. Further, note Bohle's special commissioner for the AO in Poland, Heinz Cohrs, to Propaganda Ministry, 1 June 1939 ("Betr. Schutz der Deutschen in Polen."); AA, "Massnahmen zum Schutz der Reichsdeutschen in Polen für den Ernstfall," 21 Aug. 1939, T-120/775/369885-369891; and *Mitteilungsblatt*, 8 (Aug. 1939), 2.

108. AO Treasurer (Leonhardt) to *Chef* AO, 23 Feb. 1940, T-120/78/59795; and AO, "Aktennotiz," 18 Aug. 1939 ("Streng vertraulich. betr.: Besetzung der leitenden Stellen im Falle der Übernahme jetzt polnischer Gebiete ins Reichsgebiet"), T-120/775/369897-369898.

109. According to the United States Ambassador to Poland, A. J. Drexel Biddle, Jr., Report ("Factors Contributing to Poland's Defeat"), Oct. 1939, in Cannistraro, Wynot, and Kovaleff, *Poland and the Coming of the Second World War*, p. 171; and "Confidential Order Issued by the Wehrmacht: Instructions to be Brought to the Notice of Troops Engaged Against Poland," n.d., *German Fifth Column in Poland*, pp. 149-50.

110. Ettel, "Rundschreiben—Nr. 96/39," 31 Aug. 1939, PA/*Chef* AO/Folder 55 (*Reichsdeutsche im Ausland*; *Heiraten mit Ausländer*; *Angehörige von Feindstaaten in Deutschland*): Woermann to German consuls in Poland, 25 Aug. 1939; and telegram, Bohle to *Diplogerma* Warsaw, 23 Aug. 1939, T-120/1421/D565774, D565773. See also, telegram, Woermann to German missions in London, Glasgow, Liverpool,

Paris, Bordeaux, Epinal, Le Havre, Lyons, and Marseilles, 25 Aug. 1939, T-120/ 1304/487368; Weizsäcker to Ribbentrop, 16 Aug. 1939, Nuremberg Document 2007-NG, Case 11/RG 238; and telegram, Shepherd (British Minister in Danzig) to Halifax, 21 Aug. 1939, *DBFP*, 3rd, 4, pp. 96-97.

111. From Bohle's speech, "Das Auslandsdeutschtum im Dienste des Völkerrechts," Hans Frank, E. W. Bohle, and Alfred Meyer, *Drei Reden für das Auslandsdeutschtum gehalten auf der Sondertagung des Gaues Ausland des NSRB. am 'Tag des Deutschen Rechts' in Leipzig 1939* (Berlin: Druck H. Müller und Sohn, 1939), p. 13, in the WL.

CHAPTER 6

1. LGL Rumania to the party's *Zellenleiter* in Constanza, 25 Oct. 1939, Nuremberg Document 3976-PS, *TMWC*, XXXIII:160-61.

2. "Bohle dankt," *National-Zeitung* (Basel), 30 Oct. 1939; AO Legal Office to Hess, 29 Sept. 1939, T-120/743/341927-341928; and Bohle to Seafarer Section, 10 Oct. 1939 ("Betrifft: Verkehr mit sowjetrussischen Seeleuten."), T-120/775/ 370083-370084. A bit later Bohle assumed a tighter personal rein on the Seafarer Section; *Mitteilungsblatt*, 11 (Nov. 1939), 1. Note further, Philipp W. Fabry, *Die Sowjetunion und das Dritte Reich: Eine dokumentierte Geschichte der deutschsowjetischen Beziehungen von 1933 bis 1941* (Stuttgart: Seewald, 1971), pp. 164-65; and Bohle, "Vermerk," 21 Apr. 1938, PA/ *Chef* AO/ Folder 42.

3. Telegram, *Diplogerma* Helsinki to AA (AO), 6 Dec. 1939, T-120/49/39597; "Bericht über eine Reise nach Kowno zwecks Information über die Lage der dortigen Reichs- und Volksdeutschen im Hinblick auf ihre geplante Rückführung.," n.d.; and "Vorschlag für die Aktion zur Rettung der Volks- und Reichsdeutschen aus dem Baltikum," 6 Oct. 1939, T-120/743/341937-341942, 341901. See also, *Jahrbuch der Auslands-Organisation der NSDAP, 1941* (Berlin, 1942), pp. 35-36.

4. Bohle to all diplomatic and consular officials abroad, 9 Sept. 1939, PA/ *Chef* AO/ Folder 71; Leonhardt to Reich Treasury, 8 Oct. 1941 ("Mitglieder der NSDAP in Kuba."), BDC/PK/ *Ernst Wilhelm Bohle*; AO, "Cornelius Schwarz," 30 Mar. 1942, BDC/PK/ *Cornelius Schwarz*; Bohle to *Diplogerma* Athens, 30 Oct. 1940, Nuremberg Document 3357-NG; and AO to AA, 24 Nov. 1939, Nuremberg Document 3498-NG, Case 11/RG 238.

5. "Radio Zeesen, 24.12.1941," WL/PC5/211A2; Bohle, "Aufzeichnung," 20 Aug. 1941 ("Betrifft: Ägypter in besetzten Frankreich."); German Consulate Port Said to AA, 15 Sept. 1939, PA/ *Chef* AO/ Folder 1 (*Ägypten*); Memo, Heinz Gossman, 18 Dec. 1940, T-120/78/60062; and Hirszowicz, *The Third Reich and the Arab East*, pp. 72-73. In Feb. 1940 the AO created a new Central Office for Foreign German Refugees under Hellermann, *Verfügungen/ Anordnungen/ Bekanntgaben*, III:192.

6. As, for example, the German Minister in Paraguay; German Legation Asuncion to AA, 11 Sept. 1939, T-120/218/168702-168705.

7. Which raised a bitter howl from Bohle; Bohle to Papen, 2 Feb. 1940, T-120/ 2291/E144279-E144281; and Papen, *Memoirs*, pp. 489-90.

8. Bohle to diplomatic and consular representatives abroad, 30 Sept. and 13 Oct. 1939, PA/ *Chef* AO/ Folder 72 (*Erlasse A.O. 6,7,8,9*); Bohle to AA, 12 Feb. 1940, T-120/49/39534; Bohle, Memo, 3 Apr. 1940, T-120/1454/D600869; and

Schmidt, Memo, 30 Nov. 1939 (for Ribbentrop and shown to Bohle), T-120/239/ 174513.

9. Goebbels to Bohle, 31 Aug. 1940, HA/16/294; Bohle, Memo, 15 Nov. 1939, T-120/124/119227; *Mitteilungsblatt*, 1 (Jan. 1938), 3; Bollmus, *Das Amt Rosenberg*, p. 241; Bohle, "Besprechungen mit Hoheitsträger," 4 Sept. 1939, T-120/2131/ E072920; and "Deutsche Schildwachen in aller Welt," *National Zeitung* (Essen) 8 Mar. 1941.

10. See the lengthy report, RPA, "Reichspropagandaamt Ausland," Aug. 1941, HA/16/294; discussion of German short wave radio broadcasts in Winfried B. Lerg, "Deutscher Auslandsrundfunk im zweiten Weltkrieg," *Rundfunk und Fernsehen*, 1 (1966), 25-34; and analysis of German *Radio Prieto* in Latin America, Ebel, *Das Dritte Reich und Argentinien*, p. 396.

11. LGL Italy, "Rundschreiben Nr. 22/40," 12 Feb. 1940, T-81/144/0183066- 0183067.

12. Bohle Interrogation, M-679/1/0077.

13. German Legation Stockholm to AA, 6 June 1940 ("Betrifft: Schwedische Konzentrationslager."), T-120/1847/E037507; LGL Canada to AO, 9 July 1940, T-120/38/32977-32978; German Legation Asuncion to AA, 6 July 1940, T-120/218/ 168708; and telegram, Bohle to *Germandiplo* Montevideo, 1 June 1940, T-120/178/ 141079.

14. Bohle to German diplomatic representatives abroad, 17 Jan. 1940, T-120/ 3981/E049923-E049924; and Bohle to diplomatic and consular representatives in neutral countries, 22 Nov. 1939 ("Betr.: Verkehr der Auslandsdeutschen mit Angehörigen der Feindstaaten in neutralen Ländern."), T-120/225/171143-171145.

15. V. Köllner (German Legation Berne), "Vertrauliches Rundschreiben an alle Hoheitsträger," 3 June 1940, T-120/3981/E049919-E049921; and branch of the German Embassy at Kunming to the Embassy in Shanghai, 17 Feb. 1940, T-120/ 1624/D700700-D700704. According to Kranzler, *Japanese, Nazis and Jews*, pp. 485- 504, the impact of Nazi anti-Semitic propaganda on Japan led to increased harassment of Jews in China, including the creation in Feb. 1943 of a Jewish ghetto in Shanghai.

16. Bormann, "Anordnung—A 52/40," 1 May 1940, *VOBl*, 210 (July 1940), 22.

17. Friede to Embassy, 21 May 1942 ("Betr. Jüdische Geschäfte und Lokale in Istanbul."), T-120/4721/no frame numbers; and Thermann to Farben, 10 Jan. 1941, Nuremberg Document 10712-NI, Case 11/RG 238.

18. Louis Hagen, ed., *The Schellenberg Memoirs* (London: A. Deutsch, 1956), p. 134; *Jahrbuch der Auslands-Organisation der NSDAP, 1942*, pp. 21-27; Bohle Interrogation, *TMWC*, X:28; and "Hans Thomsen," n.d., BDC/RuSHA/*Hans Thomsen*.

19. Stanley G. Payne, *Falange: A History of Spanish Fascism* (Stanford, Calif.: Stanford University Press, 1961), pp. 212-21, 233-34; Dieckhoff Interrogation, M-679/1/0261; AA to AO, 2 Jan. 1940; German Embassy San Sebastian to AA, 6 Sept. 1939, T-120/239/174533, 174433; and Klaus-Jörg Ruhl, *Spanien im Zweiten Weltkrieg: Franco, die Falange und das "Dritte Reich"* (Hamburg: Hoffmann und Campe, 1975), pp. 64, 70-71, 320-21, 328. The SS was also involved in the conspiracy.

20. Bohle Interrogation, *TMWC*, X:26. The invasion of Norway is discussed in detail by W. G. Truchanowski, ed., *Geschichte der internationalen Beziehungen* (2 vols.; [East] Berlin: Rütten und Leoning, 1965), II:36-38.

21. Bohle Interrogation, *TMWC*, X:23-25; and Scheidt to Mrs. Schickhard, 14 Mar. 1940, Nuremberg Document 2488-NG, Case 11/RG 238.

22. Gossmann, Memo, 15 Apr. 1940, T-120/1639/E022101; Gossmann, "Aufzeichnung," 11 Apr. 1940, T-120/33/29244-29245; and Gerhard Förster, Heinz Helmert, Helmut Otto, and Helmut Schnitter, "Der Überfall Hitlerdeutschlands auf Dänemark und Norwegen (Unternehmung 'Weserübung')," Zeitschrift für Geschichtswissenschaft, 8 (1960), 694.

23. Teletype, Bohle to Ribbentrop, 12 July 1940, T-120/124/119373; Bohle's Memo to Ribbentrop and AA, 24 Apr. 1940; and Zech-Burkersroda to Weizsäcker, 16 Apr. 1940, T-120/3595/E692881-E692883. Butting always complained that his work was made difficult in Holland because he held only the rank of attache at the Mission in The Hague; Fischer, Memo, 31 Oct. 1939, PA/Chef AO/Folder 42; and Konrad Kwiet, Reichskommissariat Niederlande: Versuch und Scheitern nationalsozialistischer Neuordnung (Stuttgart: Deutsche Verlags-Anstalt, 1968), p. 88.

24. Mitteilungsblatt, 6 (Aug. 1940), 7.

25. RFSS to Central SS Personnel Office, 2 Nov. 1940, BDC/RuSHA/Bernhard Ruberg; Hess, "Verfügung, V9/40," 7 Oct. 1940, BDC/Slg. Schu./Ordner 301 (Niederlande); summary of Bohle's speech at the ceremony, 27 Oct., Nuremberg Document 2108-NG, Case 11/RG 238; Verfügungen/Anordnungen/Bekanntgaben, III:198; LG Netherlands, "Anweisung Nr. 7/40," 28 June 1940; LG Netherlands, "Anweisung Nr. 8/40," 1 July 1940, T-81/134/169272a-169273, 169274-169275; Dietrich Orlow, The History of the Nazi Party: 1933-1945 (Pittsburgh: University of Pittsburgh Press, 1973), pp. 303-07; and Kwiet, Reichskommissariat Niederlande, pp. 86-89.

26. Franz Neumann, Behemoth: The Structure and Practice of National Socialism, 1933-1944 (New York: Harper and Row, 1963), pp. 538-39; AA, "Mündliche Weisungen des Herrn Reichsaussenministers an VLR von Grundherr, Gesandtschaftsrat von Neuhaus und Gesandtschaftsrat Weber (Oslo)," 25 Apr. 1940, T-120/33/29249-29252; and "Die Partei im Generalgouvernment," Die Innere Front: Pressedienst der NSDAP, 163 (16 July 1940), 3.

27. Bohle Interrogation, 26-27 July 1945, RG 165. According to Luza, Austro-German Relations, p. 373, the number of O.Gr. in the AO was to shrink to 92 by Feb. 1942.

28. Bohle to Hess, "Aufzeichnung," 7 Aug. 1940, T-120/3595/E692922-E692923; Reich Commissioner for Occupied Netherlands to Bohle, 13 June 1940 ("Betr. Internierung von holl. Staatsbürgern."), T-120/1382/D535674-D535676; Commissioner to Bohle, 22 July 1940 ("betr. Gegenmassnahme für die Niederl. Indien verhafteten Reichsdeutschen."), T-120/3782/E691844-E691845; and Kwiet, Reichskommissariat Niederlande, pp. 88-89.

29. Seyss-Inquart Interrogation, TMWC, XV:655; and Bene to AA, 8 Aug. 1942, Nuremberg Document 2607-NG, Case 11/RG 238.

30. A. Hess to Bohle, 1 July 1940, T-120/2131/E072922-E072925; and Weizsäcker, Memo to AA department heads, 30 June 1940, Nuremberg Document 1718-NG, Case 11/RG 238.

31. Louis de Jong, "Organization and Efficiency of the German Fifth Column," Maurice Baumont, John E. Fired, and Edmond Vermeil, eds., The Third Reich (New York: Praeger, 1955), p. 869.

32. As were concluded among the AA, Abwehr, and SD, Hildegard v. Kotze, "Hitlers Sicherheitsdienst im Ausland," Die politische Meinung, 86 (1963), 75-80; and AA, "Aufzeichnung," 31 Dec. 1940, T-120/357/264199-264201. Conflicts involving Abwehr, AA, and SD are amply recorded in Walter Hagen (pseud.), Die Geheime Front: Organisation, Personen und Aktionen des Deutschen Geheim-

dienstes (Linz-Vienna: Europa-Verlag, 1950), passim; and Karl Heinz Abshagen, *Canaris: Patriot und Weltburger* (Stuttgart: Union Verlag, 1959), pp. 99-203, 273-302.

33. Telegram, Schellenberg to RFSS, 5 Nov. 1942, BDC/*Slg. Schu./Ordner* 311 (*Schweiz*). Also, see Schellenberg Interrogation, 7 Mar. 1946, RG 238.

34. OKW to Bohle, 28 July 1938, T-120/1639/E022065-E022067.

35. AO to OKW, 17 Sept. 1940, T-120/124/118749; and Canaris to Bohle, 13 Dec. 1939, T-120/775/370038-370039.

36. Telegram, German Embassy Santiago to AA, 14 June 1941, T-120/225/171433; telegram, German Embassy Madrid to AA, 2 May 1941, T-120/357/261602-261603; and Papen, *Memoirs*, p. 481.

37. Chief of Security Police to AA, 15 Nov. 1940 ("*Betrifft*: Kollektive Ausbürgerung der Juden in dem besetzten Gebiet Frankreichs."), T-120/364/276136.

38. AA, Memo, 29 Mar. 1940, Nuremberg Document 3087-NG; and report of the Military Commander in Belgium and Northern France to OKW, 31 July 1940, Nuremberg Document, 2381-NG, Case 11/RG 238.

39. Eliza Campus, "Die hitlerfaschistische Infiltration Rumäniens, 1939-1940," *Zeitschrift für Geschichtswissenschaft*, 5 (1957), 213-17, 219; Leonhardt to Schwarz, 30 July 1941, BDC/PK/*Artur Konradi*; and "Artur Adolf Konradi," n.d., BDC/MF/*Artur Konradi*.

40. Bohle to Schwarz, 8 Oct. 1941, BDC/PK/*Artur Konradi*; Hill, *Die Weizsäcker-Papiere*, pp. 556-57; and Tagy-Talavera, *The Green Shirts*, p. 328.

41. Wilhelm Wrede, "Unser Kriegstagebuch," *Jahrbuch der Auslands-Organisation der NSDAP, 1942*, pp. 49-66. Wrede, born in June 1893 in Marburg/Lahn, had been head of the party in Greece since Sept. 1935; AO, "Walther Wrede," n.d., BDC/PK/*Walther Wrede*.

42. Esp, "Personalfragebogen für die Anlegung der SA-Personalakte," 2 Apr. 1942, BDC/SA/*Henry Esp*; and AO, "Henry Esp," 30 Mar. 1942, BDC/MF/*Henry Esp*.

43. AA (Martin Luther) to Schwarz, 10 Nov. 1941, T-81/145/0184211-0184212; DAI, "Stand der deutschen Volksgruppen in Europa am 12.6.41.," T-81/350/5078833; the concluding chapter of J. B. Hoptner, *Yugoslavia in Crisis, 1934-1941* (New York: Columbia University Press, 1962); and Ladislaus Hory and Martin Broszat, *Der Kroatische Ustascha-Staat, 1941-1945* (Stuttgart: Deutsche Verlags-Anstalt, 1964), pp. 39-57.

44. Bullock, *Hitler*, p. 422; and Empting's report, "Kroatien im Spiegelbild der Landesgruppe der Auslands-Organisation der NSDAP. Juni 1941-Juni 1942," T-81/136/173003-173005. On Empting's appointment, see *Mitteilungsblatt*, 2 (May 1941), 3.

45. Empting, "Kroatien im Spiegelbild . . . ," T-81/136/173007-173014, 173016-173045, 173047-173058; and U.S. Army, Military Intelligence Service in Austria, "Special Investigation and Interrogation Report: The Croatian National Independence Movement," 9 Apr. 1946, Ref. No. Special/USDIC/SIIR4, pp. 7, 11, a copy of which is in the author's possession. See also, Schirach Interrogation, *TMWC*, XIV:523-24; George H. Stein, *The Waffen SS: Hitler's Elite Guard at War* (Ithaca, N.Y.: Cornell University Press, 1967), pp. 170, 172; Hory and Broszat, *Der Kroatische Ustascha-Staat*, pp. 154-55; and "Hans Gerlach," n.d., BDC/MF/*Hans Gerlach*.

46. Hory and Broszat, *Der Kroatische Ustascha-Staat*, pp. 129-31, 138.

47. Orlow, *The Nazis in the Balkans,* pp. 97-98, 105-06, 108, 110-13, 128-33; and the excellent study by Norman Rich, *The Establishment of the New Order,* Vol. II of *Hitler's War Aims* (New York: Norton, 1974).

48. An interesting theory denied by Bullock, *Hitler,* p. 581, but noted by James Douglas-Hamilton, *Motive for a Mission: The Story Behind Hess's Flight to Britain* (London: Macmillan, 1971), p. 138; and J. R. Rees, ed., *The Case of Rudolf Hess: A Problem in Diagnosis and Forensic Psychiatry* (New York: Norton, 1948), pp. 57-58. Bohle too believed that Hitler knew of Hess's plan, Bohle Interrogation, 26-27 July 1945, RG 165. According to James Leasor, *The Uninvited Envoy* (New York: McGraw-Hill, 1962), p. 47, Hess planned to use the AO as a secret messenger service to bring an end to the war with England.

49. Telegram, Heydrich to Himmler, 15 May 1941 (copy sent to Bormann at the Obersalzburg), T-175/128/2654469; and Bohle Interrogation, 26-27 July 1945, RG 165. On Albrecht Haushofer, see Brügel, *Tschechen und Deutsche,* p. 356.

50. Bohle Interrogation, 28 July 1945, RG 165.

51. Bormann to Ley, 30 July 1941 ("Betrifft: Auslandsorganisation der NSDAP"), T-580/55/293; and Steengracht Interrogation, M-679/3/1221.

52. Bormann to Ley, 30 July 1941, T-580/55/293; and Steengracht Interrogation M-679/3/1217.

53. Bormann to Ribbentrop, 2 Aug. 1941, Nuremberg Document 118-NP, Case 11/RG 238.

54. Bohle Interrogation, 23 July 1948, and response of the Nuremberg Prosecution, "Official Court Transcript," Case 11/RG 238. In the same collection, see Lammers, Memo, 13 Nov. 1941, Nuremberg Document 3779-E-NG.

55. Lammers to Bohle, 14 Nov. 1941 ("Betrifft: Chef der Auslands-Organisation im Auswärtigen Amt."), Nuremberg Document 118-NP; and Ribbentrop, "Affidavit," 27 Sept. 1946, Nuremberg Document 167-NG, both in Case 11/RG 238. The contention by Jacobsen, *Nationalsozialistische Aussenpolitik,* p. 118, that Bohle "withdrew, disillusioned, from the Foreign Ministry," is only partly correct.

56. *Vertrauliche Informationen,* edited by NSDAP *Partei-Kanzlei,* 46 (8 Oct. 1941), *Punkt* 508; and telegram, AA to German Embassy Rome, 27 Nov. 1941, T-120/1298/482744-482748. Still, if a party member traveled abroad for longer than three weeks, he was to contact his competent party leader; *Organisationsbuch der NSDAP,* edited by *Reichsorganisationsleiter der NSDAP* (7th ed.; Munich: Zentralverlag der NSDAP, 1943), pp. 143-45. Luther's power, until he was thrown into a concentration camp for conspiring against Ribbentrop, is noted in Kordt, *Nicht aus den Akten,* p. 403.

57. Memo, by Dr. Albrecht of the AA for Ribbentrop, 4 May 1942, Nuremberg Document 4527-NG, Case 11/RG 238; and telegram, Ribbentrop to Weizsäcker, 27 May 1941, T-120/3131/E509611-E509619.

58. Joseph Goebbels, *The Goebbels Diaries, 1942-1943,* ed. and trans. Louis P. Lochner (Garden City, N.Y.: Doubleday, 1948), p. 272 (entry for 4 Mar. 1943).

59. Hildebrand, *Vom Reich zum Weltreich,* pp. 702, 707, 739, 905, 924, 934; and Wolfe W. Schmokel, *Dream of Empire: German Colonialism, 1919-1945* (New Haven and London: Yale University Press, 1964), pp. 145, 151, 154.

60. *Mitteilungsblatt,* 1 (Jan. 1940), 1; 2 (Feb. 1940), 2; 3 (Mar. 1940), 3; 4 (Apr. 1940), 4; 7 (Oct. 1940), 9; 4 (Aug. 1941), 5.

61. "Aus Brief von H. H. von Cossel," 12 Mar. 1943, T-81/289/2412951.

62. Bohle Interrogation, 26-27 July 1945, RG 165; AO Treasury, "Aufzeich-

nung," 10 Mar. 1942, T-580/56/295; Sommer, *Deutschland und Japan zwischen den Mächten*, pp. 324-49, 426-49, 481-86, and Meskill, *Hitler and Japan*, pp. 18-23, 26-27, 30, 35, 51-86, 89-124, 127-73, 191-99, dealing with the conflicts between Germany and Japan; and on Spahn, AO, "Franz Joseph Spahn," n.d., BDC/PK/*Franz Joseph Spahn*. Spahn and the LG may also have contributed (with the German Embassy in Tokyo) to the growing anti-Semitism of the Japanese government, which had led to the latter's harassment of Jews in the Philippines, the closing of Jewish newspapers and the mass indoctrination of Japanese school children in Manchuria with anti-Semitic ideas, and the creation of the Shanghai ghetto. See Kranzler, *Japanese, Nazis and Jews*, pp. 487-89.

63. *Mitteilungsblatt*, 6 (Dec. 1942), 8; Papen, *Memoirs*, p. 490, whose account is supported by the documents; "Nachrichten vom Vertrauensmann der Presse-Abteilung," 10 Sept. 1942; and Ribbentrop to Papen, 10 Sept. 1942, T-120/3973/E048780-E048781, E048782.

64. See the unpublished dissertation by Nancy Leila Sadka, "German Relations With Persia, 1921-1941," (Stanford University, 1972), chaps. 4-5, revealing there was no effective German fifth column in Iran; Hirszowicz, *The Third Reich and the Arab East*, pp. 149, 151-52, 232-33, 262, 264, 266-68; and *FZ*, 26 Nov. 1939.

65. Ettel to RFSS, 6 Dec. 1943, noting he was recalled from Teheran in Sept. 1941; Ettel to Himmler, 20 July 1942; Bohle to Himmler, 20 Sept. 1943; and SS, "Erwin Ettel," 13 Feb. 1944, BDC/RuSHA/*Erwin Ettel*.

66. Memo, Luther to Ritter, 1 Apr. 1942, Nuremberg Document 3054-NG, Case 11/RG 238.

67. Bormann, "Rundschreiben Nr. 31/42g.," 30 June 1942 ("Betrifft: Stellung und Aufgaben der Auslands-Organisation."), T-120/3973/E048783-048787.

68. Bohle to Schwarz, 30° July 1943; AA to foreign missions, 25 June 1943, T-580/55/293; and Ettel, "Notes on the possibilities of closer co-operation between Foreign Office and NSDAP Auslandsorganisation," 9 Apr. 1943, Nuremberg Document 3298-NG, Case 11/RG 238.

69. As, for instance, Bohle to Himmler, 5 Nov. 1942, Nuremberg Document 3664-NG; Bohle to Himmler, 31 Oct. 1942, Nuremberg Document 2820-NG, Case 11/RG 238; and Bohle to Himmler, 17 Feb. 1943, T-580/58/298.

70. VoMi to RFSS, 15 Feb. 1943, Nuremberg Document 5097-NG, Case 11/RG 238; Poliakov and Wulf, *Das Dritte Reich*, p. 150; and Klee Interrogation, M-679/2/0678-0680.

71. German Consulate General Marseilles, "R[Rückführung] Ausweis," 21 Sept. 1943, T-81/145/0184219-0184220; and Poliakov and Wulf, *Das Dritte Reich*, pp. 73-74, 143-44.

72. "Direct Examination [of Bohle]," 23 July 1948, "Official Court Transcript," Case 11/RG 238; no documentary evidence which the author has seen would dispute his testimony.

73. Heinz Boberach, ed., *Meldungen aus dem Reich: Auswahl aus den geheimen Lageberichten des Sicherheitsdienstes der SS, 1939-1944* (Munich: Deutscher Taschenbuch Verlag, 1968), pp. 285-86, 344-46.

74. AO, *Landesgruppe in Frankreich: Anschriftenverzeichnis* (n.p., 1944), pp. 5-13; and Otto Abetz, *Histoire d'une politique franco-allemande, 1930-1950: Mémoires d'un Ambassadeur* (9th ed.; Paris: Stock, 1953), p. 267.

75. "[Radio] Zeesen . . . , 12.7.42," and "[Radio] Zeesen . . . , 29.8.43," WL/PC5/211A2; German Military Commander of Paris to LG France, 1 July 1944,

T-81/133/166500; LG France, "Rundschreiben Nr. 93," 17 Dec. 1943, T-81/134/168936; and LG France, "Rundschreiben Nr. 50," 11 Sept. 1943 ("Betrifft: Französische Arbeiterwerbung."), T-81/135/170627-170628.

76. LG France, "Rundschreiben Nr. 94," 17 Dec. 1943; and O.Gr. Paris-Boulogne to LG France, 21 Sept. 1943, T-81/134/168940, 170109.

77. LG Belgium to RL, 17 Feb. 1943; and letters from the Nazi Welfare Office in Belgium to party districts in Germany, 25 Jan. 1943, about "Kinderlandverschickung 1943," T-81/135/171070-171080.

78. LG Italy, "Mitteilung No. 54/43," 9 Aug. 1943, T-81/136/172859-172860; Ernst Kris and Hans Speier, *German Radio Propaganda: Report on Home Broadcasts during the War* (London: Oxford University Press, 1944), pp. 5-6; and the detailed study by Jay W. Baird, *The Mythical World of Nazi War Propaganda, 1939-1945* (Minneapolis, Minn.: University of Minnesota Press, 1974), pp. 199-240.

79. LG France, "89. Rundfunksendung der AO der NSDAP Landesgruppe in Frankreich, Donnerstag, den 14. Oktober 1943, 18,15 Uhr.;" and "Presserundschau vom 5.10.1943," T-81/136/171953-171957, 171963-171965. Also, see Goebbels's article, "Der Krieg und die Juden," summer 1943, T-81/134/168933a.

80. *VB*, 21 Jan. 1944; and LG Belgium to RPA, 10 May 1943, T-81/134/169276-169278.

81. LG France, *Der Sprechabenddienst* (n.p., June 1944), pp. 5-8, 21-24.

82. O.Gr. Paris-West to one of its *Zellenleiters*, Köhler, 6 Jan. 1944; and LG France (Propaganda Office), "Rundschreiben Nr. 1/1/44," 6 Jan. 1944, T-81/134/170018, 170005-170006.

83. "Meine lieben deutschen Volksgenossen und Volksgenossinnen," Apr. 1944, BDC/PK/*Ernst Wilhelm Bohle*.

84. AO to NSDAP Reich Treasury, 14 Feb. 1944, T-580/56/295; and Frederick B. Chary, *The Bulgarian Jews and the Final Solution, 1940-1944* (Pittsburgh: University of Pittsburgh Press, 1972), p. 169. The LGL, Joseph Drechsel, was born in Feb. 1897 in Frankenthal; "Joseph Drechsel," n.d., BDC/MF/*Joseph Drechsel*.

85. Hencke, "Die Bedeutungen der Entlassungen im Jahre 1944," M-679/2/0503-0504, who also notes that some officials in the AA refused to return to Germany when recalled from their foreign missions.

86. Bohle to Himmler, 25 Sept. 1944, BDC/RuSHA/*Ernst Wilhelm Bohle*; Harold C. Deutsch, *The Conspiracy Against Hitler in the Twilight War* (Minneapolis, Minn.: University of Minnesota Press, 1968), pp. 16-17; and Hassell, *Diaries*, p. 183 (the entry for 13 July 1941).

87. Karl Stadler, *Österreich, 1938-1945: Im Spiegel der NS-Akten* (Vienna/Munich: Herold, 1966), pp. 339-40; Bohle Interrogation, M-679/1/0087, 0115, 0143, on the last months; and Bernd Martin, *Deutschland und Japan im Zweiten Weltkrieg: Vom Angriff auf Pearl Harbor bis zur deutschen Kapitulation* (Zurich/Frankfurt: Musterschmidt, 1969), p. 214. The number of persons lost on the *Wilhelm Gustloff* was more than five times that lost on the *Titanic*; John Toland, *The Last 100 Days* (New York: Random House, 1966), pp. 31-36.

88. Recounted in "Direct Examination [of Bohle]," 23 July 1948, "Official Court Transcript," Case 11/RG 238; and published in *Trials of War Criminals Before the Nuernberg Military Tribunals Under Control Council Law No. 10, Nuernberg, October 1946-April 1949* (14 vols; Washington, D.C.: U.S. Government Printing Office, 1952), XIII:1196-1204.

89. On his surrender, see NA/U.S. Army/1st Infantry Division, "G-2 Periodic Report No. 350," 24-28 May 1945 (.301-2.2 [22292]); and Percy Ernst Schramm, ed., *Die Niederlage, 1945: Aus dem Kriegstagebuch des Oberkommandos der Wehrmacht* (Munich: Deutscher Taschenbuch Verlag, 1962), pp. 427-28.

CHAPTER 7

1. "Bohle is Indicted as a War Criminal," *NYT*, 4 July 1945.
2. Bohle Interrogations, 25 Oct. 1945, RG 238; 19 July 1945, RG 165; M-679/1/0075.
3. Bohle Interrogation, *TMWC*, X:14-15. Hess, because of his amnesia, refused to recognize Bohle; J. Bernard Hutton, *Hess: The Man and His Mission* (London: David Bruce and Watson Ltd., 1970), p. 170; and Roger Manvell and Heinrich Fraenkel, *Hess: A Biography* (London: MacGibbon and Kee, 1971), p. 155.
4. Joachim von Ribbentrop, *Zwischen London und Moskau: Erinnerungen und letzte Aufzeichnungen* (Leoni am Starnberger See: Druffel-Verlag, 1961), p. 127. Also, note Papen Interrogation, 10 Sept. 1946, Nuremberg Document 165-NG; and Ribbentrop, "Affidavit," 27 Sept. 1946, Nuremberg Document 167-NG, Case 11/RG 238.
5. "Bohle Pleads 'Guilty'," *The Times* (London), 29 Mar. 1948.
6. Elisabeth Gombel, "To the Honorable Judges of Tribunal IV, Case Number 11," 27 Mar. 1948; and "Indictment," 1 Nov. 1947, "Official Court File," Case 11/RG 238.
7. On favors for Bohle, Gombel asked the Tribunal to permit him to visit his gravely ill mother in Kiel; Gombel to judges of Tribunal IV, 10 Aug. 1948, "Official Court File," Case 11/RG 238. Gombel, born in Hamburg in 1912, attended the Universities of Kiel, Berlin, and Hamburg, receiving a Doctor of Jurisprudence degree; after the war she became legal adviser to the Junkers Aircraft factory; Telford Taylor, *Final Report to the Secretary of the Army on the Nuernberg War Crimes Trials Under Control Council Law No. 10* (Washington, D.C.: U.S. Government Printing Office, 1949), pp. 336-37.
8. Quoted from "Answer of the Prosecution to the Motion of the Defendant Bohle to Change his Plea of Guilty to Counts V and VIII and to Dismiss Counts I, II and VI of the Indictment," 27 May 1948, "Official Court File," Case 11/RG 238.
9. The concept of plea bargaining may be interpreted variously, but according to a letter to the author from John Mendelsohn of the Military Archives Division of the NA, 2 May 1975, "If by plea bargaining one understands pleading guilty on one or several counts of the indictment and the dropping of one or several counts of the indictment in return, then defendant Ernst Wilhelm Bohle plea bargained."
10. "Opening Statement for Defendant Bohle," 23 July 1948, *Trials of War Criminals Before the Nuernberg Military Tribunals*, XII:271-72. Also, on his new plea and the Court's acceptance, see Gombel, "Reply of the Defendant Ernst Wilhelm Bohle to the answer of the Prosecution to defendants [sic] motion to dismiss counts 1, 2 and 6 and to change his plea of guilty to counts 5 and 8 of the indictment.," 1 June 1948; and William C. Christianson (presiding judge, Tribunal IV), "Order," 4 June 1948, "Official Court File," Case 11/RG 238.
11. "Direct Examination [of Bohle]," 23 July 1948, "Official Court Transcript," Case 11/RG 238. He testified in near perfect English.

12. Ibid.

13. See the judgments and sentence against him, *Trials of War Criminals Before the Nuernberg Military Tribunals*, XIV:552-54, 856, 866. Also, note the Tribunal's acceptance of his plea in June, Christianson, "Order," 10 Aug. 1948, "Official Court File," Case 11/RG 238; and John Alan Appleman, *Military Tribunals and International Crimes* (Indianapolis, Ind.: Bobbs-Merrill, 1954), pp. 222-23.

14. Gombel to judges of Tribunal IV, "Motion," 14 Dec. 1948, "Official Court File," Case 11/RG 238. His father died on 12 July 1943; "Ernst Bohlet," an obituary in WL/Ernst Wilhelm Bohle File.

15. *NYT*, 20 Dec. 1949; 13 Nov. 1960; "Alte und Neue Diplomaten," *Die Zeit*, 3 Dec. 1953; Kühne, "Die Fünfte Kolonne des faschistischen deutschen Imperialismus in Südwestafrika," p. 774; and "Former Nazi General Wants to Visit Britain," *New York Herald Tribune*, 18 Feb. 1950.

16. AO, "Stand der zahlenden Mitglieder lt. Reichsleitung der NSDAP," n.d., T-580/59/301; in Feb. 1942 the AO's membership was 51,797. This also appears supported by the somewhat reliable records of the U.S. War Dept., *Nazi Party Membership Records*, particularly pp. 46, 48, which reveal that the membership in Argentina dropped to 1,489 members in Dec. 1942. In the United States the membership peaked in Dec. 1940 (806 members) and dropped shortly thereafter (to 643) in Dec. 1942. Files following the latter date are not available. Membership for May 1939 in Latin America is in Ebel, *Das Dritte Reich und Argentinien*, p. 283. On Switzerland, see "Die Liste der ausgewiesenen Nationalsozialisten," *Berner Tageblatt*, 9 June 1945. Some foreign party leaders, like Thomsen in Spain, were arrested by local authorities and imprisoned; Ruhl, *Spanien im Zweiten Weltkrieg*, p. 321.

17. Kühne, "Die Fünfte Kolonne des faschistischen deutschen Imperialismus in Südwestafrika," p. 774; Smith, *Deutschtum of Nazi Germany*, p. 49; Frye, *Nazi Germany*, p. 19; Kordt, *Wahn und Wirklichkeit*, p. 98; and de Jong, *German Fifth Column*, p. 280.

18. Seabury, *Wilhelmstrasse*, p. 33; and Jacobsen, *Nationalsozialistische Aussenpolitik*, pp. 34-45, 90-160.

19. "Nazi Spy Pleads Guilty," *NYT*, 28 Mar. 1948.

20. Rauschning, *Voice of Destruction*, p. 148.

21. Hitler, *Mein Kampf*, II:439.

22. Trevor-Roper, *Hitler's Secret Conversations*, p. 461 (the entry for 20 May 1942).

BIBLIOGRAPHY

Introductory Comment on Archival Sources

Vast portions of the German archives were microfilmed after World War II, with the most extensive collection of films (nearly 30,000 rolls) located in the National Archives. Such microfilms are cited in this study according to their microcopy, roll, and frame numbers (e.g., T-120/1298/482744). The microfilmed records utilized originate primarily from the German Foreign Ministry, Reich ministries and other government agencies, offices of the Nazi party inside and outside Germany (including the *Auslands-Organisation*), Nazi cultural and research institutions, SS, and German police. A group of party and police materials was also microfilmed for the Hoover Institution at Stanford, and these are cited according to roll and folder numbers.

Most original documents in this massive collection may be found in the *Politisches Archiv des Auswärtigen Amts* in Bonn (Microcopy T-120), *Bundesarchiv* in Koblenz (Microcopy T-81, T-82, T-175, T-580), Berlin Document Center, and *Institut für Zeitgeschichte* in Munich. Among records held in Germany that were not filmed, those most valuable for this study were the biographical files at the Berlin Document Center on Bohle, Nieland, and the *Landesgruppenleiters*. The *Institut für Zeitgeschichte*, while possessing little source material on the AO that is not available in the National Archives, has a marvelous collection of German newspapers, memoirs, diaries, books, and pamphlets of the Nazi period. Similarly, the Wiener Library and Institute for Contemporary History in London has an excellent collection of newspapers, Nazi serials, press clippings, pamphlets, memoirs, and documents on several subjects that were vital

to this study: Germans abroad, propaganda, NSDAP in Spain,
Bohle, and anti-Semitism. The German documents seized by the Soviet
Union that are stored in East Germany in the *Deutsches Zentral
Archiv* in Potsdam are cited above only at second hand from East
German publications (which include journals like the *Zeitschrift für
Geschichtswissenschaft* and *Wissenschaftliche Zeitschrift der Universität Rostock*, plus a number of monographs). The Slavic and Central European Division of the Library of Congress also has various
serials published by the AO and extensive holdings of general works
on the Nazi regime. The partial membership list of the AO, which
is in the Manuscript Division of the Library of Congress, has been
published by the United States Department of War.

The Captured Records Branch of the National Archives also holds
a mass of German documents collected for the Nuremberg trials,
plus considerable postwar interrogations of German officials. Included in the latter are the papers of the special State Department
mission to Germany under DeWitt C. Poole (Microcopy M-679)
and the War Department's interrogation records (especially the
Shuster Files, or RG 165). The Archives also has original records or
reproductions of prosecution and defense documents, court tran-
scripts, and court files of the "Ministries Case" at Nuremberg, the
United States of America v. Ernst von Weizsäcker, et al. (Case
11/RG 238), which dealt with Bohle and the AO. The principal
series or collections of documents used in the Case were Nazi
Government Ministries (NG), Nazi Propaganda (NP), Nazi Industrialists (NI), and Paris-Storey (PS). A small fraction of these
documents can be found in published sources.

GUIDES, ARCHIVES INVENTORIES, HANDBOOKS,
AND OTHER REFERENCE WORKS

American Historical Association, Committee for the Study of War
    Documents, and National Archives and Records Service.
    "Guides to German Documents Microfilmed at Alexandria,
    Va." Washington, D.C.: National Archives, 1958-).
Das Deutsche Führerlexikon, 1934/1935. Berlin: Stollberg, 1935.
Facius, Friedrich; Booms, Hans; and Boberach, Heinz, *Das Bundes-
    archiv und seine Bestände.* Boppard: Harold Boldt, 1961.
Germany: A Basic Handbook. London: British Foreign Office and
    Ministry of Economic Warfare, 1944.
Heinz, Grete and Peterson, Agnes F. *NSDAP Hauptarchiv: Guide*

to the Hoover Institution Microfilm Collection. Stanford, Calif.: Hoover Institution, 1964.

Kent, George O. *A Catalog of the Files and Microfilms of the German Foreign Ministry Archives, 1920-1945,* 4 vols. Stanford, Calif.: Hoover Institution, 1962-1973.

Library of Congress. *The Nazi State, War Crimes and War Criminals.* Compiled by Helen F. Conover for the U.S. Chief of Counsel for the Prosecution of Axis Criminality. Washington, D.C.: U.S. Government Printing Office, 1945.

Library of Congress. *Newspapers in Microform: Foreign Countries, 1948-1972.* Washington, D.C.: U.S. Government Printing Office, 1973.

Petersen, Carl and Scheel, Otto. *Handwörterbuch des Grenz- und Ausland-Deutschtums.* 5 vols. Breslau: F. Hirt, 1934-1935.

Snyder, Louis L. *Encyclopedia of the Third Reich.* New York: McGraw-Hill, 1976.

Who's Who in Germany and Austria. London: British Ministry of Economic Warfare, 1945.

Winkler, Wilhelm. *Statistisches Handbuch für das gesamten Deutschtums.* Berlin: Verlag Deutsche Rundschau, 1927.

PUBLISHED SOURCES: NEWSPAPERS, JOURNALS, AND YEARBOOKS

Newspapers

Berliner Tageblatt
Berner Tageblatt
Daily Clarion (Toronto)
Daily Express (London)
Daily Telegraph (London)
Deutsche Shanghai Zeitung
Evening Standard (London)
Frankfurter Zeitung (FZ)
Germania (Berlin)
Hamburger Fremdenblatt
Italien Beobachter (Rome)
Der Kompass (Curitiba)
Manchester Guardian
Melbourne Truth
Morning Post (London)

Münchener Telegramm-Zeitung
National-Zeitung (Basel)
National Zeitung (Essen)
New York Herald Tribune
The New York Times (*NYT*)
News Chronicle (London)
NS-Dienst für auslandsdeutsche Blätter (Berlin)
Singapore Free Press
The Standard (Montreal)
Tidens Tegn (Oslo)
The Times (London)
Völkischer Beobachter (Berlin; Munich; *VB*)
Vorposten: Nachrichten der deutschen Freiheitsbewegung in den Vereinigten Staaten
Westdeutscher Beobachter (Cologne)
Die Zeit

Journals

Die Deutsche Schule im Auslande: Monatsschrift für deutsche Erziehung in Schule und Familie
Deutsches Wollen: Zeitschrift der Auslands-Organisation der NSDAP
Eigentum des Deutschen Nachrichtenbüros
Hansa
Mitteilungsblatt der Leitung der Auslands-Organisation der Nationalsozialistischen Deutschen Arbeiterpartei (*Mitteilungsblatt*)
Nachrichtenblatt des Verbandes Deutscher Kolonien in den Niederlanden
Nationalsozialistische Partei-Korrespondenz: Pressedienst der NSDAP (renamed *Die Innere Front*, Sept. 1939; *NSPK*)
Verordnungsblatt der Reichsleitung der Nationalsozialistischen Deutschen Arbeiterpartei (*VOBl*)

Yearbooks

Jahrbuch der Auslands-Organisation der NSDAP
Jahrbuch für Auswärtige Politik
Nationalsozialistisches Jahrbuch
Organisationsbuch der NSDAP
Wir Deutsche in der Welt

Published Sources: Memoirs, Diaries, Pamphlets,
and Documentary Collections

Memoirs and Diaries

Abetz, Otto. *Histoire d'une politique franco-allemande, 1930-1950. Mémoires d'un Ambassadeur.* 9th ed. Paris: Stock, 1953.

Burckhardt, Carl J. *Meiner Danziger Mission, 1937-1939.* 2nd ed. Munich: Callwey, 1960.

Diplomaticus (pseud.). *Diplomatie und Hakenkreuz: Kämpfe und Erlebnisse eines Journalisten.* Berlin: Buch- und Tiefdruck-Gesellschaft, 1934.

Dirksen, Herbert von. *Moskau-Tokio-London: Erinnerungen und Betrachtungen zu 20 Jahren deutscher Aussenpolitik, 1919-1939.* Stuttgart: Kohlhammer, 1949.

Dodd, Martha. *Through Embassy Eyes.* New York: Harcourt, Brace and Company, 1939.

Dodd, William E., Jr. and Dodd, Martha, eds. *Ambassador Dodd's Diary, 1933-1938.* New York: Harcourt, Brace and Company, 1941.

Francois-Poncet, Andre. *Botschafter in Berlin, 1931-1938.* 3rd ed. Berlin/Mainz: F. Kupferberg, 1962.

Fromm, Bella. *Blood and Banquets: A Berlin Social Diary.* New York: Harper, 1942.

Goebbels, Joseph. *The Goebbels Diaries, 1942-1943.* Ed. and trans. Louis P. Lochner. Garden City, N.Y.: Doubleday, 1948.

Hassell, Ulrich von. *The von Hassell Diaries, 1938-1944.* London: H. Hamilton, 1948.

Hillgruber, Andreas, ed. *Henry Picker: Hitlers Tischgespräche im Führerhauptquartier, 1941-1942.* Munich: Deutscher Taschenbuch Verlag, 1968.

Hitler, Adolf. *Mein Kampf.* 2 vols. Munich: F. Eher, 1943.

Hull, Cordell. *The Memoirs of Cordell Hull.* 2 vols. New York: Macmillan, 1948.

Kordt, Erich. *Nicht aus den Akten . . . Die Wilhelmstrasse in Frieden und Krieg: Erlebnisse, Begegnungen und Eindrücke, 1928-1945.* Stuttgart: Deutsche Verlags-Anstalt, 1950.

Kotze, Hildegard v., ed. *Heeresadjutant bei Hitler, 1938-1943: Aufzeichnungen des Majors Engel.* Stuttgart: Deutsche Verlags-Anstalt, 1974.

Krebs, Albert. *Tendenzen und Gestalten der NSDAP: Erinnerungen an die Frühzeit der Partei.* Stuttgart: Deutsche Verlags-Anstalt, 1959.

Kroll, Hans. *Lebenserinnerungen eines Botschafters.* Cologne: Kiepenheur und Witsch, 1968.

Ludecke, Kurt. *I Knew Hitler: The Story of a Nazi Who Escaped the Blood Purge.* New York: Scribner's, 1937.

Luther, Hans. *Politiker ohne Partei: Erinnerungen.* Stuttgart: Deutsche Verlags-Anstalt, 1960.

Papen, Franz von. *Memoirs.* Trans. Brian Connell. New York: Dutton, 1953.

Prittwitz und Gaffron, Friedrich von. *Zwischen Petersburg und Washington: Ein Diplomatenleben.* Munich: Isar Verlag, 1952.

Raeder, Erich. *Von 1935 bis Spandau 1955.* Vol. 2 of *Mein Leben.* Tübingen-Neckar: F. Schlichtenmayer, 1956.

Rauschning, Hermann. *The Voice of Destruction.* New York: G. P. Putnam's Sons, 1940.

Ribbentrop, Joachim von. *Zwischen London und Moskau: Erinnerungen und letzte Aufzeichnungen.* Leoni am Starnberger See: Druffel-Verlag, 1961.

Schellenberg, Walter. *The Schellenberg Memoirs.* Ed. and trans. Louis Hagen. London: A. Deutsch, 1956.

Schramm, Percy Ernst, ed. *Die Niederlage, 1945: Aus dem Kriegstagebuch des Oberkommandos der Wehrmacht.* Munich: Deutscher Taschenbuch Verlag, 1962.

Strasser, Otto. *Mein Kampf: Eine politische Autobiografie.* Frankfurt/Main: Heinrich Heine Verlag, 1969.

Vansittart, Sir Robert. *The Mist Procession: The Autobiography of Lord Vansittart.* London: Hutchinson, 1958.

Vogel, Georg. *Diplomat unter Hitler und Adenauer.* Düsseldorf: Econ, 1969.

Weizsäcker, Ernst von. *Memoirs of Ernst von Weizsäcker.* Trans John Andrews. London: Gollancz, 1951.

Ziehm, Ernst. *Aus Meiner Politischen Arbeit.* Marburg/Lahn: Johann Gottfried Herder-Institut, 1956.

Pamphlets

Angler, Georg. *Adolf Hitler en de door hem opgerichte Nationaal Socialistische Duitsche Arbeiderspartij.* N.p., n.d.

Arbeitsbericht für das Jahr 1934 der Abteilung "Ausland" in der Reichsjugendführung. N.p., n.d.

Auslands-Organisation. Landesgruppe in Frankreich: Anschriftenverzeichnis. N.p., 1944.

Auslands-Organisation der N.S.D.A.P.: Arbeitstagung der Politischen Leiter in Erlangen vom 6.-9. September 1935. N.p., n.d.

Frank, Hans. *Neues deutsches Recht.* Vol. 2 of *Hier spricht das neue Deutschland!* Munich: F. Eher, 1934.

Frank, Hans; Bohle, E. W.; and Meyer, Alfred. *Drei Reden für das Auslandsdeutschtum gehalten auf der Sondertagung des Gaues Ausland des NSRB. am 'Tag des Deutschen Rechts' in Leipzig 1939.* Berlin: Druck H. Müller und Sohn, 1939.

Jürges, Enrique. *Hakenkreuz am Rio de La Plata vor und hinter den Kulissen.* N.p., n.d.

Landesgruppe France. *Der Sprechabenddienst.* N.p., June 1944.

Landesgruppe Bolivia. *Tag der Arbeit, 1934: Dia del Trabajo.* N.p., 1934.

Documentary Collections

The Anti-Jewish Movements in South Africa. N.p., n.d.

Baynes, Norman H., ed. *The Speeches of Adolf Hitler: April 1922-August 1939.* 2 vols. London: Oxford University Press, 1942.

Boberach, Heinz., ed. *Meldungen aus dem Reich: Auswahl aus den geheimen Lageberichten des Sicherheitsdienstes der SS, 1939-1944.* Munich: Deutscher Taschenbuch Verlag, 1968.

Cannistraro, Philip V.; Wynot, Edward D., Jr.; and Kovaleff, Theodore P., eds. *Poland and the Coming of the Second World War: The Diplomatic Papers of A. J. Drexel Biddle, Jr., United States Ambassador to Poland, 1937-1939.* Columbus, Ohio: Ohio State University Press, 1976.

Calic, Edouard, ed. *Unmasked: Two Confidential Interviews with Hitler in 1931.* Trans. Richard Barry. London: Chatto and Windus, 1971.

Diewerge, Wolfgang. *Anschlag gegen den Frieden.* Munich: Zentralverlag der NSDAP, 1939.

Die Erhebung der österreichischen Nationalsozialisten im Juli 1934 (Akten der Historischen Kommission des Reichsführers SS). Frankfurt/Main: Europa-Verlag, 1965.

Fabry, Philipp W., ed. *Die Sowjetunion und das Dritte Reich: Eine dokumentierte Geschichte der deutsch-sowjetischen Beziehungen vom 1933 bis 1941.* Stuttgart: Seewald, 1971.

Feder, Gottfried. *Was will Adolf Hitler? Das Programm der N.S.D.A.P.* 5th ed. Munich: F. Eher, 1932.

The German Reich and Americans of German Origin. New York: Oxford University Press, 1938.

German Foreign Office. *Documents on the Events Preceding the*

Outbreak of the War. New York: German Library of Information, 1940.

Germany. *Documents on German Foreign Policy, 1918-1945.* Series C, vols. I-V (1933-1936) (Washington, D.C.: U.S. Government Printing Office, 1957-); Series D, vols. I-VII (1937-1939) (Washington, D.C.: U.S. Government Printing Office, 1949-).

Great Britain. *Documents on British Foreign Policy, 1919-1939.* Third Series, Vol. IV (1939). London: H.M. Stationery Office, 1954.

Great Britain. Parliamentary Debates, House of Commons. *Official Report.* Vol. 330. No. 41. London: H.M. Stationery Office, 1938.

———. *Official Report.* Vol. 334. No. 96. London: H.M. Stationery Office, 1938.

Grimm, Bruno. *Gau Schweiz? Dokumente über die national-sozialistische Umtriebe in der Schweiz.* Berne: Unionsdruckerei Bern, 1939.

Der Gruppe das Deutsche-Anarcho-Syndikalisten, ed. *Schwarzrotbuch: Dokumente über den Hitlerimperialismus.* Barcelona: Asy-Verlag, 1937.

Hansen, Heinrich, ed. *Der Schlüssel zum Frieden: Führertage in Italien.* Berlin, 1938.

Hess, Rudolf. *Reden.* Munich: Zentralverlag der NSDAP, 1938.

Hill, Leonidas E., ed. *Die Weizsäcker-Papiere, 1933-1950.* Frankfurt/Main: Propylaen, 1974.

Hitler, Adolf. *Reden des Führers: Politik und Propaganda Adolf Hitlers, 1922-1945.* Ed. Erhard Klöss. Munich: Deutscher Taschenbuch Verlag, 1967.

Hitlers zweites Buch: Ein Dokument aus dem Jahr 1928. Ed. Gerhard L. Weinberg. Stuttgart: Deutsche Verlags-Anstalt, 1961.

Der Hochverratsprozess gegen Dr. Guido Schmidt vor dem Wiener Volksgericht. Vienna: Österreichische Staatsdruckerei, 1947.

Hoffmann, Heinrich, ed. *Hitler in Italien.* Munich: Verlag Heinrich Hoffmann, 1938.

Hooker, Nancy Harvison, ed. *The Moffat Papers: Selections from the Diplomatic Journals of Jay Pierrepont Moffat, 1919-1943.* Cambridge, Mass.: Harvard University Press, 1956.

International Military Tribunal. *Trial of the Major War Criminals.* 42 vols. Nuremberg, 1947-1949.

Jacobsen, Hans-Adolf, ed. *Hans Steinacher: Bundesleiter des VDA,*

1933-1937. (Erinnerungen und Dokumente). Boppard/Rhine: Boldt, 1970.

Jedrzejewicz, Waclaw, ed. *Diplomat in Berlin, 1933-1939: Papers and Memoirs of Josef Lipski, Ambassador of Poland*. New York: Columbia University Press, 1968.

Jochmann, Werner, ed. *Nationalsozialismus und Revolution: Ursprung und Geschichte der NSDAP in Hamburg, 1922-33 (Dokumente)*. Frankfurt/Main: Europäische Verlagsanstalt, 1963.

Kube, Wilhelm, ed. *Almanach der nationalsozialistischen Revolution*. Berlin: Brunnen Verlag, 1934.

NSDAP. *Partei-Kanzlei*. Vol. 3 of *Verfügungen/Anordnungen/Bekanntgaben*. Munich: F. Eher, 1943.

NSDAP. *Partei-Kanzlei. Vertrauliche Informationen*. N.p., n.d.

Poliakov, Leon and Wulf, Josef, eds. *Das Dritte Reich und Seine Diener*. Berlin: Arani, 1956.

The Polish Ministry of Information, ed. *The German Fifth Column in Poland*. London: Hutchinson and Co., 1940.

Reichsgesetzblatt. Edited by the Reich Ministry of the Interior. Berlin: Reichsverlagsamt, 1933.

Spielhagen, Franz (pseud.). *Spione und Verschwörer in Spanien: Nach offiziellen nationalsozialistischen Dokumenten*. Paris: Éditions du Carrefour, 1936.

Stadler, Karl. *Österreich, 1938-1945: Im Spiegel der NS-Akten*. Vienna/Munich: Herold, 1966.

Trevor-Roper, H. R., ed. *Hitler's Secret Conversations, 1941-1944*. Trans. Norman Cameron and R. H. Stevens. New York: New American Library, 1961.

Trials of War Criminals Before the Nuernberg Military Tribunals Under Control Council Law No. 10, Nuernberg, October 1946-April 1949. 14 vols. Washington, D.C.: U.S. Government Printing Office, 1952.

United States. Department of State, Division of European Affairs. *National Socialism: Basic Principles, Their Application by the Nazi Party's Foreign Organization, and the Use of Germans Abroad for Nazi Aims*. Washington, D.C.: U.S. Government Printing Office, 1943.

United States. *Foreign Relations of the United States, 1934*, Vol. II. Washington, D.C.: U.S. Government Printing Office, 1951.

United States House of Representatives. *Investigation of Nazi Propaganda Activities and Investigation of Certain Other*

Propaganda Activities: Hearings Before the House Special Committee on Un-American Activities, 73 Cong., 2nd Sess. 2 pts. Washington, D.C.: U.S. Government Printing Office, 1934.

United States. Department of War. *Nazi Party Membership Records Submitted by the War Department to the Subcommittee on War Mobilization of the Committee on Military Affairs, United States Senate.* Washington, D.C.: U.S. Government Printing Office, 1946.

Volz, Hans, ed. *Von der Grossmacht zur Weltmacht, 1937.* Vol. 5 of *Dokumente der deutschen Politik.* Berlin: Junker und Dünnhaupt, 1938.

PUBLISHED SOURCES: SECONDARY ACCOUNTS

Abshagen, Karl Heinz. *Canaris: Patriot und Weltburger.* Stuttgart: Union Verlag, 1959.

Appleman, John Alan. *Military Tribunals and International Crimes.* Indianapolis, Ind.: Bobbs-Merrill, 1954.

Baird, Jay W. *The Mythical World of Nazi War Propaganda, 1939-1945.* Minneapolis, Minn.: University of Minnesota Press, 1974.

Bell, Leland V. *In Hitler's Shadow: The Anatomy of American Nazism.* Port Washington, N.Y.: Kennikat, 1973.

Bennett, Benjamin. *Hitler Over Africa.* London: T. Werner Laurie, 1939.

Bierschenk, Theodor. *Die Deutsche Volksgruppe in Polen, 1934-1939.* Würzburg: Holzner, 1954.

Bloch, Kurt. *German Interests and Policies in the Far East.* New York: Institute of Pacific Relations, 1940.

Bollmus, Reinhard. *Das Amt Rosenberg und seine Gegner: Zum Machtkampf im nationalsozialistischen Herrschaftssystem.* Stuttgart: Deutsche Verlags-Anstalt, 1970.

Bolloten, Burnett. *The Grand Camouflage: The Spanish Civil War and Revolution, 1936-1939.* New York: Praeger, 1968.

Borkenau, Franz. *The Spanish Cockpit. An Eye-Witness Account of the Political and Social Conflicts of the Spanish Civil War.* Ann Arbor, Mich.: University of Michigan Press, 1963.

Bourgeois, Daniel. *Le Troisème Reich et la Suisse, 1933-1941.* Neuchâtel [Switzerland]: Éditions de la Baconnière, 1974.

Bracher, Karl Dietrich; Sauer, Wolfgang; and Schulz, Gerhard. *Die nationalsozialistische Machtergreifung: Studien zur*

Errichtung des totalitären Herrschaftssystem in Deutschland, 1933/34. 2nd ed. Cologne: Westdeutscher Verlag, 1962.

Bramsted, Ernest K. *Goebbels and National Socialist Propaganda, 1925-1945.* East Lansing, Mich.: Michigan State University Press, 1965.

Das Braune Netz: Wie Hitlers Agenten im Auslande Arbeiten und den Krieg Vorbereiten. Paris: Éditions du Carrefour, 1935.

Breyer, Richard. *Das Deutsche Reich und Poland, 1932-1937: Aussenpolitik und Volksgruppenfragen.* Würzburg: Holzner, 1955.

Broszat, Martin. "Die Memeldeutschen Organisationen und der Nationalsozialismus," *Vierteljahrshefte für Zeitgeschichte,* 5 (1957), 273-78.

―――. *Nationalsozialistische Polenpolitik, 1939-1945.* Stuttgart: Deutsche Verlags-Anstalt, 1961.

―――. *Der Staat Hitlers: Grundlegung und Entwicklung seiner inneren Verfassung.* Munich: Deutscher Taschenbuch Verlag, 1969.

Brown, MacAlister. "The Third Reich's Mobilization of the German Fifth Columns in Eastern Europe," *Journal of Central European Affairs,* 19 (1959), 128-48.

[World Committee for the Victims of German Fascism]. *The Brown Network: The Activities of the Nazis in Foreign Countries.* New York: Knight Publications, 1936.

Brügel, Johann Wolfgang. *Tschechen und Deutsche, 1918-1938.* Munich: Nymphenburger Verlagshandlung, 1967.

Buchheim, Hans; Broszat, Martin; Jacobsen, Hans-Adolf; and Krausnick, Helmut. *Die SS—Das Herrschaftsinstrument, Befehl und Gehorsam.* Vol. I of *Anatomie des SS-Staates.* Freiburg: Walter-Verlag, 1965.

Bullock, Alan. *Hitler: A Study in Tyranny.* New York: Bantam Books, 1961.

Bussemeyer, Peter. *50 Jahre Argentinisches Tageblatt: Werden und Aufstieg einer Auslanddeutschen Zeitung.* N.p., n.d.

Campus, Eliza. "Die hitlerfaschistische Infiltration Rumäniens, 1939-1940," *Zeitschrift für Geschichtswissenschaft,* 5 (1957), 213-28.

Cassels, Alan. "Mussolini and German Nationalism, 1922-25," *Journal of Modern History,* 35 (1963), 137-57.

―――. *Mussolini's Early Diplomacy.* Princeton, N.J.: Princeton University Press, 1970.

Compton, James V. *The Swastika and the Eagle: Hitler, the United*

States, and the Origins of World War II. Boston: Houghton Mifflin, 1967.

Dale, C. E. *Amerikanisches Auskunftsbuch.* Union Hill, N.J., 1923.

Dallek, Robert. *Democrat and Diplomat: The Life of William E. Dodd.* New York: Oxford University Press, 1968.

Damer, Waldemar. *Unsere Brüder jenseits der Grenzen.* Berlin, n.d.

Dankelmann, Otfried. "Aus der Praxis auswärtiger Kulturpolitik des deutscher Imperialismus, 1933-1945," *Zeitschrift für Geschichtswissenschaft,* 6 (1972), 719-38.

Day, Danield Shepherd. "American Opinion of German National Socialism, 1933-1937." Unpublished Dissertation. University of California, Los Angeles, 1958.

Dedeke, Dieter. "Das Dritte Reich und die Vereinigten Staaten von Amerika, 1933-1937: Ein Beitrag zur Geschichte der deutsch-amerikanischen Beziehungen." Unpublished Dissertation. Free University of Berlin, 1969.

de Jong, Louis. *The German Fifth Column in the Second World War.* Trans. C. M. Geyl. Chicago: University of Chicago Press, 1956.

―――. "Organisation and Efficiency of the German Fifth Column," in Maurice Baumont, John E. Fired, and Edmond Vermeil, eds., *The Third Reich.* New York: Praeger, 1955, pp. 864-900.

Deutsch, Harold C. *The Conspiracy Against Hitler in the Twilight War.* Minneapolis, Minn.: University of Minnesota Press, 1968.

Diamond, Sander A. *The Nazi Movement in the United States, 1924-1941.* Ithaca, N.Y.: Cornell University Press, 1974.

Douglas-Hamilton, James. *Motive for a Mission: The Story Behind Hess's Flight to Britain.* London: Macmillan, 1971.

Drechsler, Karl. *Deutschland-China-Japan, 1933-1939: Das Dilemma der deutschen Fernostpolitik.* [East] Berlin: Akademie-Verlag, 1964.

Ebel, Arnold. *Das Dritte Reich und Argentinien: Die diplomatischen Beziehungen unter besonderer Berücksichtigung der Handelspolitik (1933-1939).* Cologne: Boehlau Verlag, 1971.

Ehrich, Emil. *Die Auslands-Organisation der NSDAP.* Berlin: Junker und Dünnhaupt, 1937.

Eichstädt, Ulrich. *Von Dollfuss zu Hitler: Geschichte des Anschlusses Österreichs, 1933-1938.* Wiesbaden: Steiner, 1955.

Einhorn, Marion. *Die ökonomischen Hintergründe der faschistischen deutschen Intervention in Spanien, 1936-1939.* [East] Berlin: Akademie-Verlag, 1962.

Eiselmeier, F. *Das Deutschtum in Angloamerika.* Brandenburg/ Havel: Deutscher Schutzbundverlag, 1926.

Fink, Carole. "Defender of Minorities: Germany in the League of Nations, 1926-1933," *Central European History,* V (1972), 330-57.

Förster, Gerhard; Helmert, Heinz; Otto, Helmut; and Schnitter, Helmut. "Der Überfall Hitlerdeutschlands auf Dänemark und Norwegen (Unternehmung 'Weserübung')," *Zeitschrift für Geschichtswissenschaft,* 8 (1960), 677-95.

Franz-Willing, Georg. *Die Hitlerbewegung: Der Ursprung, 1919-1922.* Hamburg: R. v. Decker, 1962.

Frye, Alton. *Nazi Germany and the American Hemisphere, 1933-1941.* New Haven, Conn.: Yale University Press, 1967.

Gannon, Franklin Reid. *The British Press and Germany, 1936-1939.* London: Oxford University Press, 1971.

Gauweiler, Otto. *Rechtseinrichtungen und Rechtsaufgaben der Bewegung.* Munich: F. Eher, 1939.

Gehl, Jürgen. *Austria, Germany and the Anschluss, 1931-1938.* London: Oxford University Press, 1963.

Gordon, Harold J. *Hitler and the Beer Hall Putsch.* Princeton, N.J.: Princeton University Press, 1972.

Gottlieb, Moshe. "The Anti-Nazi Boycott Movement in the United States: An Ideological and Sociological Appreciation," *Jewish Social Studies,* 35 (1973), 198-227.

Hagen, Walter (pseud.). *Die Geheime Front: Organisation, Personen und Aktionen des Deutschen Geheimdienstes.* Linz-Vienna: Europa-Verlag, 1950.

Hamburger, Ernest. "A Peculiar Pattern of the Fifth Column— The Organization of the German Seamen," *Social Research,* 9 (1942), 495-509.

Harms-Baltzer, Käte. *Die Nationalisierung der deutschen Einwanderer und ihrer Nachkommen in Brasilien als Problem der deutsch-brasilianischen Beziehungen, 1930-1938.* Berlin: Colloquium Verlag, 1970.

Harper, Glenn T. *German Economic Policy in Spain during the Spanish Civil War, 1936-1939.* The Hague: Mouton, 1967.

Heiden, Konrad. *Adolf Hitler: Das Zeitalter der Verantwortungslosigkeit.* Zurich: Europa-Verlag, 1936.

Herwig, Holger H. "Prelude to *Weltblitzkrieg*: Germany's Naval Policy toward the United States of America, 1939-41," *Journal of Modern History,* 43 (1971), 649-69.

Hilberg, Raul. *The Destruction of the European Jews.* Chicago: Quadrangle, 1961.

Hildebrand, Klaus. *The Foreign Policy of the Third Reich.* Trans. Anthony Fothergill. Berkeley: University of California Press, 1973.

———. "Hitler's War Aims," *Journal of Modern History,* 48 (1976), 522-30.

———. *Vom Reich zum Weltreich: Hitler, NSDAP und koloniale Frage, 1919-1945.* Munich: Wilhelm Fink Verlag, 1969.

Hill, Leonidas E. "The Wilhelmstrasse," *Political Science Quarterly,* 82 (1967), 546-70.

Hilton, Stanley E. *Brazil and the Great Powers, 1930-1939: The Politics of Trade Rivalry.* Austin, Texas: University of Texas Press, 1975.

Hirszowicz, Lukasz. *The Third Reich and the Arab East.* London: Routledge and Kegan Paul, 1966.

Hoptner, J. B. *Yugoslavia in Crisis, 1934-1941.* New York: Columbia University Press, 1962.

Horn, Wolfgang. *Führerideologie und Parteiorganisation in der NSDAP (1919-1933).* Düsseldorf: Droste Verlag, 1972.

Hory, Ladislaus and Broszat, Martin. *Der Kroatische Ustascha-Staat, 1941-1945.* Stuttgart: Deutsche Verlags-Anstalt, 1964.

Hutton, J. Bernard. *Hess: The Man and His Mission.* London: David Bruce and Watson Ltd., 1970.

Jäckel, Eberhard. *Hitlers Weltanschauung: Entwurf einer Herrschaft.* Tübingen: R. Wunderlich, 1969.

Jacobsen, Hans-Adolf. "Die Gruendung der Auslandsabteilung der NSDAP (1931-1933)," in *Gedenkschrift fuer Martin Goehring.* Wiesbaden: Steiner, 1968, pp. 353-68.

———. *Nationalsozialistische Aussenpolitik, 1933-1938.* Frankfurt/ Main: Alfred Metzner, 1968.

Kannapin, Klaus. "Deutschland und Argentinien von 1933 bis 1945," *Wissenschaftliche Zeitschrift der Universität Rostock,* 14 (1965), 107-17.

Kimmich, Christoph M. *Germany and the League of Nations.* Chicago: University of Chicago Press, 1976.

Kipphan, Klaus. *Deutsche Propaganda in den Vereinigten Staaten, 1933-1941.* Heidelberg: C. Winter, 1971.

Kirchner, Hellmut. *Hermann Bohle: Leben, Kämpfen und Denken eines Auslandsdeutschen.* Berlin: Junker und Dünnhaupt, n.d.

Koehl, Robert. *RKFDV: German Resettlement and Population Policy, 1939-1945.* Cambridge, Mass.: Harvard University Press, 1957.

Kordt, Erich. *Wahn und Wirklichkeit: Die Aussenpolitik des Dritten Reiches.* Stuttgart: Union Deutsche Verlagsgesellschaft, 1948.

Kotze, Hildegard v. "Hitlers Sicherheitsdienst im Ausland," *Die politische Meinung*, 86 (1963), 75-80.

Kranzler, David. *Japanese, Nazis and Jews: The Jewish Refugee Community of Shanghai, 1938-1945.* New York: Yeshiva University Press, 1976.

Kris, Ernst and Speier, Hans. *German Radio Propaganda: Report on Home Broadcasts during the War.* London: Oxford University Press, 1944.

Kühnl, Reinhard. *Die nationalsozialistische Linke, 1925-1930.* Meisenheim/Glan: Hain, 1966.

Kuhn, Axel. *Hitlers aussenpolitisches Programm: Entstehung und Entwicklung, 1919-1939.* Stuttgart: Klett, 1970.

Kühne, Horst. "Die Fünfte Kolonne des faschistischen deutschen Imperialismus in Südwestafrika (1933-1939)," *Zeitschrift für Geschichtswissenschaft*, 8 (1960), 765-90.

Kwiet, Konrad. *Reichskommissariat Niederlande: Versuch und Scheitern nationalsozialistischer Neuordnung.* Stuttgart: Deutsche Verlags-Anstalt, 1968.

―――. "Zur Geschichte der Mussert-Bewegung," *Vierteljahrshefte für Zeitgeschichte*, 18 (1970), 164-95.

Lachmann, Günter. "Der Nationalsozialismus in der Schweiz, 1931-1945: Ein Beitrag zur Geschichte der Auslandsorganisation der NSDAP." Unpublished Dissertation. Free University of Berlin, 1962.

Lange, Karl. "Der Terminus 'Lebensraum' in Hitlers 'Mein Kampf'," *Vierteljahrshefte für Zeitgeschichte*, 13 (1965), 426-38.

Langer, Walter C. *The Mind of Adolf Hitler: The Secret Wartime Report.* New York: New American Library, 1973.

Latour, Conrad F. *Südtirol und die Achse Berlin-Rom, 1938-1945.* Stuttgart: Deutsche Verlags-Anstalt, 1962.

Leasor, James. *The Uninvited Envoy.* New York: McGraw-Hill, 1962.

Lerg, Winfried B. "Deutscher Auslandsrundfunk im zweiten Weltkrieg," *Rundfunk und Fernsehen*, 1 (1966), 25-34.

Levine, Herbert S. *Hitler's Free City: A History of the Nazi Party in Danzig, 1925-39.* Chicago: University of Chicago Press, 1973.

Luza, Radomir. *Austro-German Relations in the Anschluss Era.* Princeton, N.J.: Princeton University Press, 1975.

McCann, Frank D., Jr. *The Brazilian-American Alliance, 1937-1945.* Princeton, N.J.: Princeton University Press, 1973.

McKale, Donald M. "Hitlerism for Export! The Nazi Attempt to Control Schools and Youth Clubs Outside Germany," *Journal of European Studies*, 5 (1975), 239-53.

————. *The Nazi Party Courts: Hitler's Management of Conflict in His Movement, 1921-1945*. Lawrence, Kansas: University Press of Kansas, 1974.

Manvell, Roger and Fraenkel, Heinrich. *Hess: A Biography*. London: MacGibbon and Kee, 1971.

————. *Himmler*. New York: Putnam, 1965.

Martin, Bernd. *Deutschland und Japan im Zweiten Weltkrieg: Vom Angriff auf Pearl Harbor bis zur deutschen Kapitulation*. Zurich/Frankfurt: Musterschmidt, 1969.

Maser, Werner. *Die Frühgeschichte der NSDAP: Hitlers Weg bis 1924*. Frankfurt/Main: Athenäum Verlag, 1965.

Mau, Hermann and Krausnick, Helmut. *Deutsche Geschichte der jüngsten Vergangenheit, 1933-1945*. Tübingen-Stuttgart: Casterman, 1964.

Merkes, Manfred. *Die deutsche Politik gegenüber dem spanischen Bürgerkrieg, 1936-1939*. Bonn: Röhrscheid, 1961.

Meskill, Johanna Menzel. *Hitler and Japan: The Hollow Alliance*. New York: Atherton Press, 1966.

Milward, Alan S. *The German Economy at War*. London: Athlone Press, 1965.

Neumann, Franz. *Behemoth: The Structure and Practice of National Socialism, 1933-1944*. New York: Harper and Row, 1963.

Nolte, Ernst. *Die faschistischen Bewegungen*. 2nd ed. Munich: Deutscher Taschenbuch Verlag, 1969.

Nyomarkay, Joseph. *Charisma and Factionalism in the Nazi Party*. Minneapolis, Minn.: University of Minnesota Press, 1967.

Offner, Arnold A. *American Appeasement: United States Foreign Policy and Germany, 1933-1938*. Cambridge, Mass.: Harvard University Press, 1969.

Orlow, Dietrich. *The Nazis in the Balkans: A Case Study of Totalitarian Politics*. Pittsburgh: University of Pittsburgh Press, 1968.

————. *The History of the Nazi Party: 1919-1933*. Pittsburgh: University of Pittsburgh Press, 1969.

————. *The History of the Nazi Party: 1933-1945*. Pittsburgh: University of Pittsburgh Press, 1973.

Paechter, Heinz et al., eds. *Nazi-Deutsch: A Glossary of Contemporary German Usage*. New York: Frederick Ungar, 1944.

Pauley, Bruce F. *Hahnenschwanz und Hakenkreuz: Steirischer*

Heimatschutz und österreichischer Nationalsozialismus, 1918-1934. Vienna: Europa-Verlag, 1972.

———. *The Habsburg Legacy, 1867-1939.* New York: Holt, Rinehart and Winston, 1972.

Payne, Stanley G. *Falange: A History of Spanish Fascism.* Stanford, Calif: Stanford University Press, 1961.

Petersen, Jens. *Hitler-Mussolini: Die Entstehung der Achse Berlin-Rom, 1933-1936.* Tübingen: Niemeyer, 1973.

Peterson, E. N. *The Limits of Hitler's Power.* Princeton, N.J.: Princeton University Press, 1969.

Pese, Walter Werner. "Hitler und Italien, 1920-1926," *Vierteljahrshefte für Zeitgeschichte,* 3 (1955), 113-26.

Potashnik, Michael. "*Nacismo:* National Socialism in Chile, 1932-1938." Unpublished Dissertation. University of California, Los Angeles, 1974.

Presseisen, Ernst L. *Germany and Japan: A Study in Totalitarian Diplomacy, 1933-1941.* The Hague: Nijhoff, 1958.

Rees, J. R., ed. *The Case of Rudolf Hess: A Problem in Diagnosis and Forensic Psychiatry.* New York: Norton: 1948.

Reichsstelle für das Auswanderungswesen, ed. *Die hauptsachlichsten deutschen Vereinigungen, Kirchen, Schulen und sonstige deutsche Einrichtungen im Auslande.* Berlin: Zentralverlag, 1932.

Remak, Joachim. "Friends of the New Germany: The Bund and German-American Relations," *Journal of Modern History,* 29 (1957), 38-48.

Rich, Norman. *The Establishment of the New Order.* Vol. II of *Hitler's War Aims.* New York: Norton, 1974.

Ritschel, Karl Heinz. *Diplomatie um Südtirol: Politische Hintergründe eines europäischen Versagens.* Stuttgart: Seewald, 1966.

Rogge, O. John. *The Official German Report: Nazi Penetration, 1924-1942, Pan-Arabism, 1939-Today.* New York: Yoseleff, 1961.

Rosar, Wolfgang. *Deutsche Gemeinschaft: Seyss-Inquart und der Anschluss.* Vienna: Europa-Verlag, 1971.

Ruhl, Klaus-Jörg. *Spanien im Zweiten Weltkrieg: Franco, die Falange und das "Dritte Reich."* Hamburg: Hoffmann und Campe, 1975.

Sadka, Nancy Leila. "German Relations With Persia, 1921-1941." Unpublished Dissertation. Stanford University, 1972.

Sanke, Heinz, ed. *Der deutsche Faschismus in Lateinamerika, 1933-1943.* [East] Berlin: Humboldt-Universität, 1966.

Schäfer, Wolfgang. *NSDAP: Entwicklung und Struktur der Staatspartei des Dritten Reiches.* Hanover: Norddeutsche Verlaganstalt, 1956.

Schmitz-Esser, Winfried. "Hitler-Mussolini: Das Südtiroler-Abkommen von 1939," *Aussenpolitik,* 13 (1962), 397-408.

Schmokel, Wolfe W. *Dream of Empire: German Colonialism, 1919-1945.* New Haven and London: Yale University Press, 1964.

Schröder, Hans-Jürgen. *Deutschland und die Vereinigten Staaten, 1933-1939: Wirtschaft und Politik in der Entwicklung des Deutsch-Amerikanischen Gegensatzes.* Wiesbaden: F. Steiner, 1970.

Seabury, Paul. *The Wilhelmstrasse: A Study of German Diplomats Under the Nazi Regime.* Berkeley and Los Angeles: University of California Press, 1954.

Schubert, Günter, *Anfänge nationalsozialistischer Aussenpolitik.* Cologne: Verlag Wissenschaft und Politik, 1963.

Simonson, William Newton. "Nazi Infiltration in South America, 1933-1945." Unpublished Dissertation. Fletcher School of Law and Diplomacy, 1964.

Smelser, Ronald M. "The Betrayal of a Myth: National Socialism and the Financing of Middle-Class Socialism in the Sudetenland," *Central European History,* V (1972), 256-77.

———. *The Sudeten Problem, 1933-1938: Volkstumspolitik and the Formulation of Nazi Foreign Policy.* Middletown, Conn.: Wesleyan University Press, 1975.

Smith, Arthur L., Jr. *The Deutschtum of Nazi Germany and the United States.* The Hague: Nijhoff, 1965.

———. "Hitler's *Gau Ausland,*" *Political Studies,* 14 (1966), 90-95.

———. "The Kameradschaft USA," *Journal of Modern History,* 34 (1962), 398-408.

Smith, Geoffrey S. *To Save a Nation: American Countersubversives, the New Deal, and the Coming of World War II.* New York: Basic Books, 1973.

Sommer, Theo. *Deutschland und Japan zwischen den Mächten, 1935-1940: Vom Antikominternpakt zum Dreimächtepakt.* Tübingen: Mohr, 1962.

Stein, George H. *The Waffen SS: Hitler's Elite Guard at War.* Ithaca, N.Y.: Cornell University Press, 1967.

Stuebel, Heinrich. "Die Entwicklung des Nationalsozialismus in Südwestafrika," *Vierteljahrshefte für Zeitgeschichte,* 1 (1953), 170-76.

Tagy-Talavera, Nicholas M. *The Green Shirts and the Others: A*

History of Fascism in Hungary and Rumania. Stanford, Calif.: Hoover Institution Press, 1970.

Taylor, Edmond; Snow, Edgar; and Janeway, Eliot. *Smash Hitler's International: The Strategy of a Political Offensive Against the Axis.* New York: Greystone Press, 1941.

Taylor, Telford, *Final Report to the Secretary of the Army on the Nuernberg War Crimes Trials under Control Council Law No. 10.* Washington, D.C.: U.S. Government Printing Office, 1949.

Thierfelder, Franz. *Die wirtschaftliche Bedeutung des Auslanddeutschtums.* Stuttgart: F. Enke, 1934.

Thorne, Christopher. *The Approach of War, 1938-1939.* London: Macmillan, 1971.

Tillmann, Heinz. "Tätigkeit und Ziele der Fünften Kolonne in Südafrika während der zweiten Weltkrieges," *Zeitschrift für Geschichtswissenschaft, Sonderheft* (1961), 182-209.

Toland, John. *The Last 100 Days.* New York: Random House, 1966.

Toscano, Mario. *Alto Adige-South Tyrol: Italy's Frontier with the German World.* Ed. George A. Carbone. Baltimore: Johns Hopkins University Press, 1975.

———. *The Origins of the Pact of Steel.* Baltimore: John Hopkins University Press, 1967.

Trevor-Roper, Hugh Redwald. "Hitlers Kriegsziele," *Vierteljahrshefte für Zeitgeschichte,* 8 (1960), 121-33.

Trotz, Joachim. "Zur Tätigkeit der deutschen V. Kolonne in Lateinamerika von 1933-1945," *Wissenschaftliche Zeitschrift der Universität Rostock,* 14 (1965), 119-31.

Truchanowski, W. G., ed. Vol. 2 of *Geschichte der internationalen Beziehungen.* [East] Berlin: Rütten und Leoning, 1965.

Turner, Henry Ashby, Jr., "Hitler's Secret Pamphlet for Industrialists, 1927," *Journal of Modern History,* 40 (1968), 348-74.

Volker, Nitz. *Unser Grenz- und Auslanddeutschtum.* Munich: F. Eher, 1931.

Waite, Robert G. L., *Vanguard of Nazism: The Free Corps Movement in Postwar Germany, 1918-1923.* New York: Norton, 1969.

Walsh, Billie K. "The German Military Mission in China, 1928-38," *Journal of Modern History,* 46 (1974), 502-13.

Watt, D. C. "The Rome-Berlin Axis, 1936-1940: Myth and Reality," *Review of Politics,* 22 (1960), 519-43.

Weinberg, Gerhard L. "Deutsch-Japanische Verhandlungen über

das Südseemandat, 1937-1938," *Vierteljahrshefte für Zeitgeschichte*, 4 (1956), 390-98.

— — —. *The Foreign Policy of Hitler's Germany: Diplomatic Revolution in Europe, 1933-36*. Chicago: University of Chicago Press, 1970.

— — —. "Hitler's Image of the United States," *American Historical Review*, 69 (1964), 1006-22.

— — —. "The May Crisis, 1938," *Journal of Modern History*, 29 (1957), 213-25.

— — —. "National Socialist Organization and Foreign Policy Aims in 1927," *Journal of Modern History*, 36 (1964), 428-34.

Wiskemann, Elizabeth. *The Rome-Berlin Axis: A History of the Relations Between Hitler and Mussolini*. New York: Oxford University Press, 1949.

Zeman, Z.A.B. *Nazi Propaganda*. London: Oxford University Press, 1964.

INDEX

police attaches, 128; spies on diplomats, 128, 190
—Manchuria: 182; creation of, 74
—Mexico: tie to fascist group, 144
—Netherlands: and anti-Semitism, 53; and Bohle, 77, 169-70, and Bormann, 170; dissolved, 170; and Dutch Nazis, 32, 77-78; espionage of, 169; and German colonies, 77; and German-Dutch relations, 77, 169; HJ in, 55; infiltrates police, 77; and Nieland, 32; origins of, 31-32; and propaganda, 32; and reprisals, 171; and Ribbentrop, 169; and Seyss-Inquart, 170; and undercover groups, 77; visits Hitler rally, 32
—Norway: and Bohle, 169; and German invasion, 168; and Gestapo, 168-69; origins of, 33; supplanted, 170
—Palestine: aids Arab guerillas, 126; and Arab National Socialists, 75; leader imprisoned, 163; opposes Jewish state, 125-26; origins of, 75
—Paraguay: creation of, 23; forced underground, 166
—Poland: aids invasion, 159-60, 242 (n. 107); and German schools, 159; origins of, 27, 57; propaganda of, 57, 159; and reprisals, 159; and Volksdeutsch groups, 57, 158-59
—Rumania: and Abwehr, 172; and Bohle, 172, 174; and destruction of Jews, 184; and diplomats, 156, 173; and German-Rumanian relations, 98, 141, 156; and Iron Guard, 141, 156, 173-74; leaders expelled, 174; operates undercover, 58; origins of, 58; propaganda of, 58, 141, 156, 173-74; spy tactics of, 156, 174; and Volksdeutsch groups, 58, 156, 174
—Slovakia: and Bohle, 188; and destruction of Jews, 184
—Southwest Africa: anti-Semitism of, 95; banned, 96; camouflaged, 96; colonial demands of, 94-95; and Deutsche Bund, 94-95, 96; economic plan of, 95; German opposition to, 95-96; HJ in, 94, 96; origins of, 16, 30-31
—Spain: and AA, 104-05, 167; anti-

Semitism of, 53, 81-82; and Blue Division, 167; and Bohle, 105; and Civil War, 103-05 passim; and conspiracy against Franco, 167, 244 (n. 19); and Falange, 103, 167; and German colonies, 63-64; has documents seized, 224 (n. 120); and Italian Fascists, 81; keeps tabs on diplomats, 63, 81; officials contact Hitler, 102-03; organization of, 80-81; origins of, 27; and propaganda, 81-82; and SA, 103; spies on enemies, 81; smuggles weapons to Franco, 103
—Switzerland: 80, 228 (n. 40); and AA, 99, 228 (n. 44); banned, 99; and blackmail, 25, 29; combats defeatism, 166; continues undercover, 99, 229 (n. 45); fanaticism of, 76; and front groups, 98; infiltrates Swiss government, 98; leaders expelled, 198; murder of Gustloff, 98; opposition to, 98; organization of, 98; origins of, 25-26; sends money to Hitler, 29; and Swiss elections, 29; tied to kidnaping, 98; used by Abwehr, 172
—Turkey: and AA, 182; and Abwehr, 172; anti-Jewish policy of, 166; origins of, 37, 39, 75; and SS, 184
—Uruguay: and army, 145; dissolution of, 166; and German schools, 66; headquarters bombed, 166; origins of, 33; resistance to, 66, 145; and Youth League, 145

Landesgruppenleiters ("Country Group Leaders" of the NSDAP): 200-01; anti-Jewish policies of, 125, 166; appointed as diplomats, 101, 115; and Bohle, 49-50, 59, 122, 164, 187; and contempt for diplomats, 59; corps of, 122-25; creation of office, 20; and denaturalization of Germans, 158; duties defined, 49-50, 122, 125; and Hitler, 48, 49, 100-01, 122, 207 (n. 17); and meetings in Berlin, 161, 164, 187-88; proposed as party attaches, 100-01; recruited haphazardly, 66; relations to German missions, 60-61, 112, 164; and reports on diplomats, 60, 81, 102, 115, 116, 176-77; war tasks

DATE